Praise for *Carrying a Big Schtick*

"Mora is a brilliant observer of masculinity, which we often take for granted or assume to be the default mode of being human. Drawing from politics, literature, war, sports, and popular culture, she deftly narrates a story of what it meant to be a man across nearly a century of Jewish life in the US. The story is all the more an achievement because of Mora's ability to weave together its diverse elements: Jewish men's self-representation, other Americans' assumptions, charges of effeminacy, embraces of gentleness, refusals of victimhood, and calls for military prowess are just a few of the historical developments Mora traces. American Jewish history has been waiting for this book."

—Sarah Imhoff, author of *Masculinity and the Making of American Judaism*

"This is a trenchant analysis of assimilation and otherness."

—*Publishers Weekly*

"*Carrying a Big Schtick* is an impressive work of scholarship. The breadth is outstanding. Mora's command of the material and literature is excellent."

—Mira Sucharov, professor and associate chair, Carleton University

"*Carrying a Big Schtick* is a pleasure to read. The scholarship is sound, the theoretical analysis is both frequently brilliant and always clear, and the writing is effervescent. I recommend it to anyone interested in gender history and theory and, as well, to anyone interested in Jewish life in America."

—Daniel Boyarin, professor emeritus, University of California, Berkeley

Carrying a Big Schtick

CARRYING A BIG SCHTICK

Jewish Acculturation and Masculinity
in the Twentieth Century

MIRIAM EVE MORA

WAYNE STATE UNIVERSITY PRESS
DETROIT

© 2024 by Wayne State University Press, Detroit, Michigan 48201. All rights reserved. No part of this book may be reproduced without formal permission.

ISBN 9780814349625 (paperback)
ISBN 9780814349632 (hardcover)
ISBN 9780814349649 (e-book)

Library of Congress Control Number: 2023940090

Cover photo courtesy of author's private collection. Cover design by Elke Barter.

Published with the support of the Association for Jewish Studies Jordan Schnitzer First Book Publication Award.

Wayne State University Press rests on Waawiyaataanong, also referred to as Detroit, the ancestral and contemporary homeland of the Three Fires Confederacy. These sovereign lands were granted by the Ojibwe, Odawa, Potawatomi, and Wyandot Nations, in 1807, through the Treaty of Detroit. Wayne State University Press affirms Indigenous sovereignty and honors all tribes with a connection to Detroit. With our Native neighbors, the press works to advance educational equity and promote a better future for the earth and all people.

Wayne State University Press
Leonard N. Simons Building
4809 Woodward Avenue
Detroit, Michigan 48201-1309

Visit us online at wsupress.wayne.edu.

For my children, Judah Luis and Shayna Mia, who defended the core of this work as a dissertation and signed the book contract in utero (respectively).

For my sister Shana Nova (Z"L), who believed in this project and my future, but who cannot hold this book, I hold her memory close.

And for my husband Daniel, in recognition of the difficulty of being a man married to a woman writing about masculinity. You are the best of men(ches).

Contents

Acknowledgments

As with all projects a decade in the making, I have too many people to thank, and cannot possibly do my scholarly, familial, and social support networks justice. So, I will open by simply saying thank you to every person who read a draft, approved an idea, suggested a book or article, booked a talk, approved a grant, recommended a resource, granted a fellowship, chatted about my work over coffee, or simply supported the notion that this was a topic worthy of study.

I would like to thank my graduate advisor, John Bukowczyk, for his ceaseless support, creative insight, expert guidance, thoughtful wisdom, and dry wit, without which I would never have had the strength to persevere in graduate school and beyond. I feel profoundly lucky to have found his office on my initial visit to Wayne State University, and honored to have worked closely with him for so many years. Thank you also to my nonprimary advisors and mentors for all of your support, advice, and time; to my friends in the field for your words of encouragement at every step of this process, the inspiration you provided me in your own journeys, and the commiseration over our losses and failures; my nonacademic friends who have tolerated and supported me for so long, you are like a cheering squad in my pocket and I love you; and to my various employers, who have all helped me to complete this project through their flexibility, belief in my work, and support of my scholarship.

Though this is not an exhaustive list of the above, I want to specifically thank Andrew Port, Deborah Dash Moore, David Weinberg, Howard Lupovitch, Annie Martin, Lisa Steichman, Doug Aikenhead, Marty Shichtman, Rachel Harris, Mira Sucharov, Laura Almagor, Natalia Aleksiun, Beth Fowler, Alexandra Sarkozy, Michael Varlamos, Josh Morris, Amanda Walter, Kimberly Ryder, Heather Braatz, Nancy Mayo, Amanda Rose Fell, Alexandra Boughton, Corey Tessler, Michael Eisenberg, Getty Goins, Taralyn Brinks, Ezra Graziano, Adam Steinberg, Eliot Borenstein, Fran Bernstein,

Minda Rae Amiran, Judith and David Sensibar, Larry Glasser, Shana Borenstein (Z"L), Lea Grover, Carlos and Maria Mora, and each and every JAM.

I want to thank Wayne State University Press, and my editor Sandra Korn, for helping me to make the book better at every step, and putting it out into the world. Also thank you to all the organizations that provided support for my research on this project: The Association for Jewish Studies, Wayne State University History Department, American Jewish Archives, Leo Baeck Summer University, Center for Jewish History, Wyner Family Jewish Heritage Center at the New England Genealogical Historical Society, the American Jewish Historical Society, the Cohn-Haddow Center for Jewish Studies at Wayne State University, and the Zekelman Holocaust Center. The support from these organizations helped to both fund and motivate my research and writing, providing opportunities to engage with other scholars, students, and materials I might not have accessed otherwise. The bulk of my research was conducted through the Center for Jewish History and the American Jewish Archives, both of which are home to excellent archivists and administrators who have made this research possible, and to all of whom I am indebted. Thank you also to the *Journal of Jewish Identities*, which previously published of a portion of Chapter 10 ("Militant Judaism: The Jewish Defense League") as "'Husky Jewish Boys': The Jewish Defense League and the Project of Jewish American Masculinity," in *Journal of Jewish Identities*, volume 15, no. 2 (July 2022).

I am unspeakably grateful to my parents, Trina and Nathaniel Borenstein, for their love, support, and willingness to read hundreds of papers, chapters, and excerpts over the years. Their flexible approach to my education allowed me to grow from an apathetic slacker to a Doctor of History, and they set an example of putting good into the world that few people are as fortunate as I am to have received. I could not possibly be here without their belief in me and support of my search for happiness in both work and personal life. It's not easy to live up to the example they set, and I fully intend to die trying.

And finally, thank you to my incredible partner in all things, Daniel Mora. All of this has been possible only with your love and encouragement: my work, my life, our family, and immeasurable laughter, fun, and happiness. By your example I work harder, strive to be better, and sometimes even remember to eat while I work. Thank you for supporting me in this and all things, and for collaborating with me on the greatest projects in my life.

Introduction

> We're the sons appalled by violence, with no capacity for inflicting physical pain, useless at beating and clubbing, unfit to pulverize even the most deserving enemy. . . . We have teeth as the cannibals do, but there they are, embedded in our jaws, the better to help us articulate. When we lay waste, when we efface, it isn't with raging fists or ruthless schemes or insane sprawling violence but with our words, our brains, with mentality.
>
> —Philip Roth[1]

It has never been the case that all Jewish men subscribe to a form of masculinity that lays waste with words alone, that accepts that when it comes to violence, they are unfit to engage. Certainly, American Jewish men have yearned for the rugged masculinity of John Wayne, the heroism of Sitting Bull, or the transformative frontier experience of Theodore Roosevelt. They have and they do. Over the course of the twentieth century, Jewish men have been involved in pursuits of manhood that shake old claims about Jewishness to their core. They have been soldiers, assassins, bootleggers, athletes, farmers, fighters, terrorists, heartthrobs, bodybuilders, and rebels.

Yet the image of the meek, gentle Jewish man persists, and it does so not solely because outsiders label Jews as such, but because Jews themselves buy into the stereotype and promote the image. And that image remains one of the most dominant, enduring perceptions of Jewish men in America, so much so that merely exhibiting the attributes of a stereotypical nebbish, schlemiel, or schlimazel effectively creates the impression of Jewishness. This is demonstrated in countless fictional characters, but notably in the person of Dr. John Zoidberg (*Futurama*, 1999–2003), who is tacitly but undeniably Jewish, despite the fact that he is an enormous cuttlefish-like crustacean, and, therefore, clearly unkosher.[2] He is timid (at times hiding in shells), weak, and desperate to be liked. He is generally clumsy and inept (schlemiel) and prone to misfortune (schlimazel). The recitation of these archetypes through Zoidberg conveys more Jewishness than even the stated Jewish community of the series, the robot community (who have bot-mitzvot and celebrate Robanukah). He is actually declared un-Jewish by the writers, when he is refused access to a bot-mitzvah by a Chasidic robot who sends him away, saying "no shellfish."[3] And yet, despite his being unkosher and not a practicing Jewish robot (he even mispronounces the word "roh-bit"), he is instantly, clearly, recognizable through Jewish stereotyping. He is also a failure as a male of his species, another Jewish stereotype, being told in no uncertain terms by the female he pursued, "I'm sorry, Zoidberg, you're just an inferior male specimen."[4]

While these characteristics are recognizable as stereotypically Jewish, they are indicative of a dominant archetype, not real Jewish men. In reality, there is no single Jewish masculinity, real or perceived. *Carrying a Big Schtick* demonstrates that negotiating their relationship to American hegemonic masculinity is an ongoing process for American Jews and has actually been a central aspect of acculturation for Jewish immigrants and their children. In fact, this book establishes not only that European Jewish immigrants focused on the performance of American masculinity as a central part of the American experience, but that because of the gendered nature of anti-Jewish prejudice, this tool for cultural acceptance proved to be a uniquely combative one, encountering consistent pushback.

The opening quote, taken from Philip Roth's 1996 memoir *Patrimony*, demonstrates a pervasive assumption about Jewish aversion to physical confrontation. To Roth, in life and fiction, the notion that Jews have "no capacity for inflicting physical pain" is a given. In this view, Jewish men subscribe to a unique form of masculinity, one that eschews violence and values intellect. This motif of emasculated Jewish men appears, often dominates, in nearly every venue that depicts Jews: fiction and nonfiction, by Jewish and non-Jewish creators alike, both male and female, over the previous century. Jewish men, according to religious and cultural studies, are more gentle, thoughtful, and nonviolent. In short, Jewish men are, and should be, mensches.

So why has this assumption about Jewish men followed them across centuries, continents, and oceans, despite being just one facet of Jewish masculine identity? The narrative of Jewish masculinity comprises a story of rejection from societal and cultural norms, of being blocked from accessing aspects of society and then forced to either accept and embrace their situation, or fight to change it. And in nearly all instances, reactions among Jews are mixed, some embracing, some fighting. Between these reactions, in accepting or contesting what became dominant Jewish masculine identities, the complex narrative of Jewish male identity emerges. Jewish masculinity is not, and never has been, monolithic. The story of Jewish men and masculinity in America is, therefore, not so much a continuous thread of gender norms as it is a braided and fraying twine of variant masculinities. Some Jewish men, as Daniel Boyarin has shown, accept and embrace the view of gentle Jewish masculinity as continuing in a history of rabbinic tradition that values intellect over physicality and supports a feminized or emasculated Jewish image. Others accept that such a masculinity has and does exist, but wish to change it and themselves by engaging in more traditionally masculine endeavors. Then there are others still, who accept that the *image* of Jews as feminized is real, but that the reality is quite different, and thus do not feel the need to change themselves, but instead to demonstrate and publicize the masculinity of virile Jews to alter their image and show Jewish men as more masculine figures.

These reactions would be neither interesting nor observable were it not for the persistent portrayal of Jews as outside of the masculine American hegemonic ideal. Regardless of how the stereotypes began, as a reflection of Jewish reality or as an attack on Jewish acculturation (and indeed it has been both), it is a key component of the Jewish image that affects Jewish life in very real ways. It is a substantial element of Jewish humor and self-deprecation, a tool of the antisemite, a justification for Jewish difference in American life, and a motivator for social movements within Jewish communities. For this reason, those inside and outside of the community reinforce and defend the stereotype, and it has become a constant, persistent element of Jewish life and self-image.

The story of Jewish American masculinity is one of acculturation, of acceptance and denial, of tension between native-born Jews and new immigrants, between the religious and the secular, and between generations. This study was driven by a desire to explore the concept that each of these elements of tension in Jewish life, though perhaps differently motivated, contains a gendered element, which focuses on the male as the model of a successful immigrant, making American hegemonic masculinity the highest goal of American acculturation. Instances of antisemitism in American history are similarly gendered, using the success (or lack thereof) of Jewish men to be American as motivation for discrimination.

Much of this story is the desire of middle-class, upwardly mobile Jews to acculturate, to take equal and full part in American life and society with their non-Jewish neighbors. In this case, nonpracticing (or at least not visibly practicing) Jews are much more the players in the story than the religious, as it is these acculturating Jews who are the most present and represented in entertainment media, American politics, and other American industries and professions. Who, after all, has been more influential in creating and perpetuating the image of the Jewish male nebbish than Woody Allen or Philip Roth, both self-proclaimed atheist Jews? This study is not an analysis of Jewish authorship, though it uses Jewish authors to demonstrate how Jewish men see and present themselves. This history of Jewish masculinity is one of self-representation and response to representations of themselves created by others. It considers only occasionally the culture produced by Jewish men in America and how they embody masculinity in their characters. Much more importantly it examines the ways in which actual Jewish men present themselves to the world—the real-life actions and movements they engage in with the goal of altering perceptions of Jewish manliness. The story of Jewish men is, therefore, one of a struggle to maintain the standards of masculinity by which they are judged, and the unique forms their own masculinity takes in the process.

To determine the group under examination, I use the simplest of definitions of American Jews, that of self-ascription. This is the same identification that Jacob Rader Marcus used, identifying American Jews as "anyone . . . who says he or she is and who works closely with the Jews . . . religionists, secularists, the rootless, and ideological nothingarians."[5] For the purposes of studying cultural gender identity, this breadth of subject is imperative. I include religious Jews, but only as they appear as actors in a Jewish American story that is largely secular. The Orthodox community is a world apart from the turning points in the narrative I draw in this study. The group I examine, of both religious and secular (but self-identifying) Jews, is as inclusive a representation of Jews in the United States as possible.

A word on terminology: In contemporary issues of immigration, immigration historians (myself included) generally dispose of the term *assimilation* in favor of *integration*, which more accurately represents the idyllic outcome of migration (new migrants being accepted into American society as equals, and enabling them to maintain their cultures). Throughout this book, however, I use the terms *acculturation* and *assimilation* for nearly all discussion of cultural adaptation of Jewish immigrants. *Assimilation* has many negative connotations (particularly relevant here are Jewish fears of intermarriage and abandonment of Jewish religion, life, and culture), while *acculturation* recognizes maintenance of Jewishness while adapting to mainstream American life (participating in American cultural, political, and social life, as well as primarily speaking English). When I use the term *assimilation*, I do so in dialogue with and deference to Jews of this story who not only use the term but often hold assimilation as the goal and mark of their success as immigrants.[6] When discussing the realities of Jewish adaptation to American life, I use *acculturation*, which is more historically accurate to the goals and realities of most of the American Jewish community.

Given the focus of this research on acculturated or acculturating upwardly mobile Jewish men, I have largely limited my sources to those written in English. There are some exceptions, and in these cases I have translated specific phrases or expressions from either Hebrew or Yiddish for authenticity and accurate depiction of the source. However, the key demographic of Jewish Americans under examination are those who cherish ambitions to absorb dominant, and therefore largely Protestant, male gender norms. Along with the American gender norms they emulate, many ambitious Jewish men also absorb some of the negative attitudes held by white Anglo-Saxon Protestants about Europeans, new American immigrants, and Jewish uniqueness. For this reason, the sources they produce are generally written in English, as they consider Russian, German, Polish, and Yiddish to be the languages of recent arrival, not aspirational acculturation. This distinction, therefore, is one not only of language but of socioeconomic status, as English is the language of choice for American Jews who want to identify as Americans and with rapid acculturation. The tightening of this focus, within the period considered, also narrows the Jewish subjects to a largely Ashkenormative, often East Coast centered group.

Reining in the focus of this study on those Jewish men who strive toward Americanization, I do not claim that my conclusions apply to all Jewish American men. Indeed, they are not intended to do so. Entire swaths of Jewish men in America remain unexamined, though they enter into our story as actors and help to complicate the narrative of the group on which I do focus. By focusing on one segment of American Jewish men, I highlight their specific stream of continuous attempts to attain white American masculinity, their successes and failures, and, at times, their interactions with other segments of Jewish America who did not follow the same path or share their desires for homogeneity. The term *hegemonic masculinity*, indeed the concept of its existence and necessity for historical and gender-based research, has been debated since its introduction to the field in the 1980s.[7] Loosely agreeing with a theory advocated by Robert Connell, I believe that merely recognizing the diversity within masculinity is hardly useful without also examining the relationships and power dynamics between masculinity's alternate forms.[8] By identifying and recognizing the importance of a hegemonic masculinity, we can better evaluate the gender politics taking place within varying forms of masculinity, through inclusion and exclusion of more peripheral masculinities from the hegemon. The study of masculinity, at least since Carrigan and colleagues' 1985 article "Toward a New Sociology of Masculinity," recognizes that masculinity is not dependent only on sex-role theory or the power dynamics between men and women, but can be defined by the power dynamics among men as well. Through collective practice in masculine performance, or *manhood acts*, a masculine hegemon forms and creates subordinated masculinities through a co-constitutive process. Though this work examines American Jewish masculinity, not the American hegemonic ideal, the former cannot be understood outside of its dynamic with the latter. The history of Jewish men and masculinity is largely one of interaction and negotiation with mainstream constructions of manhood.

It is imperative to focus for a moment on the definition of these gendered terms and their implications in the study of men and in this book. As a work employing gender theory to draw conclusions based on historical evidence, the term *male* refers only to an individual's biological sex. However, the term *men* is steeped in cultural and social implications. Because males and females both learn from a young age that they are to identify themselves as boys before men, and as girls before women, gender identity is clearly distinct from anatomy and is a standard to be reached, not something one is born possessing. To be recognized, therefore, as a man, and to derive the benefits from membership in that dominant group, one must compellingly perform masculinity, or (as Michael Schwalbe explains) put on a convincing *manhood act*.[9] An act of manhood is one that is not merely conducted by someone identifying as a man, but one that aims to claim privilege, elicit deference, or resist exploitation or subordination.[10] *Manhood*, for the purpose of this study, is the status of being successfully credited with the identity of manliness.

As the realities behind the *understanding* of Jewish manhood in America provide the impetus for this book, it is the performative aspects of masculine constructions that are most significant in understanding the changing of the Jewish male aesthetic over the twentieth century. *Performativity* acknowledges that there is no actual "reality/truth" of femininity and masculinity, only the reality created by performing these gender identities. Judith Butler popularized this view of the individual as a product of their place in society as determined by their language, and convention. Butler acknowledges the significance of the performance of gendered behavior as actually forming the identities and sense of self we maintain.[11] Jewish men, though not intentionally applying such a theory, attempt to change their own gendered sense of self through the performance of more mainstream conventions of masculinity imposed by a dominant concept of normative heterosexuality.

Much of the vocabulary and framework for understanding gender and sexuality in this book are drawn from the interdisciplinary field of queer theory, which I employ to deconstruct the categories of gender and sex as socially constructed and malleable. Though there are Jewish men throughout the Jewish American story who identify as queer, the language and methods of queer theory expose the categories of gender as constructed in all cases, not merely those who identify as such.[12] The term *queer* functions as a code for characteristics that oppose norms (and thereby define them) as well as those inherent within norms that continuously function to subvert them.[13] By this definition, the study of Jewish men benefits tremendously by the inclusion of queer theory, as Jewish male gender often functions in opposition to the norms of the historical context in which Jews live.[14]

The intentional actions of Jewish men to change themselves and their society, for the purpose of creating an improved or altered perception (and thus reality) of their own gender identity, is the very definition of performativity. Sociologist Michael Kimmel writes of manhood that it "is neither static nor timeless; it is historical."[15] What he acknowledges in this statement is that to understand the perception of masculinity at a given time in history, scholars must look at men's performance of gender as a response to their historical environment. In the case of Jews especially, I expand this further—Manhood is neither static nor timeless; it is historical, both a product of its time and a cause for historical change in its time. In short, Jewish masculinity is defined by Jewish men's place in society, and the resulting peripheral masculinity acts as a motivator that can also help to explain changes in Jewish history.

Through performative manhood acts, men claim their masculinity and attempt to access the male hegemon. However, in many cases certain elements of hegemonic masculinity are rejected by a male subgroup, while they embrace others to maintain a masculine identity proximate to, if not in line with, the hegemonic masculine ideal. Homosexual men, for example, reject heterosexuality as part of their masculine identity, though it is a substantial part of the hegemonic manhood performed in American society. Homosexual men and gay culture then embrace other manhood acts (glorification of large, muscular bodies; sexual voracity, conquest, and risk-taking; and macho fashion) claiming manhood status without subscribing to the full hegemonic notion of manhood.[16] Daniel Boyarin makes a similar claim of Jewish men (though he does not use this precise language), that Jewish men claim an alternate identity that pushes aside aggressive notions of manhood in favor of the gentler aspects still associated with the hegemonic ideal. Boyarin explains that in spite of a history that casts homosexual acts negatively, traditional Judaism itself was never a heterosexual culture, as heterosexuality was a concept yet to be constructed by modern society. He explains that in the absence of panic surrounding the confines of heteronormative masculinity, Jewish men are more able to embrace behaviors generally coded as "feminine."[17] I demonstrate, over the course of this book, that Jewish men did not so readily agree to put key elements of American manhood aside and accept their separate manhood, they continued to attempt to reshape themselves and their public image to escape the peripheral manhood into which they were consistently shunted.

As an example, consider the connection between manhood and nation. Scholars have taken keen interest in the connections between gender and the nation-state, using masculinity as a lens to better understand the process of nation-building and the gendered realities of nationalism. George Mosse explains in his 1996 work, *Image of Man*, how European society characterized the masculine ideal as the embodiment of the nation. Those who were nationals and members of the dominant group inherited measures of respectability and the honorable attributes of hegemonic masculinity, while those outside the favored group were stripped of such basic human gender classifications. The other side of this process was the feminization of "orientalism" as un-European, which included Jews, who were thus left out of European nationalist manliness entirely. This separation of Jews from the nation is a persistent theme in Jewish history, as non-Jews the world over have suspected and accused their Jewish countrymen of possessing dual loyalties.

Jews rejected from the nationalism of their own homelands followed this denial with their own separate nationalist movement—Zionism. A consequence of their rejection was a desire to seek out a nationalism that would include them, and also allow them access to the masculinity connected to the nation. Simon Wendt and Pablo Dominguez Andersen's 2015 edited volume of essays on the role of masculinity in national identity even uses the experiences of Jewish men and the formation of Jewish nationalism as the "best-known example of marginalized men's agency," though, interestingly, no chapter in the volume contributed an analysis of that particular example. Once Jewish nationalism (and eventual statehood) became a reality, it had a significant impact on Jewish male identity and further complicated the relationship between Jews and the masculine hegemon. It did, in many ways, redeem Jewish men through performative masculinity on a global stage, but it also did nothing to counter accusations of dual loyalty in the many nations where Jews lived as lifelong nationals and patriots.

Zionism is one of many such subjects I examine in the following chapters, not rewriting the excellent work of scholars who have studied it before, but adding to the discussion the influence of Jewish masculinity on its development and character. I am indebted to the scholars who have built the rich field of Jewish history to which this volume contributes. Without the foundational works of Jewish gender history, which focus primarily on women, this study would have no ground on which to build. Scholars of Jewish gender like Paula Hyman, Marion Kaplan, Deborah Dash Moore, Judith Baskin, Riv-Ellen Prell, Joyce Antler, and many others have expanded historical understanding of Jewish life in America and elsewhere by incorporating women fully into Jewish history, not merely inserting female sources into otherwise male narratives. Though men are certainly present in these studies, they generally appear as they relate to their dynamics with (and treatment of) Jewish women. In 2017, Sarah Imhoff opened the field of history of American Jewish masculinity with *Masculinity and the Making of American Judaism*, the first book to explore several intentional Jewish constructions of manhood in the United States from 1900 to 1924.[18] This book builds on several of Imhoff's theories, methods, and findings to expand the very necessary work that she began, and to add to the questions she raised, which I hope will be taken up in diverse future scholarly discussions.

Nearly all of the prior works written on American Jewish masculinity have emerged from cultural and literary studies, which analyze popular images of Jewish men in America and theorize about their meaning in Jewish society.[19] These studies have raised the very questions that I have set out to answer through historical analysis. What is the story of real Jewish men, not those characters who appear on the screen or in novels as nebbishes or as fully formed "tough Jews?" How have actual Jews enacted or performed masculinity in their daily lives, contributing to supposed changes to the Jewish male image, including and beyond cultural representations? This work begins the process of unearthing the underlying truths behind the characters that scholars like Paul Breines have pointed to as evidence of a changing Jewish masculinity, identifying which elements of fiction are drawn from actual Jewish men and which are merely projections of what they desired to become.

The chapters that follow cover much temporal ground, beginning with the formation of Jewish America and American perceptions of Jewish manhood at the turn of the century, and continuing through the age of mass migration, both world wars, the creation of the Israeli state, and its influence on American Jewish life. This periodization is necessary to understand the ups, downs, and subsequent redirections of Jewish masculine goals over the last century. The major upheavals to global Jewry that occurred in the middle of the twentieth century interrupted an already unique process of acculturation within an American ethnic minority. Though Jews had made progress in moving their masculine image toward an acculturated, white, heteronormative manhood, the Holocaust and subsequent creation of a Jewish nation-state disrupted this already complex process. The first two chapters lay the groundwork for examining masculinity in America among an ethnic minority. Chapter 1 examines European notions of Jewish manhood that European migrants (both Jewish and non-Jewish) brought with them to the United States. These include not only the assumptions and practices of Jewish manhood in Europe but modern Jewish reactions to existing Jewish male stereotypes, including the creation of muscular Zionism. Showing the connection between European and American views of Jewish men, the second chapter reviews those notions of masculinity popular in the United States at the turn of the century and evaluates how conceptions of Jewish men did and did not fit the American ideal.

The following two chapters focus on the tension unique to this period of rapid growth through mass immigration in Jewish America, that which existed between immigrant and native-born American Jews. These chapters include various vignettes from the first half of the century, showing how Jewish masculinity played into and was formed by Jewish crime, athleticism, agriculture, fraternalism, and Zionism. The cultural division between native-born Jewish men and newly arrived mass immigrants (as well as that between immigrants and their native-born children) is a constant theme in these venues. As accessing American masculine norms became a tool of acculturation, the tension between these groups reveals a decidedly masculine goal and produced male-centered methods for Americanizing immigrants and second-generation American Jews, as well as masculinizing the established native-born Jewish community.

Chapters 5 and 6 evaluate the role of Jewish masculinity in and around the world wars. These chapters analyze the ways in which Jewish participation and visibility in the various branches of the American military affected notions of Jewish manhood in the United States across World Wars 1 and 11, respectively. As the Second World War had such great implications for Jews, beyond military participation and the American part in the conflict, chapters 7 and 8 explore two additional areas that had a significant impact on Jewish masculine identity. Chapter 7 is devoted to the Holocaust and the effect that the atrocities committed against Jews had on perceptions of Jewish masculinity (and gender on the whole) worldwide, but particularly in the United States. Chapter 8 then examines the role of the Yishuv (Jewish settlements in pre-Israel Palestine) in creating a new image of Jews popularized in the years following the conclusion of the Second World War. The effect of Israel on American Jewish identity is also considered, as is the reconfiguring of perceptions of Jewish masculinity based on images emerging from the fledgling state. These two influences, the events of the Holocaust and the image of the Sabra (the Israeli-born Jew), immediately complicated the progress that Jewish soldiers made to popular notions of Jewish manhood during the wars.

The final two chapters focus on the fracturing and diversifying nature of the tumultuous 1960s, for both Jewish identity and gender norms. Chapter 9 is devoted to the widening Jewish middle class and the shifting norms of Jewish American identity and masculinity that accompanied the Vietnam War and the Six-Day War in Israel. In response to the Vietnam War, unlike in previous conflicts, Jewish men attempted to prove their masculinity in nonmilitary venues and introduced new masculinities to the Jewish American character in the process. Jewish men reclaimed their masculinity through activism, protest, and rebellion. The last chapter focuses on Jewish participation in reactive movements of the late 1960s, including the antiwar and civil rights protest movements and the emergence of militant Judaism. The book does not end at the Six-Day War but follows the epoch-changing ramifications of that war on American Jews until disrupted by the next major Israeli conflict, the Yom Kippur War, in 1973.

By the close of the book, I identify several variant masculinities in Jewish America and trace their progress over the century. The stopping point in the early 1970s does not only present a disruption in Israeli life with the Yom Kippur War, but also a nearly simultaneous rupture in American life following the watershed year of 1968, which redefined Americans' relationship to their nation. The war in Vietnam, the civil rights movement, and the mayhem of the Chicago Democratic National Convention all complicated American identity and patriotism. The same can be said of the American understanding of gender. The feminist movement, antiwar protest, rise of counterculture, and ethnic revival all dramatically complicated gender in the United States in the aftermath of 1968. Though it does not become impossible to identify and track Jewish masculinities after this point, it does become a more complex task after, for example, the uprising at the Stonewall Inn in 1969 brought homosexuality more prominently into the national dialogue.

Much of what I have studied for this book is not unexamined material. Historians have written extensively on Jews in sports, Jewish gangsters, muscular Zionism, Jewish fraternities, Jews in the military, and nearly every other aspect of the present study. I reexamine those histories through a lens of immigration history, focused on the Jewish journey toward American manhood through action, representation, and self-image. This meant consulting some of the same sources used in other studies but examining and using them differently, identifying that a motivating factor in changes to American Jewish manhood is persistently related to the ongoing process of acculturation. It also meant following the leads in those sources to new and exciting places and recognizing new contributors to Jewish masculine identity that I had not foreseen. It is not meant to be a history of *Jewish men and*—as others have written (Jewish men and sports, Jewish men and religious practice, Jewish men and the movies, etc.), but an inclusive collage of the contributing factors leading to the realities of Jewish American masculine identity. This book is not a complete survey or analysis of Jewish masculinities by any stretch of the imagination. The research has taken me to different sources and conclusions that I could not have predicted but have embraced and incorporated into an unexpected narrative. This work provides the historical foundation on which continuing cultural analyses and future histories dealing with issues of Jewish masculinity can build. By limiting myself to performative masculinity (or acts of manhood) visible in the mainstream Jewish American landscape, I hope I have developed an actionable (if simplified) narrative on which to build and incorporate the divergent masculinities that I was unable to research, but that richly deserve attention.

Before feminist scholarship began to balance and enrich written history (to which my generation of scholars owes a tremendous debt), Jewish history was a history of men in which women appear as supporting characters. The work in balancing the scales is not yet done, and new valuable studies of Jewish women and gender are written every year. The purpose of a history of masculinity should never be to return to a history of men, as any one-sided history is inherently flawed and spurious. Nor should it be a history of men as the dominant side of a power struggle between men and women, as masculinity is defined and achieved just as much through men's dominance over other men as it is through their historical subordination of women. The purpose is to understand how the desire to identify, earn, prove, and maintain a masculine ideal has, in itself, been a driver of historical change. Throughout this book, I demonstrate that for Jewish American men, through their unique and complex relationships with masculine identity, this driver holds firmly to the wheel.

1
The Arrow Aimed at the Mauschel's Heart

Gendered Antisemitism and the Muscle Jew

> Our character has been corrupted by oppression, and it must be restored through some other kind of pressure. . . . All these sufferings rendered us ugly and transformed our character which had in earlier times been proud and magnificent. After all, we once were men who knew how to defend the state in time of war.
> —Theodor Herzl[1]

To trace the story of Jewish masculinity in America, we must begin by examining the treatment of European Jews by the nations in which they dwelt. The growing tension between Jews and Europeans, and particularly between Jewish masculinity and hegemonic masculinity, was largely a consequence of a solidifying ideal of manhood manifested by European nationalism. By the turn of the twentieth century, nationalist movements across Europe had become inseparable from concepts of ideal manhood performed through behavior and virtue. The modern West (the United States included) defined manliness through bravery, honor, devotion to nation, and by individual physical prowess and behavior. Jews, viewed by many of their countrymen as residents but not as national brethren, held a unique place in European and American society regarding these qualifiers for manhood. Non-Jews suspected that Jews maintained dual national loyalties, and subsequently rarely granted them full acceptance into nationalist movements and ideologies. The racial science that developed in nineteenth-century Europe and the United States to justify and explain oppression of those peoples "discovered" through exploration also argued that the Jewish people maintained immutably Jewish characteristics that could not be eliminated through social adaptation to European culture.[2] In addition, Jewish performative cultural differences at times contradicted modern European and American concepts of ideal family structure and proper gendered behavior. For this reason, members of the hegemon viewed Jewish men and women as outside of this ideal—separated by customs, values, and by their lack of modern statehood. As manliness became linked to the nation, rejection from the national ideal frequently meant rejection from the masculine hegemon as well.

Gendered Antisemitism and Historical Conceptualizations of Jewish Manhood

Antisemitic accusations of Jewish weakness, femininity, and cowardice are based on long-standing and pervasive views of Jewish men. The role of masculinity in Jewish culture, at least in the rabbinic culture of the last two millennia, historically differed from the dominant European societies in which most Jews resided for the past thousand years. In nearly all commentary on Jewish men and manhood, the same value statement appears concerning intentional Jewish masculine difference: Jews value mind over muscle. The belief in this statement as a fundamental truth of Jewish life is so real, so pervasive, that academic scholars of Jewish history and culture remarking on it rarely feel the need to justify it.[3] By looking at Jewish leaders and publications of the early twentieth century, however, it is clear that Jews established a diversity of attitudes toward various forms of masculinity. In the German-Jewish magazine *Ost und West*, for example, Jewish authors of fiction and commentary grappled with different views of Jewish masculinity. In the pages of *Ost und West*, authors attempted to hold up those qualities of more traditional Jewish male behavior (piety, honor, solidarity, charity, and such) associated with a gentle Jewish male identity, while also promoting the idea that Jewish men were good German nationalists, strong soldiers, and honorable fighters.[4]

Even accepting the reality of diverse Jewish masculinities, the most dominant images of Jews routinely conflicted with images of manhood promoted by the societies in which Jews lived. It was largely out of antisemitic assumptions and beliefs that negative stereotypes against Jews emerged, much more so than by Jewish practice. The pervasive stereotype of Jewish weakness provides a constant point of reference throughout contemporary commentary, literature, modern scholarship, and even Jewish attitudes and assumptions in America today. According to the dominant stereotype, the Jewish man was physically weak, stooped and feeble, cowardly or meek, averse to physical exertion and violence, incapable at sports and athletics, and more inclined to stay indoors with his texts than to get outside in the fresh air. Stereotypes are not generally accurate, and this is no exception. However, considering the support of this idea within the Jewish community itself, and acknowledging the determination of some Jewish men to alter this perception of their own nature, it must be considered that the stereotype contains some measure of historical reality (whether the reality created the stereotype or vice versa) and that some Jews themselves embraced it as accurate.

Antisemitism has been a gendered prejudice since its inception. This is unsurprising as, to an extent, Jewish life itself has always been gendered. Some aspects of Jewish life became gendered through cultural practice while the rabbinic tradition created others, such as the passing of Jewish identity through the mother. Even the most basic Jewish covenant, male circumcision, made Jewish men physically distinct in almost any land they dwelled. Antisemites believed Jews to possess a number of unique attributes dating back to the Middle Ages: horns, tails, devilish odor, dark skin, and even the belief in Jewish male menstruation.[5] Though even the last of these can be dismissed as another absurdity of anti-Jewish prejudice (like the belief that Jews had actual horns), it remains a significant allegation, as it regularly surfaced to justify blood libel accusations. The belief supporting this connection maintained that Jewish men needed to acquire Christian or virgin blood in order to cure such distinctly Jewish diseases as male menstruation.[6] This misconception continued well into the twentieth century, as Sigmund Freud believed in male menstruation (believing that he had identified it in his own natural cycle), though he believed that it remained an unrecognized process in *all* men, not merely in Jews.[7] Years later in Nazi Germany, Theodor Fritsch published a counterargument, once again presenting male menstruation as evidence of a separate and unique Jewish sexuality.[8]

Although non-Jews propagated antisemitic notions of Jewish gender, Jews also played a role in spreading some of the least flattering stereotypes about themselves. The most notable and oft-cited and studied of these Jewish influencers of antisemitism was Otto Weininger, a Jewish-born philosopher of the late nineteenth and early twentieth centuries. His prominence, and the amount of scholarly work examining his influence on notions of Jewish gender, is particularly astounding given his very short career, as he committed suicide at the age of twenty-three. There is so much work on the life and writings of Weininger that I limit myself here to a brief commentary on his influence on antisemitic images of Jewish men through the first half of the twentieth century.[9] In his magnum opus, *Sex and Character* (1903), Weininger devotes an entire chapter to the topic of Jewishness. Weininger, himself born a Jew (though baptized as a Protestant on the day of his doctoral graduation in 1902, the year before his suicide), makes a clear distinction in his attack on Jewishness; it is not a racial failing, he speculates, but a flaw in the Jewish mental process: "Judaism must be regarded as a cast of mind, a psychic constitution, which is a *possibility* for *all* human beings and which has only found its most magnificent *realization* in historical Judaism [emphasis original]."[10]

It is worth noting that despite his disparaging language about Jewish men, he still holds them in higher esteem than women, reminding the reader that "the most superior woman is still infinitely inferior to the most inferior man."[11] However, his disparaging views on women provide a jumping-off point for his chapter on Judaism, in which he clearly impugns the manhood of the Jew, "Just as in reality there is no such thing as the 'dignity of women,' it is equally impossible to imagine a Jewish 'gentleman.'"[12] Weininger uses existing beliefs about Jews to further his gender theories around them, for example, in the belief that Jews commit fewer serious crimes. He does not attribute this quality to a higher morality but to the fact that like women, Jews lacked greatness, a quality necessary in all passionate acts, of both good and of evil.[13] Great men, he claims, require a depth that both Jews and women lack.[14] He also employs the idea that Jews focus on family life and connection as another means to equate them to women. He writes that the entire idea of family itself is maternal in origin and female in construction.[15] Though he perpetuated and even created some antisemitic conceptions of Jewish gender, Weininger's commentary also shows the degree of influence these notions of Jewish gender exerted in his time, not only in Christian circles, but among Jews themselves. Or, in his harsher assessment, "The antisemitism of the Jew . . . proves that nobody who knows the Jew regards him as lovable—not even the Jew himself."[16] Though Weininger is an extreme example, even those far less antisemitic showed degrees of this self-loathing.

Jewish sexuality, and the way antisemitic rhetoric presents it, exemplifies the ways in which antisemitic notions about Jews become gendered, in the cases of both Jewish men and women. One of the most frequent faulty assumptions about gendered antisemitism is that the representation of Jewish men as seducers of Aryan women in Nazi propaganda depicts Jews as masculine, even aggressively so.[17] Such representations of Jewish men certainly exist, but the assumption that they cast a masculine light on those men is faulty. The assumptions behind the Nuremburg Laws in Nazi Germany that dealt with Jewish gender, for example, show that this was indeed a pervasive accusation, as it assumed that Aryan women were unsafe working in Jewish homes and among Jewish men. According to Patricia Szobar, Jewish men consistently found themselves accused by Germans of hyperactive sex drives, described as deviant and animalistic, and as exploiters of Aryan women for their own sexual gratification. In truth, in the nineteenth and into the mid-twentieth century, these qualities of hypersexuality, sensuality, and seduction more often pertained to women and were considered feminine characteristics.[18] European society saw such qualities as despicable aspects of sexual femininity, embracing other manhood acts as evidence of proper manliness (such as devotion, honor, chivalry, and stoicism).[19] To ascribe such sensuality to Jewish men through accusations of seduction of gentile women was a rejection of those men from the masculine hegemon. The generally accepted distinctive difference between Jews and Christians precipitated and supported this distinction. According to popular notions of religion and manhood, Christians exemplified the aforementioned masculine qualities of goodness and European delicacy. Christians were masculine and Jews effeminate.[20]

Otto Weininger even went so far as to explain that the Jew was unmanly in his sexual desires, but still less sexually potent than Aryan men (potency being a clear marker of manhood). Sex, he claimed, drives the actions and behaviors of women. "To put it bluntly," he wrote, "Man has the penis, but the vagina has Woman."[21] The same, he believed, applied to Jewish men. He wrote, "The Jew is always more lecherous, more lustful, than the Aryan man, although, strangely enough and possibly in connection with the fact that he is not really of an anti-moral disposition, he is less sexually potent and certainly less capable of any great lust than the latter."[22]

Reducing the potency of Jewish men in rhetoric about Jews was not limited to their behavior, but attacked their spirits and bodies as well. The comparison of Jewish men to women applied in a far more physical way than merely their degree of lustfulness, as Weininger posited. Jewish men, according to Daniel Boyarin, actually view the act of circumcision as crippling, lessening a man by turning him into a Jew, no longer a true possessor of a penis.[23] This argument, based in Freud's psychoanalysis, had roots in popular Viennese society. Sander Gilman observed that not only was the circumcision diminishing to masculinity as well as the male sex organ, but physically equated Jewish men to women, as the clitoris was similarly seen as a "truncated penis." The popular Viennese view of the relationship between the body of the male Jew and women was such that in the Viennese slang of the time, the clitoris was known simply as the "Jew" (*Jud*), and female masturbation as "playing with the Jew."[24] This attack on the Jewish maleness, the physical sex organ rather than masculine behavior, undermines the ability of Jewish men to access hegemonic masculinity even through the most prominent and successful manhood acts. As Raine Dozier showed in their study on female-to-male transmen, recognition of a male body in society allows for individuals to claim more diverse masculinities, as once maleness is assumed it provides a foundation on which one can build credibility as a member of the dominant masculine group.[25] By undermining the assumption that a Jewish man is, in fact, male, larger European society made it even more difficult for Jewish men to be seen as having attained any respectable form of manhood.

Gendered antisemitism swung both ways, targeting both Jewish men and women, men as feminine and women as overly masculine. Otto Hauser's 1921 essay *Juden und Deutsche* (Jews and Germans) shows how German men perceived Jewish gender as manifesting in both the body and behavior of Jewish men and women. "In no other ethnicity," he explained, "does one find so many feminine men and masculine women as among the Jews." He further explained that Jewish women, more than others "race to enter professions of men: studying every subject imaginable from law and medicine to theology and becoming representatives of groups and of the people." He further claimed that based solely on their secondary sexual characteristics, one could only determine the sex of one-third of Jewish women accurately. He attributed this to their unfortunate possession of masculine facial hair, small breasts, and the propensity of Jewish women to wear their hair short.[26] Hauser's claims about Jewish women's appearances are more likely influenced by his perception of masculine performance by Jewish women in German society than by their actual appearance or physical characteristics. The perception of women as embodying a typical male behavior codifies their abnormal gender as it presumes inherent connection between masculine behavior and physical maleness.[27]

Jewish scholars, whether historical, religious, literary, or cultural, have long connected the uniqueness of perceived Jewish gender to Jewish religious practice, texts, and exclusion from dominant societies. According to Barbara Breitman, antisemitism totally debased and oppressed Jewish men, forcing them to construct a Jewish masculinity that valued piety over brute strength. Through this ideal, Jewish men could repress their rage and hold submission to suffering as a masculine quality.[28] This last point, submission to suffering, frequently crops up in nonreligious Jewish discussions of manliness and Jewry, in terms of military participation, sports, and public image. Theodor Herzl, for example, also believed there to be a perceptible difference in the Jewish people, that the centuries of oppression and suffering had rendered Jews not only physically weak but ugly as well.[29]

In the attempts of Jewish men and women to acculturate into larger society, there is a discernible shift for Jewish men that altered their position and character comparatively more than that of Jewish women. Like Jewish men, Jewish women held different roles than those of the dominant cultures around them, though still relegated primarily to the home. The role of women in Jewish life proved more adaptable to Western culture, as middle-class gender norms supported elements of traditional Jewish women's behavior in the home while adapting to the "cult of domesticity."[30] Women began to take on more dominant roles as transmitters of Jewish religion and identity to the children, a role that previously fell under male responsibility in traditional European Jewish culture. While women adapted to bourgeois society and their roles as women in this new environment, Jewish men found more dramatic changes affecting their conceptions of manhood. Women, for example, found it possible to remain traditionally Jewish in the home, which fell under their jurisdiction. Jewish men, however, living more public work lives, struggled to maintain religious lifestyles while fulfilling the travel and business obligations of the modern world, making it more difficult to perform religious duties.[31]

As a result of these differences unique to Jewish life, masculinity within Jewish culture is an inimitable phenomenon. Attitudes toward this unique Jewish position varied, not universally negative, positive, or even in favor of change. In mid-nineteenth-century Germany, several Jewish leaders embraced and promoted this alternate and uniquely Jewish form of masculinity. They lauded the behavior of Jewish men as particularly feminine, advocating the idea that Jewish men embodied the most positive characteristics generally attributed to women, such as devotion to family and home and compassionate dispositions.[32] Such views also appear in some Jewish representation of muscular or performatively masculine Jews as shamefully assimilated and Europeanized.[33] In *Unheroic Conduct*, Daniel Boyarin recounts growing up as a "sissy," more girl than boy, but he identifies the difference between himself and other boys as not one of gender but of culture. "I didn't think of myself so much as girlish but rather as Jewish." Boyarin explains that his gender identity is so linked to his Jewish identity as to make him feel even more connected to his Jewishness and disdainful of mainstream masculinity. Indeed, Boyarin clarifies that he penned his 1999 book to reclaim the feminine Jewish man as a tradition dating back to the Babylonian Talmud, and in doing so he thoroughly examined the origins of that character. As the counterweight to those attempts at masculinizing Jewish men (which took the form of acculturating to European non-Jewish society), the religious community began to embrace this alternate and uniquely Jewish "gentle" ideal of manhood, emphasizing more traditional Jewish life and religion.

As popular concepts of admirable manly behavior coalesced in Europe, the visual image of masculinity also, quite literally, began to take shape. Several events and trends set this ideal in motion, including the revival of Greek art and form, the German fraternity and gymnastics movements, growing nationalist movements and the heroism of military success (which both gained momentum during the Napoleonic wars), and medieval ideals of knighthood. The popular perception of the ideal man became lithe, fit, muscular, and angular. Art historian Johann Joachim Winckelmann helped to revive and popularize this image leading up to the nationalist movements in Europe, believing that the classic Greek male ideal exemplified through physical form all the attributes from medieval times that defined ideal masculinity and morality.[34] As this ideal man solidified in Europe in the late nineteenth and early twentieth centuries, Jewish men found themselves stuck in the odd position of not belonging to the newly rigid classification of *men* in Western society, but falling instead into a separate category, more analogous to the position of women.

Exclusion of Jewish men from mainstream concepts of accepted masculinity extended far beyond and outside of Western Europe. The Ottoman Empire also considered those Jews living in its territory outsiders, and so held them to a different standard of behavior and honor than the Muslim subjects of the empire. Ottomans categorized both Jews and Christians as *dhimmis* (non-Muslims living in an Islamic state), granting them legal protection while determining their inferior status (subject to special taxes and restrictions meant to degrade and visually distinguish them from Muslim subjects).[35] Yaron Ben-Naeh noted a distinction in the nature of Jewish and Muslim codes of honor in his examination of Ottoman Jews, explaining that the concept of honor in Hebrew (*kavod*) meant either an internal value or personal virtue or could be manifested as an external gesture toward another worthy person. Islamic interpretations of honor (*sheref*), by contrast, though they also recognized two kinds of honor, included separate ideals for male honor (earned through acceptable masculine behavior like courage and generosity) and female honor (referring to sexual behavior, primarily modesty and limiting their exposure to the company of men).[36] Within this gendered definition and the law of the state, one must be Muslim to have honor, and so Jews were denied such recognition and sought it among their own people instead of larger Ottoman society.

Therefore, within Ottoman Jewish communities, elements of masculine honor resembled those in much of Jewish Europe (religious piety, morality, humility, modesty, and such). A difference worth noting between the Jews of Western Europe (the primary focus of this chapter) and the Jews of the Ottoman Empire is evident in their image, and how they present masculinity to the rest of society. Adult Jewish men did, in a way separate from the Ottoman definition, assert their own masculine codes of conduct and honor, embracing a peripheral form of masculinity outside of the masculine hegemon of the empire. They considered the beard, for example, a visual representation of Jewish manhood, one which, according to Yaron Ben Naeh, was an indispensable component of Jewish male honor in the Muslim Orient. By the start of the twentieth century, the trimming of a man's beard, though more accepted, became a mark of secularism among Ottoman Jews, and therefore an embrace of another variant of Jewish manhood.[37]

Though this chapter focuses on the development of European perceptions of Jewish masculinity and Jewish responses to those assumed characteristics, by recognizing the parallel struggle of Jews across the global diaspora, a clear trend emerges. As outsiders, Jewish difference has long been identified and maintained by the dominant culture, and those cultures highlight and use Jewish manhood as distinct from the national identity and dominant perceptions of successful manhood.

Rejecting Emasculation: The Manly Foundations of the Zionist Movement in Europe

For Jews in Europe, as nationalism developed and became deeply engrained in daily life, so too did the ways in which gender determined one's place within or outside of the mainstream. Nationalism rose in popularity, and European society characterized the masculine ideal as embodying the nation. Members of the dominant national group inherited measures of respectability and honorable attributes of the masculine ideal, while stripping those outside the favored group of such basic classifications. The inclusion or exclusion of marginal groups in national martial pursuits and common practice both show this division. Jews were key among marginalized groups, belittled as they were by Western European society as particularly cowardly and effeminate.[38]

Zionism provided a Jewish answer to the question of nationalism in the late nineteenth century, as a response to rejection from both the nationalism and hegemonic masculinity of Western European nations.[39] It was one of several contemporary movements that developed as Jewish responses to the political shifts of the time across Europe. Unlike others that more closely paralleled the socialist movements of the time, such as the Bund, the Zionist movement was both easily exportable to the United States (a nation resistant to Eastern European socialism) and directly mimicked the masculine practices of Western European nationalism.

The Zionist movement gained momentum among European Jews and provided a framework to reconstruct Jewish nationalism, hand in hand with Jewish manhood, to more closely identify with contemporary non-Jewish movements and their masculine ideal. The Zionist movement, as the following chapters will examine, became a tool for constructing manhood through multiple channels in the United States as well. Hegemonic nationalist masculine ideals in European mainstream culture coalesced in the nineteenth century, following the decline of the aristocracy and the subsequent appropriation of their ideals by the middle class. Zionism owes a surprising debt to this coalescence, particularly to the nationalist embrace of the sport of dueling. The bourgeoisie adopted dueling as a valid measure and mark of honor (and proof of masculine vigor) and maintained it for decades into the twentieth century.[40] This idyllic or stereotypical image of masculinity developed from several attributes standardized by the image of knighthood and from medieval times. Such court-related traditions exemplified qualities like chivalry, loyalty, perseverance, and physical courage (most notably the act of dueling) which came to epitomize manliness both physically and morally.[41]

During the late nineteenth and early twentieth centuries, Europeans frequently denied Jews full acceptance to the middle class (despite their having gained legal equality) by refusing them the satisfaction of a duel. This denial continued long after dueling gained popularity and continued in Germany as recently as the 1920s. Dueling presented yet another hurdle for middle-class Jewish men to overcome in their long run for acceptance in European society. Merely granting an individual the opportunity to duel gave the dueler a mark of status, even if they lost the bout and ended up with the traditional facial scar of the defeated. For this reason, Europeans accused Jewish men of marking themselves on the face with fake dueling wounds—as society considered men more respectable and honorable if they had been scarred in a duel.[42] Being a

Figure 1. German fraternity students show off their fresh dueling scars on a walk. *Renommierbummel*, by George Muhlberg, postcard, circa 1910. Wikimedia Commons contributors. "File:Mühlberg—Renommierbummel.jpg," Wikimedia Commons, https://commons.wikimedia.org/w/index.php?title=File:M%C3%BChlberg_-Renommierbummel.jpg&oldid=492902234 (accessed May 11, 2023).

product of the university setting, bearing scars from duels also indicated high academic rank and social privilege.

Several famous Jewish leaders and thinkers advocated dueling as a means of achieving social status for individual Jews seeking equality and recognition and to improve the dominant population's perception of the entire Jewish people. Zionist pioneer Theodor Herzl experienced much of this exclusion and denial firsthand and cited it as formative to his worldview. Herzl advocated Jewish participation in dueling, believing that it would both raise Jewish status and advance the fight against antisemitism. Herzl was, in his own words, "exceedingly captivated by knightliness and manliness," and so sought to engage in this manliest of actions to the best of his ability.[43] This embrace of dueling to further the Jewish cause was an attempt to participate in a very clear act of manhood, which would demonstrate the Jewish ability to perform masculinity on par with their national brethren. In 1881, while attending the

University of Vienna, he joined a German nationalist dueling fraternity, Albia, one of the few that allowed Jewish participants with the caveat that the Jew joining must shed the "Jewish spirit" and loyalty to the Jewish faith, acquiring a "manly German hardness" in its place.[44]

However, he hardly managed to participate in the performative manliness he sought, as he was never in ideal physical condition. The Austrian military rejected him from enlisting for being "physically unfit" and in his time at Albia, he fought only one duel. This did not stop him from challenging other men who had offended him to duels in the following years, which he did three times, but none came to fruition. In the first two challenges, his and his opponent's selected "seconds" who resolved the issue without combat, and he withdrew himself from the last duel due to his father's illness (though it rankled him for years and made him increasingly defensive about his perceived cowardice). According to Jacques Kornberg, Herzl's writing (particularly his play, *The New Ghetto*) proved that he saw his loathsome traits of cowardice (whether real or perceived) as distinctly Jewish, and dueling as their natural antithesis and remedy.[45]

Refusing Jews the satisfaction of duels was a point of pride and access to the upper echelons of Viennese society, but it also had repercussions for the place of Jews even outside of the university. The idea that Jews lacked honor affected Jewish access to the Austrian military as well. In 1896, Herzl wrote in his diary,

> Great excitement at Vienna University. The "dueling," "Aryan" fraternities have decided to refuse satisfaction to Jews, whatever the weapons, because every Jew is supposed to be cowardly and without honour. My young friend Pollak and another Jew have challenged two antisemites who are officers in the reserve. And when they declined to fight, the two Jews laid information against them with the General Command, which referred them to the Regional Command. On its decision depends a great deal—in fact, the future position of Jews in the Austrian Army.[46]

For this reason, Herzl and other Jews on university campuses, those breeding grounds of prestige and masculinity, formed entirely Jewish groups of their own to combat the feminized Jewish stereotype and strengthen their self-confidence. Jews founded entirely Jewish fraternities in late nineteenth-century Germany that embraced the Jewishness of the members while simultaneously stressing their "German spirit," mimicking the manly behaviors of German fraternities. According to Marion Kaplan, the numerous Jewish student groups that cropped up to combat antisemitism (fraternities, nonfraternal Jewish clubs, and Zionist groups) were meant as a temporary measure to allow Jews to participate in integrated, not separate, campus life. They would cease to exist when Jews took their place among German students, but their situation did not improve enough to reach that goal.[47] Herzl himself resigned from Albia in 1883, in protest of statements released by the fraternity, in which they endorsed antisemitic views. Antisemitism in hypermasculine German and Austrian dueling societies was not a passing fancy. To this day, in Austria particularly, there are dueling societies on college campuses that promote nationalist exclusivism and far right extremism. They are secret societies, but they continue the traditions of dueling and even earning prestige by gaining facial scars. Remaining dueling clubs are generally associated with the white-nationalist far-right or identitarian movement.[48]

The same year in which Herzl resigned from Albia, Jewish students at the University of Vienna founded the first Jewish-nationalist student organization in Western Europe, Kadimah, and in their periodical, the foundations of Jewish nationalism would provide the structure for Theodor Herzl to construct the ideology of political Zionism. Though the organization began as an academic society, Kadimah changed in the early 1890s to become an entirely Jewish dueling society, full of Jewish men who wanted to fight back actively against accusations of Jewish cowardice.[49] Until the founding of the Zionist Organization in 1896, only the Jewish student body championed the Zionist movement, and several of the manly members of Kadimah became some of its most active leaders and supporters. In fact, the first Kadimah student to successfully engage an opponent in a duel was Siegmund Werner, who later became Theodor Herzl's close associate and editor in chief of the Zionist central organ, *Die Welt*.

Herzl frequently spoke and wrote about his goals to rebuild Jews into the strong and healthy Hebrew nation of biblical times. However, he focused less explicitly on the physical rebuilding of the Jewish body, concerning himself and his brand of Zionism with the national manifestation of the Jewish body, through the political construction of a Jewish state. One of Herzl's contemporaries, first Zionist converts, and arguably the second most significant name in early Zionist history, was Max Nordau, a Hungarian physician and writer, notable for his leadership in the Zionist Congress. In his 1892 book, *Degeneration*, Nordau clearly identified a degenerated type of man found in the modern world and based on current medical theories of neurosis, particularly with the recently coined condition *neurasthenia* (defined as nervous system exhaustion). An American neurologist, Dr. George Miller Beard, created the diagnosis in 1869 and defined it as a negative condition of modern society, exhibited with fatigue, anxiety, headache, impotence, neuralgia, and depression. Nordau gave several causes for the degenerated condition of afflicted modern men, linking industrialism (the increasing speed of the modern world) and dehumanization (cramped conditions of urban centers) with the shattering of men's nerves, making them degenerated, nervous, and broken down.[50] This industrial setting dictated that such degeneration afflicted members of the industrial proletariat and other city dwellers (a group including the majority of Western European Jews), not the peasants remaining in the countryside. Though a creation of the modern world, these degenerated men could not possibly compete with men of hard muscles; the comparison was so outrageous, Nordau wrote, that it "will provoke our laughter."[51] As city dwellers and intellectuals, Nordau saw Jews as particularly vulnerable to the symptoms of urban degeneration, especially given the belief in a Jewish predisposition to such symptoms based on their race. The assertion that Jews suffered disproportionately from the diseases of modernity and degeneration was not an uncommon belief, nor was it short lived. An entry in the Jewish Encyclopedia in 1906 clearly stated, "In general it may be summarized that the Jews suffer chiefly from the functional nervous diseases, particularly from hysteria and neurasthenia."[52] In 1905, American Jewish social worker Charles Seligman Bernheimer published *The Russian Jew in the United States*, which went even further, claiming that:

> Neurasthenia and hysteria are more frequent among [the Jews] than among any other race. Some physicians have even gone so far as to state that the vast majority of the Jews are neurasthenics, and

that nearly all the women are hysterical. The observations of the physicians who practice among the Russian Jews in New York sustain these contentions. Hysteria is very frequent among women, and among men is far more often met with in Jews than among any other people.[53]

Both Theodor Herzl and Max Nordau envisioned the reality of a Jewish state not only as a future for Jewish life and nationalism but as a means of redeeming Jewish masculinity, vigor, and dignity. Zionism offered one of many methods by which Jews attempted to change their effeminate image, including the Jewish presence in various European armies (where allowed to enlist), the German gymnastics movement, and other manhood acts as individuals. Zionism, however, provided a name, a unifying goal, and served as a battle cry for Jewish redemption. In Nordau's speech to the Second Zionist Congress in 1898 (frequently cited as the conceptual moment of muscular Zionism), he made this connection more firmly and blatantly, identifying Jewish weakness and demonstrating the internalized stereotype of Jewish emasculation.

The language he used when speaking about Jewish suffering mirrored his published concept of degeneration, but here he spoke of redemption from the symptoms of degeneration (a product of their mistreatment and suffering). George Mosse explains that Nordau's projection for regeneration was one based entirely on manliness and contemporary beliefs about masculinity and dignity:

> The Jew must acquire a solid stomach and hard muscles, not just to overcome his stereotype—though this was important for Nordau—but also to compete, to find his place in the world. Nordau built upon the widespread assumption that the healthiness and vigour of the body determined that of the mind as well. . . . Men who were robust and stalwart would embrace the work ethic in contrast to those whose lack of will or lack of energy made them shy away from work or any form of activity.[54]

Nordau saw the solution for Jewish redemption in the gymnastics movement (not as much in participation of sports), in the retraining of Jewish bodies to repair the Jewish condition. He advocated physical exertion not

Figure 2. Audience in the hall at the opening of the Second Zionist Congress. Basel, Switzerland, August 28, 1898. On the podium, center stage, Herzl is giving the keynote address. On Herzl's left is Max Nordau. Robert Spreng, public domain, via Wikimedia Commons. Wikimedia Commons contributors, "File:Theodor Herzl Addressing the Second Zionist Congress in Basel, 1898 AL003483697.jpg," Wikimedia Commons, https://commons .wikimedia.org/w/index.php?title=File:Theodor_Herzl_Addressing_the _Second_Zionist_Congress_in_Basel,_1898_AL003483697.jpg&oldid= 473760271 (accessed June 29, 2023).

only to improve the lives of those Jews immediately practicing, but also to revive the Jewish race.

In an article in the second issue of *Die Jüdische Turnzeitung* (*The Jewish Gymnastics Journal* published by "Bar Kochba" Gymnastics Association) in 1900, Nordau published his full idea of the muscle Jew. The idea of the muscle Jew, and muscular Judaism, was not a sudden eruption in ideology, as portrayed in past scholarship, but a continuation of the same process that led Nordau to write *Degeneration* in 1892.[55] Nordau saw the Jewish race not as degenerate in the way that he had described others, because they could improve themselves through work and rebuilding.

Jews only lost their heroic and muscular stature through years of persecution, but could regain it with effort, whereas a truly degenerated race could never be redeemed.

Muscular Judaism was not inherently Zionist, as it was frequently part of the vision held by Jewish leadership for the future of the Jewish people. However, it became manifest more in Zionist art and culture than elsewhere, which depicted Jewish men as masculine and heroic, while Jewish women stood supportively at their sides. The image of "new Jews" (men) and the movement for physical regeneration frequently appeared in materials and films emerging from Jewish settlements in Palestine, in Jewish art created in Europe reflecting life in the Yishuv, and in material disseminated in Zionist circles.[56] Zionists created sports and gymnastics clubs in which Jews would cultivate their new manhood and saw those who participated as living examples of Nordau's muscular Zionism. Demonstrations of Jewish athleticism at each Zionist congress meeting inspired attendees in their hopes of the new Jewish man, as one female attendee of the 1914 Zionist Congress remarked, "They cast from us the reproach that the Jewish race is a race of physical weaklings."[57] Nordau's view of the muscular Jewish movement, though he did not entirely neglect women, still promoted a phallocentric undertaking specifically aimed at male redemption. He wrote in the *Jewish Gymnastics Journal*:

> Our new muscle Jews have not yet regained the heroism of their forefathers . . . to take part in battles and compete with the trained Hellenic athletes and strong northern barbarians. But morally speaking, we are better off today than yesterday, for the old Jewish circus performers of yore were ashamed of their Judaism and sought, by way of a surgical pinch, to hide the sign of their religious affiliation . . . while today, the members of Bar Kochba proudly and freely proclaim their Jewishness.[58]

The statement makes clear that the ideal of muscle Jewry remained unattained, but that the movement was underway, and that Jewish men no longer felt (or resigned themselves to feel) ashamed of their circumcised penises, but manifested pride in their identifiable, visible Jewishness.

Some of Max Nordau's concept of muscular Judaism had precedent, as nearly all of what he advocated clearly reflected the preexisting muscular Christian movement of the mid-nineteenth century and elements of the valor-based heroism of the Germanic tradition to which Herzl felt so drawn. The concept driving muscular Christianity is perhaps best expressed by Thomas Hughes in his 1868 novel, *Tom Brown at Oxford: A Sequel to School Days at Rugby, Volume 2*, in which he writes,

> The least of the muscular Christians has hold of the old chivalrous and Christian belief, that a man's body is given to him to be trained and brought into subjection, and then used for the protection of the weak, the advancement of all righteous causes, and the subduing of the earth which God has given to the children of men.[59]

The similarities are undeniable, both movements calling for physical training, protection of people and promotion of good, and working toward a cause. The difference is in the need for redemption from degeneration, which is at the core of muscular Judaism.

Muscular Judaism and political Zionism often appear in historical discourse as two distinctly different phenomena, the first associated with Max Nordau, the latter with Theodor Herzl. However, this distinction fails to get at the core motivation of Theodor Herzl's experiences that drove him to Zionism. An oft-repeated narrative of Herzl's path to Zionism cited his coverage as a journalist of the Dreyfus affair as his turning point. The mythology around his conversion to Zionism states that the Dreyfus affair jolted him out of his assimilationist delusions, seeing a high-ranking assimilated Jew destroyed by persistent antisemitic notions of Jewish disloyalty. However, by the time the Dreyfus affair began in 1894, Herzl's determination to overcome his own struggles as an assimilationist Jew was already manifest in attempts to defend Jewish honor and manhood.[60] His earlier history also explains that although Nordau coined and popularized the term *muscular Judaism*, Herzl long maintained that the redemption of the Jewish people would be achieved by rebuilding their physical and moral character. He adopted the stereotypes about Jews from Austrian culture and believed that they were not merely stereotypes, but that Jews were, in fact, cowardly, inferior, effeminate, and money-grubbing (alongside their good qualities). He, like Nordau, envisioned a new Jew, built physically stronger, more heroic and masculine, and with a nationalism of his own to rival his Austrian countrymen.

Whether Herzl's belief in antisemitic notions of Jewish men was accurate or merely antisemitic is a worthwhile ongoing debate. Though Herzl is still hailed as one of the great heroes of modern Jewish history, particularly among Zionists, others maintain that his determination to remasculinize Jewish men did more harm than good. Daniel Boyarin identifies Herzl's criticism of Jewish weakness as a mentality that "triumphs over antisemitism by becoming the perpetrator of antisemitism."[61] Herzl believed in two types of Jews, as Boyarin explains, "the 'true Jews,' the manly, honorable, dueling, fighting Jacob Samuels, were the Zionists. The others were the tribe of *Mauschel*, crooked, 'low and repugnant,' frightened, unresponsive to beauty, passive, queer, effeminate."[62] Boyarin's interpretation of Herzl's writings as antisemitic for the purpose of defeating antisemitism, is supported in Herzl's own words, "Zionism's second arrow is aimed at Mauschel's heart."[63]

The movement affected Jews throughout the diaspora and met with diverse responses, both inside and outside of Jewish communities. Regardless of the positive or negative effects of the Zionist movement on Jewish life overall, it gave Jewish men an outlet to exercise their muscles, change their image, and provide an alternative to the aspirational manhood of other nations through the creation of a purely Jewish one. An alternative that, ironically, meant leaving the nations in which they had so aspired to fully engage. Jews in the United States were the diaspora community least interested in the relocation aspect of political Zionism. Their lives in America gave them unprecedented freedom and access to mainstream society. However, at the turn of the century, notions of manhood and masculinity in the United States were in dramatic flux, just as they were in Europe, and in spite of their higher levels of acceptance, Jewish men still struggled for entry into this particular aspect of American identity.

2
Jews of "Weak Physique"

Masculinity, the Strenuous Life, and Jews
in America at the Turn of the Century

> I wish to preach, not the doctrine of ignoble ease, but the doctrine of the strenuous life, the life of toil and effort, of labor and strife; to preach that highest form of success which comes, not to the man who desires mere easy peace, but to the man who does not shrink from danger, from hardship, from bitter toil, and who out of these wins the splendid ultimate triumph. . . . We do not admire the man of timid peace. We admire the man who embodies victorious effort; the man who never wrongs his neighbor, who is prompt to help a friend, but who has those virile qualities necessary to win the stern strife of actual life.
>
> —Theodore Roosevelt, 1899[1]

American Jews formed a unique case among Jewish communities around the world, as unlike their brethren in Europe, the Jewish population grew so rapidly in the United States that at the close of the mass migration period, 54 percent of Jews in America were foreign-born.[2] Therefore, the Jewish American story of the early twentieth century is as much an immigrant story as it is about established Jewish communities. In fact, the narrative hinges on the interactions between the established Jewish community (largely middle class and urban) and newly immigrated Jews. Those who recently immigrated had a great adjustment to make in acculturating to the United States, a process largely facilitated by the preexisting Jewish community. American Jews, whether native-born or those arriving in great numbers from Europe at the turn of the century, hoped that the freedoms the young nation allowed them would translate into fuller acceptance into American society. As more Jews arrived from Europe and crowded into cities with other new immigrants and native-born Americans, they encountered racialist and antisemitic attitudes and stereotypes. Some of these antisemitic notions migrated with contemporary Europeans, and some were long-established with earlier waves of immigrants. The concepts of racial science, for example, which held that Jews were unalterably separate from European white races, became part of the American vernacular, just as conceptions of Anglo-Saxon or Teutonic character had done.[3] One of the great changes that took place in their relocation to America was the very definition of what Jewishness meant in racial terms. Though Europeans of many nations had long considered Jews racially distinct, when they arrived in America they entered a new playing field of perceived whiteness, on which they were in competition with all other non-Anglo immigrants and residents. Particularly in the age of mass migration, native-born Americans were finding the language to justify their own assumed superiority to incoming groups, and *whiteness* became an aspirational goal, and firmly linked to masculinity.

Whiteness, granted to specific incoming migrants (and not initially to Jews) is a racial construct encompassing a great number of ethnicities and is connected to notions of nationalism, class, and masculinity. At the turn of the century, white masculinity was in a state of flux and deep anxiety. There were several contributing factors to the apprehension surrounding manhood in America at this time, including industrialization, the emancipation of African Americans, the entry of women into the public sphere in greater numbers; the reevaluation of the American educational system as coed, the closure of the frontier and end of the "old West," rising popularity of team sports, and a rise in American imperial aggression.[4] This period has been referred to by scholars like Michael Kimmel, Clyde Griffen, Mark Carnes, and Joe Dubbert as being subject to a "crisis of masculinity," a term that originated among critics and commentators of the late nineteenth and early twentieth centuries. William F. Pinar complicates this view, however, demonstrating instead that the flux of masculinity was a complex process by which white men redefined masculinity to support their own gender-based and racially based superiority. They often used the term "crisis" to demonstrate the sense of impending threat to their own sense of masculine identity, and to justify dramatic efforts to restore American manhood. This shaky sense of masculine self is important to the present study because in a rapid renegotiation for masculine identity, white American men drew strong lines defining who belonged inside the masculine ideal and who fell outside of it. Jews, as outsiders in several factors complicating white manhood (and their largely Christian solutions), remained outside of the American masculine hegemon as well.

Jews and their denied status as "white men" are important elements of the Jewish story in America and are a constant thread throughout this study. As was the case for Jews in Europe, being Jewish in America was at once a religious, political, and social fact of life. The view of Jewishness, as Matthew Frye Jacobson has explained, transformed (via a complex process of social value reifying as perception) from knowledge of social difference to a discernable physicality.[5] White Anglo-Saxon Americans of the late nineteenth and early twentieth centuries identified certain physical attributes they believed made Jews visually recognizable, and that embodied moral and intellectual character. These physical traits were then, in turn, also used to explain the moral character they assumed to be so inherent to the Jewish race. Certainly, many of the physical distinctions are recognizable to those versed in antisemitic literature (hook noses, physically crooked, small eyes, and such), but the determined fact of Jewish difference was not merely espoused by antisemites, but by Jewish writers and commentors as well. Joseph Jacobs, in his 1891 volume *Studies in Jewish Statistics: Social, Vital and Anthropometric*, explained that among the races, the "substantial purity of the Jewish race" was unique, the vast majority of contemporary Jews being the lineal descendants of the diaspora of the Roman Empire.

Jews fought back against these images in several ways. They could not easily alter their phenotypical appearances, but they could alter the perception that their masculinity was antithetical to white hegemonic manhood. As the default sex, men were the primary targets of such perceptions of Jewish difference, so refuting perceptions of Jewish difference often took the form of improved masculine imagery. They did not, however, replicate the European Jewish response to emasculation through commitment to the muscular Zionist movement. At the turn of the century, a dominant image of American manhood came to the fore, provided by Theodore Roosevelt, whose manly ideal was both performative and racial in nature. He saw manhood as a means to dominate and control inferior races, a strategy he and others demonstrated on the American frontier. He believed this manhood would manifest by dominating both "inferior" races and the land and fauna of the American landscape.[6] Roosevelt served not only as a masculine example but also demonstrated how a man could rebuild himself in the public eye and shake off his previously emasculated image. As such, he not only embodied American manhood but also provided an aspirational goal of improved masculinity for American Jewish men. Performing and popularizing these acts of manhood, Roosevelt stood as a shining example of reinvigorated masculinity through intentional redefinition of self.

Theodore Roosevelt, American Masculinity, and Fighting Jews

Theodore Roosevelt, for much of the twentieth century, continued to define American rugged masculinity and the power of self-determined manhood. He worked diligently to create that image, after accusations of femininity, dandyism, and weakness plagued his early days in public service. In his youth, Roosevelt was a fragile, delicate boy who suffered from physical ailments as well as timidity—a "wimpy" sort of fellow. And once he began a career in the public eye, local presses attacked his masculinity and sexuality, calling him "Jane Dandy" and mocking his timid and effeminate demeanor.[7] Roosevelt believed that America had a unique power to reform and toughen weak men by allowing them to experience life on the western frontier, and he presented himself as an example of this transformation. When elected to the New York State Assembly in 1881, he had already begun his lifelong project to reconstruct himself as hypermasculine. In 1885, he purchased a ranch in the Dakota Territories where he overcame the emasculated milk-and-water moralities of the east coast and the upper class. He wrote *Hunting Trips of a Ranchman* (1885) and *The Wilderness Hunter* (1893) at his Dakota ranch, where his love of the American West and his firm belief in the frontier as a cure for the problem of effeminate white men developed. Roosevelt believed that building physical character required more than mere presence in the wilderness; one had to endure the trials of the rugged outdoors. He maintained that he owed more than he could express to the West, to the people he met and the life he lived on the land, which eventually accepted and embraced him and enabled his transformation.[8] Roosevelt never spoke at length or advocated aggressively for American Jewish men, specifically, to rebuild themselves as *Jews*, but his references to Jews throughout his career and correspondence demonstrate his belief that Jewish men could mirror his own experiences in becoming self-made men. Roosevelt's view of Jewish manhood is significant, not only because it reflects views of the time, but because Roosevelt's obsession with masculinity *defined* manhood at the time. As president, his reinforcement or criticism of negative depictions of Jewish manliness had influence not only on how America viewed Jewish men but on how Jewish men viewed themselves.

Roosevelt valued heroics and praised America's ability to create heroes that young men could emulate. He believed that Jews were no less capable of achieving such masculine goals than any other ethnic group. In a letter to prolific author and pastor Lyman Abbott in 1908, he pointed to Oscar Solomon Straus, his secretary of commerce and labor (the first Jewish United States cabinet secretary), as an outstanding example of Jewish success. He did so, however, by comparing Straus favorably with other successful Jews in business or finance, to whom he attributed the negative characteristics associated with the antisemitic stereotypes surrounding Jews and money that were well-established by his time.[9] "I want the Jewish young man who is born in this country to feel that Straus stands for his ideal of the successful man rather than some crooked Jew money-maker."[10] While praising Straus as an "ideal successful man" Roosevelt maintained a dislike of Jews in commerce and lamented his obligation to socialize with them. In a letter to his sister Anna Roosevelt Cowles, he described a lunch he attended in New York City that "at least half the guests were Jew bankers; I felt as if I was personally realizing all of Brooks Adams' gloomiest anticipations of our gold-ridden, capitalist-bestridden, usurer-mastered future."[11]

He saw the Jewish struggle from degradation to manhood as a parallel, but not shared, quest to white Anglo Americans like himself. In this vein, he urged men of Jewish descent to embrace laudable qualities of Jewish heroes of the past that might recover their own manhood, arguing that such men suffered for lack of rugged masculinity. "The great bulk of the Jewish population," he explained, "especially immigrants from Russia or Poland, are of weak physique, and have not yet gotten far enough away from their centuries of oppression and degradation."[12] Putting it into Jewish historical context, he told Israel Zangwill (the author of the 1908 play, *The Melting Pot*, dedicated in its printed version to Roosevelt), "I made up my mind it would be a particularly good thing for men of the Jewish race to develop that side of them which I might call the Maccabee or fighting Jewish type."[13] Interestingly, Roosevelt urged Jewish men not to precisely emulate those white Americans of the western frontier. He maintained a distinction between weak Jews and Jewish heroes on the one hand, and weak white men and their masculine counterparts on the other.

Like so many of his contemporaries, Roosevelt accepted Jewish weakness as a reality. He was also not alone in his belief that they could redeem themselves, though his timeline for their redemption was far shorter than others. Edward Ross, for example, an accepted expert on immigration and assimilation at the turn of the century, believed that Jews could overcome their shortcomings, but it could take eons to do so. He argued that their weakness was both physical and spiritual, that Jews were undersized and weak-muscled, screamed at the slightest injury, and had too much damage to their potential for manhood to repair in mere generations.[14] While Roosevelt spoke disparagingly about Jewish businessmen (both American and abroad) and the unpleasantness or garishness of Jews in general, he also believed in the superior intelligence of Jews over other immigrants and remarked that they raised bright, promising children.[15] Roosevelt assumed dichotomous positions about the Jewish people: he wanted Jewish men accepted for being just as American as any other group (native-born or immigrant), yet also maintained that they were inherently different and separate from other Americans. Just as he suggested that they access that manly part of their *own* history that would enable them to attain greatness and toughness (maintaining their distinctiveness among Americans), he also defended them from prejudice in the public eye. Responding to a story by Arthur Train published in *McClure's Magazine* in August 1913, Roosevelt wrote to the author with concern about the representation of the Jewish people.

> In this story there is a native American scoundrel, which is all right. There is also a meaner Jew scoundrel, which is also all right.

But there are native American representatives of manliness and decency; and there ought also to be a Jew among them! It is very important that we shall not give the impression that we are attacking all foreigners qua foreigners. There are exceedingly bad Jews, and exceedingly bad old stock native Americans. There are exceedingly good men who are Jews, and other exceedingly good men who are native old stock Americans.[16]

Though he urged Train to also include good Jews, Roosevelt made no mention of the terribly unpleasant characteristics ascribed to the Jew in the story. Train depicted his Jewish character, Mr. Abie Rosen, as a man of "globulous" countenance with suspected connections to communism. Throughout the story, Rosen maintained shameless worry about his finances over the fate of his country.[17] Roosevelt never urged Train to reconsider these negative Jewish characteristics, as he also believed they were based in truth, just as he believed that Jews were highly intelligent and naturally dominant in higher education.

Though scholarship and outdoorsmanship may seem dichotomous, to Roosevelt the pairing constituted the ideal formula for masculine life, thus superior Jewish intelligence was a boon for those reaching for his masculine ideal. This view conflicted with many of Roosevelt's contemporaries, who argued that scholarly education had a detrimental effect on American male youth and masculinity. G. Stanley Hall, writing in the decades surrounding the turn of the century, admonished the temperance educators taught to schoolboys, fearing that education was threatening American manhood. Too much education, Hall argued, led to neurasthenia and weakened American masculinity. He found the solution to this problem in intentionally teaching young boys "savagery" and "primitive" behaviors.[18] Roosevelt, by contrast, saw education as a necessity in the creation of the ideal man. He considered education essential, but he also theorized that the issue with "modern life" included a "tendency to forget . . . the rugged virtues which lie at the back of manhood."[19] Therefore, an ideal manly education not only involved intellectual endeavors but manual labor and training, to shake the idea that in order to rise in the world, men must get themselves "into a position where they do no hard manual work whatever; where their hands will grow soft, and their working clothes will be kept clean."[20]

Roosevelt encouraged the melding of these qualities among the men he worked with and enlisted several Jewish men to work with him throughout his career. When he commanded the Rough Riders, he chose his men based on their backgrounds and merit, a combination of Ivy Leaguers and frontier ranchers, comprising an ideal masculine army. Roosevelt recruited Jewish men into his unit, who he explained (when prompted to explain his relations with Jews) had enlisted and performed well alongside their comrades, one even rose to the rank of lieutenant for acts of gallantry.[21]

Critics of ethnically and regionally mixed military units in particular faced Roosevelt's ardent defense of the practice. During his first term as president, he even wrote to the surgeon general on behalf of at least one Jewish man attempting to enlist in the armed service, who believed he was rejected because of his Jewish background.[22] He prided

Figure 3. Officers of the Rough Riders, including Theodore Roosevelt (*left of center*), at military camp, Montauk Point, New York. Frances Benjamin Johnston, photographer. Officers of the Rough Riders at military camp, Montauk Point, New York. Montauk Point, New York, 1898. Photograph. https://www.loc.gov/item/2013651521/.

himself on embracing melting-pot theory and celebrating the stew of American citizenship. When one man argued racial superiority among the enlisted men, Roosevelt called him an "addlepated ass" who "ignorantly prattles slander" about the American melting pot.[23] Despite his belief in the melting pot, however, his biases about unacculturated Jews remained in place. In a very telling correspondence with James Andrew Drain, the head of the National Rifle Association, the two men discuss the desirability of Jews in the military and in social life. Drain expressed to Roosevelt that,

> Wherever a Jew is a decent, respectable, law-abiding man he is entitled to exactly the same treatment as any other white man, no more no less. I will give that to him and you will give it to him, regardless of any consideration of incidents which occurred almost two thousand years ago . . . but with respect to the question of whether a Jew is or is not socially pleasant to us or every American, there can be but one opinion. Generally Jews are no desirable social companions. The occasional exceptions prove the rule.[24]

Though Roosevelt defended Jewish men's right to enter into the military, he abstained from commenting on Jewish sociability on paper, explaining, "I do not want to write about it," but he then invited Drain to a more frank and intimate discussion in person on Drain's next visit to New York. In the military, however, he believed that Jews should be able to prove themselves "by the scale we use with Christians." However, he also took it for granted that "a large proportion of the Jews who go into Annapolis and West Point fail, a larger proportion than that of Christians."[25]

While working for the police in New York, Roosevelt admired his Jewish colleagues in the force and used melting-pot-inspired language when he discussed diversity in police work. He spoke of the power of a fighting force, like the New York Police Department, to "weld" men of all nations (Germans, Jews, Slavs, Italians, Scandinavians, and others) into a "physically fine lot. . . . All that they need is to be given the chance to prove themselves honest, brave, and self-respecting."[26] He reasoned that Americans fighting for entry to all professions and the American ideal needed only for others to "treat them so as to appeal to their self-respect and make it easy for them to become enthusiastically loyal Americans as well as good citizens."[27] Indeed, when an anti-Jewish evangelist, Rector Alward, visited New York, Roosevelt assigned him forty Jewish policemen for protection, seeing the protection by the race he was denouncing as "the most effective answer to that denunciation."[28] Roosevelt wrote frequently about the diverse nature of his police force, which accepted Catholics, Protestants, and Jews alike. However, despite hiring Jews and praising the prowess of his Jewish officers, the New York Police Department remained minimally Jewish.[29]

Though Jewish leaders enjoyed the high praise that Roosevelt bestowed on certain successful Jews in his acquaintance, he still maintained his prejudices about Jews in everyday life. It was in service to the nation that he believed there could be equity among all men, regardless of ethnicity. He resolved that the battlefield made Americans of all men, and Jews participated eagerly. Those Jewish soldiers who fought alongside Theodore Roosevelt, and earned his praise for their actions as Rough Riders, continued in a long history of Jews serving in the American armed forces, dating back to the Revolutionary War (as both soldiers in the Continental Army and Jewish Tories fighting for the British). Few enough Jews enlisted in early American wars that, unlike the armed forces of other nations with substantial Jewish populations, it was not worth the bother to bar them from service or determine separate Jewish status as some European nations had done. Had there been more Jews present and able to enlist, such status may have been determined to control the minority of Jewish soldiers, who many leaders viewed as a threat to military security.[30]

Jews actively, even eagerly, enlisted in the United States armed forces, perhaps because European nations with historically large Jewish populations had excluded Jews from national service. As many as 120,000 American soldiers fought for the Continental Army out of a population of roughly 2,418,000, which accounted for 4.96 percent of the total population.[31] According to an 1895 study written in defense of Jews in service (and thus as men), forty-six of these soldiers were Jews.[32] This seemingly small number, however, is a much greater percentage of the American Jewish population, estimated at 2,500.[33] That the author, Simon Wolf, felt it necessary to publish his study *The American Jew as Patriot, Soldier, and Citizen* in 1895 (just two years before Roosevelt formed the Rough Riders) demonstrates the prevailing assumption of Jewish cowardice and lack of military spirit. Assuming the legitimacy of his statistics, this shows

8.69 percent of American Jews enlisted to fight against the British, showing disproportionately high levels of Jews serving in this earliest of American wars.

Jews enlisted to serve in American military units on both sides of the Civil War as well. A total of roughly 10,000 Jewish soldiers fought in the war, on both sides combined, though the majority of these Jewish soldiers served with northern states and the Union Army.[34] These high numbers in the North manifested, in part, because the majority of Jews in America resided in the North at the time.[35] However, Jewish soldiers formed specifically Jewish companies in the armies of both the North and the South, though the majority chose to serve in regular army units alongside their other, non-Jewish, countrymen. It was not until the midst of the Civil War that the army appointed the first Jewish chaplains. Prior to the Civil War, the army regulations stated, "None but regularly ordained ministers of some Christian denomination . . . shall be eligible to appointment."[36] Under pressure from the Board of Delegates of American Israelites, President Lincoln rescinded the order and appointed the first official Jewish chaplain in the military, Rabbi Jacob Frankel of the Philadelphia Congregation Rodeph Shalom, on September 18, 1862.[37] Persuading the sitting president to grant Jewish soldiers' access to chaplains of their own faith did not, however, reflect the attitudes of all American leadership, nor did it put an end to discriminatory practices. Just a few months later, in December 1862, General Ulysses S. Grant released his infamous order expelling all Jews from Kentucky, Tennessee, and Mississippi based on his belief that they operated disproportionately in the black market cotton trade.[38] The Board of Delegates used Jewish military participation as the defense against this outright discrimination, which they explained was "peculiarly painful to the Israelites of the United States, who have freely tendered their blood and treasure in defence [sic] of the Union they love."[39]

Despite their tendering of blood and treasure, the American military did not advance Jewish officers as they would white Anglo-Saxon Protestants. The growing nativist movement in the late nineteenth and early twentieth centuries ensured that the officer core consisted primarily of established upper- or middle-class white men. The so-called scientific racial theory accepted at the time argued that the American nation was a product of the purity of spirit found only in the racially unadulterated and dignified descendants of Anglo-Saxons and assumed the racial inferiority of other groups. Historian Joseph W. Bendersky calls American attitudes toward Jews, both in and out of the military, an "insecure ambivalence." Patriotic sentiment of the time hailed the power of assimilation and believed in the power of the American melting pot to absorb Jewish distinctiveness. This assumption led to a sharp distinction in the American mind (just as it did in Theodore Roosevelt's) between *good* westernized Jews and *bad* uncivilized new immigrants.[40] This view, tinged with old antisemitic wariness, meant that the American military accepted Jews but still limited their access to high-level positions.

American Jewish Conceptions of Manhood

The hegemonic masculine ideal is forever changing, and at the turn of the twentieth century, it was shifting to a more physical, rather than behavioral, definition. Norms concerning masculinity fluctuated dramatically and quickly, in what Amy Kaplan described as a redefinition of "white middle-class masculinity from a republican quality of character based on self-control and social responsibility to a corporeal essence identified with the vigor and prowess of the individual male body."[41] This meant that, as in Europe, the primary feature of manhood became the physique, a far more performative, visible, and even racial quality than social responsibility. The change posed a problem for groups like Jews, African Americans, Asian Americans, and Native Americans, who the American mainstream held apart from white manhood by presumably identifiable phenotypical features and behavioral qualities (though some more positively than others).

In addition to their presumably Jewish features, Jewish men and women experienced adjusting to American life differently. For example, Jewish migrants from Eastern Europe still saw the transmission of Jewish knowledge as a male responsibility, but acculturating to the United States altered that perception as American institutions gave women and girls more formal education (religious and otherwise).[42] Not only were they formally educated, but informally the American ideal stressed the innate religious and spiritual superiority of women. In an 1895 contribution to the Jewish women's magazine the *American Jewess*, Rev. Dr. Henry Berkowitz explained, "Physical inferiority gives [women] a moral and spiritual superiority over man. This is an established fact, and so recognized in American manhood. Woman's is the intenser [sic] nature, the tenderer susceptibility. Religion is innate in her heart."[43] So internalized was this American ideal of gender roles in this case that the author also wrote that Jewish women should learn more about economy, about the best use and spending of what men bring home. In Europe, of course, many Jewish women provided for their families as breadwinners and continued to work out of the house as immigrants after coming to America. Narrowing the women's domain to the home shifted Jewish women's daily life and served as a mark of successful upward mobility and Jewish acculturation to gender roles in the American middle class.

Some young Jewish men feared that Judaism, in its more traditional religious forms, remained incompatible with the generally accepted standards of American decorum. An entirely different set of issues concerned young men looking to make themselves into Americans in the most visible sense. At the turn of the twentieth century, it was not only important that a man be robust and healthy, but also that he ascribe to American ideas of propriety. When lamenting the loss of young Jewish men in the synagogues, a contributor to the *American Hebrew* explained:

> "Propriety" demands of the young man that he dress stylishly, that he be seen often in the society of young women, that he be able to dance. Above all it demands that he do nothing anomalous, nothing that is not "American." Overt respect for foreign-looking parents is anomalous, observance of the dietary laws is anomalous, attendance at a synagogue filled with a strange un-American congregation, a synagogue where an unintelligible and un-American language is used in the service—this above all is anomalous. And so the young man, in obedience to the laws of propriety, gives up overt filial affection, and the dietary laws and the synagogue—the last, not because Americanism disapproves of worship, but because it disapproves of the place of worship.[44]

This placed the burden of successful acculturation on the synagogues and Jewish communities, to change themselves and the way they presented Judaism to American society in order to maintain their own young membership.

This focus on the need to modernize or Americanize Judaism to keep members (not unique to the mass migration period) continued to concern American Jewish men who hoped to improve on the lack of American manhood in the Jewish community. As far back as the mid-nineteenth century, Jewish critics of the synagogue claimed that Jewish religious leaders "are not true to themselves . . . they do not exhibit the requisite energy in asserting their manhood."[45] In an 1866 cover article of the *Jewish Messenger*, one such critic argued that the space for Jewish manhood existed outside of the synagogue, by developing an organization of young Jewish men for the purpose of "developing the manhood of the New York Hebrews."

> "If we desire to create a flattering impression upon the minds of our neighbors," the article suggested, "it would seem that the picture we might thus present of our 'rising generation,' engaged in rational relaxation, mental culture, the development of artistic taste and the formation of sound opinions, would contribute to effect [*sic*] our object."[46]

Here the issue of manhood is not about the body, but suggests that Jews lack American behaviors, a failure reparable through culture, appreciation of the arts, and exercise of the mind. And it is a failing of both Jewish adulthood and coming of age, "Our 'boys' are anxious enough to display their powers of mind; but when they attain manhood and have responsibilities and cares of business thrown upon them, they appear to lose ambition for higher aims than pleasing of flattering schoolgirls." Once these "boys" attained manhood, the young man would look back at his older coreligionists from an Americanized perspective and see that when "judged by 'American' standards of propriety, all this is strange, unpardonably strange. The young man feels that he must show his superiority to this anomalous worship of his fathers, and the best declaration of superiority he can think of is to abandon the old conditions entirely." This author genuinely fears that the lack of manhood among Jews actively drove Jewish youth away from the faith and practice. Before the so-called crisis of masculinity, before the shift in hegemonic manhood to be largely focused on the physical, Jews already worried that they were not accessing proper manliness.

Through their presumably innate difference as Jews, whether American or otherwise, Jewish men struggled to be manly by the dominant standards of the day.

By altering their image, behavior, and performative gender, Jewish men attempted to refit Judaism itself to meet American standards of manhood and prestige. They believed this to be necessary, having accepted that Judaism was not a wholly *American* religion. This is what Sarah Imhoff very convincingly argued in her 2017 book, *Masculinity and the Making of American Judaism*. Imhoff hypothesized that through very intentional (and at times successful) attempts to claim American manhood, American Jews made a new Judaism through a multidirectional process of masculinization and Americanization. Imhoff argued that religion (both Jewish and Christian) influenced the way in which Jewish masculinity developed, which, by turn, influenced the American Jewish religion. This view of Jewish masculinity (all gender identity, really) as dependent on the reality of the Jewish religion, life, and practice, is reflected in both Orthodox and non-Orthodox examinations of Jewish gender. However, it is through the Reform movement, which was more able to mimic Protestant life in the United States, that Imhoff identifies the most active change in ideal masculinity (showing a very different process of the evolution of Jewish manhood than in Daniel Boyarin's work on the Orthodox). The American Jewish Reform movement allowed for Jews to alter their practices and shift the image they transmitted to the rest of American society. Methods of prayer, music, and behaviors changed to mimic Protestantism and Protestant decorum. Synagogues adopted the use of choirs, sometimes organs, so their Protestant neighbors would hear the similarities in their practices and find them less threatening. The orthodox, by contrast, as Boyarin explains, embraced the difference (not fully, but far more than the reform Jews of Germany and the United States). More importantly in this context, Orthodox Jews were not nearly as prevalent in the United States during the period of Jewish Protestant-style acculturation, arriving primarily from Eastern Europe during the mass migration period.[47]

Rabbi Max Heller provides a perfect example of an American Jewish reevaluation of manhood in America, as he attempted to blend the intellectual manliness of Jews with the courageous manliness of Christians in his sermon on American manhood:

> It was a Christian hymn that braced me with courage . . . "Dare
> to be a Daniel, dare to stand alone, dare to have a purpose strong,
> dare to make it known." There is a saying of ancient Rabbi Hillel,
> a man famous for meek patience, yet unafraid to speak bold words
> in a generation of much violence, a saying which perhaps com-
> presses into one sentence the spirit of the hymn I have quoted; "In
> a place where there are no men, strive thou to be a man."[48]

Drawing together the image of the meek Rabbi Hillel and his call to
be a man (regardless of his intention) and the Christian call to courage
and stalwart firmness, Rabbi Heller attempted to show a historical and
spiritual connection between Jews and muscular Christians. Regardless of
his and others' attempts at such connections, the gendered image of traditional Jewish life and stereotypes, so prevalent in Europe, persisted in the
United States. As Christina Von Braun explained, successful integration of
Jews into larger society failed to alleviate the aspect of antisemitism that
focused on the hate of the foreign or alien as difference disappeared. As
Jews incorporated into both European and American societies, stereotypes
of the Jew became more biological than cultural, and thus inescapable.[49]

Other aspects of Jewish life, particularly among immigrants, held
them apart and identifiable as Jews. Jews grew dominant, or at least prevalent, in several trades and professions; garment work and operating
general stores became part of the Jewish image in America. Professional
interactions between non-Jews and Jewish men conducting their business, particularly in sales, defined much of the Jewish male interface with
the public. Within the import, export, and sale of goods, peddling was a
prominent profession (and became one of the dominant images) of Jewish migrants during the nineteenth century. Many Jewish men worked as
peddlers, and Jewish peddlers acted as foundational architects of Jewish
life in the United States.[50] They served as the channels through which
many Americans first encountered Jews and Jewishness, as they traveled
across the country to enter the homes of customers, many of whom had
never seen or met a Jew. These Jewish men occupied a unique place in
American society, and as negligibly few women became peddlers, it was
an experience nearly exclusive to men.[51]

Jewish peddlers occupied an odd, in-between space of masculine
identity. Traveling alone to sell their goods on the road, the life of a

Figure 4. Jewish peddler, New York City, early twentieth century. Bain News Service, Publisher. *Jewish peddler, N.Y. City*. [No Date Recorded on Caption Card] Photograph. https://www.loc.gov/item/2014681997/.

peddler was full of hardships; they carried great loads, traversed long distances, endured financial and bodily insecurity and miserable climates, and explored areas, languages, and cultures (at times) completely alien to their own. One might believe, given the hard life involved in the profession, that Americans would have considered peddling quite the manly endeavor. However, many Americans simply considered Jewish men outside of the rules for male behavior, which, surprisingly, included the opportunities granted Jewish peddlers to married women while their husbands and fathers were away. Jewish men who worked as peddlers in nineteenth-century America received unique access to homes and formed intimate relationships with the women to whom they sold their goods. They visited the women of the household, entering while husbands worked and traveled, and even slept in the homes of the women to whom they sold their goods. Although there were instances of Jewish peddlers falling in love with, and even marrying, the daughters of some of their patrons, customers generally did not perceive a threat to the women who purchased from Jewish men.[52] In her 2015 book, *Roads Taken: The Great Jewish Migrations to the New World and the Peddlers Who Forged the Way*, Hasia Diner shows that Americans gave Jewish peddlers remarkable access to women and their homes, bringing modernity and consumerism into their lives, and dealing in what might be considered particularly intimate goods (apparel, undergarments, jewelry, and such). This comfortable welcoming of Jewish men into the lives and homes of non-Jewish women says as much about the male identity of these peddlers as it does about their lives, and more than it does about their Jewish identity. Because they were excluded from hegemonic American manhood, mainstream Americans did not fully regard Jews as men and therefore did not hold them to the same rules and standards of propriety.

Accepting Jewish Weakness

If one trend maintained the belief in Jewish particularity within American masculinity, regardless of locale or demographic, it was the tacit acceptance of Jewish weakness that Jews themselves displayed. This does not mean that all Jews believed themselves physically inferior, genetically different, or that any such difference should be cast in a negative light. What appears time and again is that the fact of Jewish male difference goes unquestioned. Even in cases in which Jewish men believed that they were physically weak as a group, they also believed that their condition could be remedied through training and performative strength and manliness. Todd Presner argued that Jews who believed in the legitimacy of this difference had internalized antisemitic notions through violent mechanisms of Jewish self-hatred.[53] More important than the question of Jewish self-hatred, however, is the fact that Jews did internalize the ideals of their dominant cultures, and, as Paul Breines wrote, "In doing so [Jews] forget that, far from being self-evident cultural universals, those ideals are predicated on a series of exclusions and erasures."[54] In some cases, of course, Jews recognized that others merely *perceived* them as weak, but the result was the same—those Jews argued that it still fell to Jews themselves to remedy the situation, to improve the appearance of the Jew in public life through physical strengthening and masculinizing. This phenomenon reappears in every chapter of this work and is reexamined in the specific condition of each context, as Jews accepted their distinctiveness and alternate masculinities. It is important to recognize that the reality of Jewish physical manliness in the early twentieth century is largely immaterial. It is these perceptions that matter, as they dictated the choices and actions of American Jewish men responding to outside influence. As masculinity is itself a social construct of gender norms, it is both pointless and unfounded to make the claim that anyone does or does not possess it. The images and ideals, however, are quite real.

The ideal American man (a rugged, tough, self-made man) emerged not on its own but by positive social comparison. Roosevelt provided a model for this type of masculinity and promoted several methods to manifest his style of American manhood. Some Jewish men adapted as Roosevelt suggested, by joining his Rough Riders or otherwise learning to balance their intellectual pursuits with those "rugged virtues which lie at the back of manhood." Though some Jews in Europe already embraced an ideal of muscular Zionism and manly Jewish virtue, the (generally antisemitic) perception of Jews as weak and enfeebled, so popular in Europe, prevailed in the United States as well. Along with muscular Jewish movements there must be (by definition) a simultaneous acceptance of Jewish deficits in manly virtue.

Among American Jewish leaders of the early twentieth century, it is evident just how prevalent Jewish attitudes toward different sorts of masculinity had become. In his speech to an interfaith audience at the University of Michigan in 1915, Rabbi Max Heller recognized traditional Jewish male intellectualism while acknowledging the value of the dominant physical form of masculinity as the American hegemon. He suggested that despite the appeals of muscle and courageous behavior, men should aim for "a higher form of courage . . . the manly vigor of intellectual independence."[55] Of course, Rabbi Heller delivered his speech to a university audience, who clearly valued education regardless of their Jewishness. Despite his emphasis on education, he still used biblical Jewish heroes who had fought physical battles to showcase manliness, for "there is no more truly magnificent picture of sublime courage, of spiritual manliness." So Jewish men, he insinuated, had the capacity for physical strength but recognized the supremacy of intellectual independence.

Marcus Eli Ravage, a Jewish American immigrant, believed in the inherent difference of Jewish men from the hegemon in America. Attempting to fit into America's ideal of manhood, he recounted his journey in his 1917 memoir, *An American in the Making*. His experiences clearly depict an America in which the backbone of the prevalent culture is masculine and aggressive, identified and proven by positive comparison against weak or soft men. Though Jewish, Ravage's memoir focused less on his Jewishness and more on his inability to fit into mainstream manly life. He wrote that "the genuine American recognized but one distinction in human society—the vital distinction between the strong, effectual, 'real' man and the soft, pleasure-loving, unreliant [sic] failure."[56] Attending university in Missouri, he learned that his background in Jewish New York left him unprepared for life in much of American society, and his peers spurned him. He depicted himself as a stranger in the strange land of American universities, though he made it clear that despite his own rejection by his peers, he "had to admire the heartiness, and the clean-cut manliness of it." For Ravage, Jewishness precipitated, but did not comprise, his primary issue, as his colleagues remained unaware of his heritage for the first three years after his arrival at the university. His Jewishness, however, was manifest as the real issue: his *maleness*. Though he tried to train himself in sports to fit in with his classmates (not because he had any personal interest), he remained inept and frustrated. He concluded that the deficits lay within him, and not with the men more interested in sports than in academic discussion:

> It was not [their] fault that I had been sewing sleeves when I ought to have been playing ball, and that I had gone to the wrong kind of school for my secondary training, where I had been made into a grind and a bore and a disputatious fanatic when I could just as well have learned to be a level-headed man among men. It was not yet too late, fortunately. The opportunities for rounding out my education were ample enough. I had but to bring my will into play.[57]

Here Ravage makes clear that no physical deficits or genetic failures made him incompetent at sports, but his Jewish upbringing had turned him into a "grind and a bore and a disputatious fanatic." He believed himself less of a "man among men," but hoped that through training and practice he could fix himself and become a real American man. That he thought the fault lay in his Jewishness is clear in his publications, having submitted a satirical article in *Century Magazine* in 1928 titled "A Real Case against the Jews," which mocked antisemites for hating Jews for all the wrong reasons. This article is still used by antisemites to prove Jewish treachery in the United States and is reprinted and illegally published for purchase on countless antisemitic conspiracy sites on the internet.

Some Jewish religious and lay leaders also took it for granted that the Jewish man differed from the ideal American man emerging from the American melting pot that Roosevelt and Israel Zangwill had praised and promoted. The most recognizable (even celebrated) image of unique Jewish manhood in the early twentieth century remained that of the scholar, whose time was better spent on intellectual pursuits (particularly the study of Jewish religious texts) than attempting to join in what Daniel Boyarin refers to as *goyim naches* (a contemptuous term meaning "the games goyim play," indicating those characteristics goyim use to describe a man as manly). However, the landscape of Jewish masculinities in America presented a far more complex scene than a simple dichotomy of those who did and did not conform to American manhood. Many Jews acknowledged that they maintained a separate form of masculinity that celebrated gentleness as a manly virtue but not one that made Jewish men "feminine" at all. It was, therefore, not accusations of *bookishness* that rankled Jewish men most, but accusations of *weakness*. Daniel Boyarin, for example, argues that a gentle form of Jewish masculinity can be traced to the Talmud and the rabbinic tradition, and that such tradition provided alternative masculinities to dominant male gender norms. Alternate masculinities developed in myriad fashions, were embraced or even celebrated by Jewish men, and scholars have explored that progress through several methodologies, primarily dealing with the modernization and Americanization of the Jewish religion.

However, Americanization of the religion was not an attempt at an alternate masculinity, but an attempt to reach the masculine space occupied by American white men. In *Masculinity and the Making of American Judaism*, Sarah Imhoff argues that American Judaism redefined itself in the early twentieth century as an unemotional (and thus a more masculine) "good" American religion. To support her argument, she provides commentary of contemporary Jewish leaders and thinkers who justify Judaism as an American religion by arguing its rationality and universalism, but, she asserts, never by mimicking muscular Christianity and its focus on the healthy body.[58] The religious element of Jewish immigrant life, however, is but one aspect of Americanization, as Eli Lederhendler explained in his 1994 book, *Jewish Responses to Modernity: New Voices in America and Eastern Europe*. He argues not that the *religion* underwent massive change through the Americanization process, but that its adherents, by way of becoming acculturated to American *secular* life, were "becoming men."[59] According to Lederhendler, the process of becoming free Americans granted Jewish men dignity, pride, and access to a more Western notion of manhood. He uses some of the same Jewish leaders that Imhoff cites to come to a broader conclusion, that the sense of liberation (real or perceived) obtained on immigrating to the United States allowed for a manlier American Jewish manhood, whether religiously or secularly identified with Judaism.

The process of becoming masculine through Americanization is not vague or elusive enough that it must be inferred through tangential writings of contemporary Jewish leaders. Commentators provided quite explicit criticisms and solutions for the issues of Jewish immigrants. This is particularly true of American Jewish philanthropic efforts to integrate newly immigrated Jews during the mass migration period. In the periodical published by the United Hebrew Charities (the official organ of the National Conference of Jewish Charities), the process of Americanizing new Jewish immigrants through physical strengthening is a common theme. David Blaustein, a Jewish charity worker (and himself an immigrant from Poland) devoted his life and career to the project of Americanizing Jewish immigrants, and he wrote of the new immigrants that in their home countries,

> The necessity of military service created a philosophy of unfitness as a means of escape. In America, where it is the "survival of the fittest," physical culture plays an important part, and when we are striving to make an American we strive to make a physically strong American, and our physical culture is by no means one of the minor branches of our work.[60]

One of the ways that Sarah Imhoff's study is most successful is how she identified those on the margins of Jewish culture to illustrate departures from masculine norms (including gentle Jewish masculinity). In the interactions between Jews on the margins (those flitting in and out of the Jewish mainstream, like converts to Christianity, agriculturalists, and criminals) and the outside world, a number of Jews attempted to escape the alternative masculinity prevalent in Jewish culture and access a more normative American masculinity. Jewish converts to Christianity accepted Jewish weakness as well and found it a motivating factor to seek a more masculine self-image outside of the Jewish faith. Imhoff examines this margin of Jewish life and unearths an interesting intersection of muscular Christianity and Jewish American identity, and she demonstrates how (though only a small element of Jewish life in the early twentieth century) conversion by Christian missionaries particularly affected Jewish men. Imhoff argues that the attraction, at least to an extent, grew from the desire to gain access to a more typically American Protestant sort of manliness or toughness. At least one of her subjects recognized that, had he known of its existence, muscular Zionism may have provided him a similar outlet without leaving the faith of his birth. According to Yaakov Ariel, Jewish men lacking father figures found parental figures in the missionaries who gave them much dedicated attention during the conversion process and became some of the most successful conversions of Jews by Protestant missionaries.[61] Though Ariel identifies a different cause for conversion, it comes down to the same issue: manhood. Converts from Judaism to Christianity, uncomfortable with their masculinity as Jews, exemplify the idea that this group subscribed particularly strongly to the idea of Jews as weak and inferior. Whether because they lacked father figures, because they lacked toughness to pass in America, or because they loathed the Jewish male gentleness, depended on the individual.[62]

For the majority of American Jewry, who remained in the Jewish community and faith, American society allowed for a specific sort of gentle manhood to flourish that found less acceptance elsewhere in the diaspora. Though not all American Jewish men embraced this view of themselves as bearers of a soft masculinity based on suffering and quiet dignity, they largely accepted its veracity. However, the difference between Jewish attitudes toward this kinder depiction of Jewish manhood and the antisemitic image of weak enfeebled Jewish men cannot be understated. Jewish men fought back against what they saw as unrealistic and insulting images of effeminate Jews. They accepted, however, that to some degree they differed in character from the American masculine norm. It is this acceptance of their outsider status that allowed them to actively work to change not only their image but their reality as men.

Jewish women also significantly influence the way Jewish men are perceived, both by themselves and by others. In Riv-Ellen Prell's *Fighting to Become Americans: Assimilation and the Trouble between Jewish Women and Jewish Men*, she explains how Jewish men ascribed negative gender stereotypes to Jewish women, thus complicating their feminine identity while they strove to acculturate into mainstream America. These include, for example, the "devouring Jewish mother" and the "Jewish American Princess."[63] This judgment operated as a two-way process in which Jewish women in turn viewed Jewish men as "indecisive, unmanly, and unable to provide for their women. If Jewish men were not '100 percent American' according to the mainstream culture, then to Jewish women they were often less than 100 percent men."[64] The tension between the sexes in Jewish life in America stands out in the words of women, who, relegated to the household in the United States, also depended on the masculinity of the men of their families and communities to acculturate.

A turn-of-the-century Detroit rabbi, Dr. Louis Grossmann, relayed a conversation with a woman in his congregation who became concerned about the negative effect that traditional Jewish life imposed on Jewish American men. She made it quite clear that the lack of manliness in the rabbinic tradition and practice was harming the Jewish people in America. He described their conversation and the concerns that she voiced:

> "You Rabbis have changed things in Judaism a good deal," a young woman said to me the other day. I confess I straightened up. I have heard the cheap remark before, though mostly from men, not from women. From men, it meant either [r]ant or fight. Neither of these fit women.[65]

The change to which the woman referred regarded the extent to which rabbis allowed others in the congregation to question them, to speak out of turn, and to dominate discussion and practice. The fact that the rabbi's reaction was to be leerier of a confrontation with a man, assuming he may want to rant or argue, is a sign of how real this change to congregation life truly was. The woman continued:

> It is quite suave and nice for you to be meek and patient and affable on all occasions; but it is not wise, and it is not manly. The business of leadership demands wisdom and manliness. If I were a man, and if I had on my shoulders the weight of public interests, I would not take my pattern for leadership from the morbid saints of Christendom, nor even from our own beautiful Hillel. The bold fellows have it all their own way, now, and are harassing us, and they are disturbing us from the confidence we had in the grand integrity of our people; this mild hot-house virtue and humble deference to every one [sic] who has tongue has done it. You Rabbis have the blame.

Though another congregant interrupted their conversation before Grossmann could respond to the woman, he explained:

> To my regret, some sociable fellow came up and broke into the conversation and snatched away any further opportunity for more of the sagacious talk. Well, perhaps it is better so. The suggestion was enough. Women are brilliant talkers; but they cannot keep up a long conversation. They scintillate for a few moments, and the brightest woman relapses into the implicit weakness of her sex.

Despite her "implicit weakness," he saw value in their brief conversation (though it is clear he did not find value in her words, only in the "suggestion" she had given him as inspiration). He mused on Jewish male temperament:

> We know something of the pathetic cost at which Power was purchased over life and conscience; and we know also that much precious blood was shed on the altar of unflinching manhood. But, just because conviction is sacred, it must be tempered with caution . . . I have seen polite gentleman made martyrs to their courteousness, and I know garrulous brain-drums, who rattle riot to logic and sense. . . . I verily believe that it is a virtue sometimes to be intolerant, and, conversely it is a vice sometimes to be overscrupulously meek.

In the op-ed he wrote on the encounter, Grossmann struggled with his role as an American Jew and his responsibility as a leader in a tradition that advocated more democratic practice, perhaps, than American manhood would allow. From this interaction, it is clear that both Jewish men and women believed that it was necessary to adhere to, and be accepted into, mainstream American masculine identity in order to successfully acculturate.

Jewish literature of the time immortalized such beliefs, much of it depicting the struggle of Jewish Americans to navigate American manhood, particularly Eastern European immigrants and their children. The novelist Anzia Yezierska provides an excellent resource for fictional representations of commonly held images of Jewish migrants in her time. Literature scholar Dana Mihăilescu highlights Yezierska's novels as particularly helpful in assessing Jewish masculine identity in the early decades of the twentieth century. Yezierska, a Jewish woman, wrote increasingly independent female characters, highly critical of their overly emotional male counterparts. The men in her novels are prone to weakness and cling to Jewish tradition. Yezierska's works represent Jewish men as performatively masculine only after they successfully distance themselves from religious tradition and Jewish life, which she depicts as culpable for their continued weakness. One of her most popular novels, *Bread Givers* (1925), provides a perfect example of this tension. The heroin of the novel, Sara Smolinsky, fights to escape her controlling father, a devout Jew, whose insistence on devoting his life to the Torah results in his inability to work and provide for his family. She gains her independence by distancing herself from her household and traditional culture and falls in love with an assimilated, respectable, more masculine Jewish Polish American. By the end of the book, Sara finds her father destitute in a gutter and resumes responsibility for his care, as he still cannot care for himself.

This story is not merely a tale of the hardship and assimilation of Jewish immigrants, it also reflects a much larger process, the interaction between migrants and native-born, more acculturated Jews. This image of the Jewish Eastern European immigrant is a common trope of the mass migration period; maintained across gender lines, both men and women contributed to its longevity and pervasiveness. The story leaves readers with a hint at the relationships between acculturated Jews and new immigrants. As Jewish immigrants crowded in cities, struggled to acculturate and to survive in a world quite different from their own, they seemed, as a group, much like Sara's father; clinging to the past and unable to care for themselves through the process of Americanization. That group, visible on the streets of America's cities, threatened to set back the image that established American Jews had worked toward for generations. For this reason, the mass migration period contained some of the most aggressive attempts to Americanize (and thus masculinize) Jews in America through physical activity, masculine institutions, and male camaraderie.

Jewish Americans did make progress in the process of masculinizing their image through Americanization. The Jewish religion itself changed to become more American and masculine in both religion and practice. Individual Jewish men strove to attain a manlier identity by accessing the manhood promoted by Roosevelt, through military enlistment and outdoorsmanship. Despite any progress made by individual Jewish men, however, both Jews and non-Jews still believed that something in Jewish heritage, culture, or physicality held them apart and necessitated an active effort to become men. Those individuals, like the men Theodore Roosevelt highlighted as manly Jewish successes, were only a small portion of American Jewish men. Their success made little impact on the general acceptance of Jewish weakness as a reality.

Likewise, Roosevelt's belief that Jews were capable of rising above their cultural/racial/social inferiority did not negate his belief that most of them did not. In fact, it is this recognition of Jewish weakness and inferiority as a curable condition (recognized by both Jews and gentiles) that further solidified the American assumption of Jewish difference and resistance to full assimilation.

3
Uptown Jews and the "Downtown Element"

Class Distinction and Jewish Manhood

The Jews "are beginning to feel their oats." I do not believe in the bullying spirit, nor in undue assertiveness, but manly defense of their rights as men will do the Jews more good than the cringing, fawning sycophantic attitude. . . . [I]n these democratic days, when a man is a man for a' that, the more sturdy the Jews are in the insistence on their right to the same treatment as all other men receive, the more likely will they be to take their proper place in the world.
—Rabbi David Philipson, 1905[1]

While native-born American Jewish communities worked to construct and maintain a firmly American masculinity, Jewish immigrants from Europe quickly diversified and complicated American Jewish identity. The growing chasm between acculturated Jews and new Jewish immigrants posed both a threat to the social successes of the former and various, often contradictory, modes of manly behavior between the two. In the early 1920s, at the peak of mass migration, American nativists (and even those merely weary of arriving immigrants) motivated acculturated Jews to help their foreign brethren Americanize, and one of the primary modes of Americanization was in the form of a definitively American masculine transformation.

Between 1880 and 1927, the Jewish population in the United States grew by roughly four million. So much of this growth was mass migration that by 1930 (in spite of the restrictive immigration acts of the 1920s cutting Jewish immigration by over 90 percent) one in two Jews in America was born overseas (the overwhelming majority of whom were Ashkenazi

Jews from Eastern Europe).[2] Differences in language, religious practice, culture, and economic class drew strong lines between new immigrants and American-born Jews and their respective variant Jewish masculinities. Immigrant communities and their children grappled with unique issues of gender and acculturation, and their behavior reflected on the preexisting Jewish communities in the United States, who had (to their minds) won a place of acceptance in American culture. As the primary port of entry for Jewish immigrants in the early twentieth century, New York City demonstrates very clearly the demarcation of Jews by levels of acculturation and economic class, which are often strongly linked.

There are many useful and insightful areas and source materials through which historians examine this separation of Jewish communities. For the current study, however, the most telling are those in which Jews contested and renegotiated masculine behaviors, as they show the very intentional, performative use of acts of manhood to redefine masculine identity. In early twentieth-century New York City, Jewish men contested notions of Jewish manhood and renegotiated Jewish masculinity through two areas: urban crime and Jewish agriculture. Though disparate issues at first glance, acculturated Jewish Americans linked the two by intervening in the process of Americanizing new immigrants and second-generation Americans, with a focus on the Jewish male. The established American Jewish community identified both crime and agriculturalism as male-gendered. The former, they believed, was a product of mass migration and overcrowding, while the latter provided the masculine solution. Through farming and a return to the outdoors, Jewish men weakened or criminalized by urban life could engage in masculine resocializing to rehabilitate and Americanize. Sarah Imhoff demonstrated this in her 2017 work on the subject, identifying the Jewish solution to weak, urban Jews as a masculine return to nature. Though she argued that the return to nature was more about the spirit than the body, in this chapter, I focus on the Jewish body and efforts of the established Jewish community to remedy Jewish manhood through relocation and physical strengthening.

This masculine retraining did not, however, apply to upper- or middle-class New York Jews, who felt that for themselves, a different means to access hegemonic masculinity was necessary, one that manifested in an approach more directly aligned with masculine behaviors of upper- or middle-class white Protestant Americans. Though aspects of the project itself demonstrated a form of masculinity among the acculturated Jews, through financial success and philanthropy, upper-class Jews also created athletic and men's institutions paralleling the white Anglo-Saxon males of the upper class in order to improve on and demonstrate their own American masculinity. Beth Wenger's article on Jewish men and the American philanthropic organizations of the twentieth century demonstrates the shift of charitable work from "women's work" to a masculine enterprise, redefining Jewish philanthropy as a male enterprise composed of large, organized philanthropic organizations and networks.[3] The masculinizing process discussed in the following pages, enacted by acculturated Jewish philanthropists and aimed at Jewish criminals and delinquents, was part of this movement as well, as male-dominated Jewish organizations created and enacted these programs.

Acculturated American Jews felt obligated to intervene in the Americanization process of new Jewish immigrants for a number of reasons, both philanthropic and self-serving. Even those Americans (Jewish and otherwise) who had no clear nativist tendencies had reason to be concerned about changes taking place in major American cities where so many immigrants arrived and most remained. Urban overcrowding led to unhealthy living conditions, unemployment, poverty, poor education among the second generation (those born into squalid urban living conditions), and a rise in street-level urban crime. Jews, like their non-Jewish American neighbors, worried about the new influx of immigrants, but for a particularly Jewish reason: new Jews from Europe, living in American cities, tarnished the image of American Jews on the whole. They threatened to undo the hard-won acceptance that many elite Jewish Americans (largely of German origin) enjoyed. The Jewish immigrant became a prime concern for Jewish organizers, leaders, philanthropists, and communities.

The actions taken by American Jewish leadership and charities demonstrate the attempts to remedy problems created by mass immigration of Eastern European Jews. Prominent Jewish men developed a solution of masculine reprogramming (though they did not name it so bluntly) and, when possible, put it into practice. Established middle-class Jewish men feared for the reputation of Jewish America, as popular opinion could be swayed by stories of criminal and unsanitary Jews in crowded centers of immigration. Not only that, they believed that new Jewish immigrants *were* a real problem, not merely a perceived one. They believed that by Americanizing immigrant Jews, they could help them to be successful in their new country, solve the public relations issues their arrival caused, and set a positive example as an American ethnic community helping their foreign brethren to acculturate. Though they focused on both men and women, one of their main and most interesting strategies specifically targeted Jewish masculinity.

Because so much of the rise in Jewish crime resulted from the living conditions of mass-migration-period Jewish immigrants in large urban centers, New York City became the center of it. New Jewish immigrants, according to Jewish philanthropic leaders of the time, came in too great a volume to integrate using the successful methods of the past. Migrants adjusted slowly and ineffectively, unable to fit the standards of acculturated American Jewish life. The massive increase in immigration created a new set of urban problems that American government, communal, and charitable organizations attempted to address. In his highly influential 1890 book, *How the Other Half Lives*, Jacob Riis publicized the severity of the unique urban issues of overcrowding, tenement slums, prostitution, drunkenness, and crime. His documentation of the squalid conditions of tenement life frightened Americans not just for the physical degradation of the impoverished, but also for their ability to maintain a healthy and moral society.

Though not a uniquely or exclusively Jewish problem, Jews immigrated to New York in tremendous numbers, and the preexisting Jewish community recognized that the problems of urban life had become Jewish problems. The newspaper the *American Hebrew* published several articles in the early years of the twentieth century regarding Jewish poverty, crime, and possible charitable solutions. By 1902, the paper informed its readers that Jews inhabited some of the most congested parts of the city, and that half of those Jews were young children.[4] Established American Jews searching for ways to resolve problems caused by overcrowding looked to the myths of American nation building for answers. Though they themselves had never worked the land or scraped by on the western frontier, they saw in these all-American experiences a sure way to instill American values and identity on new Jewish migrants and their children. As higher numbers of Jewish immigrants came to the city, Jews reached new heights of criminal behavior, among both adults and youth. The charitable community concerned themselves particularly with the children. Several organizations and leaders believed that relocating Jewish boys to the countryside would help diminish the increasingly criminal urban effects on their character and provide a perfect venue for Americanizing Jewish boys, thus instilling in them a sense of manhood unique to the American experience.

Acculturated, upwardly mobile Jewish men saw themselves as quite different from those they sought to Americanize through agricultural projects. However, they were still unable to fully access American masculinity, as the organizations and establishments where white American masculinity was most visibly enacted (country clubs, athletic organizations, fraternal brotherhoods, and such) continued to deny Jews entry. Very few proposed that acculturated Jewish men remedy their deficits in manliness by embarking on new lives and careers as farmers and agriculturists. They had, after all, already worked through several generations to establish themselves as Americans through alternate means, and reached great heights of economic and political success, if not fully successful, in reaching the upper echelons of American social hierarchy. Instead, they continued in their incremental journey of acculturation, gaining access to institutions one by one to obtain American acceptance. As they were barred entry to so many venues of American manhood, many Jews, particularly the "Uptown Jews" of New York City and Jews in higher education, started their own parallel organizations to demonstrate or manifest a more accepted American masculinity. Some publicized the Jewishness of their institutions, with the intention of changing the unfortunate views that non-Jews held about Jewish men in America, hoping to break down the discriminatory barriers between them. Others made no mention of their Jewish origins but formed organizations that hoped to improve what they believed were actual deficits in Jewish manhood (not merely biased views of Jews), bringing Jewish men up to the standard of white masculinity that would allow them acceptance and access in American society.

The following sections of this chapter examine the masculinity of Jewish crime in the early twentieth century, and the efforts of American-born Jews to make American men of immigrants and second-generation Jews. It further inspects those efforts aimed at themselves and their own journey toward recognition as American men. Several distinct and recognizable Jewish archetypes emerged in this period of flux and masculine diversity in the Jewish community; for example, the image of the religious scholar (a trope that rejects the necessity of making Jewish masculinity consistent with mainstream America), the Jewish rebel (a more aggressively masculine Jewish type that emulates the harsher aspects of mainstream masculinity), and the acculturated Jewish philanthropist (who took an active role in Americanizing Jewish immigrants for their own sakes). Though quite different, these variant Jewish masculinities were closely entwined and co-constitutive, created by, for, and against one another.

"Nothing Particularly Jewish about Them": Bad Boys from Big Cities

Criminality, though frequently waved aside as a marginal component of American Jewish behavior in the United States, comprised a significant aspect of Jewish life in major cities during the early twentieth century. Until the late 1970s, scholars of Jewish history paid little attention to Jewish crime as an area of historical interest. However, across levels of criminality varying from juvenile delinquency to organized crime on a national scale, many poor Jews from the city made their way in America through illicit means. The Jewish underworld is particularly fascinating in terms of Jewish masculinity, as it is an area dominated by men. Women participated in crime as sex workers, madams, pickpockets (or *gun-mols*), fences, or as the wives and mistresses of gangsters, but always in association with men, even when criminals themselves.[5]

Before the turn of the century, when American cities began implementing more laws based on morality and changing social conditions in the city, women involved in sex work were more in control of their own enterprise, more able to operate for themselves, not merely in association with men. However, when laws criminalized prostitution, usually couched in the language of "protection of women," men began to dominate the sex work industry, as they had access to the funds necessary to make bail for those arrested and detained.[6] In 1910, New York City assembled the Committee of Fourteen to examine the continuing "social evil" of prostitution. The report of the committee noted that when arrested for solicitation, women were often bailed out by the men who owned both the "disorderly saloons" in which women solicited and the "disorderly hotels," to which they brought their clients, giving these men control of the industry and the women who worked in it nearly as much as the venues they needed to conduct their work.[7] Even considering the central role of women in such criminal activity, early twentieth-century crime in Jewish neighborhoods was a markedly male experience, and organized crime nearly exclusively male, whether based out of New York City (by far the largest population of new Jewish immigrants) or elsewhere. Because men dominated Jewish criminal activity, a particularly masculine language surrounded crime and its proposed solutions, even beyond the masculine language that was generally prevalent at the time.

Sarah Imhoff examined this language in reference to Jewish crime at the turn of the century. Using many of the same sources and commentary, she argued that both Jews and non-Jews painted Jews as "soft criminals," not manly ones, and they both suggested that the solution lay in the Jewish religion, and a return to religious practice. Her take on Jewish crime and masculinity at the turn of the century tells us that public discussions of Jewish criminals described them as participating in the "gentlest" of crimes and even "wordy arguments" over violence, due to their physical weakness or lack of muscle. Indeed, at the turn of the century, much Jewish commentary continued to espouse the assumptions of Jewish weakness established in the previous chapter, and even to use this language as a line of defense against accusations of Jewish criminality. Banking on assumptions of the physical weakness of Jewish men, the Jewish community was able to talk about softer crime and juvenile delinquency while, as Imhoff put it, "pushing Jewish gangsters into the communal closet."[8]

Contrary to that public dialogue, however, Jewish men involved in crime in the following three decades (street-level or organized) directly rebelled against the image of Jewish men as weak, gentle, or even studious. This was particularly true of Jewish gangsters, but also of juvenile delinquents involved in violent street gangs. To understand their departure from, or rebellion against, dominant Jewish male types of the early twentieth century, generational and experiential tension between the roles of Jewish immigrants and their native-born children is key. As the Jewish population exploded, and more first- and second-generation immigrants were growing up poor in the city, the view of Jewish crime, which Imhoff described as nearly universally soft, began to break down, and by the 1920s the face of Jewish crime, and Jewish reactions to it, changed dramatically. Jewish ideals of masculinity differed between the generations, reflecting the differences in their life experiences and places in American society. American-born children of immigrants embraced more violent, tougher American masculinities than did older generations of American-born Jews in the city.

If there was a time, however, when American Jews really were "tough," it was this period of notable Jewish gang and criminal activity in the early decades of the twentieth century, particularly in New York City. Though the trope of the tough Jew really emerged in the post-World War II period, it did so largely through the glorification of *this* period, the 1910s, '20s, and '30s, when Jewish gangsters were real and Jewish boys brawled in the streets. The films and novels so many Jewish researchers have pointed to as evidence of American tough Jews in recent years have been a revival of this character in a newly positive light.[9] When Jewish criminals were active, contemporary Jews saw them as a huge problem for Jewish acceptance in American culture. It was also not until later, after both of the world wars, that the highly pervasive and long-lasting image of the "nice Jewish boy" emerge as such, but the perceived norm of Jewish gentleness set expectations for behavior of Jewish migrants and especially of the religious. The positive stereotype of the Jew as a quiet scholar permeated images of American Jews but generally only applied to those born in the United States. The archetypes ascribed to foreign-born Jewish men were far less flattering. Particularly in New York City, Jewish leadership accused the Jewish immigrant community and their children of being responsible for the majority of Jewish crime, a sign of their unassimilated nature. These elements of Jewish American life are important indicators of American Jewish manhood, as they relate to male acceptance, rebellion, and Jewish dialogue about what a good man ought to be. Some Jewish boys broke with the behavior expected of them, openly defying the image of gentleness by becoming street-brawling juvenile delinquents.[10]

As ever, the issue of Jewish physicality, or the Jewish body, is present in both Jewish and non-Jewish commentary on rising crime among American Jews during this period. In a 1921 article on the problem of Jewish immigrants, Morris Lazaron described a physical change that he claimed took place in those Jews who, in the course of adapting to a free American landscape, descended into the un-Jewish behavior of street criminals. Recalling the attitudes of Jews toward the Jewish body discussed previously, those physical changes ascribed to the criminal Jew were not becoming weaker or less attractive. In fact, according to Lazaron, the Jew is not made uglier by his descent into criminality, on the contrary, he may actually lose those features lacking masculinity that associate him with the Jewish people in the first place. "The physical characteristics of the Jew may be lost as he reacts to the environment of freedom. The back may be straightened, the form heightened, the face lose [sic] its rugged, crude, and elemental strength."[11] Undergoing these changes, new American Jews "would not be themselves." To solve this problem, Lazaron called for a closer connection to traditional Jewish life to save the American Jewish community from a life of degeneracy and transformation, and to keep at bay disdain from the rest of American society. Continuing in the tradition of previous generations, he saw connection to Jewish tradition and religion as the way to redeem Jewish manhood. The difference is in the description of Jewish criminals: form heightened, face less crude, back straightened, and not weak, physically unfit, or possessing neglected bodies.[12]

Of the socially damaging criminal behaviors American Jews displayed in the early twentieth century, prostitution played no small part in tarnishing the image of the Jewish community. Here women not only play an important role, but they highlight the differences between predicting factors of men and women involved in crime. A substantial number of Jewish female immigrants (primarily unmarried women) became sex workers, the percentage of Jews among sex workers in New York City being equal to their percentage of the population.[13] For many of these immigrants, willingly entering a life of prostitution was an escape from the miserable factory life that immigrants from so many nations and ethnicities seemed doomed to endure on arrival in New York City. Historian Albert Fried asserted that Jewish participation in prostitution outstripped that of their non-Jewish counterparts. He speculated that the reason Jewish women tended to escape in this fashion more than other immigrant groups was that Jewish women had a stronger sense of autonomy, acted more independently, and less passively (also accounting for their entry into militant union organizing).[14] Women, on the whole, also comprised a higher percentage of Jewish immigrants than of other immigrant groups. Though some Jewish male immigrants engaged sex workers as clients, criminal activity on the whole was far more likely of their American-born children, who were more apt to commit crimes themselves; American-born children also became clients of the sex industry. This is not to say that Jewish male immigrants never became involved in crime, they certainly did, in the role of cadets (pimps), for example, who tended to be young male immigrants preying on newly arrived women.[15]

The established Jewish community felt the need to run interference against the image of Jews as criminals, which gained momentum as new Jews arrived from Europe, to protect their own reputation. In a clear example of masculine performativity, speakers for the New York Jewish community couched their defense of the Jewish people in the language of masculine pride and dignity. Jews involved in New York's criminal underworld came dramatically to the fore of social commentary in New York City in 1908, when Police Commissioner Theodore A. Bingham published an article titled "Foreign Criminals in New York," in which he claimed that roughly one half of the criminals in New York City were of Hebrew origin.[16] This drew a fast and energetic response from the Jewish community, resulting in mass meetings and indignation, a response that New York Rabbi Judah Magnes argued was how "every healthy and manly people" expresses their resentment to being so insulted.[17] The indignation of New York Jews (particularly the Jewish elite) did result in an apology from the commissioner, admitting his incorrect statistics and apologizing for publishing information which reflected so poorly on the respectable Jewish community. This satisfied several Jewish leaders who responded again with masculine language of the day; Louis Marshall (constitutional lawyer and Jewish communal leader) called Bingham's admission a "manly and courageous" act that should be accepted by the Jewish community with "the same frank and manly spirit."[18] However, the energetic response to his initial statements also resulted in a great movement for remedying the Jewish criminal situation, including the formation of the New York Kehillah, a Jewish communal organization meant to unify New York Jews socially and culturally. The Bingham incident acted as fuel to incite those interested in a unifying organization to create the Kehillah, using a combination of Jewish communal leadership and the democratic method inspired by the American ethos. They hoped that it would act as a means for the acculturated, elite German-descended Uptown community to exert a "conservative restraining influence" on the "downtown element," a substantial majority comprising eighty to ninety percent of the New York City Jewish population.

Across the country, the movement to organize Jewish communities with Kehillahs was a controversial one. Rabbi David Philipson, one of the earliest leaders of the Reform Jewish movement, was very outspoken against the Kehillah structure as inherently un-American. He believed that by forming Kehillahs, Jews "stamp themselves as a separate community distinguished from the remainder of the population. . . . Kehillaism is a pendant of Zionism. Both spell a distinctive Jewish nationalism as a thing apart."[19] As a leader of the Reform movement, Rabbi Philipson was particularly concerned with the universalist and American appearances and behaviors of the American Jewish community. For the same reason, he was against Zionism among American Jews. Other Jewish leaders, primarily those in and around New York City, were quite supportive, however. Well-known Jewish philanthropist and leader Jacob Schiff was supportive of the Kehillah's work, but was stretched too thin to join the executive committee when asked to do so.[20] The New York Jewish community was distinctive in the degree of Jewish crime it was attempting to deal with, and so the New York Kehillah's response to crime was unique, due mainly to the actions of their first chairman and prominent reform rabbi, Dr. Judah Magnes. Crime in the city garnered several responses from the wealthier, acculturated uptown Jewish community, though the most typical attempts to remedy urban social issues manifested in philanthropic support. Magnes took a less common, clandestine approach in his role as Kehillah chair, made possible by working closely with members of the downtown Jewish community. In 1912, Magnes enlisted the help of Abraham Shoenfeld, a Jewish private investigator, to build a team of undercover agents to gather information on Jewish crime in the city. Shoenfeld had previous experience investigating prostitution for the Rockefellers. He also had access to the Jewish underworld, having grown up on the Lower East Side, speaking Yiddish, and knowing most of the neighborhood toughs. His (unpublished) memoir and oral testimony provide some of the most candid reflections of the seedy underworld of Jewish New York in the first decades of the twentieth century.

Shoenfeld's investigation demonstrated that though Jews may not have comprised a full half of the criminals in the city, in certain areas they did dominate, such as stuss houses (gambling clubs with betting limits, of which thirty-four of the forty-six he located were Jewish) and prostitution.[21] He investigated Jewish brothels, election corruption, and illegal "can-can clubs" and gangs. Of the characters of the underworld, Shoenfeld made clear that the gangsters (several of whom ran gambling and illegal drinking establishments) epitomized toughness and that the prostitution business may have been criminal, but it was never manly. This conclusion seems to be primarily because the men involved in running prostitution businesses were perceived as more slimy than tough; they exercised their control over women, not other men, which Shoenfeld clearly did not see as a show of strength nearly as intimidating or impressive as gangsters.

Though cases of Jewish crimes of a sexual nature did occur, they were less common, and therefore quite famous, such as the cases of Leopold and Loeb or Leo Frank.[22] In fact, some Jewish gangsters made pimps one of their main targets to rob and fight, along with those who had just struck big while gambling. When pimps committed acts of violence or intimidation against other men, it always surprised the rest of the Jewish underworld, who viewed them as weak and cowardly. Shoenfeld described a specific pimp as "a pretty tough man, something unusual for a pimping whore-master." The entire underworld was shocked when Big Jack Zelig (also known as "The Big Yid"), the notorious leader of the Eastman Gang, was killed by a pimp (and fagin) named Red Phil Davidson, asking, "How would a pimp dare do it?" and "Red Phil is not in a gang; who ever heard of him?" Apparently, he had been tricked by a rival gangster with promises of high status.[23] This view of pimping as an unmasculine criminal profession is not unique to the Jewish underworld, or even to the United States. The view of Jewish pimps as feeding off of the women they exploit, as more cowardly than tough, also appeared in conversation about sex work in Argentina in the same period.[24]

Abraham Shoenfeld's accounts provide an intimate view into a very masculine underworld and the gendered response of New York Jewish leadership. The men in his narrative all engaged, on one side or the other, in a battle for the soul of the old neighborhoods. The Kehillah hoped to be the unifying body for Jewish New York, and Magnes, chairman of the new organization and well-respected young rabbi, waged a war against the underworld, and very determinedly "manned up" to get the job done.

He convinced the Kehillah to organize a "vigilance committee" to deal with Jewish criminality, enlisting east siders to bring more of the downtown Jews into the project.[25]

Magnes invited the public to an open meeting in the David Kessler (Jewish) Theater and launched an attack on the Jewish underworld. He presented the findings of the Kehillah to the public, on the advice of Shoenfeld, who urged him to assume an air of toughness, not to pull his punches, but to face the toughs on their own terms. He called several gangsters out by name, and the rest he threatened more broadly, "You pimps, you thieves, you fixing lawyers, you rats, you weasels, we will root you out, out into the gutters and into the sewers where you belong; we know you, everyone of you; we will drive you rats out of your holes and hideaways; your days are numbered and over; we know you, everyone of you [sic]."[26] Officials collected opinions after the speech, and even among the thugs in attendance, reactions included both threats "we'll get to them," and reverence, "the man's got guts." This image of Magnes as a leader fighting the rise of crime within the Jewish community says a lot about his view of Jewish manliness, bravado, and dignity, while maintaining more traditional Jewish values regarding violence, as he was also well-known during the First World War for his leadership in the pacifist movement.[27]

The Jewish establishment's view of the Jewish criminal underworld was one of mixed admiration and disdain. A mutual respect of toughness existed between the criminals and those fighting against them. Despite the consistent name-calling in his recollections, Shoenfeld described the gangsters with reverence: bad men, certainly, but impressively brazen, daring, and tough. When describing one murderous criminal, he recalled that not only was he "the most fearless man I have ever met in all my life," but also noted proudly that the same man once said to him, "you're the toughest man I ever knew." He also describes them as impressive specimens of manhood, one particularly as "a handsome bastard, built like an Adonis." Attitudes toward Jewish crime changed over the first two decades of the twentieth century; certainly, the law-abiding community was still ashamed, but it had become commonplace enough that they had ceased mass demonstrations of shame such as the shuttering of all Jewish homes when a Jew was executed for murder. The language surrounding Jewish crime also changed, becoming distinctly more masculine and less descriptive of Jewish men inclined to nonviolent crime, as in the defenses against the Bingham accusation.

Though several historians of Jewish crime have argued that the Jewish gangster was an interwar phenomenon, the Jewish community was clearly worried about rising gang activity (and the effect it had on the image of Jews in America) for years before Prohibition.[28] It is true that Prohibition was tremendously important in exacerbating the problem of Jewish organized crime, but by the start of the Great War, Jewish newspapers already wrote regularly about the rise in Jewish criminality and gang activity. They wrote habitually and defensively about Jewish gangsters but could not deny their growing presence. Instead, they tended to argue that the criminals may be Jewish in name, but aside from that, there was "nothing particularly Jewish about them."[29] From the passing of the Eighteenth Amendment, the public desire for illegal alcohol opened a vast market for organized crime, and Jews took part along with their criminal countrymen. They bootlegged, extorted, murdered, gambled, and dealt drugs.

The question of why these Jews appeared disproportionately in organized crime is answerable, at least in part, by looking to the common elements of their backgrounds. For the most part, Jewish gangsters were second-generation immigrants, urban-dwelling, born of Eastern European, Jewish practicing (but not Orthodox), working-class parents. The majority of them were either in New York City or were transplants from New York to more western cities and markets (such as Benjamin "Bugsy" Siegel in California and Las Vegas, Meyer Lansky in Vegas and Miami, or the leaders of the Purple Gang in Detroit). By the early 1930s, gang bosses from several major cities (many of them New York Jews) joined together to form the National Crime Syndicate, connecting mob business across America for smoother operations. Some of the most recognizable and notorious names in the syndicate belonged to Jewish gangsters (including Meyer Lansky, "Bugsy" Siegel, Louis "Lepke" Buchalter, and Abner "Longie" Zwillman). One of these gangsters, Louis "Lepke" Buchalter, created a group of assassins available to all members, operating as the enforcement arm to keep the peace within the syndicate. These men became known as Murder, Inc., an intimidating group made up predominantly of New York Jewish thugs.

Residents of the neighborhoods they frequented feared them, but in some cases they were also regarded as folk heroes, recalled as a sort of holy bit of Jewish New York history by men from the neighborhood who remembered them, and by children who grew up hearing stories of their exploits. They may have been closeted by the Jewish community in newspapers and public statements, as Imhoff argued, but they were embraced by young New York Jews as pinnacles of manliness. Years after the Jewish gang heyday, when asked why the gangster Zelig had such an enormous turnout at his (Jewish) funeral on Broom Street, Shoenfeld explains that he was a bit of a hero, not so much for his action for the community (which amounted to doing more damage to non-Jews than Jews, really), but for his image. He was well-liked by Jewish sight-seers, who could appreciate his cool tough image without betraying their community.[30] The inhabitants of the Jewish communities that gangsters called home were not the only ones who saw them as heroes, and defenders of more dignified forms of upper-class masculinity attempted to downplay or diminish their influence. Fighting against the idolizing of such men, one *Washington Post* contributor, John J. Daly, suggested that the government subsidize one gang in the elimination of another as a solution to the problem of gangsters becoming the new glamorous national heroes. Even in his recrimination, however, Daly (perhaps unwittingly) raised them to an honorable and traditionally masculine status, claiming that they could eliminate one another "as in the days of knighthood . . . each foeman worthy of his steel."[31]

Although the Jewish community seldom approved of Jewish gangsters and their behavior, on multiple occasions Jewish gangsters got involved in the Jewish community to offer protection or support, regardless of the desires of Jewish religious or communal leadership. In one particularly interesting movement (short-lived in New York, but eight years long in Newark, New Jersey) a group of Jewish toughs banded together to oppose antisemitic provocation in light of growing Nazi activity in the city. They called themselves the Minutemen (after those American heroes of the Revolutionary War) and included in their ranks some notorious gangsters as well as Jewish prizefighters.

By the 1930s, the determination of the Jewish establishment to publicly deny the Jewishness of tough gangsters had dramatically waned. The Jewish War Veterans (JWV), for example, sponsored the creation of the New York City branch of the Minutemen to break up Nazi gatherings.[32] Meyer Lansky, the infamous gangster, organized the group and arranged the training of Jewish men to fight using their fists, weapons, stones, and stink bombs

Figure 5. Members of the Newark Minutemen, including boxer and Minutemen commander Nat Arno (*middle with cigar in mouth*), 1934–41. Wikimedia Commons contributors, "File:Minutemen002.jpg," Wikimedia Commons, https://commons.wikimedia.org/w/index.php?title=File: Minutemen002.jpg&oldid=757717176 (accessed May 11, 2023).

to break up rallies.[33] According to journalist Tim Newark, Rabbi Stephen Wise and Judge Nathan Perlman actually recruited Meyer Lansky to the task (though Minutemen historian Warren Grover is not convinced of the validity of the claim for Rabbi Wise). Judge Perlman reportedly asked for Lansky's help in 1935, saying, "We Jews should be more militant. Meyer, we want to take action against these Nazi sympathizers."[34] The Newark Minutemen received much of their funding from the gang boss Longie Zwillman who supported them through his own private fortune. Although he remained behind the scenes, it was common knowledge that Zwillman was involved, and this knowledge helped add to their air of menace. It also helped that their leader, Nat Arno, was a professional prizefighter from Newark. The Minutemen appeared at Nazi gatherings and broke up or intimidated the Nazis into dispersing. Max Hinkes, a Jewish thug and associate of Zwillman and Arno, recalled one of these events fondly,

The Nazi scumbags were meeting one night on the second floor. Nat Arno and I went upstairs and threw stink bombs into the room where the creeps were. As they came out of the room, running from the horrible odor of the stink bombs and running down the steps to go into the street to escape, our boys were waiting with bats and iron bars. It was like running a gauntlet. Our boys were lined up on both sides and we started hitting, aiming for their heads or any other part of their bodies, with our bats and irons. The Nazis were screaming blue murder. This was one of the most happy moments of my life.[35]

Even if some Jews felt pride with the actions of the Minutemen, and their Jewishness was not denied, the Jewish community overall disapproved of Jewish gangsters. However, several of them (like Zwillman) garnered respect, and even some recognition, from the Jewish community for their philanthropic contributions.

The Jewish gangster appealed to young Jews as an American folk hero. He was, after all, a Jew with a gun, reminiscent of the more acceptable frontiersman/cowboy type. And he appealed to the youth, as he was himself the grown-up delinquent child, disobeying societal conventions and doing as he pleased, for pleasure and for profit. Despite regular recriminations against the gangsters, men performing tough behavior embraced their image, and not only Jews. For example, in 1943, German forces downed an American flying fortress over Germany and captured the pilot as a prisoner of war. On his plane and his flight jacket were the words "Murder Inc.," which the Nazis used in much propaganda about "typical American gangsters" sent to murder German civilians.[36]

Interestingly, and consistent with their emasculated stereotypes of Jews, Nazi propaganda did not comment on the Jewishness of the gangster assassins being referenced, which would have given credibility to Jewish men as tough and intimidating. About the influence gangsters had over the youth of America, John Daly wrote, "The boys of the Nation, where once Diamond Dick and Nick Carter were their models . . . have now gone gangster themselves. The new slogan of boyhood is: 'Stick 'Em Up!'"[37]

If there is one place in which the Jewish community truly felt they could step in to halt the growing influence of organized crime among Jews, it was at the level of the juvenile delinquent. At the turn of the century, juvenile delinquency was on the rise in major cities, New York more than most. Though the Jewish population comprised less than 20 percent of the New York City population, Jews made up one-third of all of the complaints drawn in the Children's Court of the City of New York in 1904 (a rise from the one-quarter estimate by Judge Julius M. Mayer of the previous year).[38] Of those Jewish youths, only about 7 percent were native-born American children. Even non-Jewish organizations that meant to reform delinquent boys (or potential delinquents) recognized the Jew as a problem. The prime targets of these reforms were recently immigrated Eastern Jews (primarily those fleeing from Russia after the creation of the May Laws affecting Jews of the Pale) who American Jews identified as the most difficult to handle and integrate into American life.[39]

Jewish immigrants did not generally become criminals themselves, but some of their immigrant children, as well as second-generation Americans, became delinquent. According to a breakdown of Jewish boy criminality by Boris D. Bogen (the head of United Hebrew Charities of Cincinnati) in 1905, the male children of immigrants veered toward a life of crime due to separation from exactly those elements that define the gentle Jewish boy. Separated from their fatherly male role models by distinct difference in language, religious upbringing, and lifestyle, the father's authority over the child diminished, as did the boys' appreciation of a mother's love. An all but unbridgeable chasm separated immigrant fathers and their American sons, and if it could not be bridged, the responsibility of fatherhood, or raising good Jewish men, fell to the Jewish community on the whole.[40] In Bogen's evaluation (also evident in other commentary of the time), the issue was a decidedly male one. Aside from the dwindling "appreciation of a mother's love," in fact, he left women out of his analysis of Jewish criminality entirely.[41]

Observers of the time were split in their explanations for the rise in juvenile crime and gang activity, in the Jewish community and elsewhere, though even their disagreements tended to center on the gendered causes of the issue. In 1929, Dr. Frederick Thrasher (a professor of sociology at Illinois Wesleyan University) explained that all boys are inclined to form gangs, but whether those gangs turn to crime is dependent on positive male role models and father figures. Gangdom, he said, was not randomly male, because boys naturally form gangs to seek the society of other men, to engage in male play, and to revel in "masculine importance" away from girls. Forming gangs, he clarified, is an inevitable eventuality. The turn to crime, however, is only inevitable if the gang is left with no law-abiding adult male role models.[42] The trajectory of boys who turned to crime is recited in myriad articles, public statements, and reports: boys begin this life of crime by robbing fruit stands, then picking pockets and rolling drunks, after which they graduate to robbing small stores, stealing cars, and eventually, violent and perhaps more organized crime.

Not every expert shared this view, of course. Mary Antin, author of the 1912 book, *The Promised Land*, suggested that the rising criminality among Jewish boys (and the subsequent growth in numbers of Jewish gangsters) should be blamed not on a lack of father figures but on the American Jewish community's neglect of the immigrant mother.[43] Immigration and Americanization programs, she argued, focused on the masses of immigrant men, and the Americanization of young boys and girls, leaving the immigrant mother confined, alone, to her tenement. By neglecting the immigrant mother, the Jewish community removed her authority in the home, made her dependent on her Americanized children, and left them open to make their own way by whatever means appealed to them. Only by strengthening the mother's influence, she argued, could Jewish criminality be stamped out.

The immigrant Jews themselves saw the turn to crime quite differently, focusing less blame on the nature of Jewish Europeans (themselves) and more on the situation of new migrants in New York City. They also placed blame through a less gendered view, pointing to the American experience, not Jewish men or women. In contrast to the presses of the established American Jewish community (the uptown Jews), Yiddish and immigrant presses blamed the rise of criminal behavior in the New York Jewish community on the process of Americanization itself. Like both Jews and non-Jews in the first decade of the century, Yiddish presses purported that Jews had always been a nonviolent "race," and that the turn toward violent crime signified the negative effects of urban American life on new immigrants.[44]

The problem of juvenile delinquency grew so rapidly in New York City over the turn of the century that by 1902 Judge Julius M. Mayer (after years of attempting to solve the problem of delinquent Jewish boys) founded the Jewish Protectory and Aid Society, an organization specifically created to reform Jewish boys. He created it, in part, because New York Children's Court would send Jewish boys in the system to similar reformatories run by other faiths (Protestant, Catholic, and non-sectarian), which led to concerns within the Jewish community about proselytizing and potential conversion. By the spring of 1907, the Jewish Protectory opened the Hawthorne School in Westchester County and quickly reached capacity with delinquent Jewish boys.

If life in the city made menaces of Jewish boyhood, what then was the solution? How did contemporary Jews attempt to reform the Jewish delinquents of the urban landscape? Some leading Jews promoted, much like Teddy Roosevelt, a return to the land to reconnect young boys to the great outdoors. Jewish delinquency symptomized the social diseases unique to city life. Jewish boys on the street became the wrong sort of rough, and rehabilitating them required not only the religious influence of a strong Jewish community but physical training as well. To grow into manhood, a Jewish boy needed to train physically, to keep away from the city, to develop a sense of duty and pride in the Jewish people and their culture, and to train agriculturally. And indeed, the leaders at the Hawthorne School agreed that employing these changes produced fast and rewarding results. In his first annual report, the school's superintendent explained that the "physical imperfections" of the boys contributed to their so-called delinquency. To improve and cultivate these boys to grow into good Jewish American men, physical improvement was key. Through physical training (military drills, outdoor exercise, cleanliness, good habits, and athletics that furnish "the best sort of opportunities for inculcating manly standards") in combination with Jewish religious practice and "house-parents" replacing the absent father figures in their lives, the Hawthorne School manifested positive improvement in the boys.[45] This positive improvement was attributed, in part, to the imparting of Jewish religion and customs, but the manifestation of American manliness through the body and physical discipline was a primary component of the training as well.

Jewish Agriculturalism and Outdoorsmanship

Far larger than a reformatory system for juvenile delinquents, the Jewish agricultural movement affected Jews all over the United States and incoming migrants as a part of a Jewish Americanization process. The role of boys, however, was no less important. Endeavors that focused on rehabilitating Jewish youth aimed to bring Jews from the city to the country and change their lifestyles and habits to become more masculine and more American. Even to those ardent proponents of Jewish agriculture, it seemed a far worthier effort to convert the young to country life than those who had grown to maturity with preconceived notions of city life and Jewish pursuits. Adult Jewish men, already too set in their ways and too damaged by city life, could not fully adjust. Therefore, the *boys*, not the men, would benefit most from the agricultural movement of the early twentieth century.

The earliest of American Jewish agricultural experiments were unmitigated failures. Attempts at experimental Jewish settlements in rural America began in the nineteenth century, starting with Jewish playwright Manual Mordecai Noah's effort to settle Jews on Grand Island in the Niagara River.[46] He abandoned his plan for the settlement (which he called Ararat) before any colonists even settled the land in 1820. A Galician poet, Eliezer Kirschbaum, supported Noah's dream for Jewish America, believing that if 35,000 Jewish newcomers (half of them agriculturalists) were to relocate and settle the island, the United States government would be sure to give it to them as their own independent Jewish state.[47]

It was not until 1837 that Jewish settlers attempted to establish the first American Jewish agrarian society in Wawarsing, New York, which they named Sholam. According to the author of the *Olde Ulster* (a non-Jewish historical and genealogical magazine) in a retrospective on the experiment, those Jews who settled in the area of Sholam were not farmers and made no attempt to be such. They had, the magazine explained, an "aversion to manual labor peculiar to their race," making their relocation to Wawarsing "one of the facts that are stranger than fiction."[48] The *Olde Ulster* clearly demonstrates typical preconceptions about Jewish agriculture, musing that "it seems to have been the intention of the Jews to live by their wits and develop their lands by means of Gentile labor."

Jewish agriculturalists of the 1920s recounted the failures of the settlement quite differently, referring to it as a "heroic undertaking, idealistically conceived but doomed to failure," due not to a Jewish refusal to work the land but to the barren soil, short growing season, lack of farming experience, and cold mountainous terrain.[49] These factors forced them to engage in "merchandising at home and peddling abroad," the same work that *Olde Ulster* had described as their preferred alternative to farming. In truth, the story of Sholam is still mysterious, as are its intentions. Though the examples of Jewish agriculture that follow have clear motives directly connecting Jewish immigration, Americanization, and masculinity, Sholam is far less documented and less understood.

The farmers varied in their countries of origin, professions, ages, and religious beliefs. The unifying factor was their Jewishness, making it even more interesting that their experiment, in many ways, turned out to be a surprisingly un-Jewish one. It is surprising, for example, that education was not only meager but at times neglected entirely, as children raised in Sholam (before they abandoned the settlement) had to work to help support their families, and many of them neglected the study of holy books, and a few remained illiterate into adulthood. Religion, though a unifying factor, was also not the focus of the Sholam settlers, and they abandoned their small synagogue quickly as every member of the family attempted to eke out a living between the minor gains of their farms and home production. Children of Sholam recalled holding their dances and parties in the abandoned synagogue. There were some Orthodox Jews among the colonists, but there was no consistency in the devotion of Sholam residents.[50]

The initiative for a large, organized movement of Jews into an agrarian lifestyle came as a direct result of mass migration, primarily the arriving Jews fleeing from pogroms in czarist Russia starting in the early 1880s. At this time, disconnected Jewish agricultural colonies sprang up across the country without organization or large-scale planning. Though they spread nationwide, they were short-lived and ill-conceived. Some were built by families of means (like the Crémieux settlement in South Dakota), some funded by benefactors (like the Louisiana colony, initially funded by Herman Rosenthal), and still more supported through American Jewish organizations (like the Colorado settlement in Cotopaxi, created by the Hebrew Immigrant Aid Society).[51] Settlements failed due to natural disasters (crop failures, droughts, floods, and such) and human developments beyond their control (such as the completion of the railroad being built through the Jewish colony in Oregon, the construction of which had supported the businesses of Jewish settlers there).

After the turn of the century, the Jewish agricultural movement began in a much more organized and well-funded fashion, and by all accounts became far more successful than the failed colonies of the nineteenth century. This was due, in part, to the efforts of acculturated American Jewish philanthropists and organizers, who assessed the failures of the colonies as the result of injudicious selections of land, inadequate financing, lack of agricultural education, and lack of transportation. This is also the explanation for the survival of the Jewish colonies in New Jersey, which resided near enough to Philadelphia and New York to overcome several of the obstacles that befell their counterparts. The initial unifying force for the resurrection of the Jewish agricultural movement in the twentieth century came from the German-Jewish philanthropist Baron Maurice de Hirsch, an immigrant himself, who made it his mission to resettle downtrodden Eastern European Jews and help integrate them into their new country. He initially founded two organizations, the Jewish Colonization Association (to assist in emigration and resettlement from czarist Russia) and the Baron de Hirsch Fund (with a starting contribution of $2,400,000 to assist those who had made it to America on their own steam, but needed help equipping themselves as new Americans).[52] The Baron de Hirsch Fund provided personal loans, training in English language, funding for transportation, training for trades, education in American citizenship, and assistance in agricultural resettlement. The emergence of the fund injected new life into the Jewish agricultural movement, and thus into opportunities to promote Jewish manhood by working the land. However, leaders discovered quickly that settling Jewish immigrants on the soil and training them to be farmers comprised a far larger organizational task than the Baron de Hirsch Fund could handle. Therefore, in 1900, the fund chartered the Jewish Agricultural and Industrial Aid Society in New York, funded by both the Baron de Hirsch Fund and the Jewish Colonization Association.

With all of the Baron de Hirsch Fund's agricultural matters in their hands, the Jewish Agricultural and Industrial Aid Society became the main mover of Jewish agriculturalism in the United States. Though the society originally focused on industry as well, industrial aid became secondary to agricultural developments. Primarily, the Jewish Agricultural and Industrial Aid Society gave financial assistance to individual farmers. They did not focus on creating new Jewish colonies, which had proven so disastrous in the previous decades. There was a simultaneous, similarly motivated movement (also advocated, organized, and funded by New

York Jewish philanthropists) to bring new Jewish immigrants directly to the American West (specifically to Galveston, Texas), bypassing the corrupting influence of living in overcrowded and impoverished urban settlements.[53]

For those already settled in New York City, in need of redeeming masculine programming, the Baron de Hirsch fund created and sustained only one colony, in Woodbine, New Jersey. Founded in 1891 in Woodbine (a borough in Cape May County, New Jersey), the Woodbine colony was not a purely agricultural colony, as they set up industrial pursuits there as well. The history of Woodbine is a particularly interesting vignette in Jewish American history, as it separated legally from the township of Dennis and became its own borough in 1903, making it, for a time, an American municipality in which every position was filled by Jews. The school system, fire house, and all other public works were run entirely by Jews. Though originally conceived as an agricultural settlement, the number of Jews living there who engaged in and depended on agricultural pursuits for survival dwindled.[54] However, while it operated, the fund and the society focused primarily on agricultural education, establishing a Bureau of Education in 1901 and the first and only agricultural paper to be printed in Yiddish, in 1908, the *Jewish Farmer*, a product of the Jewish Agricultural and Industrial Aid Society.

The agricultural movement received its funding from the American Jewish elite, philanthropists who worried about the rising numbers of Jewish immigrants in overcrowded tenements resorting to a life of urban crime. They viewed the task of pioneering as an undeniably manly one that could remedy both the issue of immigrant masses in the city and the depleted Jewish physique, also an unfortunate result of life in urban environments. They did not move to the countryside themselves to pick up hoes and trowels and get their hands dirty, but they felt that masculinizing new immigrants and changing their physique in this way would reflect positively on the acculturated Jews themselves. Furthermore, the leaders of the organizations behind the Jewish agricultural movement attempted to present Jewish farming as being driven not by charity, but by the initiative of Jews eager to take up farming.

In 1912, the general manager of the Jewish Agricultural and Industrial Aid Society wrote that the common assumption that "the Jewish farmer of to-day is a hothouse plant carefully nurtured by the money and

Figure 6. The Woodbine Agricultural School in 1894. Baron de Hirsch Agricultural and Industrial School: Woodbine Settlement and School, Woodbine, NJ. Harvard Art Museums / Fogg Museum, Transfer from the Carpenter Center for the Visual Arts, Social Museum Collection.

efforts of his philanthropic coreligionists," was a faulty one, though this does *seem* like an accurate assessment based on the programs and successes of the aid societies of the time.[55] In nearly every available account written by a philanthropist or organizer associated with the movement, the same introduction is offered: that Jews had been denied access to agriculture for centuries, weakening their bodies and depriving them of their ancient and manly farming history, and now that America had given them access, they sprinted toward farm life with eager enthusiasm. Indeed, Morris Loeb wrote in 1912 that Jews were on the threshold of a new era, "wherein the ratio between city and country-dwellers among the Jews will be that imposed by nature rather than by restrictive tyranny."[56] The implication being, of course, that Jewish men were no less desirous of a life in agriculture than any other group, and would quickly demonstrate this, and regain the masculinity lost in the denial of this profession. However, the century since this proclamation has provided evidence that, if this is the case, perhaps farming is not truly the profession that a large proportion of Jews desire.[57]

The Jewish Agricultural and Industrial Aid Society built and sustained the Jewish agricultural movement with continued (though not massive) growth over the first few decades of its existence, at least until the Depression hit and expansion halted. The number of Jewish farmers in the United States grew from about 1,000 in 1900 to nearly 100,000 by the end of the Second World War. The society did not primarily send Jewish immigrants to the countryside with funds to start farms, as they had seen how ineffective and expensive relocation was, instead, they made several attempts to train immigrants closer to home. For example, they purchased 500 acres of land on Long Island to train farmers before moving them and their families to the countryside to fend for themselves. They called this experiment the Test Farm. This program fixated entirely on men, as heads of household, who would be hired and paid as farmhands until ready to bring their families to farms outside of the city. This focus on the men is very telling, as even in their admittance that farm work requires the willingness and participation of the wife and children, they identify changing the Jewish man as the task necessary before putting a Jewish family on a farm. They exercised the same focus on Jewish boys and men when evaluating the potential remedy of Jewish agriculturalism to juvenile delinquency.

To promote Jewish agriculturalism and save delinquent Jewish youth from the city, Jewish organizations created several agricultural programs to bring criminally inclined Jewish urbanites out of the cities to retrain them as agriculturalists. In Philadelphia, for example, Jewish leaders sent delinquent boys to live with Jewish farmers in surviving Jewish agricultural colonies in New Jersey.[58] Unlike the reformatory schools, agricultural schools aimed to reform not only delinquent boys, but welcomed all Jewish boys willing to consider a life of agricultural pursuits. The first of these schools was the Baron de Hirsch Agricultural School established in the Woodbine colony in 1894. Originally founded as a small operation for the benefit of the Woodbine farmers and their sons, soon the school also took on several boys from the New York Orphan Asylum as resident pupils. Shortly thereafter, it erected several buildings to further their work, including a dormitory prepared to house eighty youths. The Agricultural School hoped to reform Jewish boys and create Jewish men, but expected slow progress.

A Jewish agronomist, H. L. Sabsovich, helped to plan, oversee, and administer the town and school at Woodbine, serving as both the first superintendent of the school and the first mayor of the Jewish municipality. Sabsovich echoed earlier statements about the weakness of Jewish men from their shared history of persecution, in explaining that the process of turning Jews into American farmers would be a long and difficult one:

> Taking into consideration that the Jew was for centuries prevented from tilling the soil, and that centuries of physical persecution, crowding in narrow quarters, and depriving him of the advantages of a life in the open air, have weakened his body, we must not look too pessimistically on the results of the attempts of the Jew to become a farmer. We must not lose patience and become disappointed, because only a few of the Jews become farmers. The difficulties are not only innate and particularly Jewish, but they are American and European as well. I refer to the city-ward tendency of the present day. The question is not how successful are Jewish farmers and Jewish farming, but can we, so to say, ruralize the Jew; settle him in thinly populated districts; develop in him a love for nature; strengthen his body, and then let him select farming as a life occupation.[59]

According to Sabsovich's theory, to make a farmer of the Jew, the Jewish agricultural movement must first relocate adult Jewish men to the farm, even though this method seemed largely unsuccessful. Either they would take to it or they would not, but regardless of their feeling toward the farm itself, some of these men would never return to the city, choosing to take up occupations in more rural settings. In the cases of the young, and the "boy immigrant" particularly, they needed a second method, and this is where Woodbine set the example by developing farm schools. Though it seems easy to draw a direct line from this way of thinking to the kibbutzim in the Yishuv, it is important to keep in mind the particular differences in ideology driving Sabsovich versus Jewish settlers of Palestine. Sabsovich is using these methods of relocation, training, and agriculturalism to help immigrants attain the American dream, which is one of self-sufficiency, independence, and capitalism. Kibbutzniks were drawing from an Eastern European socialism-based ideology of cooperation, communal living, and collectivism.

As particularly Jewish institutions, farm schools like Woodbine had several goals in reforming Jewish men. They aimed to develop the muscles and physique of a new outdoorsman Jew while continuously promoting a life of the mind. Sabsovich argued that if the farm schools neglected regular education, the Jewish boy would begin to feel intellectually inferior to his city dwelling brother and would "turn his back on the very idea of agriculture." The flexibility of Woodbine (both the settlement and the school) allowed them to branch out from an agricultural utopian ideal, incorporating elements of industry that help to account for their success. Though they could not thrive as a purely agricultural settlement, they became quite successful as an agro-industrial colony. Other Jewish agricultural schools formed, such as the National Farm School outside of Philadelphia in 1897, aimed at preparing young men to enter state agricultural colleges.

It is important to note that even among American Jews who settled in the country or smaller rural towns, Jewish people did not unanimously agree that they were well-suited to a life of farming. In an early report on an attempt to relocate Jews from the city to more rustic areas (in this case Warren, Pennsylvania), local Jewish leadership explained that Jews who relocated to small towns needed to be trained as artisans, as Jews were simply ill-suited to farm life. Jewish men were too intent on profitable enterprise, and Jewish women not content with the isolated life that agriculture provided. Of course, these claims assume a universality of Jewish tendencies that recalls precisely the antisemitic archetypes that American Jews hoped to dispel through agricultural enterprise. The confident recitation of such Jewish stereotypes by Jews themselves to explain failures in this area of work points to the degree to which Jews had internalized and believed these attributes to be truly Jewish ones. After the business that brought about sixty Jewish men to Warren closed permanently, only three remaining employees attempted to become farmers, but even in these cases, they gave it up quickly.[60]

These farming movements were but one way in which acculturated city Jews attempted to masculinize the wayward city-dwelling Jewish youth. It was meant for Jewish immigrants and their children to Americanize through masculinization. Jewish American philanthropists also developed quite different programs for their own offspring, coming from greater means, which intended to bring middle- and upper-class Jewish city boys of more respectable sorts out to the country to make American men of them. In the interwar years particularly, summer camps, which exclusively invited Jewish boys, opened for business and were founded and operated through the Young Men's Hebrew Association (YMHA), local congregations, Jewish philanthropic organizations, and even some under fully private ownership. In large part, their records, advertisements, and other ephemera read like any other summer camp, stressing the camaraderie, sports, crafts, and song that children will enjoy during their stay. That one of their primary purposes was a masculinizing mission for Jewish boys is clear in a close reading of their activities, goals, and statements by camp leadership.

Between 1910 and 1933, the camping movement in the United States expanded tremendously, as over one hundred summer camps (of all sorts) existed in the United States in 1910, and by 1933 that number had grown to almost 3,500.[61] Though the nondenominational, private Jewish camps had their boom and heyday in the 1940s and the years of prosperity after the Second World War, the goals of these camps were different. It is the antimodernist, return to nature, "strenuous" lifestyle camps, aimed specifically at Jewish boys, that are of interest in this context. Not all of these camps admitted only boys, some focused on girls as well, and they had various missions, but for the most part they all embraced the theory of the "strenuous" life that Theodore Roosevelt made popular in the early twentieth century. They stressed outdoorsmanship and health, and they all sought the restorative qualities of experiencing the great outdoors. Most of the camps accepted exclusively male campers, stressing an overarching agenda of making men of soft urban Jewish boys.

A few Jews from Philadelphia opened a private camp in Maine, Camp Kennebec, with the expressed goal of implementing the ideals of the strenuous life, and the secondary goal of working to overcome antisemitic stereotypes of Jewish weakness by promoting manly Americanization. At Camp Kennebec, camper experiences did not focus primarily on Jewishness. According to historian Jonathan Sarna, the camp downplayed Jewish activities for a more American experience, to "breathe in the 'pure sweet air of American mountains, lakes and forests' and to exhale any residual foreign traits."[62] Camp Wah-Kon-Dah in Rocky Mount, Missouri, exemplified this, with practically no Jewishness in the programming, though parents clearly thought of it as a Jewish experience. Judging by the materials available from the camp, the name Wah-Kon-Dah has no actual meaning, but is meant to sound like an Indian name or tribe. Though no longer in existence, the camp reopened under new management in 1970 as "Camp Sabra," a term with its own attachments to Jewish man-making.[63]

Not all Jewish camps operated with so little Jewish programming, of course, some focused more on combining a Jewish male experience (including study of Jewish texts and prayers) with an American experience in the great outdoors. In 1915, Bernard C. Ehrenreich, a popular rabbi from Alabama, bought a large plot of land in the Northwoods of Wisconsin and opened his own camp for Jewish boys, Camp Kawaga. Ehrenreich believed that not only could manhood be attained in the great outdoors, but that God resided in nature. By combining Jewish life with the strenuous life, a Jewish boy could blossom into full Jewish American manhood. The early promotional material for the camp shows this in its language and stated goals (even hinting at the goal of attaining "whiteness"). One flyer contains a poem with the stanza:

> Four great tall pines lived ages thru
> And saw pines die and others grew
> To shelter man again.
> The white man's child comes here to grow
> In health and strength and learns to know
> The life of now and then.
> In play and work and campfire song
> The pines—they watch for eight weeks long
> The boys grow into men.[64]

Kawaga was one of the first twenty-five camps in the country (according to their current promotional material) and still maintains the restriction against girls, and the mission of "helping boys develop meaningfully into manhood."[65]

In 1923, the Young Men's Hebrew Association of Philadelphia opened a camp an hour outside of the city, in Betzwood, Pennsylvania, called Camp Port Indian. Camp Port Indian invited only Jewish boys between the ages of twelve and eighteen years for a summer of manly pursuits. Their marketing materials made the masculinizing mission of the camp quite explicit. They topped their newspaper advertisements for the camp with the words, "Health. Recreation. Manliness."[66]

The camp mission statement clearly defines their purpose to "inculcate through the medium of a wonderfully wholesome recreation, the finest traits of manhood" and includes deliberate mention of the weakness and physical frailties of Jewish boys. "A feature of the camp will be the special attention paid to boys whose constitutions need upbuilding. Special exercises and weight gaining play will be prescribed for those boys who need such special attention." "Manliness," according to the opening statement of a camp brochure, "is developed, not invented or inherited. Camp life offers every opportunity for developing courage, sportsmanship and a rugged constitution, under excellent supervision. . . . It is just the place to send your son."[67] This statement is a perfect example of constructing Jewish masculinity through intentional acts of manhood, though the language and understanding of gender construction now are quite different.

These Jewish boys' camps did not use only the physical rebuilding of the Jewish boys into men to promote a masculine image, they also played into a popular embrace of Indian identity (as is clear from the rhetoric and names of the camps) to connect to their own Americanness. The use of Indian names and imagery in summer camps across the country was a way of claiming a deep-rooted American manliness associated with the land and its indigenous inhabitants. Historians have mused about this fantastic connection and what it meant to the men attempting to manifest it. In *Masculinity and the Making of American Judaism*, Sarah Imhoff examines the ways in which Jewish men linked Jews to Indians through their relationship to the land, Christianity, and the mythology that Native Americans descended from one of the ten lost tribes of Israel. She argues that Jewish men used these connections to Indians to boost their own masculine image.[68] In these camps, however, though the names sound Indian, the campers are not compared to Indians at all but

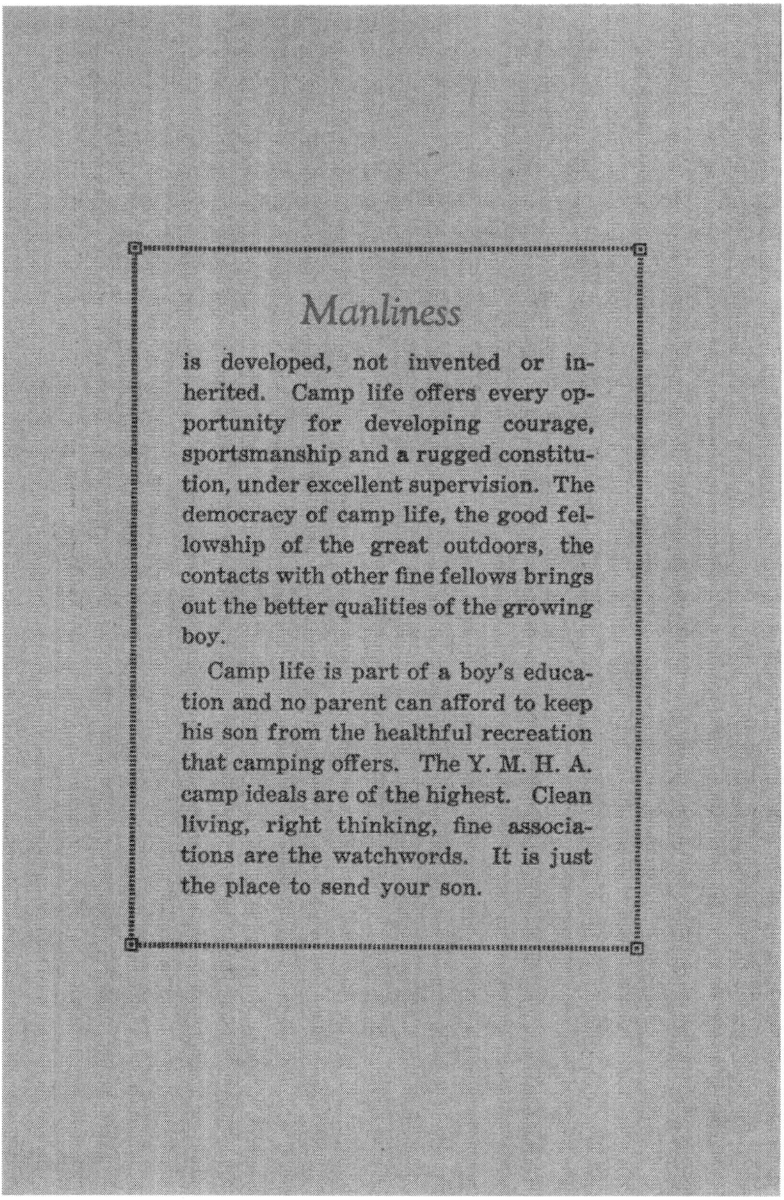

Manliness

is developed, not invented or inherited. Camp life offers every opportunity for developing courage, sportsmanship and a rugged constitution, under excellent supervision. The democracy of camp life, the good fellowship of the great outdoors, the contacts with other fine fellows brings out the better qualities of the growing boy.

Camp life is part of a boy's education and no parent can afford to keep his son from the healthful recreation that camping offers. The Y. M. H. A. camp ideals are of the highest. Clean living, right thinking, fine associations are the watchwords. It is just the place to send your son.

Figure 7. Interior page from a Camp Port Indian brochure. Courtesy of the Jacob Rader Marcus Center of the American Jewish Archives, Cincinnati, Ohio, at americanjewisharchives.org.

identified as *white*, as in the poem from Kawaga, "The white man's child comes here to grow, in health and strength and learns to know."

Contrary to Imhoff's analysis, which stresses the connection of Jewish camps to indigenous people as a lost tribe, these camps overtly identified their campers as white, which, while painting a picture in which they are surrounded by native land and spirit, does not actually serve to connect Jews to Native Americans. Instead, it connects them to the American frontier experience, mimicking Roosevelt's beliefs about the frontier making Americans and making men, and maintaining that whiteness is the masculine goal far more than what was then called "noble savagery." There is certainly an established connection of American men proving themselves by donning red-face and feathers, particularly in terms of American mascots.[69] However, such a minute number of Jewish authors and scholars are engaged in the comparison of Jews to Native Americans that it is unlikely that proving their masculinity by highlighting this connection was a very common occurrence or theme. More importantly, though Americans of European descent considered Indians fiercely masculine, they did not consider them the height of manhood, white men still presented themselves as more masculine by their creation and embrace of modern civilization. It was, in fact, not an original movement but a facsimile of the camps made so popular by Ernest Thompson Seton's Woodcraft League of America (originally called the Woodcraft Indians and League of Woodcraft Indians), the Boy Scouts, the Young Men's Christian Association (YMCA), and similar groups, who wove together lore about Indians and Christian spirituality.[70] Creating Jewish camps in the image of the popular Christian Indian-themed camps shows the desire to be seen as parallel to their Christian countrymen, more so than to native culture and mythology.

Even so, the primary mission of the camps was to masculinize the boys through connection to nature, and that is where they focused their activities and rhetoric. To help make men of boys, Camps Indian Port, Kawaga, Kennebec, Wah-Kon-Dah, and others of their ilk aimed to supplement urban or suburban lives with outdoorsmanship. They were, after all, summer programs only, not life-altering changes or relocations. For the problems of urban overcrowding, crime, new immigrants, and the image of Jewish America, prospective solutions were both more permanent and more philanthropic, in line with the endeavor to create large

Jewish agricultural ventures. Camping presented a solution based on the same ideas, but for the middle class, those who could afford to send their sons to summer camps (although some camp leaders, like Rabbi Ehrenreich, did provide scholarships for underprivileged youth) and wanted to make men of their boys.

The problems of Jewish manhood during this period and their masculine solutions in nature show distinctly separate problems for different Jewish communities, but with the same remedy. The upper- and middle-class Jews *needed* to become tougher, while the poor, urban Jew had become too much so. Wealthy Jews promoted the same solution for both, but whereas the return to nature was only temporary for those with means, they expected the poor to adapt to a new agrarian lifestyle for the sake of the Jewish American image and spirit. Of course, wealthier Jewish men from the city did not themselves engage in the same sort of summer camp masculinity building exercises to which they subjected their sons, but they were not exempt from their own criticisms of having become soft.

Acculturated upper- and middle-class Jewish men who accepted notions of Jewish weakness as a reality and believed in masculine remedies, did not generally escape the city to heal their masculinity out in nature with their sons. More appropriate to their own social standing in the larger American middle class, they saw participation in masculine institutions of the time as an attainable method of altering both themselves and their public image. In part because American men's social clubs, athletic institutions, and fraternities were exclusive in male membership, they served as the stages on which masculine identities were built and men were made.[71] However, a number of the institutions promoting and celebrating male camaraderie and athletics among affluent men barred even the most respectable and prosperous Jews from entry. This was true of urban athletic and social clubs, suburban country and golf clubs, city and university clubs, and university Greek life across the nation. Discriminatory practices against Jews in purely social organizations helped to determine the place of American Jews in the early twentieth century as outside of the masculine hegemon. They were largely acculturated, accepted as peers politically and economically, but were still socially restricted, particularly as men.

An unidentified American Jewish man wrote, in a 1924 issue of *The Atlantic*, that "we regard our country still as the land of opportunity where no white man, at least, is denied the fruits of his toil in every direction and where, at least, all white folk are created free and equal and remain so throughout good behavior." He continues that although Jews are included in this glorious white equality, "Americans are prone to lay too much stress upon *political* equality as distinguished from *social* equality," and it is the latter to which Jews are still denied entry.[72] The Americanization process, he believed, was being undermined by this discrimination, as life in the suburbs especially was built on congenial social interactions between men and between suburban families. Unless one resided in a city like New York, with a booming Jewish population, they would be unlikely to find fellow Jews with common interests with whom they could create parallel Jewish institutions. As a particular and very small subgroup of white men, he believed that in some respects, this made the Jewish experience "worse than that of the Negroes because, being fewer in number, they are unable to find a sufficient number of congenial spirits among their own people with whom to associate." He believed that the generally high status and education level of acculturated Jews meant their chosen associations were more particular than those of the laboring class, including the Black community. "What the lot of a really educated Negro in this country is," he mused, "I hardly dare contemplate." This article is especially fascinating as the author laments his status as a socially restricted Jewish man while demonstrating his successful aspirational whiteness by highlighting his own educational and economic advantages over African Americans and others in the laboring class.

In cities and settings with more Jews, Jewish men did exactly as the unidentified *Atlantic* author of the above quote thought they would, they constructed institutions of exclusively Jewish clientele and leadership to provide such social venues for themselves and their communities. The most notable of these particularly male institutions were fraternal and athletic organizations. Though the author feared this would reinforce ethnic group cohesion and impede Americanization efforts, the Jews who created these groups had the same goal of Americanization in mind, just with different methods to achieve it.

Jewish Athleticism

The American proving grounds of masculinity differed from those in the countries across Europe where Jews had dwelled for centuries and from which they were immigrating to the United States in record numbers. Along with the great waves of migrants from Europe during the late nineteenth and early twentieth centuries came European attitudes (among both Jews and non-Jews) about Jewish physicality and sportsmanship. Across Europe, Jews had tried to prove their mettle as fighters and athletes, and by dueling, of course, which became so popular among students in Germany that it was the primary activity of fraternities at German universities.[73] Dueling never became popular in the same fashion in the United States as in Germany, nor did it elicit the same Jewish backlash against antisemitism that evolved into the theories of Theodor Herzl and Max Nordau. Most American duels, for example, involved pistols, not swords, the intention of the duels being far less a fraternal "hazing" tool than a means to settle grievances, even if it ended in death. German students wore protective padding with full coverage, aside from their cheeks and chins, making the facial scars both prized and public. Given the American propensity to duel with firearms, however, the facial marks or scars of having fought a duel were not prized as a symbol of masculine status.[74]

Among the second generation of European Jewish migrants, more American and more accustomed to city street life, many saw fighting as their opportunity to become American men through performance, to protect themselves from other scrappy immigrant boys in the slums, and to disprove the accusations those other boys made against Jews for their assumed cowardice and meek nature. Tension between ethnic groups among children on the streets persisted as a part of everyday life in immigrant neighborhoods in the city and was not limited to boys on the street. In his study of the death of a young Jewish girl in 1918, Gil Ribak demonstrated how much these ethnic tensions had solidified (and how much of the Jewish attitude toward other immigrant groups grew from deep-rooted attitudes toward gentiles in Europe). Jews in the girl's neighborhood quickly sensationalized the tragedy with accusations against Irish "hooligans" and "murderers" for her death, despite the ample evidence of her suicide. Negative though some of their attitudes and presumptions about the Irish were, Jewish immigrants also tended to commend them as "straight-thinking people who could defend their group's honor."[75] At times emulating the Irish and Italian toughs with whom they tussled, Jewish boys learned to fight and prove themselves, and several notable Jewish pugilists emerged as heroes of the neighborhood gangs.

Figure 8. Boxing match between two young men from the Jewish Education League in Toledo, Ohio. Photo was taken around 1920. Toledo-Lucas County Public Library, Public domain, via Wikimedia Commons. Wikimedia Commons contributors, "File:Jewish Educational League Boxing Match—DPLA—74f841f3b0f085e12b23ebefe5e62d2a.jpg," Wikimedia Commons, https://commons.wikimedia.org/w/index.php?title=File:Jewish_Educational _League_Boxing_Match_-_DPLA_-_74f841f3b0f085e12b23ebefe5e62d2a.jpg &oldid=747435795 (accessed June 29, 2023).

In the early twentieth century, boxing was both the most masculine sport of the day (as it was generally illegal, rough, and associated with gambling and gang activity) and the most Jewish sport of its time. Jews entered the ring, shaking the perception of Jews as weak and cowardly by becoming leading prizefighters of the day. According to Steven Riess, the majority of Jewish prizefighters in the United States (in New York, San Francisco, Chicago, and other major cities) came from the poor sons of Eastern European immigrants, living in slums and trying to earn their way out.[76] They differed from their parents, who kept to more Old World practices and avoided *goyim naches*. Herbert Sussman claimed that "playing professional sports and losing the self in sports fandom provided a way of rejecting the Jewish heritage of the pallid student. The true American was the athlete, and Jewish males coveted this identity."[77] Though the latter holds true, the assertion that Jewish athletes, particularly boxers, rejected their Jewish heritage in order to access this American identity does not. Jewish men who became prizefighters largely continued to behave, in their families and communities, as nice Jewish boys. They embraced more masculine images, in this case professional fighters, in order to access the masculine element of Americanness that might help them acculturate and find acceptance in the American landscape. Though they coveted the masculine American identity, they did not reject their Jewish heritage. For example, to protect their parents from the potentially devastating reality that their nice Jewish boys fought in the streets (and for money!), many Jewish boxers fought under aliases, hoping to avoid disappointing their immigrant mothers. Boxer Morris Sheer fought as Mushy Callahan, for example, and Beryl Rasofsky as Barney Ross.[78] In fact, one of the all-time great Jewish boxers, Benny Leonard, left the profession "for the love of my mother, who has begged me not to fight again."[79] But in their own lives, they remained participatory members of their Jewish communities and families.

Though they worried about disappointing or embarrassing their families, Jewish boxers received praise not only for their skill in the ring but also for their character. Benny Leonard was flattered by Theodore Roosevelt, who admired him for "fighting clean," and by the mayor of Philadelphia for his "gentlemanly conduct."[80] The dominance of Jewish pugilists, as a product of the struggles faced by second-generation Jewish immigrants, was not built to last. The generations that followed acculturated more successfully, had access to better education, and faced a less urgent need to escape the slums than their fathers. The social and economic mobility that they gained as second-generation immigrants provided their children with better routes for success.[81]

The stereotype against which Jewish fighters struggled also affected regular Jewish men who otherwise occupied themselves in sales, business, medicine, finance, and other professions and skilled trades. For those men, becoming a famous professional boxer was not an option or even particularly desirable. American institutions already existed for the purpose of masculinizing American men (and male camaraderie) through social and physical training. Even in New York City, where the largest population of American Jews resided during the mass migration period, several of these athletic and social institutions rejected Jewish participation. For Jews to achieve American manhood, and for comfortable acculturation into mainstream American culture, access to institutions that fostered male camaraderie and masculine disciplines was a necessity. Of particular interest presently are those institutions that were not only predominantly male, but exclusively so, like athletic, sporting, or country clubs and organizations.

Jewish men responded in a number of ways to their exclusion from non-Jewish athletic clubs, as they have historically when denied entry from groups, clubs, and institutions of all sorts. As they had in many other areas of discrimination, Jews responded to exclusion from athletic endeavors by fighting for entry or creating parallel Jewish institutions showcasing Jewish capabilities and adequacy for participation in similar activities. In addition, at least in the case of some New York City Jews, they also created gyms and athletic clubs for Jewish men that avoided mention of their Jewishness nearly entirely. The goal was not to change the way that outsiders viewed Jews, but to change the nature of Jewish sportsmanship and encourage behaviors more in line with American mainstream masculinity. In other words, Jews did not create these clubs to prove the manliness of Jews, but to *improve* their manliness by providing a venue in which they could participate and progress.

In 1906, a group of male Jewish New Yorkers founded the City Athletic Club in response to discriminatory policies and practices barring them from non-Jewish clubs that offered access to American manhood through physical training. They intended to "give to the Jewish young man of character a club which will fill a long-felt want."[82] Shortly after its founding, the secretary for the club interviewed with the *American Hebrew and Jewish Messenger*, which quoted him as saying:

> We have had this project under consideration for some time. Many of us, all Jewish young men, have long felt the difficulties that the Jew has experienced when he endeavored to gain admittance to any of the leading clubs in the city. The objections usually were two-fold. Either the club was entirely social, card parties being the predominant feature, or else the doors of the organization were closed to the Jew, if not by direct legislation, then through such discrimination that no self-respecting Jew could care to be enrolled. Recognizing these difficulties, a committee . . . started

this movement to combine physical development with social activity.[83]

The organization was not founded to give athletes a venue in which to thrive and compete (the goal of other leading athletic clubs of the time), but to make athletic men out of the Jewish membership. "Our sole object in organizing this club," the secretary continued, "is to draw as fine a line of distinction as possible between an organization which supports 'The Athlete' and one which is organized for the athletic welfare of its members." The City Athletic Club supported a variety of activities to promote their goal of athletic welfare, including both team sports (like basketball and baseball) and individual sports (handball, tennis, squash, and swimming).[84]

One of the fascinating elements of the City Athletic Club is that despite its undeniably Jewish nature, it did not publicly (or even within its own internal institutional documents) discuss Jewishness or publicize the successes of its members as Jews. The previous quotes came from the pages of a Jewish paper. The *New York Times*, by contrast, did report on the opening, development, membership, controversies, and expansion of the club over the years, but never mentioned their Jewishness. The *New York Times* was committed to remaining objective, particularly on Jewish issues and news from the Jewish community (for fear of accusations of bias), and so was loathe to identify any institution or business as a Jewish one.[85] Within a few months of its founding, the *Times* reported that with full membership so quickly achieved, the organization was sure to rival the New York Athletic Club and the Irish American Athletic Club, but did not mention the fact that the organization, and all its members, were Jewish.[86]

The lack of mention of the Jewishness of members, not just in the press but in their own institutional documents, makes apparent the transformative goals of the founders and leaders of the club. Though prosperous New York Jews formed the club for Jewish athletics, an examination of even the private records of the City Athletic Club shows no mention of the organization's (or its members') Jewish identity.[87] The word *Jew*, in fact, does not appear in either institutional records or club newsletters, though other ethnic groups are discussed. Omitting the Jewishness of members seems especially intentional when examining the Temple Bulletin Collections, which show how the club was involved in Jewish activities and philanthropy across New York City.[88] That this organization aimed to promote masculinity is evident in their own original constitution, which states, "The objects of this organization shall be: to encourage all manly sports and to promote physical culture; to maintain a club house and athletic grounds for the use of its members, and generally to add to their comfort and entertainment."[89] And it inarguably succeeded at meeting these objectives. Jewish presses hailed the success of the club as a sign of the virility of club members, "one of the results of clean athletics."[90]

Similar movements emerged for the younger generation of New York Jews to get them involved in strength building athletic activities. And several did include the added goal of larger inclusivity to their missions. The Grand Street Boy's Club, for example, founded in 1916, originally began as a reunion of men who had grown up in the neighborhood of the Lower East Side. It served as a hangout for men from the neighborhood in all walks of life. Members included judges, pickpockets, thugs, politicians, and every type of "Downtown kid."[91] Although not their initial intention, the club got involved in athletics because other athletic clubs in the city discriminated against Jewish boys. By the end of the Second World War, the club was also advocating civil rights and boycotting associations with groups in the Jim Crow South that discriminated against African American athletes.[92] Addressing the issues of urban life and trying to positively alter the image of Jews among their non-Jewish neighbors, several Jewish organizations encouraged Jewish inner-city children, particularly the children of immigrants, to engage in athletic activities to address the negative press about Jewish physicality. "The children of the poor," one commentator explains, "are often consecrated to a noble cause; they are to be the pioneers of a new life for their race. . . . Thus, physical culture is taught, not because it is to benefit the physique of the individual, but for the sake of the argument that the Jews are able to become athletes."[93]

While Jewish men trained in the gyms and tracks of the City Athletic Club and others like it, Jewish commentators refuted preconceived notions of Jews as unathletic. Even some of these excited supporters of Jewish athleticism accepted a physical disadvantage of brute strength (compared with, say, their Irish neighbors in the slums) when they highlighted the advantages of the Jew in certain sports based on those same stereotypes about Jewish physicality and intellect. "It is a well established fact," the *American Hebrew and Jewish Messenger* asserts, "that in basketball the Jew has no superior. This game requires a good deal of quick thinking, lighting like rapidity of movement, and endurance; it does not call for brutality and brute strength, and this is why the Jews excel in it."[94] In his excitement to extoll the virtue of Jewish basketball players, the author buttressed elements of a stereotype regularly used as a negative portrayal of Jews, that they are historically cunning and clever ("quick thinking").

These clubs participated in a larger movement, according to one contemporary commentator—that of expanding athletics in Jewish life to extend beyond athletes to everyday Jewish men:

> The Jew is not content with having only stars, but is endeavoring to encourage and develop athletics. As a result, we have witnessed within the last few years the wonderful growth of the country club and the Y.M.H.A. . . . the Jewish business man is learning to engage in athletics as well as support it, while the Jewish youth is participating actively. The wonderful result has been that with these two forces cooperating, the Jew as an athlete and as a supporter and developer of athletics has made a prominent showing, and it is no overburst of exuberance which leads one to predict that the position of the Jew in this branch of American life is due for still greater progress.[95]

The phrase "this branch of American life," as supporters and developers of athletics, is a telling one, as it indicates not only that being athletic is American, but that Jews have to make this active effort to change their position, as they had previously not met the standard of American athleticism. It was an intentional change to what the Jewish community believed was a very real deficit, but one they were confident they could overcome. More difficult than the athletics, however, was the social standing of Jews in America. As the secretary of the City Athletic Club explained, the final goal necessitated that they "combine physical development with social activity."[96] In many ways, this second demand presented a harder goal, as it necessitated not merely exercise and training but broader acceptance in American society. It was not only Jewish athletic clubs that promoted the lofty goal of social respectability among Jewish men, but academic and purely social ones as well. Foremost among these, the academic fraternal organizations of the day.

Jewish Fraternalism

In 1908, a Brooklyn rabbi explained of discrimination, "The leading manifestations of anti-Judaism are social—the fraternal societies particularly—societies whose very foundation sentiment is the promotion of universal brotherhood, make use of all sorts of excuses to keep out Jews."[97] The accuracy of this claim is evident in the response it generated: "Admit Jews into your club or fraternity and you will find that they are not content with a modest place. They must lead. They push their way forward indefatigable, and if repulsed or rebuffed cry out, 'Race prejudice! We are persecuted on account of our Religion.'"[98] In fact, Jews rejected from fraternal societies *did* feel wronged by what they saw as racial prejudice and religious persecution. However, they still saw participation in these groups as a necessary component of American college life, and so fought for acceptance.

Figure 9. Jewish fraternity brothers pose for homecoming celebration. Ezra Sensibar pictured on right, other men unknown. Evanston, Illinois, 1923. Sensibar Family Collection, personal collection of author.

Dating from before the Civil War, Greek letter societies in America served as a training ground for middle- and upper-class masculinity, reflecting the practices and methods used by their European counterparts. Most of these fraternities had the goal of promoting male bonding through rough play, Christian values and service, and the maintenance of the American male elite. Excluding or involving Jews in these societies followed the same trajectories as many of the Jewish struggles for manhood examined in the progress of muscular Zionism in chapter 1.[99] American fraternal organizations, though in existence from the early nineteenth century, got their great push in its last decades, as fears of loss of homosocial white camaraderie grew in light of new and diverse populations seeking admission to universities during the period of mass migration. The fear of diversity extended to include women, African Americans, and new immigrants, including Jews. Fraternal organizations grew more popular, particularly in state schools (which were required to admit all state residents and so rapidly became more diverse), because social clubs could maintain their focused membership and exclusivity without breaking any rules or codes of conduct.

Jews responded to exclusion from these Greek organizations by forming their own fraternities, many of which had the same stringent admission policies, allowing only Jews to pledge. Interestingly, some of these Jewish groups were the last holdouts of discriminatory admission practices in the 1950s and '60s when policy shifted to eliminate discrimination based on ethnicity or religion. Though all founded for similar reasons (primarily other groups excluding Jews), Jewish fraternities differed in their attitudes about the public nature of their Jewishness. Some, like the athletic organizations discussed in the previous section, desired only to participate, to have access to Greek campus life and the benefits that such activities bestowed upon their members, without any mention or publicizing of their Jewish heritage. Others, mimicking their white counterparts in the universities, focused on camaraderie and brotherhood through mutually shared characteristics, and in this vein, they had a quite different mission regarding their Jewishness. This second type tended to be more open about their Jewish identity, their purpose in instilling Jewish values and culture, and their pride in Jewish heritage. Even this professed Jewish pride did not guarantee entry to all Jewish students, however, as some Jewish fraternity brothers had internalized antisemitic notions of Jewish unsuitability to fraternal life. According to

Marianne Sanua, the leadership of these Jewish fraternities was careful in their selection to avoid diminishing the prestige of their group by admitting only those "as far as possible from negative Jewish stereotypes."[100]

The difference in attitudes of Jewish fraternities and their missions shows a change over the turn of the century. The first Jewish fraternity, Pi Lambda Phi (founded at Yale University in 1895), had no goal of promoting Jewish values or publicizing Jewish participation. In fact, much like the City Athletic Club in New York, they either willfully forgot or refused to admit that all their founders and early members had been Jews who had created the institution to participate in fraternity life despite being initially excluded. In the decades following the founding of Pi Lambda Phi and its subsequent chapters at several additional universities, the foundation mythology changed, and the three original Jewish founders (Frederick Manfred Werner, Louis Samter Levy, and Henry Mark Fisher) ceased to be acknowledged as Jews and came to be identified as "a Protestant, a Catholic, and a Jew."[101] Still in existence today, Pi Lambda Phi defines itself as a nonsectarian fraternity with no mention whatsoever of its Jewish foundation, claiming as recently as 2018 that "the early period of Pi Lambda Phi is wrapped in a veil of mystery and has, thus far, defied efforts to research thoroughly."[102] The website has since been updated to include the founders goal of creating "a fraternity in which all men were brothers, no matter what their religion," but still without their Jewish identities recognized openly.

It should come as no surprise that the first college fraternity exclusively for Jewish men, Zeta Beta Tau, began not in a public university but at the Jewish Theological Seminary in 1898. Originally named for the acronym Z.B.T., for their Hebrew motto, "Zion Be-mishpat Tipadeh," (Isaiah 1:27, "Zion shall with judgment be redeemed"), they began not as a Greek fraternity, but as a Zionist organization to be modeled after the Viennese student group "Kadimah," a club formed as a Jewish alternative to the dueling clubs in Vienna that barred Jewish membership.[103] Z.B.T. quickly evolved into a national Jewish fraternity, aiming to include all Jewish men on campus, not only those who had already taken a Zionist stance. Once determined to admit more diverse Jewish students into the brotherhood, they had more potential members excited to participate in Greek campus life. When they formally became a college fraternity, they chose the Greek letters Zeta Beta Tau as a stand-in to maintain the original acronym for "Zion Be-mishpat Tipadeh."

The goals of this openly Jewish fraternity differed from those of Pi Lambda Phi. They did not wish to quietly participate without showcasing their Jewish identities. Instead, they recognized among their leadership that Jews possessed deficits that could be remedied by the social niceties that would help the Jewish man on campus who was "inferior to his colleagues in his social training." This attitude is reflected in the ideals and aims of other Jewish fraternal organizations as well, such as Pi Tau Pi, to whom the national vice president said in a 1914 address that they were, in terms of their place in the Jewish community, "banded together to improve our 'social' condition . . . that is to say from the point of view of human society in general."[104] Not only would Jewish men be redeemed on a personal level through the vigor and excellence of Jewish manhood, but their position on campus and in the public eye would reflect this redemption. The primary mission of the fraternity in its first few decades exemplified this goal, "an experiment of pro-Semitism." Elucidating their mission, the organization explained:

> From every section of the land young men come to the Universities bringing with them all manner of prejudices, preferences, and predispositions. Many of these relate to the Jew. Rarely perhaps, but too often, in a mind poisoned by a slander, or a tale that is told, is the conception of the Jew painted in the colors of physical and moral cowardice, greed, ostentation, unsociability and anti-social proclivity.

It is interesting to note that the author categorizes the conception of Jews as greedy cowards as *either* slander (false information) *or* tales (which could be either a fictitious or true narrative).

> From the universities, young men go to every section of the land—young men who will one day lead the thought in their local communities. What impression do they carry back of the Jew? Much depends upon the kind of Jew they meet in college.

The fraternity insinuates here that the "kind of Jew" that a college student meets is the remediable situation. They accept the unpleasant, socially untrained Jew as a very real figure that needed to be addressed, not a falsehood to be disproved. In fact, they explain,

> One does not dissipate a prejudice by denying, however vigorously, its soundness or justice. A prejudice knows but one mortal enemy—a series of demonstrated facts that are obviously wholly inconsistent with the prejudice.

Whether it be true or false is less the concern than that it be disproved through "demonstration." Theirs was a proselytizing mission, to change the minds of non-Jewish students through action, by putting the best foot of Jewish manhood forward. In more theoretical terms, their goal was to engage members in outwardly visible acts of American manhood.

> It is the mission of the Jewish student to have contact with his non-Jewish comrades on the athletic field, in journalism, debate, dramatics, and in every field of campus activity which affords expression to that moral and physical courage, that capacity for sportsmanship, generosity, sociability and social conscience which form part and parcel of the Jewish racial heritage. To stimulate this missionary effort, to tide the individual over the depression of temporary defeat, to launch him anew into the combat to ultimate victory as a Jew. . . . This is a labor that distinguishes from the others this Zeta Beta Tau—this group of socially congenial Jewish collegemen banded together to demonstrate by their every word and deed in public and in private the best of which Jewish manhood is capable and the inherent excellence of the Jewish character.[105]

In addition to concerns over antisemitism on campuses, the issue of assimilation and the disappearance of Jewish men into non-Jewish life never left the minds of fraternity leadership. The more accepted the fraternity became and the closer its behaviors drifted toward other non-Jewish Greek societies, the more likely it would be that "the average college man [would be] apt to forget that the successful Jew is a Jew."[106] Those Jewish college men who had proven their mettle might forget their Jewishness, as might the rest of the college population in looking at Jewish successes. They needed to show the rest of the student body that Jews could participate *as Jews* and be successful in college campus life, not to lose their Jewishness or to show so much of it as to make other people uncomfortable. "It is enough," an editorial in a Z.B.T. bulletin reads, "if we make them realize that we are Jews: we need not accentuate our Jewishness."[107]

Unfortunately for Z.B.T., their openly Jewish nature did not merely make others aware of their Jewishness but had negative repercussions that made some members of the larger Jewish community uncomfortable. An Ohio Jewish newspaper, the *American Israelite*, took an actively anti-Jewish fraternity stance. In an article on the issue, Jewish American lawyer and magician Bernard M. L. Ernst wrote that after the "exceedingly ill-advised" founding of Pi Lambda Phi (which Ernst argued inflamed latent antisemitism in every institution in which it opened a chapter), the founding of Zeta Beta Tau had "been noted by the Greek press, and a movement is now on foot to withdraw the charters of the several prominent organization chapters at this institution, thus removing the possibility of the initiation of Hebrews in these societies at this institution. . . . Whatever the objects of Zeta Beta Tau may be," he continued, "its methods are to be deplored and its members are simply inviting another wave of anti-Semitism in the colleges which will affect Jewish students throughout the East."[108]

Hyperbolic though this may seem, it does reflect some very real reactions from non-Jews on campus. The president of Harvard said that Jews "are hardly justified in complaining as they do that they are discriminated against if they attempt by the forming of associations to keep themselves apart."[109] As more Jewish fraternities began cropping up all over the country, Jews inside of the fledgling organizations debated the divisive nature of Jewish fraternities as well. In the pages of the *Octagonian* (the publication of the exclusively Jewish fraternity Sigma Alpha Mu), a debate took place about the advisability of creating "artificial castes" in collegiate life by growing a separate Jewish fraternal system in an American landscape where Jews already faced scrutiny for their exclusivity.[110]

There are several examples, like Z.B.T., of proudly Jewish fraternities. The fraternity Hai Resh shared at least part of the mission of Z.B.T., in that they aimed to actively change the image of Jews in America to one of manly respectability. This is partially shown through their determination to use Hebrew letters (Hai Resh) instead of Greek, while participating in Greek life on campuses. They debated the issue over decades of fraternity leadership, as some members repeatedly called for a change of name to better blend into larger university Greek life. In fact, during the First World War, nearly every issue of the *Hai Resh Bulletin* included letters from various members questioning the necessity of keeping the Hebrew name, suggesting that if they adopted Greek letters, they might stand out less starkly among other campus organizations and show unity with their gentile friends. The same argument always won out; that Jews would earn more respect and admiration as Jews by sticking "to what is rightfully ours" than by behaving as if ashamed of their Jewishness.[111] One poem written by a founder of the fraternity in a 1917 issue of the *Hai Resh Bulletin* showcases the Jewish pride that Hai Resh leadership felt necessary to the groups survival, and the spiteful rebuttal to the suggestion of a name change:

Aye, change our honored symbol!
    Too long has it stood the test
And held its place in Fratdom,
    Along with all the best.
Cast to the winds, without remorse,
    The work of ten long years,
And start anew to build a Frat
    The brave need have no fears.

Forget your age. Tho' growing old,
    You've many years to live,
And to your New Fraternity
    Your close attention give.
Throw up your jobs, you'll need the time
    As you have much to do,
For now the much-esteemed Greek Frat
    Supplants the spurned Jew.

Go! Your Gentile friends await you,
    Their arms outstretched in "Love,"
They're pleased at your desertion,
    While God Supreme, above,
Looks down with gentle pity
    That you so weak should be,
To put a moment's favor
    Above Eternity.[112]

The entrance of the United States into the First World War shifted the focus of those fraternity brothers remaining in the United States from reaching that coveted position of equality without separateness to that of disproving accusations of Jewish cowardice and meekness. Honor rolls of servicemen from each fraternity appeared in every publication during the war, and the praise of their heroism, volunteerism, and self-sacrifice is ever present in the pages of fraternity wartime publications. During the war, fraternities saw a drop in their numbers as a great number of their members (both Jewish and non-Jewish) served in the armed forces. This was certainly the case for Hai Resh, who saw such a drop in their leadership (who were of military age) that there were talks of suspending all fraternity activity until the war was over.[113]

By 1937, another Jewish fraternity, Pi Tau Pi, absorbed Hai Resh, and along with the loss of Hai Resh's Jewish letters came the loss of their particular determined Jewish public presence. The two fraternities joined together, only using the name Hai Resh as a subline on official documents, not in campus life, which all fell under the fraternity letters of Pi Tau Pi. The Pi Tau Pi publications, as well as those published after the two fraternities merged, do not ignore their Jewishness. In fact, during the Second World War it is again a point of pride, the number of members, and Jews overall, in service to the country. However, the determination to change the *image* of Jews in America became less important, and certainly less discussed from their merging until the collapse of the organization in the 1960s. Until its last days, members of Pi Tau Pi continued to debate dropping the "Hai Resh" byline, some arguing that the organization was a thing of the past, while remaining old Hai Reshers insisted the Hebrew letters remain to show their history.[114]

The Jewish fraternal system relied heavily on American Jewish professional and lay leaders for organizational and experiential leadership. They gathered honorary members, advisors, and local rabbis and congregations to support the growth and maintenance of the fraternities. For the older generation, who had passed through college life before the creation of a Jewish fraternal system, Greek campus life did not necessarily bring fond memories. For many of this generation, news of budding Jewish fraternities in their communities proved an unwelcome or uncomfortable addition, as Greek life left impressions of snobbery and undemocratic practices in their own memories, which, according to Rabbi Sol. L. Kory of Mississippi, "went against my Jewish grain."[115] In Rabbi Kory's case, his mind was eased by the fact that the members of Pi Tau Pi (the Jewish fraternity opening in his community of Vicksburg, Mississippi) obligated themselves to proclaim themselves publicly as Jews, and to indeed *be* Jews, safeguarding against assimilation of the best and brightest of Jewish manhood. Indeed, the members appealed to new recruits explaining that "to enlist in the ranks of this fraternity is to . . . afford your manliness and character a broad and stimulating field in which to assert themselves. . . . Our weaknesses are reduced, as our virtues encouraged."[116]

The degree to which Jewish fraternities and athletic clubs succeeded in their respective goals of improving Jewish manhood, or changing existing perceptions of it, is not truly quantifiable. Indeed, given the changes that occurred in American social and cultural life in the mid-twentieth century, most of these exclusive organizations (both Jewish and otherwise) would cease their exclusivity in membership by the end of the 1960s, particularly those that had racial or ethnic requirements or prohibitions. However, the consistent determination with which Jewish men created such institutions, and the stated purpose of their missions to improve Jewish American manhood, is a critical glimpse into the Jewish American man's perceived place in the American masculine milieu. At least through the world wars, Jewish men were actively combating their exclusion from the masculine hegemon, enacting/performing manhood to improve their image as socially respectable American men.

4

We'll Take Your Rejection and Raise You One Nationalism

American Jews and Zionism

One might almost assert that a new Jewish folk is being created in Palestine: the vast majority almost a head taller than their parents, a sturdy people more a throwback to the farmers and fishermen of Jesus' day than products of the sons and daughters of the cities of Eastern and Central Europe.

—Bartley C. Crum, 1947[1]

The greatest change to Jewish masculinity, and the image of Jews worldwide, came in the form of the Zionist movement. In the early development of the Zionist movement in Europe, Zionism called for the rejection of the Jewish fragility of the diaspora, and for Jewish men to claim for themselves the hegemonic masculinity that Western Europe had long denied them. The same was true for Jews in the United States, though the situation was quite different. Jews had come much closer to fully accessing acceptance and hegemonic masculinity in America than they had in Europe, and they already had a very strong sense of American nationalism and loyalty. For this reason, the American Jewish community leadership was torn. Some identified with the Zionist movement as one of redemptive manliness for the Jewish people, and saw it as working in cooperation with American ideals and nationalism, and so embraced Zionism while defending their status as loyal Americans. Others believed that if American Jews joined the ranks of Zionists the world over, they would be forfeiting their hard-won acceptance in American society, claiming an identity that paralleled American nationalism, but was incompatible with it.[2]

For the purposes of this study, I distinguish Zionists in very inclusive terms. Contemporary associations with the term at the time of this publication are, of course, quite different from those maintained by the historical actors in this narrative. Even at the time of writing, there is no simple accord among Jews or non-Jews as to what Zionism is, as an ideal or a practice. Walter Laqueur's definition of Zionism as "the belief in the existence of a common past and a common future for the Jewish people," functions as a broad enough view to be inclusive of all who might identify, representing a great diversity of positions on the future of world Jewry throughout history.[3] This includes those who believe that a Jewish state *in the land of Palestine* is a necessity for the survival and happiness of the Jewish people, but is not exclusive to that belief, as some diaspora Zionists did not see it that way (a particularly prominent attitude among American Jews). This definition does not preclude non-Jews or any religious denominations, ethnic identities, or regional affiliations. Because the attitudes of the historical characters examined presently are not only different from one another but also go through massive changes individually, this inclusive definition helps to observe the attitudes of various groups and individuals as complex elements of, and reactions to, the Zionist enterprise.

Like other issues in Jewish religious and communal life, no consensus was reached among Zionist Jews, thus they created a great number of both cooperative and contradictory Zionist organizations to promote their various interpretations of the ideology. The attitudes of Jewish Americans toward Zionism, therefore, followed several nonlinear, weaving paths. There are, however, a few large and traceable shifts and events that Jewish historians have highlighted as significant turning points in Jewish American Zionism. Several of these directly responded to the efforts already underway to construct the Yishuv, primarily by Eastern European Jews, and often with funds provided by wealthy American Jews.

Regardless of their support or opposition to Jewish statehood, the developing Jewish community in Eretz Israel (traditional Jewish name for the pre-statehood Land of Israel), and the image it broadcast across the globe, affected Jewish Americans and their self-image. It gave them a contemporary masculine Jewish image they could be proud of and tout as evidence of their own potential for Jewish manhood, if only they were given the same opportunities to grow and thrive (physically and socially) in the United States as they had in Palestine. In addition, the existence of a growing and thriving Jewish presence in Palestine promised to provide American Jews with something other immigrant communities had long enjoyed: an external land they could include in their own American immigrant mythologies, making it acceptable to be American patriots while supporting the foundation of a Jewish religious state.

Masculinity in the Early Years of the Yishuv

By the turn of the twentieth century, as political Zionism firmly took hold of the imagination of the international Jewish community, it began to manifest physically as European Jews made their way to Palestine to construct their utopia (often built with socialist ideals prevalent in their countries of origin). The international Jewish community witnessed a new breed of Jews emerging as they created and improved the Yishuv. They lived lifestyles previously denied them in their old countries, settling the land and engaging in agriculture and communal living. Jews raised in Palestinian settlements presented themselves (and their supporters presented them) as harder, tougher, more muscular, and connected to the soil. In 1933, the Jewish author William Schack wrote of the first generation of Eastern European Zionist Jews born in Palestine:

> Although few have reached their teens, they already reveal a certain cast of character, the more positively indicated by contrast with the children of the orthodox . . . compared to them, the youngsters of the professional and working classes are as those born outside a ghetto must have been to those within. They are stronger physically, being better fed and more active. They are freer mentally, as a result of both their freer bodies and their more varied educational fare.[4]

The "new Jew" conceived and promoted by Max Nordau started emerging as a reality and was consistently presented as evidence of the success and necessity of Palestinian settlement and the Zionist cause.[5] Some American Jews saw these Jewish pioneers as kindred to themselves, not only as heroes of the Jewish people but also as a people whose ideals were related to their own American principles of pioneering, progress, and self-reliance.

In the praises Jewish leaders sang about the Jews in Palestine, they signaled toward the idea that in Palestine there may be a corrective element to some of the issues plaguing American Jews themselves. For example, in the first few decades of the century, Jewish crime in the United States was a principal concern for Jewish American leadership. But despite the lack of police forces, army, or formal government in Palestine, American Jewish leaders pointed out that in the Yishuv, there was no Jewish crime. American lawyer (and later Supreme Court justice) Louis Brandeis wrote in 1915 that no Jews committed crimes in the Palestinian colonies because every Jew there was "led to feel the glory of his people and his obligation to carry forward its ideals."[6] In reality there was certainly crime committed by Jews and other inhabitants of pre-state Palestine, and books were published on the subject within a decade of this statement by Brandeis. One such book was *Crime and Criminals in Eretz Yisrael*, written by David Tidhar, a law officer under the British Mandate and himself a personification of the manly hero of the Yishuv. He was a native-born Palestinian Jew (the seventh of his parents children, but the first to survive), soldier of the Jewish Legion in World War I, athlete, police officer, private eye, writer, and community leader.[7] Though not every member of the Yishuv was a model citizen, the pervasive images of pioneers in the United States were of the Palestinian equivalent of cowboys and farmers, the *shomrim* and *halutzim* (guards and pioneers). Though debates fumed among European Zionists about the ideal manifestation of the halutz (clashes between the right and left over the best methods for construction of the settlement of Jews in Palestine), Jews in the United States did not engage in the discussion that was distant both in proximity and language (the European discussion taking place in Yiddish and Hebrew). Instead, American Jews embraced the image of the halutz as the idyllic Zionist pioneer.

The *halutzim* in Palestine provided a visual remedy to the stereotypes that had afflicted American Jews, and that they attempted to fight through American Jewish agricultural pursuits. The image of the Zionist pioneer proved far more effective, however, as the Jewish farming enterprise in the United States never made such headway. The image of the halutz in Palestine became part of the American Jewish self-image. In materials created in Palestine as well as in the United States, Jewish pioneers (draining swamps or working fields) seemed not only heroic and strong, but very gendered. This is especially observable in material created for young children learning about life in the Yishuv. Jewish Americans did not only praise their brawn but their intellect as well, depicting them as educated men of Europe who had left their studies and high-minded professions to take part in the great rebuilding project of the Yishuv. One visiting American Zionist recalled the pioneers of Palestine in this way, explaining, "You can see men crushing the rocks or digging the soil, and talking about Nietzsche, Wagner or Weininger, Strindberg or Ibsen, Maeterlinck or Anatol France, Wagner or Beethoven."[8]

Zionism remained a contentious subject in the years before the First World War, so did not make its way into American Jewish schoolbooks until the interwar period. When it did, however, they adopted an interesting reverence of the halutz. The image of Jewish farmers "making the desert bloom" strongly counteracted American antisemitic projections of Jews as overly urbanized and unable to connect to the land.[9] Thus, the halutz allowed American Jews to identify the Jewish people with popular American cowboy fantasies of the time. For this reason, authors of American Jewish schoolbooks in the 1920s began to tell the story of Palestine as one of brave frontiersmen, mimicking the American West. The primary difference in representation between the halutz and the American frontiersman was that the scout on the Western frontier had always been a solitary hero, and American ideals had valorized rugged individualism. In Palestine, as they depicted it to American children, Jews were working in cooperation, looking out for one another and the collective. This difference reflects a combination of Jewish and American influences and ideals. Jewish culture has long emphasized the well-being of the collective, the survival of the people, and the importance of social responsibility in both Jewish and larger society. By emphasizing the collective, Jewish schoolbooks were able to highlight the Jewishness of the frontiersman without any of the negative Jewish tropes, instead embracing the socialist principles prevalent in the Yishuv. In his analysis of two prominent publishers of Jewish schoolbooks of the time, Jonathan Krasner found that both publishers included multiple photographs of halutzim in their books:

> The photographs typically depicted individuals involved in physical labor, mostly agricultural in nature. Men, in particular, were shown irrigating, plowing and carrying heavy bundles, while both

men and women were photographed harvesting fruit. Both books also included photographs of Jews engaged in other occupations that defied conventional stereotypes, including merchant mariners, fishermen and longshoremen. The vast majority of the non-scenic photographs depicted young men.[10]

He also found the depiction of the Jewish male body eroticized to an unprecedented degree in the photographs chosen for the books, sometimes even obscuring the face of a man to emphasize his musculature and perspiration as he toiled in the Palestinian sun.

The Jewish woman, by contrast, had various images: mother and caretaker, modestly clad harvester, or sporting anachronistically revealing clothes in the hot sun. Outside of Jewish schoolbooks and within Zionist circles, female halutzim appeared in even more diverse scenes, at times as strong and muscular, like the men working in the Yishuv. Arthur Goren explained the representation of the sexes in American Zionist circles, noting that American Zionists admired women for serving alongside their male comrades. He also found, however, that many of the American Zionist women commenting on these female pioneers believed the workload would be too much for most women, including themselves.[11]

A romantic ideology emerged surrounding not just those Jewish pioneers of the Yishuv but also the Jewish defense groups who protected them. Young American Jews habitually applied American mythology to their commentary venerating Palestinian Jewish groups like the *shomrim* (Hebrew watchmen of the Palestinian settlements). In one such case, they even labeled the shomrim "Jewish Minute Men" and explained that by their "fearlessness, by undying devotion and loyalty to duty, [the Jewish protectors] finally won the admiration of everyone."[12] As Mark Raider observed, such praise of the shomrim and halutzim mixed symbolism and mythology from Jewish and American pasts, functionally "Americanizing" the image of the *shomer*. He explains, "Like the patriots of the American Revolution and the cowboys of the Wild West, the shomrim ride horses, protect the frontier, and defy the 'half-savage' and 'lawless' indigenous inhabitants."[13] Regardless of their actual resemblance to American cowboys and revolutionaries, American Jewish men used the image of the shomer and halutz to lessen their anxiety about their own masculinity.

Jews were not the only Americans to form a romantic narrative around the rebuilding of the Jewish people in Palestine. American politicians and journalists became involved in the politics of Jewish settlement, and the image of heroic halutzim in the Yishuv began to solidify in the American imagination. In their role as members of the Anglo-American Committee of Inquiry (non-Jewish men from England and America tasked with the political fate of the land at the close of the Second World War), members recollected the stark difference between the Arabs and Jews as they passed from one territory to another. One member, an American attorney, explained that as soon as the train reached the Jewish settlements in Palestine, "the tempo and color of life changes sharply. Things seemed to quicken, to become more alive; children suddenly were no longer tiny bundles of rags, but youngsters, wearing shorts, with sturdy arms and legs and open smiling faces and bright eyes—alert and human again."[14] So deep was his conviction of the evident physical rebuilding of the Jewish people on their ancestral land that he believed they were not only becoming stronger, but taller, blonder, and bluer-eyed as well. He saw their regeneration as a process that made them more muscular, whiter, and therefore, more American. As scientifically untrue as this assertion was, it does reveal to us the connection in the American mind between physical vigor and phenotypical whiteness. It also makes clear the degree to which this particular (non-Jewish) American saw Jewishness as antithetical to physical health and attractiveness.

In Jewish periodicals of the early twentieth century, the physical rebuilding of the Jewish people was attributed not only to political Zionism and the Yishuv but also to Jewish American nationalism. In 1904, a contributor to the *Jewish Exponent* explained that historically athletics were little known to European Jews, and it fell to America "to teach the Jew the value of bodily exercise," the success of which was visible if not yet ideal, in that "now we frequently meet with Jewish names in the lists of the athletic societies, although not as frequently as in the lists of the debating teams."[15] He continued, however, giving credit to the Yishuv, that Zionism "may justly claim priority in inculcating a desire for physical culture among the Jewish people." And that priority was not only for Jews facing persecution in faraway lands but for Jews in America as well. Zionism inspired Americans (both Jewish and non-Jewish) to assess the physical condition of Jews anew. Charles W. Eliot, president of Harvard

University from 1869 to 1909, was a particularly interesting and visible non-Jewish convert to Zionism and adherent of its desire to rebuild the Jewish people physically. Though not a Jew, he saw in the American Jewish body a people with "no courage or bearing," through no fault of their own. They were, he explained, victims of millennia of torment, even those Jews living in the United States. "I didn't understand the physical condition to which thousands of American Jews had been reduced by the sufferings of their ancestors," he lamented after seeing a procession of Jews, heads bowed, knees bent, "crouching along" their route.[16] He encouraged the Jews of Boston to train physically for combat, "what I thought they needed most was to send all their young men into the militia of Massachusetts, where they could learn to bear arms, to fight in the defense of their rights and their people's rights." Eliot is particularly interesting in this assertion as such militarism was not his modus operandi, having famously fought to end football at Harvard University, explaining that the sport had the "barbarous ethics of warfare."[17] In the case of Jews, however, he believed that the physical rebuilding must be enacted through such barbarism, as was successfully being carried out in Palestine.

American Jewish leaders and rabbis did not uniformly believe that political Zionism provided the best possible solution to Jewish problems in the modern world. However, it does seem to be a consistent attitude among Jewish Americans that regardless of the advisability of a Jewish state, the work done in the Yishuv provided an effective remedy to the stereotype of Jews as physically weak, victims to a meek nature, and unable or unwilling to work the land. One visiting rabbi's report from Palestine in 1913 shows the enthusiasm of this experience at the Passover gathering of Jewish Palestinian agriculturalists:

> What a happy, healthy, sturdy, vigorous, well dressed crowd they were—the boys muscular, brown and straight as a mountain ash, the girls fresh-looking ruddy-faced and right of eye—farmer boys and farmer girls that it did one good to look upon. I challenge the most vicious and rabid Anti-semite [sic] to look upon scenes like these and to repeat the lie that the Jew has an ingrained disinclination to handle the plow, to scatter the seed, to break the sod and to woo and win the treasures of the earth.

Though this exultant praise of Jewish pioneers might sound like the words of an ardent Zionist, the rabbi continues:

> I am not a Zionist. I do not agree with the despairing voices that tell us that the Jew can never gain the fullest recognition in other lands and must go back to Palestine to realize his fondest dreams. But as the pleasant pictures of those smiling fields and spreading orchards rise again in memory and as I see again the sturdy, healthy, broad-chested, large limbed generation growing up upon the sacred soil and when I compare those pictures with the sombre [*sic*] scenes in the ghettos of the world that I have visited . . . the cramped and stunted life, the bent and stooping narrow-chested figures, the poor physiques, the evils physical and moral to which these dreadfully congested quarters are exposed—I raise my voice in unstinted praise of those Jews who have disproved the charge[s] of the Antisemites. . . . I glory in the work of these sturdy sons of Israel.[18]

Though not a Zionist, it was the bodies of the halutzim that he gloried in, not the pride of financial contribution or Zionist ideals. Louis Marshall, then serving as the chairman of the Board of Directors of the Jewish Theological Seminary of America, also wrote that he was "not a Zionist, and probably will never become a Zionist," largely due to his complete disbelief that the exercise of political Zionism could be successful, or result in anything more than "bitter disappointment."[19] However, among the qualities that Zionism had contributed to Jewish life, Marshall noted that it had "given birth to a manly Jewish consciousness, in refreshing contrast with the apologetic attitude which precedes it."

Both Zionists and non- or even anti-Zionists used the exact same language to describe these changes in Jewish manhood. However, they did not all agree on (or perhaps did not all hazard to comment on) the cause. Muscular Zionism may not have appealed to anti-Zionists like Reform Rabbi David Philipson, for example, but that did not mean that muscular *Judaism* and this change in Jewish attitudes did not appear in his life and congregation. He wrote in his diary in 1905 of an "amusing experience . . . which showed me that 'muscular Judaism' is not non-existent." This experience occurred after a Christian preacher made antisemitic attacks on Rabbi Philipson about his attitudes on teaching the Bible in public schools. In response to these attacks, a Jewish athletics teacher wrote to the preacher telling him that he "would be glad to meet him anywhere and at any time and would encounter him, as he might choose, 'with or without gloves.'" Philipson added, "this incident is characteristic of the spirit now largely pervading Jewry. The apologetic attitude is giving way to an attitude of self-respect and even aggressiveness."[20]

American-Made: Muscular Zionism in the States

American Jews found an answer to some of the exclusion they felt as an immigrant community in American society through the international Zionist movement. The Zionist promise, the idea of a Jewish nation-state allowing for full participation in society, religious and cultural pride, and physical rejuvenation appealed to many. For the most part they did not feel the need to migrate to Palestine themselves, but instead saw an opportunity in the political manifestation of a Zionist state for equity among their American peers by possessing a homeland to link to their ethnicity. This was a link that most American ethnic enclaves had maintained for generations after immigrating to the United States, but which many European Jews did not feel with their own nation of origin, particularly if it was acts of antisemitism that drove them to migrate. Louis Marshall (though he never considered himself a Zionist) saw the desirability of such a connection, writing that the Zionist spirit was in no way unpatriotic to American ideals, as it mimicked the feelings of so many other "good citizens [of the United States] whose love for their land and its institutions does not militate against their American citizenship," despite the "love and most ardent attachment" to their ancestral homes and mythologies.[21]

Louis Marshall's comparison between Jewish Americans and other patriotic immigrant groups with connections to ancestral homelands was surprisingly prescient, as the future connection between America and Israel became so dependent on foundational mythology. Literary historian Orm Øverland identified three genres of homemaking myths that help American immigrant groups to become a part of the American landscape: foundational, sacrificial, and ideological. The foundational genre portrays an early presence of members of the group on the continent, before or simultaneous with the British. With the claim of early arrival, immigrants declare their right to an American identity and equality with the Anglo-Saxons as discoverers and founders of the American nation. Jews, as seen previously, pointed to their participation in the American Revolution to cement this foundation. Mythology around blood sacrifice for America in times of war made evident American Jewish willingness to fight for American ideals. Lastly, the ideological claim to have an inherent connection to American ideals—which is traditionally presented as having originated in their own home country. Zionism is a sort of inverse ideological connection. American Zionists saw, in the prospective nation, a country that could be built with ideals similar to those of the United States and supported by Jewish communities in America.

In her 2018 book *Our American Israel*, Amy Kaplan makes a compelling argument that not only the Jews of America, but large swaths of American nationalists made this argument to buttress their support for the fledgling state. They saw in Israel a nation being built in their own image, with connecting threads of religious persecution, revolutionary democracy, rugged individualism, and collective nationalism. The mythmaking that formed around a potential Zionist state served not only to provide American Jews with immigrant mythologies that could link to an outside homeland (like so many of their countrymen) but also to Americanize the Zionist ideology, allowing them to maintain their own American patriotism while supporting the foundation of a Jewish religious state.

Zionism, very much a product of the *Galut* (the diaspora or exile), discovered its foundational ideas as a product of Jewish life in Europe, not in America. As Evyatar Friesel explains, American Zionism, if wholly dependent on the experiences of those suffering from life in the Galut, would have been a hopeless proposition.[22] Those foundational ideas of Herzlian Zionism are by their nature products of the conditions of diaspora Jews living in Europe and had little to no bearing on American Jewish life (aside from connection to relatives and communities abroad). Participating Jewish leaders, pillars of the acculturated Jewish community, led the process of Americanizing Zionism to fit into a distinctly American Jewish ideology, just as they had taken it on themselves to support the Americanization of new Jewish immigrants. Not all Jewish American leadership (religious or laypersons) became Zionists or attempted to create an American Zionism. In fact, the debate over the ideological principles of Jewish America, Zionist and Americanist (largely in opposition to each other), formed one of the great tensions of Jewish leadership in the first half of the twentieth century. They held conferences, developed schisms, and tested loyalties in the debate over the coexistence of Zionism and Americanism.

As American Jews were debating the necessity and advisability of American Jewish support for the Zionist cause, there was no single unified Zionist cause on which to base decisions. At no point were Zionists across Europe and in Palestine in agreement about best practices or even guiding Zionist ideologies. As different Zionist movements and perspectives among Jews in Europe solidified, small (and often weak) branches of those movements would organize in the Unites States as well. The religious Zionist Mizrahi and the socialist Zionist Poalei-Zion, for example, both had weak branches of supportive American Jewish organizations. Though the foundational groups in Europe quarreled with one another, regional and religious affiliations and differences died out in American Zionist discussions, as European concerns were no longer central to the issues concerning Zionists in the United States.[23] One group that becomes particularly important to this study in the following chapters is the emergence of the Revisionist Zionists, led by Vladimir Jabotinsky, a Russian Jewish soldier and leader.

The Revisionist movement (which would eventually reform into the nonreligious right in the Israeli state) promoted a modern form of political Zionism that they believed was more faithful to the original ideas of Theodor Herzl. The group emerged from a commitment to revising the official policies of the World Zionist Organization to emphasize the goal of establishing a Jewish state on both sides of the Jordan River through massive Jewish settlement and the creation of a Jewish army in Palestine.[24] In 1933, the Revisionists broke away from the World Zionist Organization, forming instead the New Zionist Organization in London, which aggressively petitioned the British government for free Jewish migration to Palestine. Even within the Yishuv, Revisionists remained at odds with the labor movement, which did not agree with their aggressive tactics. The Irgun, a Jewish underground organization founded by members of the Haganah (Jewish paramilitary in British Mandate Palestine, eventually the core of the Israel Defense Forces), split away from the main body in 1937. Disagreeing with the Haganah's policy of restraint, the Irgun followed the Revisionist movement and their leader Jabotinsky, carrying out armed attacks on local Arabs. The Revisionist's militant brand of Zionism appealed to some Americans, growing in support through the 1930s in response to international Jewish crises, though never becoming a very large movement in America.[25]

The Zionist Movement in America was highly masculine, both in its imagery and its intention. Jewish men used hypermasculine imagery and language in their discussions and depictions of the Zionist movement, in part to show that Jewish men could "normalize" themselves on the world stage of competing nationalisms by attaining a nation-state in Palestine. Mary McCune identified this gendered difference in her 1998 research into the relief activities of Jewish women during the First World War, but the flip side of her study of Zionist women highlights a masculine agenda in the enterprise that is valuable as well. American Zionist leaders saw the movement as one of male redemption, a remedy to the lack of understanding among diaspora Jews that "life [is not] worth the sacrifice of manhood."[26] These men echoed much of the masculine rhetoric of the muscular Zionists in Europe. Many attended the Zionist Congresses and were in close communication with European Zionist leaders. American Zionism was a manly enterprise on two counts as it aimed to physically redeem Jews worldwide, and because it gave them the opportunity to show their strength through support of the settlements in Palestine.

Contributing in the form of political clout, financial support, and providing social service provided an opportunity for Jewish men to be manly as both Jews and as Americans. "We in America now have the good fortune," Shmaryahu Levin wrote in the *Maccabean* in 1914, "to show our manhood in this emergency, and it is our duty to meet it with earnestness, willingness and optimism."[27] This is an example of what Sarah Imhoff identified as a manifestation of manliness through Zionist philanthropy. It showed, she explained, that:

> Courage need not be located in the body, and manly bodies need not be located in Palestine. Instead, [American Zionist men] abstracted courage and manliness into the political realm, where they focused on forming political bodies more than fleshy ones. Building and securing a society for the vulnerable was the central

task of American Zionist masculinity—not bodybuilding, but society-building.[28]

However, this is but one side of a many-faceted and complex masculinity that emerged in light of the Zionist project in Palestine, which *did* include upbuilding the body as well. It is certainly true to an extent; elite acculturated Jewish men (both in American and elsewhere) contributed financially while basking in the physical improvement of the Jews of Palestine, and not necessarily attending a gym or taking up arms themselves. Their statements about progress in Palestine, the meeting minutes and missions of philanthropic organizations, and the correspondence between Jewish philanthropists and the halutzim show the importance of philanthropy to the American Zionist enterprise, but also highlight the significance of the body in the image of Jewish settlements. Thanking the Jewish Colonization Association for their financial contributions, pioneers wrote of their efforts to build in Palestine:

> We bring to it will-power, patience, muscle, and ability to execute. We want to stand up to our necks in the swamps . . . for us no labor is too hard: we have no fear of death. To create and to upbuild is our task . . . if [it] demands human sacrifices from us, it shall have them. Even so, we shall have far more courage and far more vigor than if others were to fall on our field of honor.[29]

The reflected glory felt by those contributing monetarily to the "heroic" work of the Yishuv provided the sort of philanthropic and political muscle of which Imhoff spoke. However, American Jewish men were not only contributing financially, they were themselves participating in physical manly endeavors disconnected from the Zionist enterprise. They were building athletic institutions, becoming prizefighters and gangsters, they fought Nazis in the streets of American cities, and they worked to prove themselves in Greek life on college campuses. Men from each of these categories venerated the physical rebuilding of the Jewish people in Eretz Israel, but their participation in the masculine project was more diverse than mere praise and philanthropy. Those who closely watched the manly progress of the Yishuv celebrated their manhood as a physical manifestation that benefited all Jews, including themselves.

The gendered dynamic of Jewish philanthropy, both within and outside of the Zionist enterprise, was complex and subject to a tremendous shift from the nineteenth to the twentieth century. When it came to Zionism, leadership in philanthropy was the cause of much tension between Jewish men and women. Philanthropy was only an aspect of this tension, and though many Jewish philanthropic organizations were by this time run by men, not women, it was not seen as the manliest aspect either, as it was used to dismiss the work of Zionist women who engaged primarily in charitable contributions. In a 1917 bulletin, women of Hadassah (Women's Zionist Organization of America) expressed their frustration at their exclusion from a masculine movement:

> Even when [our detractors] concede our claims to the Zionist heritage, they dub us lachrymose, whining sisters of a brotherhood that stands for staunch manhood and dignified self-assertion, and looks upon charity as a necessary evil at best, and the need for exercising it as a blot upon civilization's escutcheon.[30]

Note that the manly detractors of female Zionism loathe charity, they do not consider it a masculine and prideful endeavor in the Zionist enterprise. Through this critique, they emphasize an interesting distinction, that though charity was the work of women, *philanthropy* was the work of men.[31]

It would be misleading to insinuate that the Zionist movement (in the United States or elsewhere) was an entirely male movement or ideology. Jewish women participated eagerly, actively, and with more influence and leadership than many American women had in non-Jewish politics and public life.[32] Theodor Herzl himself invited Rosa Sonnenschein (writer and editor of the *American Jewess*) to participate in the First Zionist Congress in Basel in 1897, where there were a total of twelve female delegates. Though these delegates were not granted voting rights in the first congress, this changed by the second congress when they were accorded voting rights in full.[33] Louis Brandeis also consistently supported women participating in the American Zionist enterprise, and his support became institutionalized once he assumed leadership of the Provisional Executive Committee for General Zionist Affairs (PZA). Henrietta Szold, founder and leader of Hadassah, had a friendly relationship with Brandeis. At the 1924 Hadassah convention, she recounted a story of a discussion with Brandeis in which he made clear that he believed the work of the Zionist women in Hadassah to be indispensable.[34] "Every Jew a Zionist," Brandeis explained, "we are making no distinction[,] men and women, both, are equally welcome."[35] That does not mean, of course, that women in the American Zionist enterprise were treated equally, given equal representation, or recognized and respected for their contributions as much as their male counterparts.

Some Jewish Zionist women considered themselves apart from the masculine aspects of the movement, contributing in ways that they saw as specifically American, Jewish, and female.[36] The United States movement divided along gender lines, with women contributing (through groups like Hadassah) medical and social welfare support for Jewish settlements in Palestine, and men pushing for more political and territorial ambitions. This was an acknowledged difference for female Zionists, who maintained that the practical work they were doing on the ground in Palestine was every bit as worthwhile and Zionist as the lofty goals of the leading Zionist men. Henrietta Szold explained to the Hadassah convention in 1924:

> What our lords and masters do not seem to understand is that true pedagogy, a wise insight into psychology, means waiting for results. They want you to utter promises and pious wishes that cannot be carried out. I am not a man-hater, but I would like you, for instance, to compare our resolutions with the resolutions that have been adopted by the men's convention; and you will find that we have uttered no pious wishes, that whatever we have resolved upon is practical and can be carried out, and that it is thoroughly Jewish.

Here she makes clear that women's work is the more practical, even the more useful of the two spheres of contributions to the Zionist enterprise in Palestine. She goes even further, as she continues, in explaining that to do practical work is not just valuable, but more Jewish than to make impossible promises.

> I would like to say to our lords and masters—of whom a few at least are present—it is thoroughly Jewish and it has been pointed

out in this: that the Jewish version of the Golden Rule is "Do unto others as you would have others do unto you." The Christian version is "Do not unto others as you would not be done by." This is an impossibility. That is a pious wish. They cannot be carried out. Or again, we say, "Love thy neighbor as thyself." And the Christian religion says, "Love thy enemies." You cannot love your enemies. That is also a pious wish.[37]

The pious promises of Zionist men, she explains, mean nothing, and are, in fact, more Christian than Jewish. The practical work of American women in the Zionist cause, by contrast, is measurable and more Jewish.

Some Jewish women, however, were far more excited to join in the masculine side of the movement and embraced and extolled the value of muscular Zionism as an idea and a practice. Reporting on the Eleventh Zionist Congress (1914) in Vienna, an American Jewish woman, Judith Solis Cohen, wrote excitedly about the athletic demonstration at that event, which involved both men and women. She explained, "Fourteen hundred young men and women in blue and white uniform with the 'Mogen David,' the Zionist insignia upon their breasts, gave a display of what we proudly designated as 'muscular' Zionism. They cast from us the reproach that the Jewish race is a race of physical weaklings."[38] Despite women being included and participating, Zionism was a male-dominated movement, just as most spheres of public life in the early twentieth century were male dominated. However, it was more than just a reflection of a male-dominant society, as manliness was an integral part of the Zionist project in Herzl's original conception. As Michael Berkowitz wrote, "To be a Zionist was to 'take a manly stand' and be a manly man, asserting the Jews' rightful place among the people of the world."[39]

On both sides of this debate American Jewish leaders used the language of aspirational masculinity to promote their cause. Unlike the masculine language linking Zionism and the Yishuv, among the Reform movement, perhaps the most ardent Jewish promoters of Americanization and Americanism, there was great opposition to the Zionist cause, which attempted masculinity in a non-American way. Though some religious Jews opposed Zionism on theological grounds, leaders in the Reform movement, more determined to acculturate, did so as defenders of a patriotic universalist American Judaism.[40] Rabbi Isaac Wise, one

Figure 10. Provisional Executive Committee for General Zionist Affairs. *Left to right*: Seated, Henrietta Szold, Rabbi Stephen S. Wise, Jacob de Haas, Robert Kesselman, Louis Lipsky, Charles Cowen, Dr. Shmaryahu Levin, and Rabbi Meir Berlin. Standing, Blanche Jacobson, Adolph Hubbard, and A. H. Fromenson. 1918. Papers of Elihu David Stone Addendum, P-555A, box 80S, folder 6, Wyner Family Jewish Heritage Center at NEHGS, Boston, Massachusetts.

of the leading Reform rabbis of the nineteenth century, was staunchly opposed to the Zionist idea, favoring more aggressive Americanization. He wrote that "the Jew must become an American in order to gain the proud self-consciousness of the free born man." As an immigrant himself, he did so fervently, and encouraged all Jewish immigrants to do the same, to become "not only American citizens but [to] become Americans through and through outside of the synagogue."[41]

David Philipson, a member of the first graduating class from Hebrew Union College in 1883, author, and founder the Central Conference of

American Rabbis (CCAR) in 1889, was, like Wise, a staunch advocate of Americanism and felt that Zionism flew in the face of that cause and the fight for Jewish acceptance in all aspects of American life and patriotism. He called both Zionism and the creation of the New York Kehillah "neo-ghettoism" and dangerously separatist.[42] In his opposition to Zionism, he used the image of the passive, powerless Jew, claiming that historically, Jews had maintained a passive acceptance of the challenges from the outside world, and that Zionism's answer was "at bottom [a] confession of surrender and defeat."[43] The entire CCAR came out against Zionism from the start of its political program, and (at least Rabbi Philipson) believed that it would be a short-lived fad.[44] The prevalence of this attitude in conjunction with the presence of Zionists among Reform leadership led to a conflict at Hebrew Union College that ended with the firing of three professors.[45]

Though most Reform Jewish leaders opposed Zionism, public opposition was a complex issue, both within and outside of the Jewish American community. Jacob Schiff, though opposed to "the menace of Zionism," was concerned about openly disparaging it. He wrote that regardless of his feelings toward American Zionism, openly combating the movement was bound to cause "too much antagonism and bad blood," adding, "it never pays to make martyrs to religious or semi-religious beliefs."[46] The opposition to Zionism also waned considering the worsening conditions for Jews in Europe. Though originally Jacob Schiff expressed hostility to the idea of Zionism and merely worried about conflict within the American Jewish community, his view changed shortly after the Bolshevik Revolution. In 1918, Schiff wrote to Dr. Philipson about this shift, "the conditions in Russia, Poland, Romania, Austria, perhaps even Germany and elsewhere foretold that considerable unhappiness, if not suffering, is likely in store . . . for the Jewish population."[47] Jacob Schiff is an excellent example of the complexity of the Zionist problem for American Jewish leadership. His views advanced and shifted enough to create a very interesting historical debate about his eventual stance on Zionism. While many historians have argued that Schiff became a reluctant Zionist throughout the First World War, historian Caitlin Carenen recently argued that he never came to fully embrace Zionism, remaining distant from the idea due to practical issues (like disbursing aid to Palestine, the proportionally large solicitation of aid from American Jewry, and the lack of cooperation in Palestine with non-Zionist groups), along with his own ideological inconsistencies.[48]

The real shift in attitudes toward Zionism in America came as a response to a public statement issued by the British government during the First World War, declaring England's support of the Zionist goal of establishing a "national home for the Jewish people" in Palestine (which was then an Ottoman controlled region with a minority Jewish population). Though the declaration promised a "national home" it did not guarantee statehood or independence for the Jewish people in Palestine. The Balfour Declaration (so named because Foreign Secretary Arthur Balfour made the statement in a letter to Lord Rothschild, a leader in the British Jewish community) brought disparate groups and leaders who had drawn away from Zionism back into the Zionist fold. It even brought back other brands of territorialists, like Israel Zangwill, who then believed that any opposition to a Jewish home in Palestine would be "treason to the Jewish people."[49] The reaction in the Jewish press in America was jubilant, though there were still anti-Zionists unwilling to accept a homeland outside of the United States. Reform leaders felt particularly incensed at the idea that they should be expected to count Palestine as their homeland (though no one said they would have to do so). Rabbi Philipson remained an anti-Zionist for the rest of his life, even as some of his colleagues warmed to the idea of a Jewish nation in Palestine.

Despite Schiff's warning of divisive opposition, Philipson attempted to organize a conference of rabbis and Jewish laypeople to oppose Zionism in 1918. He reached out to Jewish leaders all around the country and from several areas of Jewish life. The conference collapsed after substantial opposition to this idea was voiced from notable figures like Jacob Schiff (who had previously been an ally of Philipson in anti-Zionism), Louis Marshall, Cyrus Adler (a prominent Jewish leader who served as president of the Jewish Theological Seminary and of the American Jewish Committee, as well as co-chair of the Council for the Jewish Agency), and Oscar Straus (Theodore Roosevelt's secretary of commerce and labor). In the end, both Zionist and non-Zionist leaders opposed the conference as they struggled to keep Jews together despite the tensions in the American Jewish community.[50]

There were some concessions and cooperation between the Zionist and non-Zionist leaders over the following decade. For example, in 1927 the Weizmann-Marshall agreement on the Jewish Agency drew support from both sides for the migration and settlement of Jewish refugees to Palestine, if not the Zionist idea. Judge William Lewis (serving as president of the Appeal) wrote:

> The recent publication of this accord, auguring as it does the establishment of harmony and cooperation in American Israel on behalf of Palestine, has brought added strength and zeal to the men and women who, through the United Palestine Appeal, and the funds that are associated in it, have borne the major part of the labor and responsibility involved in the rebuilding of the Jewish National Home.[51]

Nonreligious Jews opposed to Zionism in America were largely acting on their determination to maintain the degree of success and acculturation they had earned. Even after such understandings had been reached, acculturated American Jews fought to keep the public aware that Jews were not all Zionists, and that not all American Jews believed they should have national pride for any other nation than the United States. The Reform movement adopted a more positive attitude toward Zionism in 1937 at the convention of the CCAR, though the demographics of its leadership were quite different by then. In their 1937 "Columbus Platform," the CCAR reversed its stand on Jewish peoplehood, declaring that "Judaism is the soul of which Israel [the people] is the body." The platform continues, "We affirm the obligation of all Jewry to aid in its [Palestine's] up-building as a Jewish homeland by endeavoring to make it not only a haven of refuge for the oppressed but also a center of Jewish culture and spiritual life."[52] Anti-Zionists, like Rabbi Philipson, continued to speak out against Zionism, though their organizations were small until 1943, when they joined to establish the anti-Zionist American Council for Judaism.[53]

In its early years, and through both world wars, the Zionist movement provided a new image of, and argument for, muscular Jewry the world over. In the United States, though views of the enterprise itself varied, the influence of the "new Jew" making the desert bloom by his own hands and through his dominance over nature, had significant and lasting effect. The defenses for and arguments against supporting the

Zionist endeavor in Palestine demonstrated the strength of this influence. American Jewish men did not only bask in the reflected glow of Jewish masculinity in Palestine, they popularized images of men in the Yishuv as Jewish heroes to which they could aspire and with whom they maintained affinity.

In the midst of negotiating the relationship between American Jewry and the Zionist enterprise, the Great War broke out in Europe, complicating the place of Jews and Zionists everywhere, as they fought with armies on both sides of the conflict across European nations and empires. Jews around the world were pulled in several directions and underwent rapid changes during the war: the world center for Zionist activities shifted from Berlin to London, the publication of the Balfour Declaration changed the tone and timeline of the Zionist territorial ambitions, and the entry of the United States into the war brought American Jewry into an unprecedented leadership position in the councils of world Jewry.[54] For American Jewish men, the war presented opportunities to prove themselves, first fighting as Jews, then, once the United States entered the war, fighting as Americans.

5

The Hardiest Canard

Jewish Participation in the Great War

> Myths die *hard* and one of the *hardiest* is the canard that the Jew
> does not make a good soldier.
> —Jewish War Veterans of the United States[1]

The First World War marked an important moment in the history of masculinity, not just for Jewish men but throughout the industrialized world. In the last decades of the nineteenth century, western concepts of qualities of masculinity (physical health, beauty, strength, valor, honor, and duty to family) served as the foundation for a middle-class dominant masculinity. The Great War, a culmination of modernism and nationalism including unprecedented global participation and technology, provided a theater for men to play out (and indeed resurrect) these solidifying ideas of masculinity through warfare (camaraderie, violence, valor, and duty to country). The Great War did not change the dominant masculine ideal in Europe and America, but strengthened those concepts of masculinity that had already begun to form and tied masculinity to nationalism in a new and lasting way. The trauma men who fought in the war experienced, unique in its mechanized nature, was acute. However, regardless of the trauma caused by new methods of warfare, in the popular imagination (cultural imagery and depictions of war), war still made men of boys. For soldiers who emerged unbroken, the Great War was a masculine rite of passage, traditional in its manly connection to the fight and unique in its facing down the technological advancements of the industrial age.

As citizens of many nations with connections to the Jewish diaspora, Jewish detractors of a certain ideology viewed Jews as *disconnected* from land and nation, and for this reason, from modern manhood as well. The most obvious proponents of this theory were those functioning within German *Volkisch* ideology, which believed that as a people are inextricably linked to their land, Jews can be viewed as either a landless, soulless people, or a desert people, devoid of the richness of the lands of Europe. Contemporary American Jews tried very hard to combat the idea that they held unpatriotic dual loyalties, particularly in times of war. There was still a tendency among both Jews and non-Jews, however, to ascribe a gentle nature to the Jewish religion and texts, promoting the idea that Jews detest warfare overall. Even those stories of Jewish heroes are pointedly discussed by the rabbinic tradition with ambivalence, sometimes antagonism, when it comes to militarism and martial tradition.[2] In a speech delivered to Jewish audiences in 1914, Rabbi Gustav N. Hausmann demonstrated very well the confusing position in which Jews found themselves with regard to the fight. In defending Jewish patriotism, Hausmann extolled Jewish battle readiness and prowess, explaining (perhaps overly optimistically):

> Judaism exalts patriotism into a law. There can be no good Jew who is not a complete patriot. . . . All now admit, even those anti-Semitic countries who pointed at him suspiciously as an alien, as a foreigner, sometimes even as a traitor, that the Jew has the gift of patriotism for his country. The Jew is not only unswervingly *loyal*, but he has also been fearlessly *brave* on the battlefield. [italics original][3]

He continued, also adhering to classic explanations of meek Jewish nature, claiming, "The Jew comes into the World Arena with an altogether different weapon, the weapon of weakness, of submission, of suffering. Ours has been the power of endurance; it is better to suffer than to die." He summarizes, confusingly, "Fearlessly brave is the Jew on the battlefield. Judaism and Peace are one and interchangeable. Force is not to be relied upon. Might meets with defeat by might. Often weakness, based on right, defeats power. God is on the side of the weak."[4]

Though not as befuddling as Hausmann's assessment of Jewish valor, patriotism, and pacifism, attitudes of American Jews fighting in the Great War show equal complexity. Jews, in large part, eagerly joined the fight before America even entered the war. Veterans recall the need to disprove stereotypes of Jewish weakness, and to show Jews as equal to all other modern men in war, the manliest of pursuits. The rise in militance as the mark of a man is clear in their accounts, but so is the need to persist against continued accusations of Jewish cowardice and evasion. Jewish men intended to prove their mettle by joining the fight and salvaging the image of Jewish heroism and manliness.

The Myth of Jewish Evasion

For Jews in the United States, scrutiny of their manliness, as exemplified by the willingness and capacity to fight, was an ever-present impediment. Jewish men struggled against accusations of Jews as evasive of duty, but distinguished clearly between American Jews and Jewish immigrants. Such accusations remained throughout the duration of the war, regardless of the realities of Jewish enlistment. In June 1918, just a few months before the war officially ended, an American Jew, Lewis Brown, published an article in the *North American Review* addressing the supposed determination of American Jews not to fight in the war. In this article, Brown examined a statement from the instruction manual for the Medical Advisory Board of the draft, stating that, "The foreign born, especially the Jews, are more apt to malinger than the native born."[5] Interestingly, Brown did not deny that *foreign-born* Jews may be prone to malingering, but he explained that it was only those who had not Americanized fully. He even defended their slacking by claiming that it was unique, "They are 'slackers,' of course, but their 'slacking' is not sneaky, mean, and 'yellow.' It is 'red'; it is imbued with a peculiar zeal and passion. It is a type of 'slacking' altogether anomalous—and for that reason, most impressive—to the American born and bred."[6]

Brown clarified for his readers the difference between Jews who had absorbed the American manly character and those who were still too foreign in their Jewishness. He provided a threefold explanation for Jewish malingering; the first element argued that the Jew is naturally averse to war because of his teachings, that he is indeed "constitutionally antipathetic to physical violence. He has nothing of the berserker in him." The second mirrored statements from Roosevelt and Herzl about the historical emasculation of Jewish men. Brown argued that among Jews, the martial spirit "has been almost crushed beneath centuries of servility and oppression . . . powers neglected tend to atrophy . . . and so men unable to use physical force lose altogether the sense of fight. Their bodies wither . . . they must live by their wits." The third reason he gave for foreign-born Jewish malingering regarded the memories they retained of the brutal draft and military in their home countries (primarily those from Russia). He explained that though he may have done the same if he had been in the old country, as an American Jew, he knew "that here the soldiery is clean and fine and manly." "Yes," he continued, "*I* know all this, but—and here lies the root of the evil—my un-Americanized brother does not." The Medical Advisory Board removed the slur on Jews from the manual in February 1918. President Wilson ordered the removal of the offensive paragraph himself, in response to a telegram from Louis Marshall, the president of the American Jewish Committee, protesting the slander.

Not all Jewish leaders agreed with Brown's assessment of the "slacking nature" of foreign-born Jews, and several made very public efforts to combat the image of Jews as slackers or malingerers. A New York rabbi, Samuel Buchler, president of the Federation of Hungarian Jews in America, led a call to enlist Austro-Hungarian Jews in the American military and planned to expand his efforts to men of other foreign birth as well. Several notable leaders of the time (mostly of German-Jewish heritage, including Jacob Schiff) formed a Jewish antipacifist group in New York called the American League of Jewish Patriots, in April 1917. The group existed to encourage Jewish American men to enlist in the American armed forces. Their leaders claimed that through the Americanization process, the values of democracy would inspire men to act. They explained that "he who originally was a 'slacker' is among the first to volunteer, and on the field of battle he is the renowned hero."[7] However, the desire on the part of these Jews reads less as a desire to "win" either the war or Jewish freedoms abroad (though that certainly does concern them) than it does the need to disprove the continued criticism that Jews are somehow different and cannot become American men, patriots, and soldiers. In all, approximately 225,000 Jews (both native-born and immigrants) served as Americans in the First World War.[8]

In 1919, as the war wrapped up, the American Jewish Committee's Office of Jewish War Records released a report on Jewish participation "as an instrument wherewith to combat certain manifestations of anti-Jewish prejudice in the immediate present."[9] This report reveals several things about American antisemitism, its emphasis on emasculation, and American Jewish reactions to such prejudice. The Office of Jewish War Records released the report prematurely, as there were still troops mobilized, and so they could not yet count many of the soldiers, medals of valor, casualties, and so on, that would be in the final tally. The American Jewish Committee released this material to the American public early as a direct reaction to antisemitic claims of malingering and draft dodging, which constituted an attack on the manliness and honor of American Jews. The sense of urgency for such reports doubtlessly increased in response to aggressive accusations of Jewish evasion made by the German government. In 1916, the German military conducted the *Judenstatistik* (Jew census) to catalog the number of Jews serving at the front, though they did not release the numbers until the war had ended. Both the fact that the German government considered this census necessary and the lack of information published only served to increase suspicion of Jewish evasion among antisemitic circles, and it continued to represent one of the key points of German antisemitic propaganda.[10]

It is clear in the report that the Office of Jewish War Records interpreted antisemitic claims of malingering and evasion as an attack on Jewish manliness and honor (and were not apt to agree to the veracity of such ideas as did Lewis Brown), because it reads less as a record of participation than it does a determined effort to prove Jewish grit. A section devoted to the role of Jewish soldiers as combatants versus noncombatants explains that far more Jews wished to fight than to organize. Another section on volunteers explains that so many Jews in service were outside the draft age that their excessive numbers could not be coincidence or happenstance, but that Jews were surely overrepresented due to high levels of patriotism and valor. The office's director, Julian Leavitt, concluded the report:

> Jews of America have contributed their full quota to the winning of the war, and a generous margin beyond their quota; that they have enlisted cheerfully, fought gallantly and died bravely for the United States. . . . The qualities which [have] enabled the Jew to survive through the centuries—his capacity to endure, without breaking, prolonged and intense nerve strain; his qualities of initiative, his elasticity of mind, his capacity for organization, and

above all, his idealism—[enabled] him to fit himself successfully into a democratic army fighting for world democracy.

He explained that it was for the outside world, those who still did not recognize or believe the facts of Jewish valor, that the Jewish War Records office must exist and compile this data.

When Jews did receive high praise for their strength and battle prowess (from their fellow officers and superiors), their Jewishness was determinedly highlighted by both the Jews themselves and the commentator, upholding the notion that theirs was an exceptional case (whether or not that was their intent), and that the particular Jew in question was an exceptional specimen of Jewish manhood. This certainly held true in the case of Sam Dreben, the heroic soldier about whom author Damon Runyon composed the following poem:

There's a story in that paper

I just tossed upon the floor
That speaks of prejudice against the Jews.
There's a photo on the table
That's a memory of the war.
And a man who never figured in the news.
There's a cross upon his breast—
That's the D.S.C.,
The Croix de Guerre, the Militaire,
These, too.
And there's a heart beneath the medals
That beats loyal, brave and true—
That's Dreben,
A Jew!

He is short, and fat, and funny,
And the nose upon his face
Is about the size of Buglar Dugan's horn.
But the grin that plays behind it
Is wide, and soft, and sunny,
And he wore it from the day that he was born.

There's a cross upon his chest—
That's the D.S.C.,
The Croix de Guerre, the Militaire,
Mon Dieu!
He's a He-Man out of Texas,
And he's all man through and through—
That's Dreben,
A Jew!

Now whenever I read articles
That breathe of racial hate,
Or hear arguments that hold his kind to scorn,
I always see that photo
With the cap upon the pate
And the nose the size of Bugler Dugan's horn.
I see upon his breast
The D.S.C.,
The Croix de Guerre, the Militaire—
These, too.
And I think, Thank God Almighty
We will always have a few
Like Dreben,
A Jew![11]

Sam Dreben, known in the American army as "the fighting Jew," immigrated to the United States from Russia and proved himself in battle on multiple fronts, having fought in several wars and for several nations. Dreben was honored as one of the outstanding heroes of the First World War. He fought in the Philippines, China (and Peking), Panama, and Mexico, before entering the Great War, serving in Europe until the war came to a close. According to Martin Zielonka, Dreben "never allowed any one to doubt his Jewish origin and his pride in it. . . . He was a living example that the Jew is not a malingerer."[12] The poem, clearly written from the perspective that it was shocking and unusual for a Jew of such valor to emerge among the ranks, paints a picture of Dreben as a short, fat, funny, big-nosed, smiling Jew who to everyone's surprise, emerged as a "He-Man out of Texas, and he's all man through and through." Dreben was not from Texas (though that is the state in which he enlisted to fight in the First World War), but was a Polish immigrant, the foreign-born Jewish man that Lewis Brown believed more apt to malinger.

Even Jews who believed that assumptions of Jewish cowardice were mere prejudice still acknowledged the need for individual Jews to disprove them. The Jewish Welfare Board (JWB) was established during the war as the Jewish civilian agency to aid soldiers in wartime and acted as Jewish representatives to the American War Department. Jewish men serving in the American military during the war largely got along with their non-Jewish comrades, but such connections did not knock down the fences between Protestant, Catholic, and Jew. While considering his own military service, Jacob Rader Marcus (who later became a Reform rabbi, scholar of Jewish history, and the founder of the American Jewish Archives) believed that all Jewish soldiers had a responsibility to maintain a high standard of behavior, but that even the best of behavior could not rid American men of their assumptions of Jewish cowardice or evasion.[13] Much like Dreben, Marcus explained that be believed he was accepted among his non-Jewish compatriots because his Jewishness was ambiguous enough that they saw him as "one of those Jews who are not really Jews." The "real" Jews in this case, as identified by Marcus's contemporaries, were foreign-born Jews, Yiddish speakers from Eastern Europe, Orthodox in religious practice, and more left-leaning politically. As a Reform Jew, Marcus was more Americanized and less seemingly foreign, he was more able to "pass" among the other men. He believed, as did his contemporaries discussed in the previous chapter, that time spent in the American environment, around American men, would help foreign Jews to improve themselves and better reach the standard of American manhood, therefore lessening the degree of antisemitic attacks against them.

The Jewish Legion

Before America joined the Great War, Jews in the United States were gratefully left out of what Horace Kallen, in 1914, called their unique position of "fratricide," as Jews fought in every army involved in the conflict. Recounting an anecdote from the battlefields, Rabbi Hausmann demonstrates the fratricidal nature of the war in Europe, "In a bayonet charge, a Russian Jewish soldier stabbed an Austrian Jewish soldier to death. The former heard the latter utter with his last dying gasp: 'Shema Isroel'–God is one [*sic*]."[14]

Kallen argued that the Jewish struggle for equality and freedom to practice their religion and tradition while simultaneously contributing to the various societies in which they lived was the "great historical incarnation of the *casus belli*" (justification for war).[15] And indeed, American and Palestinian Jews did see the poor and unequal situation of European Jews in various nations as justification to join the fight (even before America entered the war). This was certainly the case among those Jews expelled from settlements in and around Jaffa by the Turkish

Figure 11. Two distantly related Jewish soldiers meet—Bernard Gorfinkle of the US Army (*left*) and Captain Isaac Gorfinkle of Belfast (*right*). Belfast, Ireland, c. 1917. Herbert Gorfinkle Papers, P-904, box 1, folder 10, Wyner Family Jewish Heritage Center at NEHGS, Boston, Massachusetts.

government in 1914. Among the over ten thousand Jewish refugees gathered in Alexandria (Egypt) were Jewish veterans of Russian and Yishuv fighting and defense groups. Two of these veterans, Captain Joseph Trumpeldor and Vladimir Jabotinsky (who would later become a leader in the Revisionist Zionist movement), proposed an all-Jewish army to fight under British command, on the Sinai Desert, which would inevitably become a fighting front. Initially turned down for work as soldiers by the British government, these 652 Jewish would-be soldiers became the Zion Mule Corps, carrying food and ammunition to British men in the trenches, proving their resolve to the British government. By 1917, British forces began training a group of these men in London to be the leaders of a new Jewish Legion (known in Hebrew as *Hagdud Haivri*), an actual combat unit, which officially formed at the end of 1916.[16]

Subject to American influences and trends, Jews from the United States eagerly joined to prove themselves, as Roosevelt had advocated, in the theater of war. Even more so than other American groups, perhaps, as they remained excluded from so many venues of masculine performance. The Great War provided the occasion to do so, and a great number of Jews took the opportunity. The formation of a Jewish Legion abroad, paired with the fact that the United States had not yet joined the fight, gave Jewish Americans an unprecedented opportunity to fight *as Jews*. Interest in the fight increased when Balfour issued his 1917 declaration in England, spurring hope for a Jewish homeland in Palestine. In response, American Jewish men interested in enlisting volunteered to join the Jewish Legion in their battles against the Ottoman Empire. Within the Jewish Legion, North American men constituted the largest contingent of volunteers, forming entirely American battalions making their way to Palestine via training camps in Canada.[17]

American Jews volunteering in the legion faced several impediments (especially after America joined the war), primarily age and American citizenship that strictly prohibited citizens from serving in a foreign army. For those exempted from the American draft, however, these restrictions were not insurmountable. At least a few underage Jews lied about their age (if under twenty-one) to fight. Those who wished to join but were fully eligible for the American draft went so far as to forfeit their American citizenship to join the legion. William Braiterman was one such underage recruit who wished to join the legion. A child

Figure 12. Jewish Legion soldiers in their daily dress at their camp, n.d. Courtesy of The Jewish Museum of Maryland. 1992.154.4.

immigrant from Russia, on his arrival in the United States Braiterman very quickly began to Americanize, primarily by participating in American sports (through the available Jewish organizations) and engaging in more elements of American (and English-speaking) culture. Delighted with America but appalled by the antisemitic lynching of Leo Frank (so reminiscent of similar blood libel charges his family witnessed in Russia), he became an ardent Zionist in his teens. The legion came to his attention when he ran across a Baltimore recruiter who called to him on the street, "You look like a strong Jewish Boy. Do you want to fight for your homeland?"[18] Braiterman ran away from Baltimore to Philadelphia (against his parents' wishes) to enlist in the British army under a false name and lying about his age. He fought in the Jewish Legion, bolstered by the Balfour Declaration and the promise of a homeland for the Jewish people. An entire gang of Jewish toughs (gamblers and prizefighters) from Brooklyn also joined up, following their leader's call of "Boys, let's go fight for the Jews!"[19] It was not only Jewish boys who ran off to join the Jewish Legion to fight. Jewish girls also showed interest but were turned away from the all-male unit. One of the rejected girls who attempted to enlist in the legion was a young Golda Meir (first female prime minister of Israel), who was crushed by being turned away from the fight.[20]

Outspoken antiwar Jewish men who otherwise might have registered as conscientious objectors, like Russian immigrant Elias Gilner, weighed the duties to their various convictions, and some decided, as he did, that deplorable as he found war, fighting for the Jewish Legion was something altogether different. He explained how determined a pacifist he had been at the start of the war, that he had advocated peace publicly, and in response, "Invectives were flung at me; fists were raised at me; chairs were hurled at me; but I stood my ground." He fled New York City, trying to escape antipacifist aggression, and ended up in St. Louis, where he found no relief. "I was socially ostracized as a slacker and I could find no peace as a man." Still, he held fast to his pacifism. But when he saw the call to fight for the Jewish people, in an all-Jewish battalion, "the pacifist arguments fell flat. I could not stir. The simple sentence [enlist in the Jewish Legion!] clearly possessed an irresistible power. It did not mean war to me. It meant the discovery of a road to peace."[21] He registered on the spot.

Though the United States government had allowed the Jewish Legion to recruit men who were otherwise not subject to the American draft, several American Jews remained torn about the legion. Some Jewish assimilationists, anti-Zionists, and even Zionists concerned about the perception of Jewish dual loyalties objected to the recruiting of American Jews to the legion. They argued that American Jews owed their full allegiance to the United States and should therefore enlist only in the American armed forces. For the most part, however, American Jews viewed the recruits as heroes and received them as such, even before they reached basic training. One recruit recalled, about his journey to the legion training ground:

> The battlefield was still far. Our deeds of valor farther. But our heroism, offered in the open market, was guaranteed in advance, underwritten, and floated by pompous personages or by lean, anaemic [sic], and pious-looking individuals in bombastic speeches, lyric, ecstatic, or prayerful effusions. Small wonder that the issue was subscribed to and oversubscribed by generous matrons and their charming daughters. We were dined, petted, cuddled, worshipped,

bemoaned, glorified, supplied with comforters and socks and sent on our way. Grapefruit, roast chicken, speeches, and kisses were bestowed upon us in Detroit, Montreal, and St. John's, Newfoundland. Speeches and kisses without grapefruit in a number of minor stopovers. We arrived in camp sore-lipped, heavy-limbed, swellheaded, hot under our shirts from carrying our luggage and under our skins from the sense of self-importance pumped into us by silver-tongued toastmasters and red-lipped girls.[22]

The end of the war in 1918 cut off the flow of American Jewish volunteers at its height. Though about five thousand volunteers actively fought in Palestine, on Armistice Day, 5,600 more (predominantly American) Jewish men were in training or transit to join the battle.[23]

The Jewish Legion was the first fighting Jewish military body since the Roman Empire and served as inspiration for the future iterations of Jewish militaries and defense forces of what would become the State of Israel. Jewish men found, in the legion, a stage on which to demonstrate (or manifest) their strength, Jewish nationalism, pride, honor, and courage. One Jewish colonel, Eliezer Margolin, wanted his battalion "to be brave and heroic, knowing well that the eyes of the Gentile world were upon them—the Gentile world which, for centuries, mocked the Jews as cowards." According to fellow legionnaire, Roman Freulich, when his battalion captured a village (Es-Salt) in Palestine, they "proved that they were real men—brave men."[24]

Yet even among the real, brave men of the Jewish Legion, the image of the Jew as coward did not die. Within their recollections, writings, and recordings, it is clear that even among the rank and file of the Jewish battalions, stereotypes about Jews lacking manliness persisted and served to support their praise of their fellow soldiers as exceptions to the rule of Jewish meekness. After training, one Jewish recruit noted, "the frail and pallid tailors left the camp as tough and hardened soldiers."[25] In this fashion, Major H. D. Myer, a Jewish English officer who had transferred to the Jewish Legion from his assignment in Europe, wrote to his fiancée that the Jews in his unit were far preferable to the "regular" Jews of England: "They are people with ideas and ideals of things besides mere money making, and the soil of Palestine is suited to such. They are well developed mentally and physically and they are men."[26]

The successes and failures of the Jewish Legion were as mixed as the intentions of the enterprise. In some respects, they were highly successful. For example, the Jewish men who fought in the legion considered themselves *redeemed* men, as is clear from their accounts. However, the ultimate goal of the legion was to become a militia security force to protect the Zionist enterprise, and this never came to fruition. They succeeded in convincing British forces to let them fight as a Jewish combat unit, but the British kept their opportunities for combat infrequent and held them back from forming their militia when the war closed. In America, Jews venerated the legion and took pride in Jewish soldiering; however, the call for an all Jewish army was never realized, even though the idea did gain some popularity in the decades that followed. In truth, the legion maintained a good combat record and provided cause for Jewish pride, but it had little impact on the continuing view of Jews (in America and elsewhere) as physically weak and violence averse.

As the persecution of Jews in Europe increased, Jews in America fought to maintain what little momentum of manliness and bravado they won through their militarism in the Great War, both in the American service and for the Jewish Legion. This positive progress was limited to individuals who served, and they were still seen as outliers. There is no evidence that the larger American perception of Jewish men reflected such change, however, Jewish men's attempts to prove themselves and the manliness of the American Jew did not go entirely unrewarded. The Jewish War Veterans of the United States (JWV) formed before the turn of the century, and their work during and after the war, particularly in promoting the image of Jewish men of valor, helped lessen the view of Jewish men as evasive of duty. The JWV, addressing rising antisemitism at home, claimed that the need for "an aggressive, militant organization like the Jewish War Veterans of the U.S.—whose existence refutes most of the falsehoods used—is becoming more evident in Jewish American life." They saw it as their duty to "uphold the fair name of the Jew."[27] The American Jewish Committee also served to weaken the myth of Jewish evasion with their report, as did the successful retracting of the offensive statements in the *Manual of Instructions for Medical Advisory Boards*. In addition, the JWB also worked to promote a positive image of Jews as patriotic Americans during the war. Enough Jewish men served, and sufficient numbers of American leaders supported their claims of manly equality, that by the start of the Second World War, Jewish *evasion* was not the common attack on Jewish manhood it had been previously.

Being Jewish became slightly less of an impediment to success every year in the interwar period. By the mid-1930s, Jews were taking their place on the American scene more visibly and prominently than they ever had previously. Jews served as Supreme Court justices, remained influential in arts, literature, music, theater, and many other spheres of public life without hiding their Jewishness as some had done in previous decades and generations. Antisemitism, however, also increased to an unprecedented degree in the United States. Between 1933 and 1941, over one hundred antisemitic groups formed in the United States, a tremendous increase from the five that existed before that time.[28] This movement was largely fringe and lost some of the respect they gained from key antisemitic American figures like Henry Ford supporting their rhetoric. Additional antisemitic leaders, like Father Charles Coughlin (the "Radio Priest"), and Charles Lindbergh (and his America First Committee) became more typical on the American landscape.

The Second World War created several challenges to Jewish manhood, as events of the war itself, the Holocaust, and the ensuing crisis of displaced Jews in and from Europe, had a tremendous impact on Jewish life across the globe and brought much attention to global Jewry, engendering both compassion and defamation. These events transformed the image of Jews in Europe, put an international spotlight on Jews residing in Palestine, and altered the self-image of Jews (and the functions of Jewish life) throughout the diaspora, and particularly in the United States.

6
"Shalom with Honor"

American Men and the Second World War

Jews fight too! Perhaps they do not fight any better, nor more heroically than any other people—but certainly no less bravely do they
fight.

—Mac Davis, 1944[1]

American Jews joining the Second World War were in a distinctly different position than in the Great War, as there was a clear Jewish interest in
American participation in Europe. America did not join the war in order
to fight for or protect the Jews of Europe, but the war had a Jewish element
that could not be overlooked, even before the full extent of the atrocities
against Jews was common knowledge. Jewish Americans could not join
the Jewish Legion as they had decades prior to prove their mettle and fight
for a Jewish ideal. Joining this war meant fighting for the United States,
though it tangentially included a fight for Jewish interests and protection
worldwide (a fact recognized by both Jews and non-Jews, with varying
positive and negative reactions). America's entry into the war, however,
was heavy with masculine rhetoric, promoting the idea that service, for
Jews and others, spoke directly to their manhood, bravery, and heroism.
The American government intentionally promoted this view, with an eye
to the future of the postwar world and America's potential role. They also
had to entice an American population to fight who were still reeling from
the previous war, and initiated several direct tactics to do so.

Uncle Sam Wants YOU!

As it became ever clearer that America would soon enter the Second World War, recruiters for the American armed forces took on an

enormous task in persuading the American people to willingly join in another international conflict. From the moment America joined the fight, the Roosevelt administration saw an end-goal of America as a powerful international leader and began building up America's image of strength and stability. If America were to take part in this international conflict, it would commit to serving as peacekeeper after the war had concluded, ensuring American dominance in the postwar world. In 1942, the United States government created the Office of War Information (OWI) to persuade the American people not only to join the rank and file of the armed forces but to contribute to the war effort in every imaginable way by creating a supporting home front. This was a particularly difficult task as citizens still felt the effects of the First World War and were not eager to suffer further.

In addition to the remaining trauma of the previous war in everyday life, unforeseen challenges threatened traditional gender roles in interwar America. Women achieved new levels of mobility, won access to the vote, and participated in more areas of American life than had ever been possible previously. The confusion of these years created a tension around transforming gender roles, and a perceived threat to preexisting notions of manhood. As a result, when America entered and fought in the Second World War, traditional images of manliness (the role of the protector, obligation to family, community, and country) were already being stressed. Once again, the war provided an opportunity for boys to become men, and for men to reclaim and prove their manhood in a time of uncertainty and confusion. The American military employed strong concepts of gender in recruiting materials that reveal some notions about masculinity in the United States. During the war, the OWI ran recruiting campaigns that stressed how manly it was to voluntarily enlist in service to the country. The stated goal of their campaign was not to create an impossible ideal but to represent what Americans already were at their best. Since its inception, the OWI adopted a "strategy of truth" based on the presumption that informed citizens could be trusted to make up their own minds, and that disseminating truth promoted trust in the American government.[2] This was a double-edged sword, however, as while the truth of American manhood and patriotism held aloft the ideals of American manhood, it also disdained those classified unfit for service as unmanly and pitiable. Conscientious objectors and those who attempted to avoid the draft were presented as worthy of the meanest contempt and punishment.

The American government very intentionally monitored and controlled the national view of military service through popular consumable media. The image of the enlisted man American officials promoted was a maverick who *chose* to commit to the war effort and transformed from an everyday man (or a weak, incomplete man) to a heroic soldier. American propaganda contrasted this image with the people of enemy nations who lacked the freedom to make their own choice to heroically take up the charge, but whose governments forced them to do so instead. The freedom inherent in American identity enabled Americans to be their own men. Hollywood film productions provided one of the most effective methods of spreading this message. The OWl monitored, and at times censored, these productions and successfully used them to spread their message. The office even published a *Manual for the Motion-Picture Industry* as a guide for American movie-makers to properly represent America and the war.

Hollywood image-makers and the OWl (working together a great deal throughout the Second World War) saw in the war a chance to rebuild American manhood from the disillusion and depression of the interwar period. The war was an opportunity to reconstruct manhood and character by providing a unifying "cause worth dying for." During the Depression, popular films had depicted evil forces corrupting and degrading American society, dragging it down into debauchery and chaos. Wartime films, however, featured American heroes representing the melting pot in their diversity (though still mostly white native-born Americans, new immigrants, southerners, and Jews) using popular and patriotic volunteerism to bring people together for a common cause.[3] Wartime recruiting imagery, which targeted both men and women for different roles, was highly gendered. The posters recruiting men to fight for the Marine Corps, the Navy, and the Army depicted well-muscled men (often shirtless) storming beaches, destroying enemy submarines, and flying planes. The same visual tactics appeared in numerous depictions of Uncle Sam: often with the more formal American flag top hat tossed aside in favor of an unbuttoned jacket or shirt, or even rolling up his sleeves for the fight.

Though gender relations remained tense during the war, the armed forces still needed women to serve in support roles. Attempting to

Figures 13 and 14. Compare the famous Army recruiting poster from World War I (*left*), with the one from World War II (*right*). The former features Uncle Sam and the now famous phrase "I want you for U.S. Army," as the character points his finger at the viewer, appealing to their sense of duty and patriotism, and asking for their help. The latter shows the character engaging with the enemy, not the potential recruit, appealing to the viewer's eagerness to join the fight. Hat and coat tossed aside, shirt unbuttoned, not asking for help but already in action. *Left*: Army Recruiting Poster, by James Montgomery Flagg. Library of Congress Prints and Photographs Division Washington, DC 20540. loc.gov/pictures/item/96507165/. *Right*: Army Recruiting Poster. Office for Emergency Management. Office of War Information. Domestic Operations Branch. Bureau of Special Services. National Archives at College Park, Public domain, via Wikimedia Commons. Wikimedia Commons contributors, "File:'Defend Your Country'—NARA—513694.jpg," Wikimedia Commons, https://commons.wikimedia.org/w/index.php?title=File:%22Defend_Your_Country%22_-_NARA_-_513694.jpg&oldid=731741943 (accessed June 29, 2023).

maintain gender division, the military restricted women's work to more traditionally female tasks. Recruiting posters targeting women showed well-put-together women in uniform, committed to serve in order to relieve men of the tasks that kept them from the fight. One such Marine Corps poster, for example, showed a woman in uniform standing beside a fighter plane with a clipboard. The caption read, "Be a Marine: Free a Marine to Fight." These posters showed women rigging parachutes, on WAVES duty (Women Accepted for Voluntary Emergency Service) in control towers, and at Coast Guard shore stations with SPARS (Coast Guard Women's Reserve). One recruiting pamphlet read:

> This is total war—a war in which every woman as well as every man must play a part. The men in the Navy and Coast Guard are in for one reason alone—to fight! They're in to fly the planes, man the ships, smash the Nazis and Japs. But to keep them fighting, there are important service jobs that must be carried on at home—man-size, full-time jobs which you, the women of America, can fill—jobs in which you can serve your country in your country and release the men to fight at sea.[4]

The campaign for women in the military showed women in picture-perfect uniforms, hair and makeup well in place, never fighting or getting dirty. This was still much more inclusive of women than the recruiting materials of the First World War, which showed pretty civilian women and slogans like, "Gee!! I wish I were a man—I'd join the Navy." Throughout World War II, women served in the United States Army in the Women's Auxiliary Corps (WACS), the Naval Reserve as WAVES, in an experimental Army Air Corps program (WASPS), and in the SPARS.

Images of wartime women diverged from the pristine female ideal only in the images depicting women working wartime production jobs on the home front. These occasionally showed women with their sleeves rolled up as well, mimicking the men in the military posters, the most famous being the "We can do it" campaign featuring Rosie the Riveter. But for the most part, even women working in wartime productions were still urged to maintain their femininity, as in the instructional posters featuring "Jenny on the Job," who worked hard, but got her beauty sleep and kept herself "fresh as a daisy."[5] Military recruiting did not use

Figures 15 and 16. Compare the Navy recruiting poster from World War I (*left*), with the Coast Guard recruiting poster from World War II (*right*). The former features a girl in uniform, playfully dressed as a sailor, with the phrase, "Gee!! I wish I were a man," and following with, "be a man and do it." By the start of the next war, however, women *were* being recruited, but their appeals were gendered very differently. The latter shows the woman in SPARs in clean, crisp, gloved attire, contrasted boldly with the man in the Coast Guard, holding a weapon, engaged in action behind her. Her presence in a supportive role frees him to fight like a man. *Left*: Gee!! I wish I were a man, I'd join the Navy Be a man and do it—United States Navy recruiting station. Howard Chandler Christy, 1917. Courtesy of Library of Congress Prints and Photographs Division Washington, DC 20540 USA. *Right*: *Your Duty Ashore . . . His Afloat.* Graphic image of a woman in US Coast Guard (SPARS) military dress uniform holding binoculars, with a sailor holding a rifle in the background. Illustrated by Floherty Jr. Image courtesy of Northwestern University Libraries.

such images, as propogandists working for the armed forces kept the genders quite separate in their tasks and recruiting techniques. Indeed, even women entering the wartime workforce presented a challenge to American manhood. Men across the country (and fighting overseas) worried about job competition from women after the war. They also fretted about maintaining traditional family structure as women emerged from their homes and homemaking roles to fulfill an unprecedented number of duties in the public sphere. Fears of damage to the social fabric of America remained, as women went out alone more, attended public dances, and spent more time in the world without men. There were also fears that boys raised in female-headed households during the war would become feminized, their male identity somehow undermined by the lack of a strong male figure in the home. In 1942, Philip Wylie coined the term "momism" as a critique of the influence of overly present maternal figures in the lives of American boys, making them less manly and tough than the enemies they faced in Nazi-occupied Europe.[6]

Though of great concern to American men overall, this may not have troubled Jewish men as much as it did American gentiles. Jewish life had long employed women in more trades, and therefore Jews (at least immigrant and first generation) most likely felt less troubled by the thought of their "breadwinner" roles weakening due to female labor and inclusion. Many Jewish immigrants accepted women as breadwinners, working outside of the home, and taking part in the larger community. Though Jewish men felt more comfortable with a diversity of roles for both men and women in the public sphere, they still responded to the propaganda campaigns of the military, which reinforced an American masculinity based on willingness to fight for one's country. Fighting in the war gave them the opportunity to transform themselves into warriors and connected them to American manhood and other American men who were serving or had served.

Your Best Isn't Good Enough: Jewish Enlistment and the American Military

Just as in the First World War, Jews volunteered for the American armed forces in the face of criticisms from all tiers of American society, criticisms that targeted their abilities, strength, and willingness to enter the fight. This is not to say that Jewish men entered the war for the sole purpose of altering their masculine image in America, but their volunteerism highlighted Jewish manhood and bravery through military service and wartime martyrdom. Leading up to and during the Second World War, Jewish men entered the military with a twofold motivation: patriotic duty and duty to their Jewish brethren in Europe. The Great War drew Jewish Americans overseas to fight against the Ottoman Empire in the hopes of establishing Jewish territory in Palestine, but at the start of this second war, the Third Reich directly threatened the Jews of Europe, making the need to join far more urgent. Whereas numbers range among sources, there is a consensus that Jewish participation was at least proportionate to the Jewish American population, and many argue that the number of Jews enlisted in the military was overrepresentative of their population. Approximately 550,000 self-identifying Jewish men and women served in the American armed forces during the Second World War, accounting for between 4 and 5 percent of the soldiers serving in the United States. According to the numbers of the total American Jewish population found in the Jewish Yearbook from 1940, Jews constituted 3.6 percent of Americans, showing that Jewish participation was, in fact, higher than their proportion of the American population. With a sense of patriotic duty in line with their neighbors of other backgrounds, Jewish men entered the war as American citizens, like members of any other ethnic, religious, or migrant group.

Despite Jews enlisting voluntarily, non-Jews still viewed Jewish men as too cowardly, weak, and selfish to sacrifice themselves for their country. It is possible, given the small percentage (and visibility in the public sphere) of Jews compared to other ethnicities in the general population of United States, that non-Jews saw few Jews among their ranks and assumed low participation. Complaints voiced in the American military, government, and public echoed those of Americans and Europeans of the past (and particularly during the First World War) that Jewish men evaded military service and patriotic duty, although these accusations were less common (and less institutionalized) than in the previous war. The American government, for example, did not publish such offensive statements as were in the *Manual of Instructions for Medical Advisory Boards* from the First World War. Even within the government, accusations of Jewish cowardice still cropped up, at times propagated by national leadership. A congressman speaking in front of the House Military Affairs Committee, for example, believed that few Jews would willingly fight and argued that those who inevitably tried to escape their service should not be allowed to go "scot free."[7] The congressman was not alone in his stance, and it crops up in other places among military recruiters throughout the rest of the twentieth century. There was a move, in 1980, for example, to explicitly recruit Jewish men on Long

Island, on the premise that their numbers in the enlisted services were shamefully low, due, in no small part, from a report by a Lieutenant Colonel Phillips to that effect. The report and solicitation of recruits specifically from the Jewish community (which promoted the assumption that few Jews enlisted) brought recriminations from both rabbis and the Jewish War Veterans of the United States.[8]

In the years that elapsed since the First World War, the belief that Jews were unwilling or incapable of taking part in the fight was not merely perpetuated by antisemites, it also had its basis in contemporary behavior. There were Jews volunteering, certainly, but there were also others (primarily the religious community) who did not want to fight and voiced their preferences publicly. As committed pacifists, they argued that religious men should not be punished for refusing to join up or answer the call of the draft. A good number of Jews believed that a softer form of masculinity, one that focused on the life of the mind and promoted peace, should indeed be the primary role of Jewish men. This concurs with Daniel Boyarin's description of Jews as contemptuous of such *goyim naches* as included such physical behavior as violence, fighting, sporting, and other activities associated with the ideals of European manliness.

Religious Jews throughout the diaspora fought the masculinization of Jewish men to assimilate with their gentile neighbors. For example, a fascinating illustration from Budapest in 1938 shows the "wicked son" of the Passover Haggadah as both muscular and modern, defying Jewish gentle tradition.[9] Those Jews who considered such masculinization of Jewish culture to be a detriment to the Jewish people believed that service in the armed forces should be avoided. American Jews debated whether voluntary exclusion should be allowed for religious Jewish men. This would not detract from their view of themselves as manly or as Jews, of course, if their view of manhood avoided such *goyim naches*, as Boyarin argues. Though not necessarily intentional, this attitude among Jewish leaders helped to perpetuate the view of Jews as timid, even cowardly, by fighting for the rights of Jews to avoid military service on the grounds of religious belief. In June 1936, the Central Conference of American Rabbis (CCAR) adopted a resolution at their forty-seventh annual convention seeking the exemption of Jews from military service "in accordance with the highest interpretation of Judaism."[10] They included in their resolution that exemption from military service had long been granted to members of the Quaker Society of Friends and similar religious organizations. This pronouncement met with an immense backlash from the Jewish community, particularly from Jewish veterans of the First World War, who viewed this as a slap in the face not only to their service to country but also to their service in the image of American Jewry and Jewish men. Julius Klausner Jr., the national intelligence officer for the Jewish War Veterans, wrote, in response to the resolution, that American Jews were "painfully shocked" by the pronouncement.[11]

Although the CCAR eventually amended their original pronouncement, assuring that they never intended the exemption for *all* Jews, only conscientious objectors, the situation was further complicated by the history of conscientious objectors in the previous war. During World War I, conscientious objectors stated their case for exemption without any sort of statement by Jewish leadership demanding exemption or drawing the disdain of the American public.[12] Why should it be necessary, detractors of the CCAR asked, for American Jewry to take such a stance now, given the equal opportunity for conscientious objectors in the previous war? In fact, there was another recommendation for a resolution (which, after much debate, was not passed at the convention) for the CCAR to adopt the stance that Jewish leadership should urge the "uniform continuance of nonviolent resistance to evil as a basic principle in Jewish life."[13] This was a particularly weighted statement, given the plight of European Jews at the time.

Shortly after the resolution (and a short article drawing attention to it in the *New York Times* titled "War Duty Exemption for All Jews Urged"), the Jewish War Veterans adopted a resolution of their own, firmly against this stance, staunchly reaffirming the "heroic record" of Jewish fighters. "Categorically, we deny that fighting for one's country is inconsistent with 'the highest interpretation of Judaism'; we deny that patriotism is to be confused with militarism; we deny the right of any Jew to exemption on religious grounds; we deny that patriotic veterans love peace any less than do selfstyled pacifists [*sic*]. JWV stands for sholem—with honor."[14] "In one fell stroke," wrote a national intelligence officer with the JWV, "do those rabbis . . . give credence and support to the charge that the Jew is a pacifist and a cowardly avoider of the obligations of citizenship." The JWV officer added that in the biblical history of the Jews, the passage to "go forth and smite thine enemies" was a "command to walk among our fellow man with dignity and not as flinching cowards. . . . The modern Jew, the American Jew, must be prepared to fight . . . just as did the Maccabees and the Jewish military heroes of Biblical, medieval, and modern history."[15] While clearly arguing that Jewish men are not weak and that Jews have a history of heroism in battle, the recrimination, "flinching cowards," is clearly a jab at those rabbis within the Central Conference who were behaving just as they are expected to by antisemites who claimed that Jews could not truly be patriots.

The accusations against the CCAR were, at times, even more extreme in their condemnation of rabbinical cowardice. Leon Schwarz, a former Jewish major in Mobile, Alabama, went so far as to write that if the CCAR could secure military exemption for Jewish men, they should adopt one further resolution, to endorse Adolf Hitler, as he also believed that a Jew is never really a citizen, merely a Jewish person living in someone else's country.[16] One of the greatest fears he voiced to the CCAR was the reaction of those men from other faiths serving in the armed forces. These men might end up far away defending their country while Jews remained at home, enjoying peace and the fruits of war. These letters show a fear that the hard work that Jewish veterans had put into correcting an old image was being nullified, and that the American masses would once again see the Jew as a coward. They were clearly worried, not that Jewish men would refuse to fight if permitted to avoid service (they themselves fought, after all), but that the *image* of Jews as men would be damaged.

Regardless of growing American antisemitism, and of the option to refuse military service as a conscientious objector, the Second World War showed no decline in Jewish participation in the military. Just as in the First World War, enlisting was not always easy for Jews who wanted to fight. Several volunteers fought antisemitism in army recruiting offices just to be allowed to enlist. This war did, however, show the army beginning to take on Jewish officers in unprecedented numbers.[17] The disproportionate number of Jewish men of fighting age (roughly 50 percent of men between ages eighteen and forty-four) meant that most American Jews had close ties to someone serving in the armed forces.[18] Many American Jewish families lost loved ones. In fact, Jewish percentages of military combat dead and wounded were high enough to equal their proportion of the American population.

It is a common misconception (which some Jewish historians like Solomon Grayzel have promoted) that high levels of Jews enlisting in the Allied forces against Germany in the Second World War was a rare or spectacular occurrence. This is partially due to the fact that many Americans at the time viewed Jews as being personally invested in the outcome of the war in Europe. A good number of those joining the United States armed forces never went to Europe at all, serving in the navy and fighting the war in the Pacific against the Japanese. These soldiers had little to no contact with (or impact on) the war against Nazi fascism in Europe. This did not mean, however, that the navy was free of antisemitism. In her examination of Jewish GIs in World War II, Deborah Dash Moore unearthed a popular doggerel that spread through the American armed forces in the testimony of a Jewish naval officer, who had admonished one of his subordinates for passing it along.

> First man to sink an enemy battleship—Colin Kelly.
> First man to set foot on enemy territory—Robert O'Hara.
> First woman to lose five sons—Mrs. Sullivan Etc.
> First son of a bitch to get four new tires—Nathan Goldstein.[19]

It is also a common misconception about American Jews that serving in the Second World War was a purely unifying experience, which slashed away at antisemitic feeling in the military. Certainly, some Jewish soldiers felt that their lives in the military were less likely to contain antisemitism than civilian life, given the fraternal bonds formed by serving with their comrades in arms. However, the unifying argument has been posed primarily in the case of racial or ethnic minorities, such as African Americans, Hispanics, or ethnic whites. Jews presented a minority trifecta, as they were considered an ethnic, religious, and racial group. In the cases of racial minorities, it is, perhaps, more accurate to claim a unifying experience than for the Jewish American minority, which was still suffering from rising antisemitic feelings within and outside the military.

Indeed, while service alongside Jewish Americans dispelled some of the more common antisemitic myths (such as the belief that all Jews have physical horns), pervasive Jewish stereotypes about masculinity and fear of confrontation persisted. The stereotype that Jewish men are bookish and feminine rears its head in the very same oral testimonies of those who make clear statements *against* racism and for ethnic equality in the United States. So well-established were these views on Jewish behavior that those perpetuating them did not even think themselves intolerant. World War II veteran Ben Ewing, speaking about his own battle with prejudice in the military, explained that he had gotten teased for being a racist redneck, by the very same soldiers who, while "kidding" him for being racist, made terrible statements about Jews. While he prided himself by the time of his interview on having overcome his own prejudices, he still used typically disparaging language to describe the Jewish men being picked on by other soldiers. He explained that the Jew most ridiculed in his platoon "was a typical non-athletic scholarly type sheltered lad" and that he "wasn't physically able."[20] Despite his loathing of prejudice, this was clearly standard of "typical" Jewish men in Ewing's view.

By 1942, in the midst of the war, American discussion of Jewish soldiers and their mettle was far from over, and the language used in commentary, op-ed pieces, and public defenses of Jewish heroism continued to be gendered. The JWB published a hefty pamphlet, *In the Nation's Service*, which collected articles, obituaries, and statements by public officials celebrating brave Jewish Americans fighting in the war. The articles addressed and refuted disparaging statements about Jewish cowardice. Damon Runyon argued, in an included article, that the belief that Jews were different or inferior had been clearly disproved, "for the American sons of Israel are writing their names in imperishable letters of fire across the skies of glory along with the Americans of every other religious faith and racial origin. The Jewish boys in this war are no more heroic than anybody else, but surely they are not any less."[21] Indeed, *In the Nation's Service* painted a picture of a numerical overrepresentation of Jewish Americans proudly joining the fight, and the antisemitism of the past melting away. However, the very fact that the JWB published the piece one year into the war demonstrated their belief in the necessity of disproving criticisms of Jewish cowardice. The urgency with which the organization published *In the Nation's Service* is highly reminiscent of the American Jewish Committee's "First Report of the Office of War Records" which was rushed to publication at the close of the First World War, before all information could even be gathered.

The publications of Jewish fraternities reacted similarly (as organizations particularly affected by the sudden absence of young Jewish men): they constantly engaged in a one-way argument with invisible accusations of Jewish evasion. The Jewish fraternity Pi Tau Pi, for example, continued publishing their periodical, the *Pitaupian*, throughout the war. The pages of the wartime publication are scattered with commentary on Jewish bravery and heroism on the front, letters from soldiers, and assurances back to Jewish servicemen receiving the *Pitaupian* that every Pi Tau Pi brother is constantly working to be "an alert true American citizen at home."[22] Some articles or letters in the *Pitaupian* delicately finessed the issue of Jewish fragility or lack of enthusiasm for the war. Every May during the war, pages entirely devoted to the fraternity's Mother's Day celebrations appeared, with statements for, by, and about the mothers of fraternity brothers and servicemen. Jewish mothers wrote in, assuring Jewish boys that to show sentiment during times of war does not make them "sissies." One mother wrote that "the greatest men, the men who best serve mankind are men of sentiment." She continued that although those men fighting in the war should be praised, "other, less spectacular deeds deserve praise too . . . let each Jew be a man of absolute integrity."[23] These clues to fraternity brothers' relationships with their Jewish mothers ran contrary to larger American wartime fears that American men would become feminized through momism. They demonstrate that Jewish boys, at least those who put such letters from their mothers in the pages of the *Pitaupian*, remained unafraid that their male identity was being undermined by the influence of a loving and concerned mothering figure.

Contrary reactions also line the pages, as the fraternity urged men to action. Rabbi and National Chaplain of Pi Tau Pi Dr. Phillip David Bookstaber berated complacent Jews for not being involved in the fight, for assuming that they would continue "business as usual" during the war. "Any Jewish group today that desists from cooperating with any part of the world struggle commits itself to serious and deserved criticism."[24] Those who vocalized accusations of antisemitism within the military were (even in publications cheering the heroism of Jewish soldiers) met with recriminations about oversensitivity, understandable though it may be, given the situation of world Jewry. Even the Army and Navy Public Relations Committee of the National Jewish Welfare Board uses familiar language about Jewish boys, many of whom "enter upon their new associations in the armed forces timidly, some even fearfully." Complaints of antisemitism in the ranks were often, though not always, the result of "oversensitivity" on the part of Jewish boys, as "it can be said unequivocally that the position of the Jew in the army is better than that of the Jew in civilian life."[25]

Among those who did fight, Jewish soldiers appeared in every theater of the war, mostly serving alongside their fellow Americans with no complaints about antisemitism within the ranks. Accounts show that Jewish soldiers felt that the degree of antisemitism in the military mirrored that of American society at large, meaning a smattering of comments and minor discriminations, but nothing more threatening. Others, however, came back determined to prove themselves as men, having heard soldiers, even high-ranking ones, jeering about Jewish cowardice and determination not to fight. This seems to be a particularly sensitive issue among soldiers who participated in the liberation of Nazi concentration and death camps, an experience that will be discussed at length in the following pages. This may have contributed to what one journalist referred to as a whispering campaign intent on promoting the idea that Jews were evading service, despite their numerically high participation in the war outstripping their population in the country.[26] Rumors of draft dodging were common and are evident in the wartime correspondence of the National Jewish Welfare Board's Bureau of War Records, which show complaints by local Jews from all over the country that Jews evaded the draft with the help of the Jewish community. In one letter to Samuel Leff, a field secretary for the JWB, a colleague informed him of a Polish demonstration in New York in front of the Selective Service Board. This particular accusation involved a Jewish doctor giving Jewish boys "some kind of injection affecting their hearts, for draft evasion purposes."[27] These complaints spurred studies by local Jewish community leadership, collecting and compiling all available data on Jewish boys in the service. The earliest example of these studies was in Trenton, New Jersey, conducted by a Dr. Louis Dublin in response to accusations of draft evasion by the non-Jewish community. This was a great effort, including records from draft boards, but also a citywide house-to-house canvass, conducted largely by the War Records Committee of the Jewish Federation of Trenton.[28]

Although some Jewish soldiers found it difficult to dispel stereotypes about themselves, others changed their comrades' views by engaging in the most masculine of activities, like fighting other soldiers in their platoons. Corporal Morris Eisenstein, after a supply sergeant harassed him for being Jewish, attacked the sergeant and "kicked the daylights out of him." "After that," Eisenstein explains, "all of a sudden, everybody was my buddy."[29] Such brawls and conflicts brought on by prejudice and resentment were common in the American military during World War II. Petty harassment of the seemingly or assumed "weak" was abhorred by many soldiers, Jewish and gentile alike, and was known within the military as "chickenshit," bothersome behavior that had nothing to do with winning the war or succeeding in battles. Fighting against this behavior was a means of building respect and camaraderie among the troops. Tension, and even fighting between Jews and antisemitic soldiers broke out on the European front. Reaching the limit of his tolerance for antisemitic slander, Paul Steinfeld fought a fellow soldier in a foxhole, yelling for him to "go over and join Hitler's Army."[30] The lack of understanding that the offending soldier registered was not unusual among non-Jewish soldiers. Throughout correspondence from the front, Lee Kennett explains, one group that remained consistently politically and morally aware and committed to the opposition of fascism and Nazism were the Jewish soldiers.[31]

One might assume that although antisemitism was present on the European front, on naval ships in the Pacific, and in training camps in the United States, once soldiers had entered the fight (especially those who were tasked with liberating Nazi concentration camps), they might have been more sympathetic to their Jewish comrades. This was not, however, always the case. Instances of antisemitic action were not as rare among camp liberators as one might expect, given their experiences. Emotions ran high after observing the horrors of Nazi brutality firsthand. Bearing witness to the terrors of the camps affected soldiers in varying ways. Some found themselves frightened by their own racial prejudice, which they reconsidered after their experiences on the front, and resolved to leave with a new respect for all men, regardless of race, religion, or background. Their individual reactions aside, the experience of liberating the Nazi concentration and death camps changed those who participated. The wide range of actions taken by soldiers immediately following liberation attests to the complexity of the experience. A small percentage of those American soldiers liberating the camps were Jewish, reflecting their overall percentages in the military. These Jewish soldiers faced an odd mirror when they liberated surviving Jews from the concentration camps in Nazi-occupied Europe. Jewish American soldiers recognized that their connection to the Jewish victims was more than a common humanity; they were part of the same international religious and cultural community. They had a particularly complex reaction to the victims that greeted them in the camps, as their feeling of pity and disgust were tinged with recognition and commonality.

It seems counterintuitive to imagine that the soldiers liberating the camps continued to be (or even became) antisemitic, considering their own experiences, both with Jewish soldiers and in light of Nazi atrocities. Although most soldiers did not engage in such activity, the psychological distress of liberating the German concentration camps prompted a number of antisemitic actions against Jews by American soldiers. Some of these soldiers targeted their fellow Jewish American comrades, and some even took action against Jewish camp survivors. In 1945, after liberating Buchenwald Concentration Camp, Private Howard Cwick, a Jewish soldier in the Unites States military, nearly killed a fellow US soldier for antisemitism. Cwick walked in on a Sergeant Cooley, tormenting a group of liberated Jews. He was force-feeding one man and shouting them all down with insults and slurs. "It horrified me," Cwick explained, "This was a man, a Jew, from a camp. And Cooley, the antisemite, was doing this to him." Cwick entered, drew his gun, brought back the hammer, and threatened the sergeant's life. He warned Cooley, "If I ever see you treat another Jew like this again, I'll kill you." The sergeant left in shock. Although Cwick did not shoot the man, he never knew, thinking back, what he would have done had Cooley fought back.[32] The interaction between Sergeant Cooley and Private Cwick is one particularly ugly manifestation of antisemitism during liberation, directed at the recently liberated. Similar surges of violence cropped up directed not only at the liberated victims of Nazi brutality but at local townsfolk in occupied Europe and fellow soldiers of Jewish descent. In some cases, American soldiers took out their aggression on local women, through forcible rape and abuse.[33] Of course, this is only one form of response to the events they witnessed, but it is one deserving of more scholarly attention than it has received.

Perhaps the most surprising antisemitic statements made after liberation were indeed those made against comrades in arms. Harry Zaslow, a Jewish soldier from Philadelphia, experienced instances of antisemitism directly following and even during his platoon's liberation of Dachau. The military frequently granted looting rights to American soldiers in German territory, officially and unofficially. When Zaslow's platoon approached the camp (not having a clue what they would find there), they were giddy to open the trains halted outside of the camp, sure that they would be full of Nazi loot. When they opened them, however, they were full of piled corpses. Upon opening the boxcars, a comrade told him, "Zaslow, if you're not careful, you're gonna be in that boxcar." Recalling this statement, Zaslow explained, "He meant that because I was Jewish . . . that I *should* have been in that boxcar." He explained that some of his fellow soldiers were so entrenched in antisemitism that even seeing the camps and all the suffering inside did not change their views.[34] Tensions among liberators continued as soldiers became restless with their duties in helping the displaced persons and clearing out the camps. Shortly after the liberation, Harry Zaslow was performing watch duty at night in a prison tower. Carved into the wooden railing were the words, "Zaslow is a dirty Jew." Within days of arriving, and certainly during the process of liberation and rescue, at least one of his comrades expressed his own antisemitism at Dachau. Recalling this incident, Zaslow said, "Here I am standing in this tower isolated all by myself with my own thoughts. Here's what I felt . . . this is a tragedy. I mean, we fought the Germans to liberate the country and the Jewish people who were in the camps, and the Germans were our enemies. And now, a few American soldiers are my enemies as well."[35]

Outbreaks of antisemitism within the military continued even after soldiers had returned home to the United States. Some remained bitter at the Jewish people for what they themselves went through in the process of liberation. Upon his return to the States, Harold Baldwin, a non-Jewish Dachau liberator from Brooklyn, was shocked at such attitudes when speaking with fellow soldiers from his own platoon shortly after the end of the war. Catching up with an army buddy, Baldwin explained, "he said one thing about this war I don't like, he said, 'we should have killed all the bastards, the Jewish people.'"[36] When asked about personal experiences with antisemitism in the American military, nearly all World

War II veteran interviewees responded with firsthand knowledge and experience of antisemitic actions by individuals or institutions within the American armed forces. At the same time, several recall their experiences in the war as eye-opening to the importance of and need for tolerance of ethnic and religious diversity. From this range of experiences, it is clear that service in the Second World War did, in fact, mark a pivotal time in the perception of ethnic and racial diversity among those who served. Liberating the camps did not unify all participating soldiers against hate and discrimination. For some, it even solidified negative perceptions of Jews as weak and helpless and provided them an opportunity to vent their anger on Jewish soldiers and survivors.

However, the majority of soldiers in the liberating units did not turn on their Jewish comrades, or on the inmates of the camps, but they did express their anger in other brutal ways. Americans took some of the SS as prisoners, as protocol dictated, and some shot them on the spot. When asked what happened to SS prisoners captured by American liberators, a veteran answered, "It's a black mark upon the United States Army, what we did. We shot them. I had a complete hatred for them. I shot them. I was part of that. In fact, I looked at 'em and I spit at 'em."[37] Some non-Jewish soldiers even urged the killing and interrogation of captured SS by Jewish soldiers. One veteran recalled, "We had the Jewish boys do the interrogation. . . . Scared the daylights out of our prisoners. They had a Jewish fellow that was interrogating them, and the Jewish fellow had the upper hand. Oh, that guy had a lot of fun. He enjoyed it. We enjoyed it too."[38]

Too Young to Fight: Big Boys at War and Little Boys at Home

Those too young to fight overseas weighed varying ideals of Jewish masculinity and militarism presented by the adult Jewish community. For Jewish youth, just as for Jewish adults, the events of World War II and the Holocaust had deep and complex emotional effects. This generation, however, came of age at a time when Jews fought for their very survival, and inevitably encountered (if they did not know personally) several American Jews in uniform. If the estimated 50 percent of Jewish men between ages eighteen and forty-four were enlisted, most American Jews had close ties to someone serving in the armed forces. Participation in Jewish youth organizations in the United States intensified during this period, and several groups came together in the shadow of the conflict abroad. The National Federation of Temple Youth (NFTY) organized and held its first convention in 1939 and addressed the international state of the Jewish people. Though at its inception it primarily reached out to college-aged students, in the era immediately after the war, the target age dropped from college to high school.

The Jewish youths in NFTY were motivated and invested in the war effort, but discussions among adult religious leadership reflected more traditional Jewish ideals and defended Jews investing in scholarship and prayer rather than brute strength. As with these Jewish youth groups, adult mentorship came from both the secular and religious community and reflected the conflicting views of those groups with regard to Jewish enlistment. Addressing the full assembly at the first ever NFTY conference in 1939, Rabbi David Polish, in the last speech of the convention, addressed the temptation of Jewish boys to join the fight. He acknowledged that they "cried out in rage against the seemingly servile and craven resort to mere spiritual defense when fire and sword would have conveyed a more coherent message to the enemy." But his sermon still supported the claim that the Jewish people, by their very nature, were not fighters, and that they could not and should not attempt to become so. He explained:

> Each people possesses its own particular strength. It can successfully contend against adversity only with that strength. Resort to any other is like attempting to pass a counterfeit coin. Some people thrive on their military might, others on their fleets, others on their colonies. But our strength lies in the inner sanctuary, the Torah. Do not laugh it off! Perhaps most comparable to this paradox of triumphant weakness is that weazened [sic], puny giant of India, Mahatma Gandhi. In his fasts, his penances, his prayers, lies his empire defying might. If one man by faith alone can withstand a world, what hidden powers yet await a whole people whose might lies hidden in its Torah.[39]

Youth leadership at the same conference voiced their concern for Jews abroad, and their desire to become a stronger, more virile people. They saw Jewish torment abroad and weakness at home. The youth may not have "laughed off" the argument that their true strength lay in the Torah (as Rabbi Polish had said), but their pride was in those Jews residing in Palestine who were actively fighting. One youth leader claimed that Palestine was "the only country on the face of the earth in which the Jew does not run away, nor hide, nor meekly bend his back to receive another blow, nor stand hopeless, helpless, spat upon. There he fights back! There he defends his home, his hearth, his life!"[40] It is particularly interesting, at this gathering of young American Jews, that America is not considered a country in which no Jew stands helpless. Again, even the young Jews at this conference did not deny antisemitic notions of Jewish meekness; they accepted the criticism's basis in reality and argued for change. Throughout the war, in the speeches and op-ed pieces in NFTY publications, there is a mix of pride in Palestinian Jewishness and bitterness at the docility of Jewish life in the United States. One particularly frustrated young man railed against the inaction of American Jewish boys to take part in the manlier practices of American life: sports, fighting, and military endeavors. He argued that Jewish boys did not take part because they were merely "tolerated" in American society, therefore making waves would immediately elicit accusations of communism or of un-Americanism, so they remained quiet out of fear of reprisal. Again, the Yishuv, not American Jewish men, provides the example of manliness for American Jewish youth embittered by their own perceived weakness.[41]

The idolizing of the Palestinian Jew and Jewish soldier as aspirational Jewish manhood for American Jewish boys was at its strongest at the close of the war, not because of their accomplishments on the frontier of the desert, but in contrast to new images emerging from Europe. Images of devastated, starved, beaten, downtrodden, and murdered Jews would soon flood the airwaves and newspapers of the industrialized world and provide one of the greatest impediments with which Jewish men have ever had to contend.

7
The Noble Perished and Ignoble Survivors

The Holocaust and Jewish Manhood

> The imagination of the six million who went to their death, more or less with the cooperation of other Europeans, was simple and naïve . . . few of those millions could have imagined that [the world], instead of feeling shame . . . would set him, the murdered Jew, on the witness stand and cry accusingly, "Coward! Why didn't you defend yourself?" How much more inconceivable is it that any of those six million could imagine such an accusation or question from the lips of Jews.
>
> —K. Shabbetai[1]

Starting in 1933, and for the duration of the war, Nazi oppression and murder of Jewish Europeans aroused horror and sympathy in the United States, but the traumatic victimization of Jews also altered the international perception of the Jewish people and increased the desire for a revival of Jewish strength. At the close of the European theater of war, the dominant images of Jews changed, very suddenly, over the course of a three-week period. This dramatic transformation came in the form of photographs and news of Jewish victims and survivors pouring out of Europe and dominating the American press after the liberation of Nazi camps by American GIs. A new and pervasive image of Jews emerged: the camp survivor or living skeleton, personifying victimhood, became a new archetype of the Jewish image. This chapter examines the effect of that archetype, and the liberation of Nazi concentration and death camps, on the Jewish American self-image through the accounts of Jewish leadership, youth groups, and soldiers.

Images of Jews emerging from Europe during and after the war quickly overshadowed the progress that Jewish men in the American armed forces had made to overcome the image of Jewish male softness. The Nazi assault on Jewish life, which began before the wholesale murder of European Jewry, continued throughout the war and had a significant impact on the ways Jews were viewed by others and by themselves. Discriminatory German policies stifled and dictated Jewish life in Germany, and then in Nazi-occupied Europe, several of which focused on the destruction of group cohesion. In practice, these biased policies were highly gendered. To simply state that Jews seemed emasculated as victims of Nazi persecution fails to identify how directly this persecution attacked Jewish masculinity.

Gendered Persecution

Nazis instituted an intentional process of emasculating Jews with discriminatory policies, which affected European Jews directly and global Jewry indirectly. The early stages of persecution under the Third Reich discriminated against all Jews, certainly, but Jewish men were particularly targeted. And though Nazi policies had no direct influence on the lives of American Jewish men, the changes to the international perception of Jews that the Holocaust created affected American Jews during and after the war. The Nuremberg Laws, in their original form in September 1935, laid out two discriminatory policies: the Reich Citizenship Law and the Law for the Protection of German Blood and German Honour. The former stated that only those of German or related blood remained eligible to be Reich citizens; all "alien" races became subjects without citizenship rights. The following month, a supplementary statement defined who the government identified as Jewish, and its release coincided with the Reich Citizenship Law coming into practice. The Law for the Protection of German Blood and German Honour prohibited marriages and sexual intercourse between Jews and Germans. It also forbade Jews from employing German women under the age of forty-five to work in their homes, or in homes that boarded even a single Jewish man.

The Nazi government, by subjugating and excommunicating Jews from the public sphere, forced the Jewish communities of Europe into a sort of *social death* before ever forcing them into concentration or death camps. In her 1998 book *Between Dignity and Despair*, Marion Kaplan argues, very convincingly, that the destruction of Jews' social lives was a prerequisite for the coming genocide. She also argued that the destruction of social cohesion is best evaluated by examining the lives of women. In doing so, however, she lays the framework to examine Jewish men in the process of German persecution. The ways in which women suffer differently from men, which Kaplan analyzes so well, also highlight the very particular way that men suffered, for having been born Jewish and male, through policies that specifically targeted their manhood. The Reich Citizenship Law attempted precisely that. By taking away their citizenship and civil rights, the government disenfranchised Jews politically, socially, and commercially, forcing them into a perpetual state of dishonor. Jews found themselves barred from elements of German society that they had enjoyed since their emancipation in the late nineteenth century. In September 1942, they were forced to endure a return of medieval sumptuary laws requiring them to identify themselves with a Star of David. According to Joseph Goebbels, chief propagandist for the Nazi Party, Germans in Berlin initially responded with horror at the treatment of Jews, so much so that many banded together and protested with their Jewish neighbors against the new laws, sharing their own rations with deprived Jews, and trying to protect them. "Suddenly," Goebbels explained, "all the Jews in Berlin are nothing but quaint little babies, moving by their helplessness, or frail old women."[2] In this statement, Goebbels lamented the affection that German citizens had for some of their Jewish neighbors, but though frustrated, he also highlighted the lack of agency Jews felt, and the infantilizing (or emasculating) nature of their new position, requiring the charity and protection of their German friends and neighbors.

In response to violations of the second of these laws, the Law for the Protection of German Blood and German Honour, the Nazi government dealt with Jewish men more harshly than women. When the law was first put into effect, women were not subject to prosecution for the violation of racial purity laws at all. The Nazi government assumed that men comprised the responsible parties in sexual relationships, and women existed merely as objects of men's desires. Hitler's own writing and the larger Nazi propaganda machine portrayed Jews as rapists of Christian women. The sexual nature of this act did not make Jewish men more masculine in the view of Nazi antisemites, but more animal. The idea that a Jewish man could become so dehumanized and dangerous that he needed to be fixed by physical removal of male organs implies that the exclusion of Jews from Christian society could result not only in their emasculation and comparison to women, but in their exclusion from manhood altogether.[3] Although eventually Nazis also prosecuted Jewish women for race mixing, the initial punishment was specific to Jewish men, to eradicate their more primal, masculine desires. This view of male responsibility was a close reflection of Hitler's personal views on the issue. He had, in the initial years of the law, intervened in individual cases to ensure that women would not receive criminal sentences for a male crime.[4] Marked as such, it was an attack on Jewish men and their ability to engage women with the same freedom that was granted to German citizens. Even in those marriages that predated the Nuremberg Laws, intermarried couples with a Jewish woman and Aryan man were not as harshly condemned as those with a Jewish man and Aryan woman.

According to Maddy Carey's 2017 book, *Jewish Masculinity in the Holocaust: Between Destruction and Construction*, the Nazi genocide against European Jewish men attacked their masculinity twice over: Nazis emasculated Jews as victims and then feminized them as passive in their own destruction. The first expands on Kaplan's work concerning Jewish women, the latter will be discussed in more detail in the following section on Jewish American reactions to the Holocaust. The Jewish position leading up to and during the Second World War, according to Carey, eliminated Jews' *ability* to be masculine in the ways that normative society dictated they must. A Jewish man would have previously been able to meet some European qualifications for manhood: he was able to work and provide for his family, protect his loved ones, and hold a position of respect in the community. The Nazi assault on Jewish businesses and exclusion from professions left Jewish men unable to provide for their families and maintain their livelihoods. It affected the roles of women as well, as when the Nazi machine destroyed a Jewish man's career, their wives, mothers, and daughters had to carry the financial burden and the task of maintaining family cohesion. The attack on Jewish professions and incomes also left Jewish men largely unable to protect their families and loved ones from harm, deportation, forced labor, and public assault/humiliation. Those who could protect their loved ones from such assaults did so by use of bribery, an option that was not available to those already stripped of their professions and ability to work.

The last element, in Carey's estimation, concerned the social standing of a Jewish man within his community. Eliminating Jewish access to the public sphere (the social death about which Marion Kaplan wrote) inhibited their standing, a condition further exacerbated by the public humiliations that Jewish men were forced to endure (such as the cutting of Jewish men's beards, removal of their hats, and forced deference to German officers). This is the state in which the Jews of Germany and occupied territories found themselves in the years leading up to the mass killings and physical genocide: robbed of their social standing as men, denied the right to fraternize with the women of their choice, and minimizing their ability to provide for their loved ones.

The rounding up, sorting, and killing of Jews that followed this social discrimination was also largely dictated by age and gender. In keeping with fears of racial mixing and the dilution of German bloodlines, Nazis viewed Jewish women (the bearers of Jewish children) as enemies in the Nazi war for long-term racial domination, but they saw Jewish men as an immediate threat. They attacked Jewish men, therefore, in very different ways, the results of which were devastating for Jews of both sexes. The targeted attacks on Jewish men fit Mary Anne Warren's definition of *gendercide* as a sex-neutral term (in this case applied to the Jewish male population) for the deliberate destruction of a group based on their particular sex. Once the murders began, Nazi forces killed young and able Jewish men first, as the first stage of a genocide they would escalate to include women, children, the elderly, and the infirm. Though Nazi death programs had largely begun with the infirm as part of their "euthanasia" program, this was not targeting Jews, but *all* German citizens they deemed as "unworthy of life."

The *Einsatzgruppen* (Nazi killing squads) initially selected only Jewish men for the earliest killings, maintaining the traditional taboo around killing women and children, which they did not routinely break until 1941. It is clear based on firsthand accounts by the killers themselves that the male victims were less traumatic to kill; they were more of a perceived threat to the nation, and therefore the killings were more justifiable.[5] The early orders to begin the mass killings with only male victims helped to acclimate the shooters to murder, without the trauma of killing women and children, possibly violating their sense of chivalry. The mass murder of men *was* traumatic to the killers, but by the time the killings began, the process of emasculating Jewish men and stripping them of their dignity was well underway, easing this process for German soldiers recruited for the job.

American Jewish Reactions

The Nazi policies and procedures that emasculated European Jews had a highly damaging effect on the global perception of the Jewish people: that their apparent passivity had aided their own destruction. American Jews acknowledged this process, even as it was occurring, and were concerned about its influence on outsider opinions about them, as well as their own self-image as Jews. Of course, American Jewish reactions to Nazi persecution of their European brethren were not monolithic. Although Jewish leaders in the United States were sympathetic to the plight of European Jews, and called for assistance and philanthropy, even some of the most concerned Jewish leaders supported President Roosevelt's noninterventionist stance.[6] Early in Hitler's rule, Jewish leadership (both in and outside of Germany) worried that Jewish intervention from abroad would solidify in the minds of the German people that Jews were themselves a foreign element and make the situation for German Jews even worse.[7]

American Jewry long held themselves apart from other Jews of the diaspora. To their minds, they were able to access more equality and opportunity for acculturation than any other diaspora community. Still, some worried that if Germany successfully suppressed its Jewish population, there would be a detrimental influence on public opinion of Jews in the United States, adversely affecting their position. New York City served as the hub for Jewish American discussion and reaction to the events abroad, comprising hundreds of Jewish organizations with various goals, strategies, affiliations, and viewpoints. Many Jewish religious groups mobilized to send aid in the years leading up to the Holocaust, some Orthodox rabbis even driving around wealthy Jewish neighborhoods on the Sabbath to solicit funds to aid Jews in Europe.[8] Many organized to lobby the American government to act, including the Rabbis' March on Washington (October 6, 1943), in which over four hundred Orthodox rabbis marched on the capitol.

Many other Zionist and Jewish communal organizations also mobilized for aid, some of them directly involved with Jewish communities in Europe, such as the Joint Distribution Committee, American Jewish Committee, various *landsmanschaftn* (mutual benefit societies built around the town of origin for community organizing within a regional group of Jewish immigrants), and several Jewish labor organizations. Determination to help, however, did not nullify the influence that images of despicable Jews emerging from Germany (and German occupied territory) presented. Even among those who mobilized support, some American Jewish leaders still derided those Jews suffering under German oppression. Blaming the victim might be too harsh an assertion, but it is accurate to say that some leaders criticized and lamented the passivity of European Jews in the face of their own destruction, even though those same leaders mobilized to send aid. It was not a universal attitude, but this judgment on the part of some Jewish leadership does show the influence that the treatment of German Jewry had on American Jewish men's sense of masculinity and strength.

Before the scope of oppression and murder became clear to Jewish leadership in the United States, Rabbi Stephen Wise, one of the most influential American Jewish leaders of his time, used the passivity of the German Jewry, and their failure to protect themselves, as a negative example for American Jews. He sympathized with the deteriorating situation of the Jews in Nazi Germany and called repeatedly for support, migration assistance, boycotts, and other measures to help and protect European Jewry as the Nazi threat loomed ever larger. However, he presented a clear difference between the type of Jews that remained in Europe and the distinctly American Jews that he was leading and helping to mold.

In 1938, still unaware of the extent of the atrocities in Europe, Wise criticized the impulse on the part of some American Jews to adopt a strategy of identifying themselves as Americans who *happened* to be Jewish but were Americans foremost. This emphasized their nationalism and patriotism and minimized their outsider status. Wise distinguished between proud American Jews like himself and the "tragic cowardice" of the Jews of Germany who had defended themselves against antisemitic accusations by claiming, "We are not Jews; we are German citizens of the Jewish faith" (referring here, presumably, to the *Centralverein*, the liberal political organization of "German citizens of the Jewish faith," to counter antisemitic propaganda).[9] He proclaimed his own identity as an American Jew (*not* an American who happened to be a Jew). There were some American Jews who expressed outrage at his proclamation and critique, but Wise considered it "one of the chiefest distinctions of my life" to have earned the resentment and enmity of those fellow Jews who disliked him for the fact that he consistently "insisted upon the end of a policy of evasion and timidity on the part of the Jews."[10] "Let us have an end," he said, "of the cowardice of Jews who speak of themselves as Americans who are Jews." Rabbi Wise was lauded for his strength and courage, often in the manliest imaginable language. In 1932, a Boston newspaper referred to Wise as "one of the most courageous men of our times," one who "appeals to men as a 'two-fisted, red-blooded fighter who asks for no quarter and gives none in his battle for his ideals.'"[11]

Wise condemned the Nazi explanation for their defeat of Jews, that they were simply *minderwertig* (inferior), but he submitted that the "pitiably timorous" Jews of Germany allowed themselves to be "broken and oppressed." In doing so, he attributed their emasculation and passivity as their undoing. "It was unwise and fatal," he said in a radio broadcast, for Jews to leave unanswered the charges leveled against them by Hitler and his party.[12] To the question of how Hitler's persecution of Jews should be met, Wise answered in the most chivalrous language, "We who are Jews are resolved to meet it as men, to dare do all that doth become men, to defend ourselves in every honorable, peaceable and just way. Better that Jews nobly perish than ignobly survive."[13]

Naturally, Wise represented only one man's attitude of Jewish American leadership, but it is one that reflected the American Jewish sense of distinctiveness in the world of diaspora Jewry. It is also not one that could be lost among the varied reactions of America's Jews, as Rabbi Wise was such a dominating figure of the time in American Jewish life. He was not only the founding president of the World Jewish Congress, but he also founded the Jewish Institute of Religion (later merged with Hebrew Union College), served as president of the Zionist Organization of America, was a close friend and advisor to President Franklin D. Roosevelt, served as a New York delegate to the 1924 Democratic National Convention, acted as president for the American Jewish Congress, and served as co-chair of the American Zionist Emergency Council during the war.

Figure 17. Rabbi Stephen Wise at a World War 1 Liberty Bond rally in front of Federal Hall, Wall Street, New York City, 1918. Bain News Service, publisher. Courtesy of Flickr Commons project, 2016.

Indeed, when the World Jewish Congress in Geneva sent reports of the German plan for the Final Solution to the United States, representative Dr. Gerhart Riegner requested that they be sent to the American and Allied governments, and to Rabbi Stephen Wise in New York City. Once Jewish leaders were aware of and speaking out about the atrocities in Germany, Rabbi Wise called together a group of seven Jewish organizations united to form the Joint Emergency Committee on European Jewish Affairs to organize a Jewish relief response (the groups included were the American Jewish Committee, American Jewish Congress, Jewish Labor Committee, B'nai B'rith, Word Jewish Congress, Synagogue Council of America, and Agudath Israel of America). Even once the Emergency Committee was formed, Rabbi Wise remained tempered in his calls for American action to aid European Jews. The most outspoken opponents of Rabbi Wise and the Emergency Committee's lack of action were not, primarily, American Jews, but Revisionist Zionists from Palestine (to whom the committee had refused entry to participate). The Revisionist critics of this tempered response remained separate, working to rally a more aggressive response, to which we will return in the following chapter on Palestinian Jews and the American imagination.

The Walking Dead

After Wise's press conference on November 24, 1942, announcing that Nazi Germany was implementing a policy to annihilate the Jews of Europe, the American public was at last aware of the Final Solution and the goal to exterminate the Jews of Europe.[14] Americans knew the goal was present but had no way of understanding the extent to which it had been carried out, in spite of the fact that even the earliest reports leading to this announcement estimated that two million Jews had already been murdered. Sporadic reports emerged from Europe of unimaginable horrors, occasional occurrences of defiance, and death immeasurable. Jewish American reactions to events in Europe were as diverse as the Jewish communities themselves. Within New York City alone, hundreds of Jewish groups (religious, political, social, and such) organized and reacted, reaching out to government officials in Washington, holding rallies and marches in New York City, publishing papers for Jewish and non-Jewish audiences, and disseminating information about Jewish events abroad.[15]

As Allied troops liberated concentration and death camps, the picture of European Jewry abroad was quickly dominated by the unimaginably vast destruction the Nazis delivered to the Jewish people, and by the visages of the skeletal camp survivors. The helplessness (real or perceived) of the Jews of Europe supported some of the most pervasive antisemitic assumptions about Jewish weakness. This was true not only for antisemites, but among Palestinian Jews and American Jewish communities as well. In his 1963 book, *As Sheep to the Slaughter? The Myth of Jewish Cowardice*, K. Shabbetai recounted the Jews who themselves concluded that the slaughter of European Jewry was due to the cowardice of diaspora Jews. This included Israeli children, the Israeli attorney general, American Jewish Psychologist Bruno Bettelheim, Raul Hilberg, and various others.[16] That the Jewish dead were victims of atrocity was not denied, but the view that they went without a fight, or that they had no fight in them to begin with, supported negative preconceptions about the Jewish people. As did arguments made by American Jews that by embracing masculine American ideals of virile tenacity, they were cut of a different cloth than those allowing their own destructing. The process of camp liberation and the resulting media coverage became disastrous for the image of strength that American Jewish men were fighting to construct.

The prime goal of winning the war was what guided the progress of Allied troops through Europe, liberating concentration and death camps was merely a by-product of their presence, not a planned rescue mission. As such, liberating the camps did not constitute a turning point in the war so much as an inevitable task of the war's end. However, the photographs and films of camp liberations did mark a turning point in the world's awareness of the atrocities that had taken place during the war. These are the images that haunt the mind when imagining and remembering the Holocaust. That soldiers arrived with both still and motion cameras, and were allowed and encouraged to share them with the public, has made these scenes some of the most recognizable imagery of the Holocaust and possibly of the war.[17] The American armed forces not only encouraged, but sometimes even ordered soldiers to take pictures of the most gruesome sights, particularly of suffering camp prisoners, to document and publicize Nazi cruelty.

This became the first well-documented genocide, helped by vastly improved photographic technology. The standards for publicized images

Figure 18. Portrait of Buchenwald liberator and Army photographer Herbert Gorfinkle, with camera, 1945. Image from Private First Class Herbert Gorfinkle "GOTE: Goofing Off through Europe" Scrapbook, c. 1940s; Herbert Gorfinkle Papers, P-904, box 1, folder 18, page 15, Wyner Family Jewish Heritage Center at NEHGS, Boston, Massachusetts.

showing the realities of war (which had been set by previous wars) was shattered because of the graphic nature of what troops found in German territories. Although photographic technology dated back to the American Civil War, by this war it was more advanced, more portable, and more accessible than in previous conflicts. By 1942, the United States military attached a photographic team to nearly every fighting unit, adding to the personal cameras that soldiers brought with them. In addition to the availability of equipment, the United States had a vested interest in showing the world the cruelties of totalitarianism as tensions rose with the fear surrounding the spread of Soviet communism.

American soldiers and journalists in Europe released shocking and haunting photographs, and the extent of their effect was incalculable. The American press did not, for the most part, release photographs of Nazi atrocities against Jews in Europe until the end of the war in 1945. At that time, General Eisenhower mandated that the visual records of camp liberations (still and moving pictures) be distributed over a three-week

Figure 19. Portrait of Buchenwald liberator and Army photographer Herbert Gorfinkle in his trailer darkroom in the European theater, 1945. Image from Private First Class Herbert Gorfinkle "GOTE: Goofing Off through Europe" Scrapbook, c. 1940s; Herbert Gorfinkle Papers, P-904, box 1, folder 18, page 29, Wyner Family Jewish Heritage Center at NEHGS, Boston, Massachusetts.

period in the spring of 1945 to help persuade civilians that descriptions of the atrocities were accurate. Photographs flowed so quickly (and in such quantities) out of the camps and into British and American presses that the media struggled to determine how many images they should print, and how graphic those images should be. The image of atrocity became an essential aspect of liberation. These photographs served as evidence to convince a public who could not imagine what soldiers were seeing as they combed across the German-held territories. At that time, it was still a commonly held belief that photographs contained an undeniable degree of accuracy and truth (a belief that is now completely absent thanks to the digital manipulation of both still and moving images), and were particularly important to the collective understanding of Nazi atrocities. Therefore, the collection of photos bearing witness to atrocities was a mark of verisimilitude.[18] Images of bodies stacked like corded wood, and piles of corpses so large they necessitated a bulldozer to move them into mass graves, accompanied news of camp liberation to audiences at home. These masses of bodies made the magnitude of the Nazi death machine a reality for American viewers. This was one of Eisenhower's goals in demanding a mass witnessing of the camps: to visualize the unimaginable scope of the killings.

Though the release of these photographs made the reality of the killings more real for audiences reading American newspapers, the identity of the victims was less clear. Presses publishing the photographs of mass graves did not identify the masses as Jewish, as they were not, in fact, all Jews. News outlets largely mentioned the victim groups all together, with Jews included, but making no mention of the specific targeting of Jews among these persecuted groups. Though some scholars have criticized this omission as a willful blindness to the reality of the Jewish Holocaust, historian Peter Novick rightly points out that those liberated from camps were *not* in fact primarily Jews. There were Jews among the liberated, but the death camps devoted to the methodical murder of Jews were largely destroyed and abandoned in the German retreat from Allied forces. It was in the years *after* the war that Jewish Americans began to see all survivors as Jewish, in photos and otherwise. Following the liberation and the knowledge of the scope of Jewish tragedy, all images of mass graves, displaced persons (DPs), and murder victims became associated with Jews, regardless of the actual identity of those individuals photographed. Within the liberation photographs, for example, some survivors are clearly Jewish, like those conducting Jewish services, but at least a few of them are merely presumed to be Jewish by those who originally created and captioned the images. This false assumption was certainly not lost on the other victim/survivor groups after the Holocaust, who were not associated with the same suffering as those Jewish survivors, and not included in the postwar settlement at Yalta.

Through the photographs of Nazi atrocities, the image of the survivor (the "walking dead" as some liberators called them) emerged and dominated collective Holocaust memory. The image of skeletal survivors, sores on their bodies and eyes deep-set, was one of a people completely stripped of their dignity. This is not to say that there was no sympathy for the abused masses of survivors, but there was an undeniable repulsion at the sight of them. Once again, the same question is asked of them as of the dead: why did they not fight back, how could they *let* this happen? According to Richard Middleton-Kaplan, the "sheep to the slaughter myth" really took hold at the end of the Holocaust in response to photographs from within the ghettos and liberated camps that made their way to the United States. He particularly recognized the photographs of skeletal corpses and survivors, and the very famous photograph of a young boy in the Warsaw ghetto with his arms raised in surrender, as culprits for the cold response of so many Americans.[19] Representations of Jews as passive in their own destruction did more than elicit disdain, it damaged the perceived manhood of the victims. Of course, it had an effect on the view of Jewish women as well, but passivity was not seen as incongruous with femininity, as it is with masculinity.[20] In addition to the actual photographs of the walking dead, Nazi propaganda films also made their way back to the United States, where they fostered an unfortunately harsh response from the American public. These films often showed fabricated life in ghettos or camps, giving those who viewed clips of them in postwar documentaries no identification of their original source and very unrealistic views of Jews before and during the war.

Liberating forces also sought answers to the question of passivity, and the remaining survivors were the only place to look for answers. Entering the camps and encountering the horrors of the systematic slaughter of Europe's Jews, American soldiers (both Jewish and otherwise) reacted in various ways, though all with shock, revulsion, anger, and disbelief. For some Jewish American soldiers, their heartbreak for their European brethren at times conflicted with their pride in themselves as Jewish American soldiers. One liberator, recalling that he refused to enter the camp himself, explained, "We didn't want our buddies to see how cheap Jewish life is . . . we didn't want to be there when the goyim see it."[21] Reactions were varied, even among Jewish soldiers. Many not only entered the camps, but made it their purpose to stay there as long as possible, initiating what would become American and international relief and relocation efforts for Jewish survivors.[22]

Liberating soldiers were responsible for caring, at least in part, for the survivors they had liberated. Caring for such infirm and mistreated people was not easy on Allied soldiers, who, of course, had no training to do so. In some cases, the American soldiers' sympathy for these beleaguered Jews turned to repulsion, both toward the individual survivors and the group at large. Leon Bass, a liberator from Philadelphia, described how the behavior of the living victims at Buchenwald shocked and sickened him:

> He was skin and bone. And he stopped right there in front of me, he undid what was holding his trousers, he let them fall, he squatted down, and he began to defecate. Right in front of me. And I couldn't believe this. He was so thin it looked like the bones of his buttocks would come through his skin, but I stood there saying no, no, you don't do this in public! Where is your dignity![23]

In cases like Bass, the soldiers' revulsion was visceral but did not lead to disdain of the prisoners themselves. As previously mentioned, the weakness of these Jews not only repulsed them, but even led to antisemitic actions committed by liberators against surviving camp victims.

Although camp prisoners had been "liberated," they were not yet *free* people, a fact that only added to the pitiable nature of the Jewish character in Europe at this time. Survivors were, for all intents and purposes, still prisoners of the concentration and death camps that they had inhabited before their captors abandoned their posts or were caught by American, Soviet, or British troops. Their continued captivity impeded their ability to regain their masculinity, as they had no control over their lives or destinies. Restricted to the camps, they continued to wear their camp uniforms (or the uniforms of their former captors) and subsisted on 2,000 calories a day, 1,250 of which came from rations of black bread.[24] They had no homes to return to, no means to travel, and no way to take care of themselves or any remaining family they may have had. Their status may have changed from *prisoner* to *displaced person*, but they were still unable to leave and had to rely on military personnel to provide them with food, shelter, and information about the outside world. The victorious Allied Powers, along with several American politicians lobbying for the release of displaced people from German camps, discussed the issue of what to do with displaced people. Congressman Melvin Price, for example, pleaded before congress for the American president to release imprisoned Jews from liberated Nazi camps, where they had been held for four months following victory in Europe. Harry Truman, in his public response to the report from Earl G. Harrison on displaced persons, was particularly concerned with descriptions of the conditions for Jewish refugees, "As matters now stand, we appear to be treating the Jews as the Nazis treated them except that we do not exterminate them. They are in concentration camps in large numbers under our military guard instead of SS troops."[25]

In spite of their pitiable and helpless position, Jews were blamed by some soldiers for the trauma that they *themselves* were experiencing, believing that it was because of Jews that America had gone to war, and thus, the reason that soldiers became responsible for the unpleasant task of cleaning up the mess. This view was by no means limited to the American military. Throughout the war, American press outlets determinedly avoided identifying the victims as Jews. Roosevelt, when referring to victims of the Nazi regime called them *unfortunates* but refrained from saying that the majority were Jews. The *New York Times*, in articles about both Dachau and Auschwitz during the liberation, referred to the victims as citizens of various nations, but neither mentioned the word Jew.[26] By 1938 both the press and the Roosevelt administration avoided drawing attention to the Jewishness of the victims. James Carroll has argued that this omission was intended to undercut public knowledge, which might spur indignation about the inaction of the American government in the plight of the Jewish people. But it also reflects the very real resentment harbored toward Jews, once America seemed destined to enter the war, and after the war ended. There was arguably more sympathy for the unidentified masses of "citizens" than there would have been for masses of murdered Jews, as by 1944, 44 percent of Americans believed that Jews were the main cause of the war.[27]

American servicemen on the front were resentful of having to provide for the survivors, and felt, in some cases, that the survivors expected and took too much from the liberating forces. Many soldiers believed that Jews were too destroyed as people to understand how to be civilized again, and in Austria local police were even authorized (by American forces) to shoot uncooperative survivors, since it was all they were capable of understanding. Even beyond soldiers who had personally liberated or visited camps in Europe, many American soldiers stationed in all US occupied territories (Allied or Nazi) felt no love for the Jewish people and blamed them for having to remain on the continent. In the fall of 1945, the American Army took a poll that showed that 51 percent believed that Hitler "did the Reich a lot of good before 1939," 30 percent preferred the Germans to both the French and the English, 24 percent were willing to concede a German right to rule Europe, and 22 percent were satisfied that the Germans had "good reasons" for their persecution of Jews, with another 10 percent undecided.[28] In their helpless and weakened position, displaced persons quickly transformed, in the minds of many, from helpless victims to needy, demanding, homeless masses.

This view of Jewish survivors as pathetic, needy, and passive in their own destruction was a common one, and not one reserved to antisemites. In fact, those who were sympathetic to the plight of European Jews may have been more susceptible to the assumption that the victims were pathetic than those who believed the Jews were truly at fault or undeserving of support. In her work on the advancement of human rights through victim storytelling, Diana Meyers speculates that there are two common "types" of victims: the pathetic and the heroic. According to Meyers, to earn a place as a truly pathetic victim and to avoid the contempt of observers for their own plight, not only must one have endured horrific suffering, but the part they played in that suffering must be beyond reproach.[29] If they are deserving of compassion, then they must be fully innocent and functionally passive (their oppressors must so thoroughly disempower them as to leave no doubt of their innocence; this entails shame and passivity in exchange for blamelessness and sympathy). Agency and victimization, she argues, are therefore incompatible in the minds of many people and the policies of aid organizations.[30] The shift from prisoner to displaced person granted the prisoners a sliver of agency. They were no longer entirely powerless against their fate (at least this is what an outside observer might believe, if only witnessing their plight through American presses, which patriotically heroized the American liberators). This supposed agency helps, in some part, to explain the attitudes of American Jews, like Rabbi Wise, or members of NFTY, who at times harshly criticized the lack of resistance by European Jewry. Because American masculinity is so firmly connected to ideas of self-sufficiency and independence, if Jews were fully deserving of compassion as victims, they could not also be men.

What information American observers received about the liberation (particularly the abundance of liberation photographs that emerged in that three-week period in the spring of 1945) represented men and women very differently. Images of women after the liberation reinforced preconceived notions of gender identity. Photographs of women with children, cleaning or collecting items in groups, caring for the dead, and preparing food featured prominently in both British and American newspapers. Journalist and academic Barbie Zelizer argues that the way photographers chose to show female survivors depicted a community of women resuming their nurturing and domestic routines. Survival, then, was presented as the act of resuming normal female routine. The captions for the photographs reinforced this idea, presuming that if women were preparing food, cleaning, or gathering items, each was an act of nurturing the community of survivors. These captions appeared even if the reality of the photos was an individualistic act of survival. One photograph of female survivors pilfering the clothes of corpses, for example, was published in three different papers, with three different captions: hinting that the women were gathering for the community, taking care to prepare the dead for burial, or gathering the clothes to prevent the spread of lice.[31] Although the actual experiences of female survivors varied, women were presented as monolithically helpless victims. Captions attached to photographs of women stress their womanhood while additionally condemning the perpetrators for their violations of female dignity. In photographs of men, by contrast, gender is not highlighted at all; they are merely victims of Nazi atrocity, struggling to survive as displaced persons. This total apparent helplessness does not, as Diana

Meyers indicated, grant them much in the way of agency. It presents them as fully victimized, and therefore lacking in those American qualities so necessary for establishing dignified manhood.

Though Zelizer's chapter on gender and atrocities focuses on the injustices of the representation of women as universally helpless victims, it raises a very important question about the male side of that representation. It is, of course, unreasonable to hope to find images of former camp inmates playing football, wrestling, or generally horsing around, given their circumstances and physical condition. However, that does not mean that photographs of male survivors did not gender them in other ways. Liberation photos do at times depict men reclaiming some sort of male gender identity, and this comes in two varieties; the first is through a typical masculine norm (and is rare among liberation photos), and the other is decidedly Jewish (and far more numerous).

The former depicts Jewish male survivors engaging in the typically masculine norm of physical violence. This can be found in personal accounts (memoir, testimony, and such) as well as in photographs of former camp inmates beating, berating, or in some way exerting power over the SS and guards who had been left behind and captured by liberating forces. The most famous images of men taking revenge on captured Nazis were not photographs of Jews, but of Allied soldiers committing violence against them, forcing them to labor in some way (usually in the moving and burial of corpses) or forcing them into some other act of humiliation. There are some photographs of Jewish prisoners doing the same, but they are not as numerous.

The more common representation of Jewish men reclaiming masculine identity is in a typically Jewish fashion. There are many pictures and recollections of Jewish men trying to return to normalcy through some of their studious religious practices, behavior that might be interpreted by pious Jews as masculine, but not by the American public. Countless photographs circulated of freed but displaced Jewish men praying and leading others in prayer. Jewish chaplains arriving with American forces found Jewish survivors eager to participate in funeral rites, holy days, and daily prayer. Letters to American Jewish organizations from Jewish soldiers and chaplains asked for American Jews to send clothes, toiletries, English-German dictionaries, and religious articles (prayer books, talleisim, tefillin, and such) for the survivors.[32]

In many ways, the Jewish chaplains of the United States military had the most functional and difficult responsibilities toward survivors in displaced persons camps. They served as intermediaries between Jewish religious and social organizations in America, provided the only available religious support, acted as the primary contacts for survivors to learn news of their loved ones, and sent out word of their survival to relatives in the United States. The rabbinate attempted to supply the materials necessary for the religious needs of Jewish DPs, establishing synagogues, providing Torah scrolls, building ritual baths, and even overseeing the kosher slaughter of animals. The United States Army, responsible for many DP camps, redistributed prayer books in enormous numbers for prisoner use, including a loan of 25,000 books so Jews in the camps could carry out their services.[33] These responsibilities were thrust on Jewish American clergymen as the only available option, they were initially sent to Europe, of course, to provide religious support for the Jewish military personnel serving in Europe and had no idea what they would encounter in the camps, or what work would be expected of them.

The presence of American rabbis serving as military chaplains, and their religious support to help Jewish survivors return to prayer (and when possible, to reading Jewish texts), was significant. Daniel Boyarin's assertion that Jewish men maintained a separate, gentler form of masculinity to begin with might suggest that this was an expression of that particular Jewish masculinity and therefore a reclamation of their identities as Jews and as men. The traditional *edelkayt*, as Boyarin describes, is gentle, timid, studious, and dates back to the Babylonian Talmud. A return, then, to this style of male behavior might have served as a way for Jewish survivors to reclaim not only their masculinity, but specifically their manhood as Jews.[34] Most generally accepted standards of masculinity were otherwise impossible to manifest in the camps; they could not form communities, had no families to support, no work to conduct, and no physical strength with which to conduct it. Even if religious learning and practice were acknowledged in the United States as form of empowered masculinity, it would not provide an equally normalizing image to that of female survivors prepping dinner. In short, it does not serve to make these surviving Jews seem more powerful and masculine, only more Jewish.

Gendered perspectives on surviving victims came to condemn male Jews in two ways: they were pitied as pathetic victims or, when they were not, they were instead disdained as having survived the camps through some deplorable or duplicitous qualities. Much evidence supports that it was a common view among Jewish leaders that the surviving Jews of Europe must somehow be the worst of the lot, that the best had all "perished nobly." In an article in the *Saturday Evening Post* in 1946, Samuel Lubell explained that a grim social Darwinism prevailed in the Nazi concentration camps, one that "toughened the bodies, hardened the hearts and sharpened the wits of the few who survived. . . . It was a survival not of the fittest, not of the most high-minded or reasonable and certainly not of the meekest, but of the toughest."[35] It was possible then, to escape the stigma of lambs to the slaughter, but only by forfeiting those qualities that made victims most sympathetic. This was common enough that survivors commonly felt the need to explain or excuse their survival in positive terms, asserting their moral and physical strength. A group of Jewish youths who had survived internment, concentration camps, death marches, and escape attempts wrote in 1945 to the Joint Distribution Committee in the United States seeking help. They wrote, "You will no doubt want to know how we survived. The answer is simple: We not only had more physical endurance, but also moral endurance. We told ourselves that we must heroically bear all suffering and we lived through."[36]

Though it was a common perception, not all commentary represented Jews as having gone passively as sheep to the slaughter. Stories of resistance were circulated widely in the cases where it did occur. The Warsaw Ghetto Uprising got much attention from American Jewish groups as an exception to the submissive behavior that was attributed to Jews in Europe. Even in their appreciation of the uprising, however, the perception was still that "the majority of Jews submitted passively to the German terror," according to a World Jewish Congress report published in 1943.[37] This resulting change to the image of Jews the world over (to be seen as even more meek and passive than ever) did have positive effects for international Jewry. The Zionist cause was taken up by Jews and non-Jews around the world in the hopes of providing a safe haven for European Jewish survivors, and to ensure that such a thing never happened again. However, the image of a frail survivor as the dominant Jewish type in the years following the war set American Jews back, in terms of the mainstream public perception of Jews as men.

In the aftermath of the war, American Jews work to glorify and popularize the Jewish resistance fighters (like those of the Warsaw ghetto, the armed Jewish partisans in the forests of Belarus, and their like), but this began a few years after the war, in tandem with the emergence of a new international Jewish hero: the *sabra*. The sabra (meaning a Jew born in Palestine) became the counterbalance to the withered camp survivor, playing a vital role in both the rescue and relocation of Jewish displaced persons, and in the revival of a more aggressive Jewish masculine identity.

8
From Sabra to Citizen

The Yishuv, the Jewish State, and the American Imagination

> Our return will only succeed if it will be marked, along with its spiritual glory, by a physical return which will create healthy flesh and blood, strong and well-formed bodies, and a fiery spirit encased in powerful muscles. Then the once weak soul will shine forth from strong and holy flesh, as a symbol of the physical resurrection of the dead.
>
> —Rabbi Abraham Isaac Kook (first Ashkenazic chief rabbi in pre-state Israel)[1]

In contrast to the image of enfeebled Jewish survivors in Europe, the international perception of Jews living in the Yishuv was that of strong, wilderness-taming pioneers, evocative of Teddy Roosevelt's idea of manhood through the taming of the wilderness in the Dakotas.[2] For nearly a century before World War II (even before the agricultural aliyah in 1882), Zionists had been traveling to Palestine from Europe, so there was a multigenerational Jewish community present. At the close of the war, not all surviving European Jews yearned to build a new life for themselves in Palestine, but an unprecedented number did attempt the migration, supported, in part, by the international Jewish community.[3] The attempts of survivors to reach the Yishuv were legendarily difficult, as many displaced Jews remained stuck in camps in Europe, and when they did begin the migration, were halted by British troops and turned away or interned in one of the twelve British deportation camps on the island of Cyprus. While survivors attempted to make their way to Mandatory Palestine, the political situation there was fraught, and the masses of victims were left largely at the mercy of the Allied powers.

The Jewish pioneer existed in Palestine well before the Holocaust, but the image of that pioneer (rugged, muscular, and able) became particularly stark when set next to the emerging victims of Nazi brutality (emasculated, passive, and helpless). These dichotomous images of Jewish strength became new archetypes for the Jewish man in the twentieth century, but transitioning from one to the other was not an easy process. Many refugees trekked toward Palestine where the promise of political Zionism would transform them from victims to fighters and the land of Palestine to a Jewish nation. The organizations that evolved into Israel's military (the Israel Defense Forces) were operating long before statehood was declared and acted as the training ground for the halutzim (and then sabras) to reconstruct Jewish masculinity and shed the weakness of the ghetto Jew and the Galut. These pre-state defense organizations developed into the successful Israeli fighting forces that continued to ward off attacking countries in the decades following independence and began to establish the unique Jewish masculinity of the Yishuv. Though they could not have predicted exactly how the state would be established, the ideal new Jew that Herzl and Nordau popularized was manifest in the Yishuv and grew, as they had hoped, into a European-style masculine modern Jewish nation.

Constructing Israeli Masculinity

Though numerous and haphazardly organized, Jewish military organizations in Palestine from the turn of the century to the declaration of statehood served as the training ground for a new Jewish manhood. Initially put together for self-defense during conflicts with the local Arab population, they lacked both training and arms. As they operated within an externally controlled territory, Jews in Palestine made efforts to keep peaceful relations with the ruling authority of the time (be it Ottoman or British). For that reason, they constructed their defense organizations underground. The earliest of these groups were Ha-shomer and Bar Giora (eventually absorbed into Ha-Shomer), which consisted primarily of male Jewish immigrants from Eastern Europe. A small number of women served in Ha-shomer, and their work remained within the confines of traditionally female tasks such as cooking, laundry, and medical care.[4] These groups acted as incubators for Israeli masculinity in its infancy, in part fulfilling the prophecies of Rabbi Abraham Isaac Kook, Theodor Herzl, and Max Nordau. They manifested a new Jewish manhood by rebuilding the Jewish body with muscles and by redefining Jewish manhood through the performance of manly purpose. They sought to actively correct the flaws that they believed to be characteristic of diaspora Jews through physical training (both before and after the establishment of the state) and believed that they presented measurable positive results.[5]

The desire to become more masculine is evident in the actions carried out by Ha-shomer, a group that sought to protect their new lands and shed their old, ghetto Jew image and mentality. They became a very different "tough Jew" from that imagined by European Zionist thinkers. In the case of Herzl, his ambition to fight in duels and his urging other Jewish men to do likewise was a matter of dignity and prestige in bourgeois European society. When Max Nordau spoke of the "muscle Jew," he did so in terms of mind and body regaining vitality. He spoke of training in the gymnasium, and restoring masculine dignity and health. These Zionist leaders advocated equal social status and a return to a healthy and strong masculine Jew created in the image of masculine Europeans, not of those fighting clandestine and bloody battles in the desert. Although the Zionist settlers and farmers largely shared the Herzlian desire for European manhood, Ha-shomer prioritized battle as a primary part of the new Jewish masculinity. As Martin Van Creveld writes, "Self-defense apart, the first concern of the *shomrim* or 'guards' was to put as much distance as possible between themselves and the small towns from which they came and that, to them, stood for everything that was base, cowardly, and weak. Accordingly, they modeled themselves on the Circessians [*sic*], who enjoyed a reputation for bravery and whose place, after all, they sought to take."[6] The *shomrim* incorporated elements of local Arab culture, learned some of the language, and defended Jewish farms and settlements from Arabs who might attack. These Jewish men grew their mustaches to emulate local Arabs, as they viewed the locals as epitomic masculine figures; they were connected to the land, protected their people, and were fierce in battle. Not all the Jews of the Yishuv took part in, or even approved of, these tactics, or of the new self-image the shomrim adapted. Ha-shomer's interest in forming this new self-image bothered some Jewish settlers, who the shomrim sometimes even bullied into paying them for protection. These Jewish settlers prioritized creating a full religious Jewish life and encouraging a renaissance of labor over reconstructing the Jewish image.

The goals of the organization changed with the circumstances of Jews in Palestine. By 1920, Ha-shomer was a relic of the Ottoman period, created to protect Jewish settlements from marauders but not equipped to deal with the new struggles settlers faced in the fight for a Jewish national homeland. It was replaced in 1920 with the Haganah, which developed slowly over the course of the next decade, under the British Mandate. The Haganah, along with several other small military organizations, stayed in place until the end of British rule and the declaration of the Jewish State of Israel. After statehood was established, the Haganah became the core of the Israel Defense Forces. The story of Jewish military strength in Palestine (and therefore Israeli masculinity as well) could not have occurred as it did were it not for the participation and support of the British Empire. The British government declared support for the formation of a Jewish homeland in the Balfour Declaration of 1917, and although statehood was not yet in sight, many Zionists counted on this support to construct and institutionalize a Jewish homeland and eventual Jewish state. In the early years of the Yishuv, while England still controlled Palestine under the British Mandate, the British accommodated Jewish immigrants to a degree, though they remained reluctant to fulfill the Balfour Declaration for fear of Arab retaliation.

In addition to the support Zionists found within the British government, England had a well-established Jewish community with a highly respected group of Zionists advocating the Jewish cause in Palestine. The British Board of Deputies (the main representative body of the British Jewish community) actively participated in internal British affairs and earned the respect of many elites in larger British society. Jews served as British citizens during the First World War, and so established a military history for themselves in England, and had general support in the English army, navy, and air force. Forming British Jewish regiments and Jewish battalions (the Jewish Legion) represented very deliberate attempts by British Zionists to showcase British and foreign-born Jews as soldiers capable of fighting with honor.[7]

British support of the developing Jewish military in Palestine involved several key British military experts and veterans, primary among them, British Army Captain Orde Wingate. Wingate began a tour of Palestine in 1936 as captain of an infantry division in intelligence. He arrived on a mission to Palestine to collect intelligence for England while the tensions between Jewish settlers and Arab locals were rising. At the time, the British Army leaned more toward the side of the Arabs, according to Major General Derek Tulloch, sympathizing with them as an overpowered and backward people (though a people with whom the British had to deal to maintain their access to Arab oil resources). Upon arriving, Wingate believed that the Arabs had become the oppressors, and the Jews their victims.[8] He became an ardent Zionist after a short time in Haifa and surpassed the expectations of Yishuv leadership through his willingness to disobey commands, placing the Zionist cause above the British crown. His motivations were varied, as he believed there was an injustice and wished to right it, but he also believed that Zionism was inherently correct for religious reasons. His religious beliefs, more than his politics, made him a Zionist supporter. In fact, he was not at all well-read in Zionist literature, claiming, "There is only one important book on the subject, the Bible, and I've read it thoroughly."[9] Wingate was a Christian and a millenarian. This meant that he subscribed to the belief in a future millennium following the Second Coming of Christ (based on the Book of Revelation 20:1–5), brought about by the return of the Jewish people to the land of Israel. This belief was common among non-Jewish Zionists and was one motivation for British interventions on behalf of the Jewish people, most notably, the Balfour Declaration of 1917, which formalized British support for the creation of a Jewish homeland in Palestine. Wingate believed not only that the Jewish people should remain in Palestine, but that they had the makings of an elite and powerful fighting force, which, if properly trained, would be more than capable of defending itself. He helped, over the course of his stay in Palestine, to manifest a new Israeli manhood through defense and military strength.

Wingate sided with a portion of Palestinian Jews who believed in the full formation of a Jewish Army, which Wingate could lead into battle in the inevitable all-out war with the Arab population. The policy of the British Army and of the Jewish Agency, however, supported only peaceful, defensive preparations on the part of the Haganah. In 1937, the British military authorized Wingate to organize patrols composed of British soldiers and Haganah members (all male) called the Special Night Squads (funded by the Jewish Agency), which quickly became the elite force in the defense against Arab revolts. Wingate became a symbol of hardened manly virtue and military strength among Jewish fighters. He was notoriously hard on all his men during training, sometimes even hitting them with his rifle butt, or striking them with his hand for misreading maps or making unnecessary noises. Yet, when off duty, he was informal with his Jewish trainees, calling them by their first names, and generally mingling with the troops. It was said of his military prowess, "after three weeks under Wingate a squadman [sic] was made a soldier."[10] The men who trained with him did not call him by his first name, but called him "Hayedid" (the Friend). Though he did not live to see Israel become a Jewish state, his influence on the Israel Defense Forces and in cementing physical strength in the Israeli psyche is memorialized in the Wingate Institute, Israel's National Center for Physical Education and Sport in Netanya, created in 1957, and named in memory of the famous national hero. Since its founding, the facility has trained military personnel in combat, served as a center for nutrition and health education, and still trains the Israeli national sports and Olympic teams. In essence, the Wingate Institute is the place where muscle Jews are built. Over the years, both men and women have attended the institute for training or sport, fulfilling Wingate's desire and hope for the people of Israel to learn to defend and protect themselves, and perpetuate ideals of Israeli strength and masculinity.

After the end of the Second World War, when Jewish refugees attempted to migrate to Palestine, the international Jewish community applied pressure on the British to grant Israel its independence, fulfilling and building on the promise of the Balfour Declaration. The State of Israel declared itself as a new nation in May 1948, and the unification of Israel's paramilitary units into the IDF (Israel Defense Forces) was one of the first actions taken by the new Israeli government and David Ben-Gurion, the first Israeli prime minister. He intended to showcase the importance of the Jewish military presence in the upheaval surrounding the declaration of statehood as well as to prevent the breakup of the new state by the factionalism of different ideological and political groups. Combining the Jewish paramilitary troops was not without incident, as several groups (such as the Irgun) wished to remain independent, or at least to maintain some level of autonomy, within the IDF. There was little time to squabble, however, as immediately after Ben-Gurion declared Israeli independence, the state was at war. They had, of course, been fighting continually, but the War of Independence followed the termination of the British Mandate and the presence of the British military in Palestine.

The Jews attempting to form the Jewish state could not have won the War for Independence, also known as the 1948 Arab-Israeli War, without a massive influx of men, material, and economic support from the Jewish diaspora (particularly America and Western Europe). The *Machal* (the Hebrew acronym for overseas volunteers) comprised volunteers from fifty-six countries, mostly World War II veterans from various nations, many of whom hailed from the United States.[11] Though Jews born in the Yishuv presented the image of ideal Israeli soldiers, in truth, in the early years of the war, 80 percent of the early military force was made up of newcomers who had been in Palestine for less than a year, and so made up a vital majority of Jewish fighters.

By the 1950s, the Israeli fighter began to transition from a social ideal to a soldierly profession. The myth of the desert fighter gradually shrank away, replaced by a new dominant figure of more aggressive masculinity, the emphases shifting from pioneer values to combat capabilities and masculinity of the new fighting Jew. Israeli children's stories of the 1950s idolized the "boy fighter" who joined more combat-hardened fighters to become heroes themselves in the continuing war of retribution and vengeance with neighboring Arabs.[12] This view of the heroic young soldier fighting on the Israeli frontier appealed not only to Israeli children but also to American audiences, both Jewish and otherwise. Americans saw in the fledgling state a modern re-creation of their own mythical nation-making story, with heroic frontiersman fighting to secure the land ordained to them by divine providence.

The Sabra: A Real Jewish Hero

American Jews saw the Yishuv and its Jewish inhabitants as a beacon of hope for the Jewish people. The generations of Jews born in the ancestral homeland presented a "new Jew," the fruition of Max Nordau's muscular Zionist dream. These new Jews called themselves *sabras*, a term that applied only to those born on the soil of Eretz Israel. The name was drawn from a comparison of the people to the thorny prickly pear, bearing a harsh exterior but containing sustenance and sweetness. According to Oz Almog, the sabra "was taken as a metaphor for the native Israeli, whose rough, masculine manner was said to hide a delicate and sensitive soul."[13] The sabras (both men and women are included in this description) were held as the ideal of Jewish strength and were glorified in American Jewish literature, film, and culture, especially prominently after the Israeli state was declared.

Even before the Holocaust, Jewish pioneers in Palestine maintained a sense of superiority supported by their belief in the socialist ideal that they were bringing to fruition, largely in the *kibbutz* movement (collectives in Palestine, usually agricultural), and by the fulfillment of the Zionist dream. Jews raised in the Yishuv were taught from their early years that they were the manifestation of Jewish chosenness. Not only were sabras "chosen people" as Jews, but also the fruits born of a socialist utopian society, the combination of which seemed destined to be "a light unto the nations," as Hebrew texts had long promised. Nahum Sokolow epitomized this attitude when he wrote that the task of progressing the whole human race could not be carried out by oppressed, downtrodden, or assimilated Jews but that it "may be fulfilled by a national self-centred [*sic*] Jewish people."[14] This is reflected in Zionist recollections, literature, and art from in and outside of the Yishuv. Of Palestinian Jewish fictional literature in the 1940s, Tom Segev wrote: "Their main subject was the mythical Sabra, the native-born soldier boy. Handsome, upright, honest, bold and hounded by none of the complexes of the Diaspora, he was always ready to die in defense of his home and the life of his 'girl.'"[15] Though this does seem an overgeneralization of what was a wide breadth of writers, it certainly shows a consistency in themes. Even in this reflection from the 1980s, Segev identifies the sabra as male not only in the male-as-default sense but very specifically by referencing "his girl." In fact, both men and women born in Palestine were sabras, but this does show the tendency to associate the figure with manliness.

This did not make for an affinity with Jews of the diaspora, but a sense of superiority and even contempt for the diaspora Jew. Masculine vitality was stressed in early descriptions of the Jews of the Yishuv, in sharp contrast to the weak, ugly, feeble nature of more traditional, religious Jews.[16] This view was particularly harsh considering those Jewish survivors attempting to get to Palestine after the end of the war. Though Zionist, and believing that Jews should migrate to Eretz Israel, sabras were not universally pleased to join forces with their weak counterparts from Europe. Many sabras looked down on those Jews (on all the Jewish diaspora, really) as weaker, pathetic, unfulfilled versions of themselves. When pondering how the Jews of Europe came to be destroyed, how they put up so little fight, some young sabras assumed that they "let themselves be slaughtered" due to "the cowardice of the Diaspora Jews."[17]

That such tension between young sabras and Holocaust survivors existed is not disputed. According to Avner Holtzman in his 1995 lecture at Yad Vashem:

> The accepted view is that the Israelis were uniformly alienating and patronizing toward the survivors, a posture that derived from the "negation of the Diaspora," a basic concept of their parents. Translated into practical terms, this concept meant that the Hebrew-Zionist education given the new generation in Palestine/Israel sought to create an unbridgeable chasm between the "new Hebrews" and the old Jewish world, with its contemptible "ghetto mentality." It was precisely against this mentality that the parents of the "Generation of 1948" had rebelled. That education bore fruit, according to the detractors of the "Generation of 1948," when the sabras, the native-born Israelis, took a position of pronounced superiority toward the broken and downtrodden Holocaust survivors who arrived in the country after 1945.[18]

Yishuv life was meant, on several counts, to shed all of the emasculating practices of European Jews, imposed from within or without. This meant that working the land was particularly important in developing the new Jews of Palestine, as Jews had not been eligible for landownership and agricultural pursuits in Europe. It meant shedding some religious practices and lifestyles, for example, replacing traditional prayer and study with manual labor and physicality, to rebuild the Jewish nation that diasporic life had so enfeebled. As Holtzman said, the "ghetto mentality" is precisely what the migrants (those who migrated by choice rather than by postwar necessity) were trying to eradicate by relocating to raise their children as sabras. Sabras were raised speaking Hebrew, disdaining Yiddish as the language of the Galut. Upon entering Palestine at the close of the First World War, Jewish Legionnaire Elias Gilner recalls meeting a sabra who refused to acknowledge the Jewish Legion soldiers while they spoke Yiddish, forcing them to ask him for directions in Hebrew.[19] This attitude, and the attempts to quash the weaker tendencies of diaspora Jews, assumed veracity in some European antisemitic notions of Jewish life and practices and saw these qualities as flaws in need of restructuring. Health, vigor, a muscled body, and dedicated Jewish soul would redefine these new Jews.

But the sabras did not come to replace feeble, bookish, or emasculated Jews in popular representation or understanding of worldwide Jewry. They coexisted as contrasting images of modern Jews. Indeed, those already living in Palestine were indispensable in the transport of survivors out of Europe. Though they varied in their feelings toward survivors, they expended great efforts in getting as many refugees as possible settled in Eretz Israel. Their efforts to relocate survivors in the wake of the genocide of European Jewry contributed to the influence that the image of the sabra had on the hearts and minds of Jews in America. This influence has helped to define the American Jewish (and larger American) relationship with Israel in the nearly seventy-five years since its founding.

Uncle Sam and the Srulik

American Jews were not just admirers from a distance of the tough, fighting sabra. Palestinian Jews reached out to the American Jewish community for support, calling on them to join their more masculine brethren in the fight for Jewish survival (though they requested monetary support more than fighting bodies). During the war, a branch of Revisionist Zionists from Palestine working with the Irgun sent delegates to the United States for the express purpose of garnering American support for the Jewish state and for the creation of a Jewish army. They operated under several group titles, including the American League for a Free Palestine (ALFP), American Friends of a Jewish Palestine, the Committee for a Jewish Army of Stateless and Palestinian Jews, and the Emergency Committee to Save the Jewish People of Europe.

These men brought a militant, masculine Zionism to the United States, which some American Jewish men felt compelled to support. Many found the idea of Jews fighting, while the news from Europe was all of Jews being abused, very attractive. The prospect of an internationally gathered all-Jewish army was not entirely novel, as the Jewish Legion fought under the command of the British during the First World War. The proposed Jewish army was, in fact, being promoted most fiercely by the leading Revisionist Zionist, Ze'ev Jabotinsky, who had been the mind behind the original Jewish Legion. As a Jewish soldier, Jabotinsky had also founded the Jewish Self-Defense Organization in Russia and, eventually, cofounded the Irgun in pre-state Palestine.

Jabotinsky came to New York in 1940, trying to rally American Zionist support for the creation of a Jewish army, made up primarily of Palestinian and European Jews. There was still time, he argued, to get Jewish volunteer fighters from European areas not yet occupied by the Nazis (like Romania and Hungary), as well as those who managed to escape from Poland. He believed that in addition to the 50,000 troops that would join from Palestine, a force of an additional 120,000 volunteers could be raised from American and European Jewish communities.[20] What he sought from American Jews was less a supply of men to join his ranks as a financial and political support for his plan. Though he died of a heart attack during his visit, his ideas did not die with him. Supporters of his vision remained in the United States to continue spreading his ideas and gathering support. Keeping in close contact with the Irgun back in Palestine, these representatives rallied support for the Zionist cause, helped to acquire weapons and munitions, and collected funds to maintain the struggle.

Another of the creators of the Irgun, Hillel Kook, came to the United States, following Jabotinsky, to garner support for a Jewish Army in Palestine during the Second World War. Hillel Kook was the nephew of Rabbi Abraham Isaac Kook, the first chief rabbi of the Yishuv. Hillel Kook took on an alias, Peter Bergson, to avoid embarrassing his uncle with his clandestine actions in the United States.[21] As Peter Bergson, he was instrumental in popularizing the image of the tough Jews of the Yishuv, and in revitalizing the image of Jewish men in America and the American national consciousness.

Public discourse about the war and the need for America to join was limited in the American Jewish community, for fear of inviting antagonism in an already fraught climate. There were, after all, Nazi rallies held in the United States (the largest held by the German American Bund), and blame of Jews for American involvement in the war (or fear of involvement) was on the rise (the America First Committee was particularly open in calling American Jews "war agitators"). But Bergson made his priority the rallying of larger support and awareness by reaching greater audiences. American presses were covering very little about the destruction of European Jewry during the war, staying under the radar. The Committee for a Jewish Army (started by Bergson and other members of his group), on the other hand, were advertising to the American public, publishing full-page advertisements in the *New York Times*, and advocating an all-Jewish army in Palestine.

In 1942, the Committee for a Jewish Army took out a full-page advertisement in the *New York Times* titled, "Jews Fight for the Right to Fight," which bluntly asserted that not only were Jews fighting along with the rest of the world but they were desperate for opportunities to fight more. "What are Jews doing in this war? In England, the United States and in Russia this question has an easy answer: They are fighting. But there are thousands upon thousands of Jews who are not fighting." The statement continues to explain that there are "fearless Palestinian Jews," stateless Jews sent adrift by persecution in Europe, and those diaspora Jews in countries that are not yet involved in the war, all "eager to fight back and to avenge." Speaking for Jews everywhere (including in the United States) the committee asserts that *all* Jews, everywhere, want to fight, united, under one flag of liberty, and under Allied command. Jews in Palestine, they argue, must be trained and given arms, planes, tanks, and guns, so they will not be "slaughtered . . . as helpless children." "A powerful and courageous army ready to give its life for the ideals that mark the Allied cause lies waiting to be born."[22] Through the language of toughness, duty, and honor, as well as the inclusion of Jews "in countries which are not yet involved in the war" (like America), the committee expanded their own Palestinian Jewish masculinity like an umbrella over the diaspora, inviting Jewish men to join them in their redemptive manhood.

The advertisements got more desperate as the situation of Jews in Europe deteriorated and American knowledge of the situation grew.

Figure 20. Committee for a Jewish Army advertisement, run in the *New York Times*, December 7, 1942, 14. I-613, American League for a Free Palestine—Lena Cohen Kleinberg Collection, box 1, folder 19. Photo courtesy of the American Jewish Historical Society.

After Rabbi Wise alerted the public to the mass murder in November 1942, the Committee for a Jewish Army redoubled its publicity efforts with a new full-page *New York Times* spread, headed by an Arthur Szyk illustration in which a screaming Jewish soldier, half buried in a pile of his murdered relatives, sheds a tear and holds his gun aloft. The bodies include a mother and infant, an elderly woman, a man in chains, and an elderly bearded man wearing a Star of David armband and clutching a torah, with swastika-hilted knife in his back. Underneath this figure, the words, "We shall no longer witness with pity alone." "All they ask," the text reads, "is the right to fight, and die, if need be, for democracy, and the survival of their people. Though still unwanted and unarmed, they still do not give up. They are awaiting the signal from America—the moral and military arsenal of World Democracy." The committee urged the

American public to support a change in the status of Jews, from being "compelled to haunt the corridors of Time as ghosts and beggars and waifs," to the "Fighting Jew, arising from 'blood, sweat, toil and tears,' marching shoulder to shoulder with the Legions of the United Nations to ultimate victory."[23]

The committee dedicated its efforts to building political support from US senators and congressmen and worked as the public face of the Irgun in the United States. Kook was particularly interested in cultivating American Jewish pride and dignity, an idea closely following Jabotinsky's concept of *hadar*, the pride of bearing that, if adopted, would deliver and rehabilitate the new Jew from the diaspora, giving him the social graces, strength, and dignity that was lacking in diaspora Jews. Throughout the course of the war, a rift also grew between Kook and Revisionist Irgun leadership in Palestine. The younger generation (led by Menachem Begin) focused their efforts on arming and training fighters, not publicizing the work and achievements of what was still supposed to be an underground organization.[24] They saw the old guard (including the movement's creator, Ze'ev Jabotinsky) speaking the language of action and strength, but not prepared to apply their rhetoric to the battlefield.

This translated, in their actions in the United States, into a boastful American campaign, celebrating Jewish strength in Palestine and publicizing the plight of European Jews. This was not, however, representative of most American Zionist leadership. In fact, when Jabotinsky arrived in New York and began to rally support in earnest, American Jewish leadership (Stephen Wise chief among them) were particularly concerned that fighting for the creation of a Jewish army might increase antisemitism and claims of Jewish war-mongering, and intensify doubt of Jewish American loyalty to the United States.[25] Stephen Wise (and the American Jewish Congress) believed in and trusted American leadership (particularly Franklin D. Roosevelt) to act in the best interest of American Jews, whereas the Revisionist movement and its followers did not, and so took very different approaches to dealing with the American government.

Emerging truths of the destruction of European Jewry under the Nazis shocked and devastated Jews in the United States. Some also became defensive in their attitudes toward surviving Jews and the view of Jewish weakness that they perceived as being cast on themselves as part of the international Jewish people. American Jews throughout the war contrasted the weak Jews of Europe with the strength and success of Jews in America, who had instilled within themselves American pride and self-determination. These qualities, they argued, complemented their Jewishness and set them apart from the starving, wounded masses in Europe. The example of the sabra, an image that made its way quickly into American Jewish art and literature, helped to give American Jews an archetype of a "new Jew" to which American Jewry could aspire and of which it could be proud. Youth groups quickly gravitated to these soldiers as new Jewish heroes (recall the earlier quote from the first meeting of the North American Federation of Temple Youth who held the sabra in such high esteem).

American Jews defensively fought to develop their masculine image. They held aloft the sabra and the Jewish soldier as positive examples, refocused their attention on the Jews who fought during (and in the case of the sabras, after) the war, and, when promoting the manly Jewish image, largely left the Holocaust out of their discussion. This is not to say that there were not popular depictions of Holocaust narratives in the immediate postwar years, or that those narratives left European victims out of the story. In fact, five of the *New York Times* best sellers in 1948 were books dealing with the Holocaust, and all five stories focused on Jewish soldiers fighting in Europe, and liberating concentration camps.[26] That these narratives dealt with Jewish soldiers struggling against antisemitism from their own comrades was a means of highlighting both the Jewishness of the heroes and the toughness of American Jews. Authors also glorified the sabra as a strong hero in a wave of representations of Jewish men in the years following the close of World War II. Eretz Israel became the focus in much of American Jewish life, and a new trend began to emerge when Holocaust films became popular, a trend that depicted sabra heroes, strong and battle-worthy (though often blond haired and blue eyed), as in *Exodus* (1958 novel adapted to film in 1960), *Judith* (1965), *Cast a Giant Shadow* (1966), and *Tobruk* (1967).

Once the Second World War concluded and the Jewish state was established, the image of Jews in Israel changed. Sabras evolved from the land-working pioneers of the 1920s, '30s, and '40s to the fighting heroes of the new state's military. New images of Israelis, national heroes, and even mascots emerged to support this change in Israeli culture. A visual representation of this change came in the form of a new popular character named Srulik. Kariel Gardosh (known to his fans as "Dosh"), a Hungarian Jewish newspaper cartoonist who had escaped Europe during the war, set out to produce a personification of the fledgling Israeli state. He intended to create an image that would "concisely and accurately symbolize the young State of Israel . . . like other national figures such as American Uncle Sam, the Russian bear and Marianne, or the heroine of the French Revolution."[27] His caricature was of a young man in a cap and shorts named Srulik, who personified Israel as a young, innocent sabra, surrounded by bigger, meaner enemies (though with a little characteristic sabra *chutzpah*). In the early years, Srulik was frequently surrounded by full-grown international and political figures, trying to find his way in an established world of politics. As the state matured, however, Srulik enlisted in the military, grew taller, donned a uniform and combat boots, and came to personify Israel less as a child, and more as a "new Jew." He was not the established, well-dressed, or flamboyantly suited Uncle Sam, but a young, plucky, and boyish personification of the sabra.[28]

Changes to Israeli life and self-image went far beyond Israeli pop culture and the new Israeli borders. From the moment of Israeli independence, Jewish life throughout the diaspora began to change, as large pockets of Jewish communities refocused on developing, supporting, and even migrating to the new state. This change affected American Jewry and their perceptions of Jewish manhood as well. As the sabras and *halutzim* evolved into the Israeli soldier, American Jews had a new rubric for manhood against which to compare themselves and to which they might aspire. Over the following decades, the effects of military successes and international acclaim of Israeli manhood can be seen in all aspects of Jewish American life, from religious practice to youth programs, in film, literature, and television, and in their reactions and participation to the world around them.

American Jews and the Creation of a Jewish State

American Jews were instrumental in the promotion of a heroic Jewish image in Israel. In the initial decades of Israeli statehood, the international Zionist community disseminated newsreels, journals, press, images, and propaganda about the new state and glorifying the heroism of the fighting Jew. Though a lot of this material emerged from Israel, much of it was created within the United States. American Jews celebrated those Americans who served in Israel's fight for statehood in popular representations such as the 1966 film, *Cast a Giant Shadow*, starring Kirk Douglas as American Machal commander Colonel David Marcus. From Brooklyn, but having attended West Point and law school, Marcus became commissioner of the New York City Corrections Department and was the subject of another Hollywood film in 1939, *Blackwood's Island*. American Jews lauded Marcus as a shining example of their American success as well as their contribution to Israeli defense. He volunteered to support what he saw as a fight parallel in many ways to the American struggle for independence, one that, like the American struggle, necessitated support from friends abroad with like-minded beliefs in democracy and freedom.

Though American Jews celebrated their own contributions to the war effort in Israel, they volunteered in much smaller numbers than those Machalniks from Canada, South Africa, England, and France. This reflected, at least in part, the significant impediments for American volunteerism in the shape of strictly enforced American laws forbidding participation in foreign military conflicts.[29] In addition, Derek Penslar argues that "American Jewry was less connected with Palestine than its diaspora counterparts, and its Zionism was far more likely to be philanthropic, manifested through donations of money, not bodies."[30] Those Americans who went to Palestine to join the fight, however, were unlikely to have been ardent Zionists before the war. Their motivation was far more personal (several experienced acute, personal losses of family overseas during the war) and more in reaction to the Holocaust and the sight of displaced Jews being pulled off ships heading for Palestine. They did not come out of the woodwork to volunteer but were recruited, targeted by Irgun and Haganah operatives in the United States who reached out to Jewish war veterans individually and through public displays (like those of the American League for a Free Palestine [ALFP]). Overall, it is true that American Zionism was manifest largely on paper (both political and monetary). American Zionists supported the Israeli cause by sending money and weapons, rallying for the cause, and even undermining American policy to get resources to Israeli forces.

Jewish American philanthropists saw their financial support not as less masculine than military volunteerism but as their best way to contribute to a new developing Jewish strength overseas. In fact, since the United States banned the transport of arms to Israeli paramilitary groups, American Jewish philanthropists committed an act of defiance against the American government through their contribution. President Truman invoked the Neutrality Act on December 14, 1947, imposing a unilateral embargo on weapons to both sides in the Zionist-Arab conflict.[31] Successful American Jewish entrepreneurs and Zionists formed a secretive volunteer network known as the Sonneborn Institute (so named for its founder, Rudolph G. Sonneborn), whose main goals were the acquisition of weapons for Israel and support for Aliyah Bet.[32] The Sonneborn Institute worked very closely with the Haganah, contributing in intelligence, arms, funds, and influence.

Group membership grew to several thousand by 1947, and members recognized the new Israeli hero emerging to fill the void of Jewish masculinity left in the wake of the Second World War. One member recalled, "I have known Jews all my life who were waiting for the day that they could point to another Jew that carried a gun and say, 'he represents me.' Meaning not to a gangster but a hero, and in the last few weeks the papers have come forth and they mention Haganah with respect."[33] This quote is particularly interesting as it reflects not only the recognition of the Israeli fighter as a new hero, but also, perhaps unintentionally, undermines the notion that contributors to the institute vicariously became heroes themselves. They engaged in illegal activity but were not gangsters, and fought for Jews by supporting those in Israel, but none of them were themselves the "Jew that carried a gun." Sarah Imhoff argues that earlier Jewish philanthropists (of the early interwar period), though not traveling to Palestine to become men, were claiming an American Jewish masculine identity through their support of the homeless Jews of Europe. She explained that "in their eyes . . . they were already doing an excellent job of Jewish manliness."[34] This was not the case, however, in the years of the Second World War and the early years of Israeli statehood. Though they did view this monetary and organizational support as a manly endeavor, they still continued to recognize Israeli fighters as the new ideal and manifestation of Jewish manhood, and supported it from afar. In this way, Jewish American Zionists were indeed embodying a dignified, supportive aspect of manhood, but they were also helping to establish a new aspect for the future, of which they could or would not participate themselves.

These fighters presented a new sort of role model for Jewish manhood, unique to their time and place. The masculine Israeli was not the chivalrous soldier of the Middle Ages, the Civil War, or even the First World War. Supporting the Irgun meant supporting a clandestine operation, which, at times, carried out acts of terrorism. The fighting Jew was not the same as the knightly soldier or volunteer, he was fighting for the survival of his people by whatever means necessary. In some respects, the Irgun's actions had the side effects of reinforcing some of the negative stereotypes about Jews being sneaky and self-serving, which the American Jewish establishment fought. For this reason, quite a different demographic of American Jews supported the Irgun over the Haganah. Members of the Sonneborn Institute, for example, gave exclusively to the military organizations they felt represented Jews in a more positive light. However, the Jewish underworld also played a role in funding and arming the Haganah. Members of the Haganah sent to the United States to garner assistance for the Israeli struggle ended up making several useful contacts among Jewish gangs and mobsters. Jews in criminal enterprises in New York, Miami, Los Angeles, Baltimore, and Las Vegas provided both the Haganah and the Irgun with weapons, ammunition, cash, and connections in South America to help in the illegal transport of materials to Israel.

That Jewish American gangsters, largely uninvolved with organized American Jewry on the whole, vehemently supported the upbuilding of a fighting Israeli state demonstrates how important the image of tough Jews was to American Jewish men. Interactions between Haganah emissaries working in the United States and Jewish criminals show just how much Jewish gangsters reveled in Jews taking up arms and fighting as men. When speaking with a Haganah emissary, Bugsy Siegel (one of the most infamous Los Angeles mobsters, Jewish or otherwise) asked, "You mean to tell me Jews are fighting? Fighting as in killing?" Once assured that righteous Jewish violence was indeed becoming a reality in Palestine, he began donating large sums of cash, estimated at a total of $50,000.[35] Similarly, the American League for a Free Palestine received a check from Meyer Lansky for $25,000 to support the cause.[36] These and other American Jews saw the desire of fighting Jews come to fruition most publicly in the actions and publications of the defiant and militant Irgun, whereas the Haganah worked largely under the radar in the United States, with some support from leading American Jewish organizations.

In defiance of several American Jewish organizations, the Revisionist Zionists continued their efforts to rally diaspora Jews to the fight in Palestine and to garner American support for the idea of a confrontational and rebellious Jewish Army, based on the urgent need for a "Hebrew fight for freedom." This was the phrase that the American League for a Free Palestine used in their campaign to enlist public support when starting a "Palestine Resistance Month," to get Jews "home" to Palestine from Europe.[37] These efforts came primarily from the national director of the Committee for a Jewish Army, Peter Bergson, and by the American League for a Free Palestine. The difference in terms between *Jewish* and *Hebrew* was particularly important to Bergson, who explained that Hebrews were descendants of an ancient Hebrew nation, composed of the Jews of Europe and the Jews living in Palestine (who owed national allegiance to no one). The Jews in America, he said, were not members of the Hebrew Nation but were American Jews of Hebrew descent. This distinction was intended to free American Jews from their wariness about potential accusations of double loyalty between the American and Hebrew nations (though it put Bergson at odds with Revisionist leaders in the Irgun).[38] The American League for a Free Palestine began seeking support for a Jewish Army early in the war with the arrival of Jabotinsky in the United States, and continued after the war ended and through the fight for Israeli statehood. The ALFP and its brother organizations tried to rally support through the image of Jewish/Hebrew toughness, determination, and fighting spirit. Though the Irgun was a clandestine organization, this group was far from it. They organized huge publicity campaigns (like the full-page *New York Times* advertisements discussed previously), and collected well-known, recognizable American men to be the faces of the organization, most notably, a US senator from Iowa, Guy Gillette, who served as the league president.

The league, though not an exclusively male organization, was saturated in the language and imagery of chivalry and manliness. The league's materials presented images of Jewish Palestinian fighters resembling the masculine war posters put out by the Office of War Information (OWI). Shirtless men or men with rolled-up sleeves, carrying a variety of weapons, tools, and uniforms or flags adorned with the

Star of David. The texts consistently referred to members, supporters, and leaders within the movement in the language of chivalrous manhood: defiance, bravery, free and mighty, fighters, stalwart heroes, and so on.[39] In a thirty-page booklet published on the history of the "Hebrew Freedom Movement," the ALFP laid out the struggle of Hebrew heroes fighting for a greater cause. The booklet depicted ten heroic Hebrew emissaries who came to the United States on a selfless and gallant quest. Throughout the publication, these heroes and their American allies are lauded as having "fearlessly challenged the mighty of this world, caring little for the consequences to their personal welfare," by creating and orchestrating the necessary organizations in America to protect Hebrew freedom abroad.[40]

The league produced as much attention-grabbing publicity material as they could muster during the war. They credited the full-page *New York Times* advertisements (which the Committee for a Jewish Army had released early in the war) with breaking the conspiracy of silence in the American press and beginning a constant flow of public information from then forward. In a full two-page spread in the *Times*, the league published their "Proclamation on the Moral Rights of the Stateless and Palestinian Jews," one full page was devoted to the names of many (though not all) of the 5,000 American leaders who signed their names to the proclamation (a good number of their impressive supporters were not Jewish), which recognized the right of all members of the Hebrew Nation to fight in their own army, with their own insignia.[41]

They intended, through these efforts, to inspire action through public opinion and outrage. They created grand and ostentatious spectacles, like their 1943 pageant at Madison Square Garden, *We Will Never Die*, which then toured, performing in several other major American cities. In the four months following the opening of the pageant, over 100,000 people attended different productions across the country funded by local communities. The author of the pageant, and one of the most important voices in the movement, was Jewish American playwright, journalist, screenwriter, and novelist Ben Hecht. Hecht created the most striking of the league's publicity and work, and it demonstrates powerfully the American Jewish perceptions of the feeble survivor and the aspirational fighting Jew in Palestine. Working with Peter Bergson, Hecht wrote the scathing ads and inspirational poetry the league published during the war

Figure 21. Photo of the American League for a Free Palestine pageant, *We Will Never Die*, which premiered at Madison Square Garden in New York City, March 1943, to a sold-out crowd of 20,000. I-613, American League for a Free Palestine—Lena Cohen Kleinberg Collection, box 1, folder 20. Photo courtesy of the American Jewish Historical Society.

and gave the movement a voice. This voice, through his writing and the league's events, had a decidedly masculine tone that was particularly critical of the American Jewish and Zionist philanthropic communities. Hecht even tailored a production of *We Will Never Die* specifically for the benefit of government officials in Washington, DC, to more directly accuse American politicians of inaction.[42]

In 1946, Hecht's play *A Flag Is Born* (published and produced by the ALFP) opened on Broadway to sold-out crowds. It meant to inspire Americans from all backgrounds to support the creation of a Jewish state. *A Flag Is Born* is a self-identified propaganda piece, following in the footsteps of *The Eternal Road* (a philosemitic spectacle of biblical proportions released in 1937 as a response to the appointment of Hitler as chancellor in Germany).[43] Indeed, Kurt Weill (the composer behind *The Eternal Road*) wrote the music for *A Flag Is Born* as well. The play centers on three survivors of the Holocaust, all embarking on a journey to Palestine by foot, who meet by chance in a European cemetery and consider aloud the position of the Jews of the world who remained alive. The play depicts two types of survivors, an older couple (Tevya and Zelda) who lost everything but retained their Jewish beliefs and practices, and a bitter young Jew, resentful of the weakness of European Jewry. It takes place on the sabbath, and as the older Jewish couple prays, Tevya has visions that connect him to the heroes of Jewish history. Tevya has several visions during his prayer, and in one of them he confronts the leaders of the world to ask that they grant Jews their homeland. This part of the play is biting satire, showing the nations of the world refusing action, and the British as an irrational, foolish empire. The biblical heroes he connects with are all men: Solomon, David, Saul, and so on. There are some visions of women, but only as parts of celebrations of the kings. The play is decidedly male. Zelda, the only female character, is present primarily to weep for her lost children, but she does not experience the visions, or express her own longing for the Jewish homeland, she merely doubts aloud if they will ever make it. In fact, while Tevya prays and connects himself to Jewish history, and while he argues with his great enemy (the entire world) for the rights of Jews to a homeland, Zelda (quietly and unnoticed) dies in the background, which Tevya only realizes after his confrontation with world leadership has ended.

Hecht presents his audience initially with two types of Jewish men: David, the bitter young Jew, and Tevya, the traditional ghetto Jew, and the two argue throughout the play. The play is led along by a detached narrator, who makes it clear to the audience that diaspora Jews do not only need to fight for their homeland, but for their manhood as well.

> The inner eyes of the ghetto Jew of Europe were not for seeing God only but for looking on his own manhood. This is Tevya's last secret in the graveyard—that he dreams of the glory of being a man. His soul has not accepted the lower levels designed for it by the hate and villainy of a world. It will not bow to contempt or murder. Condemned to survive as human rubbish, it will lift itself up out of the dusts and move bewilderedly toward its destiny—manhood.

David (Marlon Brando), Zelda (Celia Adler) and Tevya (Paul Muni)

Figure 22. Pictured (*from left to right*): Marlon Brando, Celia Adler, and Paul Muni (as David, Zelda, and Tevya) in the play *A Flag Is Born*. American League for a Free Palestine—Lena Cohen Kleinberg Collection, box 1, folder 6. Photo courtesy of the American Jewish Historical Society.

> Such is the reason of Tevya's journey to Palestine. There his man-
> hood lies. There he will go—or die reaching for it.[44]

Tevya does indeed die reaching for it. Upon discovering that Zelda has died
during his prayer, he gives in and lies down to die beside her. Only David,
fueled by the hatred in his heart, survives the night. He nearly kills himself
following the couple's deaths, forfeiting any hope of dying at the hands of
an enemy (his greatest wish), when he is called forward in a vision by the
heroic Jewish soldiers of Palestine, introducing a third image of Jewish
manhood.

> Don't you hear our guns, David? We battle the English—the sly and
> powerful English. We speak to them in a new Jewish language, the
> language of guns. We fling no more prayers or tears at the world.
> We fling bullets. We fling barrages. The manhood the world took
> from us roars again in Palestine.

The target of the play was an American audience, to appeal to the guilt
or shame of American Jews for their inaction. Throughout the play, Hecht
attacks affluent American Jewry through David, who, in response to the
thought of the monetary charity American Jews sent abroad to Europe's
Jews, rages, "I spit on their food." He glares into the audience and asks,

> Where was your voice crying out against the slaughter? We didn't
> hear any voice. There was no voice. You Jews of America! . . . Strong
> Jews, rich Jews, high-up Jews; Jews of power and genius! . . . A curse
> on your silence! That frightened silence of Jews that made the Ger-
> mans laugh as they slaughtered. You with your Jewish hearts hidden
> in your American boots!

The appeal to Americans was a complex one. While harshly criticizing American Jews and their fearful complicity, Hecht also called to their American identity, to their desire to be stronger, to reclaim their Jewish manhood. It was,
after all, written by an American Jew who maintained a strong yet conflicted connection between his Jewish and American identities. Hecht
wrote that it was not until the mass murder of Jews in Germany began
that he "became a Jew" in his anger and determination to fight. In doing

so, he explained, he simultaneously became an American in a truer sense than his having simply been born in the United States.[45] Jewish Americans like Hecht may not have wanted to move to Palestine themselves, but they recognized it as the training ground for Jewish masculinity and praised the muscular form of Judaism developing there. At the close of the play, spectral Jewish Palestinian soldiers appear to David and promise him to "wrest our homeland out of British claws—as the Americans once did." Hecht here appeals to American pride and equates the fight in Palestine with American independence. The soldiers tell David that his connection (and the implied connection of any other diaspora Jews that may have been in the audience) to his people and his land would rescue him from the degradation of diasporic Jewry and lead him, they promise, "to the land where manhood and a gun wait for you."

Though Hecht was American, many of his colleagues in the league were not. They were Palestinian Jews whose actions, statements, and publicity efforts not only caused anger and resistance from the American Zionist elites but also inspired them to deplore the ALFP as counterproductive to the cause of Jewish survival. Leading American Jewish organizations denounced the actions of these newly formed groups for creating a misleading representation of the Zionist struggle by a few unsupported and unqualified adventurers from Palestine. Bergson and his group refused to cooperate with the preexisting American Jewish establishment, and his publications undermined them by claiming that his were the only groups taking measurable action. In truth, Bergson initially believed that he *could* work with the American Jewish and Zionist establishment. However, though he cooperated with their early requests for him not to publish incendiary material, when they stopped inviting him to the table or responding to his queries, he stopped attempting to appease them.[46] The American Zionist Emergency Council (AZEC) referred to them as "a handful of young men . . . attempting to perpetrate a colossal hoax upon the American people." They urged the public, "Do not be misled by this group's publicity—remember that full-page advertisements will not rebuild the Jewish National Home."[47] They stressed that true American Zionists should not patronize the league's pageant, *We Will Never Die*, or give any funds to the league.[48] In fact, the Jewish establishment was so unhappy with the pageant that they actively attempted to shut down the production. Rabbi Stephen Wise, as the head of AZEC, particularly disliked Bergson, calling him a rabble-rouser and a troublemaker.[49]

Despite the friction within American Zionist circles, the material released by the Committee for a Jewish Army of Stateless and Palestinian Jews that promoted the Jewish state and Jewish manhood galvanized at least a few Jewish American men into defining themselves anew with each military, social, and agricultural success in Israel. It provided them a concrete example of the modern Jewish military hero they had longed for during the war, and missed all the more because of the piteous image of European Jewry in light of the Holocaust. Israel did not attempt to incorporate the Holocaust or the image of the wizened survivors into international relations or culture from the start of their nation through the late 1960s. In fact, they attempted to downplay the role of the European Jewish tragedy in their national story. The new Israeli state welcomed all Jews, but survivors from Europe were not sabras, they were not representative of the new state or the new Jew. The goal of the state was to create an entirely new life for Jews, allowing them to shed their ghetto mentalities and diaspora weaknesses, precisely what the Palestinian Jewish heroes of *A Flag Is Born* had promised.

American Jewish Youth and Israel

American Zionist youth transformed in the years surrounding the creation of the Israeli state. Over about a decade, from the close of the war to the mid-1950s, the focus of Zionist youth organizations shifted from zealous support for the creation of a state (and rallying American youth to migrate themselves to Palestine to fight for independence) to a stance that supported the State of Israel but accepted the reality of Zionism in America without the necessity of aliyah (immigration of Jews from diaspora communities to the land of Israel/Palestine). The earlier part of this support, the push for American migration to Israel, emerged in the form of physical training, camps, and militaristic education. Zionist youth groups used the fight for Israeli statehood, a uniquely *Jewish* fight, to rally support. Once statehood had been declared and the war for independence won, however, the urgent need for migration became a harder sell.

Jewish American youth began idolizing the Israeli fighter during the Second World War, comparing him to the weaker, defenseless Jews of

Europe and even diaspora Jews in the United States. The generational difference in American Zionist ideology during the war demonstrates the hero worshipping attitude of the younger generation. There were separate youth movements, Zionist and Revisionist, leading up to the war (just as there were in the adult Zionist organizations), but as the war raged on, young American Zionist leadership militarized on both sides. The Revisionist youth movement, Betar (created by Jabotinsky), reflected the same militaristic and antiestablishment sentiments as did the adult movement. Even the name, Betar, pays homage to a Palestinian hero, as it is short for Brith Trumpeldor, so named for Captain Joseph Trumpeldor, who cofounded the Jewish Legion with Jabotinsky and whom the group hailed as one of the first real Jewish heroes of modern-day Palestine.

In 1931, Zionist youth founded the American branch of Betar, and the material they distributed (like the materials produced by the Hebrew Freedom Movement) depicted the halutz as a brawny Jewish hero, a physical redemption of the male Jewish body. The American Betar movement grew as news of the Jewish plight in Europe trickled into American newspapers. Also like the Revisionist adult leadership, Betar disparaged the American Jewish establishment for throwing money at the problem of Israel, assuming charity would help to eventually create a state, instead of leaving for Palestine to fight like men. By the end of the war, Betar criticized their own prewar movement as well, saying that when the war began American Zionist youth was fully unprepared to fight the necessary battles, that they were "still busy collecting pennies to plant and build houses."[50] Much like the ALFP, they saw the Holocaust as a rallying cry for young Zionists to take measurable action.

Betar's practical goals included educating Jewish American youth to enable them to fulfil their Zionist duty through psychological, moral, and physical training. They aimed to create a new Jew "out of decay and disintegration, through sweat and blood, a new people—proud, kind and refined, and tough."[51] They drew on the imagery of the Maccabees, taking the menorah as their emblem, and teaching Jewish boys to be militant Zionists. Betar opened a summer camp, Camp Betar, in Hunter, New York, that educated Jewish boys in Zionist ideology and history and trained them militarily and physically to join the fight in Palestine. Jabotinsky died while visiting this camp for an inspection of the Betarim (Revisionist Zionist youths) in 1940. Upon his arrival at the camp, he was greeted by youths in military formation. They also opened the Jabotinsky Aviation School in Queens, New York, in the hopes that once a Jewish Legion was again established, as it had been (by Jabotinsky and Trumpeldor) in the First World War, the hundreds of attending Jewish boys would be ready to join the fight at a moment's notice. After Pearl Harbor, however, once America entered the war, the government shut down all private aviation schools and (according to Betar ephemera) every boy from the Jabotinsky school joined the United States Army.

At the close of the war, however, the Revisionist movement resumed their training of American youth. Brith Trumpeldor of America Inc., an affiliate of the New World Zionist Organization of America (NZOA) which Jabotinsky founded when he broke away from the World Zionist Organization in 1935, opened a school to train Jewish American teens (sixteen and over) to fight in Palestine. The two-month course included military drills, jiu jitsu, map reading and sketching, Palestinian geography, radio communications, Hebrew and Arabic language, hand-to-hand fighting, and wrestling. After completion of the course, students were expected to leave for Palestine to fight, or to remain in America to train "the thousands who look to Betar for guidance and adequate preparation for the task confronting them and Jewry." They made no attempt to hide the rebellious nature of their recruiting or their disdain for the practices of the American Zionist establishment: "If you are ready for action, if you want more than demonstrations, if you believe as we do that in the hands of American Jewish youth lies the future of Palestine, if you are a proud and militant Jew, then you will join our school."[52]

Though Betar remained the official Revisionist movement youth group on college campuses, other Zionist groups looked to the Revisionist movement for answers to questions raised by the inaction of the leading Zionist establishment. The Zionist Organization of America and Hadassah joined together in 1940 to create the American Zionist Youth Commission (AZYC) to support organized Zionist education for American Jewish youth, from a perspective compliant with the goals and policies of the World Zionist Organization. Several Jewish campus groups operated as affiliates of the AZYC (and were provided some funding through the parent organizations), including Hillel and Avukah (The American Student Zionist Federation). The ZOA recognized Avukah in 1925 as the only officially supported campus Zionist organization.

To their displeasure, however, Avukah also began to harshly criticize the ZOA for what they considered feeble wartime actions and Zionist leadership. The youth leadership, by 1942, had radicalized and begun to stray from American Zionist institutions. They disagreed on several points and became determined to recognize three goals for their organization: the security of Jews in America, the fight against fascism, and their connection to a Jewish Palestine. These points helped the group fashion a more militant, radical agenda. Nonmilitant American Zionism as it stood, they argued, should be considered "historically and politically non-existent."[53]

American Zionist leadership grew increasingly uncomfortable with the more right-wing, militant language emerging from Avukah and attempted to negotiate with the youth groups to bring their policies back in line with those of the ZOA, in order to prevent alienating possible recruits or the larger campus communities. After eighteen months of negotiation with AZYC, Avukah leadership concluded that mainstream American Zionist leadership was weak, preferring a "hush-hush" and "be nice" policy to actual Zionist action. "The only adult Zionist group that is bringing up political issues today is the Revisionist. . . . The ZOA today has a 'class Zionism' which does not tolerate Avukah."[54] More than anything, Avukah became frustrated with the establishment's determination to 'toe the line,' to remain inconspicuous, and avoid publicity for Jewish action on campus. Though not an exclusively male group, Avukah's leadership (nearly all those railing against the establishment) were male, aside from the position of executive secretary, which a female student occupied. In the AZYC report on the "Avukah problem" in 1942, the chairman made a point of explaining that the two female student representatives who appeared to meet with the adult organization were merely sent as props. The commission realized, when checking the backgrounds of the two women, that neither of them actually acted as leaders in Avukah (as they claimed), but were wives of ex-chairmen, presently serving as adult advisors for the organization. This was explained as particularly duplicitous since the women used their maiden names to obscure their relationships with the men in charge.[55] In light of their growing militancy, Herman Weisman (chairman of the commission) urged the ZOA and Hadassah to rescind recognition of Avukah as the only university campus Zionist organization.

In Jewish youth groups across the country, manliness took a primary role in the goals and imagery of Zionist students, as the strength, stoicism, and success of the Israeli soldier became an aspirational goal for Jewish American boys. Though aliyah of their core membership had never been the primary objective of the majority of even the most ardent of American Zionist youth groups before the war, in 1945 the goals of organized Jewish youth showed a quick movement toward migration to Palestine. Before the war, several different Zionist American youth groups existed (such as Hashomer Hatzair, Avukah, and Left Labor Zionists), and many lost some of their wartime membership to the war efforts, as young Jewish boys volunteered to serve. When the war ended, several of these diminished groups reorganized themselves into the Intercollegiate Zionist Federation of America (IZFA), which included both the AZYC and Avukah. Their new program worked with unprecedented effort to send as many young Jews as possible to migrate to Palestine to live in kibbutzim and help build the Jewish state.[56]

The IZFA gathered a core group of student leaders, the *Haoleh*, to promote aliyah among members. The *Haoleh* brought students on weekend trips from college campuses to *halutziut* (pioneering) training farms to indoctrinate and prepare participants for aliyah. The farms were modeled on and run by Israelis, as American Jewish youth's role models for rugged Judaism. When the war broke out in Israel, they increased efforts to send young American Jews to Israel to fight and to support the Haganah.[57] The core group of IZFA members put a good deal of effort into proselytizing to other Jewish groups (like college campus Hillel organizations), and by the mid-1950s most of the original members made aliyah, and the remainder of the group reformed into a less zealous migration-based organization, the Student Zionist Organization (SZO).

The generational tension between Zionist youth groups and the Jewish establishment only grew in the decades that followed, as Jews in the United States watched the developing Israeli nation from afar, contemplated their own lack of action during the Holocaust, and debated their current responsibility to the Jewish state. Zionist youth, frustrated with the American Jewish establishment, continued to distance themselves and move further to the left. The sense of responsibility became more complex as America entered an unprecedented age of affluence in the postwar years. This affluence provided many Americans access to the middle class and altered several facets of life in America for Jews and non-Jews alike. Unlike the burgeoning State of Israel, American masculinity quickly shifted, becoming less measured through physical prowess and fighting power and more associated with affluence and conformity in suburban life. By the mid-1960s, American Jewish youth explored their frustration and anxiety over the tension between these conflicting masculine ideals in an era of rapid and dramatic social and political change.

9

"Israel Is We"

Jewish America, Postwar Affluence, and the Six-Day War

"Gutsy fighters, those Israelis," I hear all around me. "Gutsy fighters, those Nazis," I hear Lenny Bruce from above. "Blitzed those Polacks and Frogs right off the map." "Gutsy fighters, those Americans . . . Gutsy fighters, those Russians . . . Gutsy fighters, those Viet Cong . . . Gutsy fighters, those Japs . . . Gutsy fighters, those Romans . . . Gutsy fighters, those Greeks . . ." The applause echoes throughout history. Someone's missed the point.

—Martin Jezer[1]

The affluence of postwar America altered the definition of manhood in the United States and presented new challenges to the rugged Judaism emerging simultaneously in Israel. American suburbs provided a new standard for masculinity and became the proving ground for American men struggling to conform and adhere to universalized ideas of normalcy. This provided alternate avenues to masculine identity, apart from military service and outward toughness. Fear of communism and difference in the early years of the Cold War further added to the frantic need to prove oneself, as cold warriors like Joseph McCarthy equated communism and socialism with homosexuality, effete intellectuals, and soft men. Such crises in gender identity affected some groups more quickly and powerfully than others, particularly those already experiencing differences in perceived masculinity. Jewish Americans had struggled throughout the Second World War to prove themselves and continually encountered resistance and bigotry. But in postwar America, Jewish manhood (and Jewish identity on the whole) entered a complex period of flux and crisis.

American Jewish youth particularly felt the dual influences of changing masculine norms in the United States (both the ever-present military hero and the newly established suburban man) and the new image of Jewish strength coalescing in Palestine.

In the postwar years, as the American middle class expanded and suburban life grew to represent the dominant American dream, conformity became the watchword of the day and Jewish America followed suit. Where a life of scholarly interest and study had previously been so esteemed, Jewish America came to embrace the more mainstream goals of achieving manhood by acquiring and maintaining bread-winning positions, enabling Jewish fathers to support wives and children who need not work themselves. This change in Jewish life, and indeed it constituted a measurable change from prewar Jewish occupations and affluence, stirred up concerns in the Jewish community about a growing crisis of Jewish identity, as tension built between the conflicting images of the scholar, the sabra, the American war hero, and the American middle-class businessman.

As many middle-class Jews settled into suburban life and relative wealth, they simultaneously embraced the rugged image of Jewish men emerging from the Middle East. After Israel emerged victorious in the War for Independence and declared their statehood, Israeli men and women struggled to build the new state, resettle refugees, and "make the desert bloom." Some Jewish American men, themselves veterans of the Second World War, went to Israel to help fight, build, and to popularize the new emerging Jewish image from Palestine. The popularization of the image was a far more common and meaningful endeavor in the United States than actual travel to and work for the new state. The films, literature, and media that emerged from American Jewish life throughout the 1950s and '60s sharply contrasted the image of increasingly soft suburban men in the United States with the sturdy men building a new society in the Palestinian desert.

Jews, the Widening Middle Class, and Masculine Reconstruction

Unease regarding growing Jewish American affluence abounded in the late 1950s and early '60s, as much of the middle-class Jewish community experienced very real societal advances, while others saw this progress as detrimental to Jewish religious life and intellectual tradition. Criticism of upward mobility, and the type of men it created, laid the foundation for the Jewish archetypes in film and fiction that still define Jewish American life today, both within and outside the Jewish community. The preexisting image of bookish Jewish intellectuals was buttressed by the newly emerging Jewish businessman, career-driven and (though not scholarly in the traditional Jewish sense) living the life of an educated and successful elite. Criticism of Jewish American affluence by militant Zionists (both in and outside of the country) reached its height during the war. Betar programming taught participants that the movement had failed to gain ground in time to be of real help during the war because American Zionists believed that what was needed of them was money, not blood and sweat, in the fight for a Zionist state. The movement resented assimilation in the United States as the cause, calling it "ugly, disgusting and bankrupt."[2] They referred to an American Zionism they dubbed "Zionism deluxe," in which the only obligation of the Zionist was to help provide refuge through charity to poor Jews overseas. This view of American Zionism was widespread even before the war, enough so that there was a well-known joke that defined an American Zionist as: one Jew who collects funds from a second Jew to send a third Jew to Palestine. Much of this changed, however, in the conditions of the postwar world. Once Israel established statehood, the urgent need to help overseas evaporated and American Jews enjoyed the economic boom of the years following the war.

The postwar shift in American manhood, from cities to suburbs, affected all American men but reached Jews in even greater proportions than most American communities, as larger percentages of Jewish men entered professional fields. Rachel Kranson outlined this shift in her 2017 work, *Ambivalent Embrace: Jewish Upward Mobility in Postwar America*, and demonstrated the complexity of Jewish upward mobility in the immediate postwar years. In Jewish American literature of the 1950s, three Jewish types interact and compete in a constant reevaluation of Jewish manhood: the tough Israeli (the halutz or the sabra); the suburban Jew of American affluence; and the traditional bookish Jewish intellectual. The journey that Jews made to the middle class, attempting to navigate these newfound identities, was complex, multifaceted, and often anxiety producing.[3]

Jewish writers, producers, and media-makers used these contrasting images of Jewish manhood to comment on and evaluate Jewish life in postwar America. In the following pages, this negotiation of American Jewish masculinities is illustrated using the exchanges of a few prominent American Jewish authors, whose works have been frequently used as evidence of changing Jewish masculinities. As noted in earlier chapters, nearly all of the prior works written on American Jewish masculinity have emerged from cultural and literary studies and use authors of this period like Leon Uris, Philip Roth, Normal Mailer, Saul Bellow, and the various authors of what Paul Breines calls "the Rambowitz novels," to demonstrate the desires of Jewish American men to access or resist the allure of American hegemonic masculinity.[4] It is not the intention of this chapter to engage in literary analysis or criticism as evidence of changing American Jewish masculinities. Instead, the dynamic between the authors themselves, their public statements about each other's works, and the ways in which they differ from one another in their appeals to American Jewish men is used as evidence of the tension over the conflicting images of Jewish manhood in postwar America that they themselves popularized.

No single event or historical figure was as influential in the popularization of the hypermasculine sabra as the novel *Exodus* by Jewish American novelist Leon Uris. Uris, himself a Jewish American World War II Marine Corps veteran and best-selling author, wrote a fictionalized account of a ship of Jewish refugees attempting to get to Palestine, aided by Israeli sabras. The novel was based on the *Exodus*, one of the most famous ships that the British turned away, which carried 4,515 passengers, most of them Jewish refugees from Europe, and was piloted by Palestinian Jews. The British forced the actual *Exodus* to turn around and return to Germany, but Uris's account earns the refugees safe passage through the tenacity of their sabra leaders. The book paints a picture of the Jewish men of Palestine as kindred to young American marines: brave, noble, stoic, and physically superior. He was well-prepared to rewrite the Palestinian Jew in this light, as his best-selling novels and successful screenplays before *Exodus* all featured military heroes, rebels, and cowboys (all tropes he applied to the sabra).

Uris accomplished a tremendously influential feat with the publication of *Exodus*, he managed to redefine Jewish masculinity to an American audience by creating a tangible, accessible Jewish hero out of the

Sabra. The main character, an all-American hero (aside from the fact that he was a Palestinian Jew), was Ari Ben Canaan. Ari served as the prototype for a new hypermasculine Jewish trope in American film and literature, what historian Paul Breines called the "tough Jew."[5] Even Ari's name was carefully crafted to recall Jewish heroes throughout history. His first name recalled Joseph Trumpeldor (Ari means "lion," and evokes the Roaring Lion monument to Trumpeldor's last battle at Tel Hai), and his last name recalled the biblical conquest of Canaan.[6] Ari contradicted every emasculating stereotype and commonly held belief about Jews in his action and physicality. Uris refers to him as "big," "handsome," "hard," as having "ice-blue eyes," and his love interest explains that he also does not act like any Jew she's come across. In the movie version (1960), Ari is played by Paul Newman, a heartthrob from Hollywood's golden age. The film adaptation of Exodus drew a particularly stark contrast between the Holocaust survivor and the sabra, showing the heroic Ari Ben Canaan alongside the Auschwitz survivor, personified by Dov Landau, an angry, bitter, desperate teenager. Dov is eventually redeemed by his migration to Palestine and acceptance into the Irgun, but is also feminized by his suffering, particularly by his sexual abuse at the hands of German soldiers and his confession to having been used "like you use a woman."

Uris's accomplishment was greater than the creation of a manly Jew for American audiences. He also helped to redefine the relationship between Israel and the United States for the next three decades by equating the foundation of the Jewish state to the American story, for contemporary audiences. Until the war in Lebanon in 1982, Americans would see Israel as a righteous phoenix risen from the ashes of the Holocaust to heroically defend land that, according to the popular Pat Boone title song for the film, God gave to the Jewish people.[7] According to Amy Kaplan's analysis of the book's influence on the American psyche, Uris's creation of the Palestinian hero and careful recasting of the Palestinian Arab into the role of criminal sanctified the creation of the Israeli state in the American imagination as anticolonial. The sabras were fighting against the British Empire, they were not themselves a conquering power (thus erasing the issue of Arab self-determination). This distinction is vital not only for understanding the Israeli-American relationship but also for determining the source and veracity of the heroic sabra archetype in American media.

Philip Roth, in contrast to Uris, was one of the most prominent and frequently referenced authors of fiction depicting the discomfort of postwar Jewish men in America. Roth's protagonists sat on the uncomfortable dividing line of traditional Jewish intellectualism and postwar acculturation, watching with trepidation as Jewish manhood changed, and trying to find their place in the changing male landscape. The characters that Roth created present as simultaneously superior in their traditional intellectualism and inferior in their earning potential and place in larger society's expectations for American men. They are also sexually aberrant, in much the way that early twentieth-century critics of Jewish men believed them to be, but overtly so, as Roth makes sexual obsession a primary part of his characters. This overt sexuality did not serve to make Jewish men more masculine, merely more deviant from acceptable gender norms. As Otto Weininger explains, "the Jew is always more lecherous, more lustful, than the Aryan man," but he concludes, is also "less sexually potent."[8] Roth's characters illustrate this perfectly, for example, the primary character of *Portnoy's Complaint* (the entire book is framed as a session with the protagonist's analyst) is sexually obsessed, but not arguably successful.[9]

Roth, the most notable content creator of his time to popularize his particular Jewish archetype, was an active participant in a very public renegotiation of acceptable and popular notions of Jewish masculinity in the postwar years. His Jewish male characters reflected long-standing criticisms of modern Jewry as physically or culturally inferior, building on themes present in Jewish commentary dating back to early German Zionist ideas of Jewish regeneration. Max Nordau's critique of European Jews in the mid-nineteenth century as degenerate, weak, and disconnected from their stronger ancestors reemerged here as a stark and unfavorable contrast to images of Jewish manhood emerging from the Israeli state. Just like earlier views presented through muscular Zionism, Roth's neurotic intellectual American Jewish male characters also internalized antisemitic views, this time with an added caricature of the Jew as corrupted by his monetary success and sexual desire. Those Zionists active in the Unites States who extolled the virtues of the Israeli fighting forces tended to criticize Jewish middle-class upward mobility as unmanly and degenerate. These critics held wealthy American Jews as examples of the deterioration of Jewish life against which Jews in Israel must fight.

Interestingly, there is a marked difference in the way various Zionists drew this comparison and criticism. The Revisionists, those in the ALFP (who supported the Irgun and more militant rebellion), harshly criticized American Jewish men, presumably to shame them into action to support Israeli fighters. Peter H. Bergson and Zionist leader Chaim Weizmann engaged in a public exchange in which Bergson repeatedly attacked Weizmann and American Jewish leaders as continuing a status quo that was both "disastrous for us Hebrews and most harmful and potentially explosive for Jews everywhere" by denying support to the cause of an independent Jewish Palestine. "You and all these good people," Bergson explained of American Jewish organizations, "must understand how futile and ridiculous and harmful this all is."[10] Those supporting the leading American Zionist institutions and the Haganah's tactics for more gradual independence recognized that their own strengths as Jewish American businessmen were not physical or heroic, and so they appealed to their sense of pride in their success rather than their sense of shame in not being "tough" themselves. Contributing support to manly Jews abroad allowed these American Jewish men, including, and like, those in the Sonneborn Institute, to feel as though they were underwriting the fight to improve the image of Jews everywhere. Both, by different means, held American Jewish men as weak counterparts to the heroes of Palestine. An excellent example of these different strategies can be found in comparing the goals of Revisionist Ben Hecht and Zionist author Leon Uris in their respective works, *A Flag Is Born* (1946) and *Exodus* (1958).

If Ben Hecht was, in his desire to prompt immediate action, harshly critical of the American Jewish and Zionist philanthropic community, Leon Uris wrote *Exodus* with the opposite intention. *Exodus* attempted to foster support through pride in Jewish progress in Israel by appealing to an American sense of kinship with the fledgling state, not by shaming American Jews into action. Though Jewish audiences around the world adored the new perception of Jews that Uris promoted, the glorification of Palestinian (and Israeli) Jews targeted primarily American audiences. Uris explained, "I wrote *Exodus* because I was just sick of apologizing—or feeling that it was necessary to apologize. The Jewish community of this country has contributed far more greatly than its numbers. . . . I am definitely biased. I am definitely pro-Jewish."[11] His goal was less to affect Israelis or any of the key players in the story, but to emotionally move (and even redeem) Jewish

Americans through his retelling of the foundational Israeli story. And indeed, some of the historical actors on which he based the book expressed discomfort at the "toughness" that Uris had retroactively granted them in his retelling. One of the captains of the real-life *Exodus*, Captain Yehiel Aranowicz, told *Time* magazine, "Israelis were pretty disappointed in the book, to put it lightly. The types that are described in it never existed in Israel. The novel is neither history nor literature."[12]

Philip Roth reciprocally disparaged the new tough Jewish image in America, just as content creators who promoted it disparaged him. Just a few years after the publication of *Exodus*, Roth exchanged public criticisms with Leon Uris. Their published back-and-forth provides an excellent example of the growing tensions in popular depictions of American Jewish masculinity. While Uris attempted to put a masculine and heroic shine on the American Jewish community by glorious representations of Israelis and Jewish family life, Roth wrote about what he saw as the unique family problems found in Jewish American homes, which, quite contrary to Uris's work, showed emasculated men closely guarded by their doting Jewish mothers. According to Uris there was, in the late 1950s, a certain school of Jewish American writers who:

> spend their time damning their fathers, hating their mothers, wringing their hands and wondering why they were born. This isn't art or literature. It's psychiatry. These writers are professional apologists. Every year you find one of their works on the best-seller lists. They do a disservice to the Jewish people. Their work is obnoxious and makes me sick to my stomach.[13]

For his part, Roth points to the mendacity of the depictions of Jewish heroes in novels by Uris and those of his ilk. He explained that they (in this case specifically Uris and Golden, author of *Only in America*):

> burden no one with anything. Indeed, much of their appeal lies in the fact that they help to dissipate guilt, real and imagined. It turns out that the Jews are not innocent victims after all—all the time they were supposed to be persecuted, humiliated, and mocked, they were having a good time being warm to one another and having their wonderful family lives.[14]

The real problem with this happy view of Jewish life, Roth explains, is that Jews are never the only consumers of this popular media. While it may improve public relations for American Jews, and make those who read it feel good, he argued that it contained a significant secondary statement, which is that "if the victim is not a victim, then the victimizer is not a victimizer either." By relieving Jews of their weakness and persecution, Uris also relieved their enemies, both in America and abroad, of culpability for the oppression that created the Jewish neuroses that plagued Roth and his literary characters.

The contrasting goals of Uris's and Roth's Jewish representation reflect the dichotomous identities (or preferred identities) among actual American Jews of the time. Not all Jews in America enthusiastically embraced the image of tough Jews, which for some, was a long welcome (and even hard-won) reward. And, perhaps even more importantly, not all those who embraced the image managed to demonstrate it in their own lives, regardless of the delight they took in promoting, reading, and writing about it. Uris is a perfect example of this inner conflict, as he had more in common with Roth's writing in his real life than his published back-and-forth with Roth might indicate. Deride the image of the hated, doting, typical American Jewish mother though he might, Uris himself had a relationship with his own mother that reads quite like characters in a Philip Roth novel. M. M. Silver, in his book on Leon Uris and the writing of *Exodus*, even conjectured that "*Exodus* was one massive and theatrical way to win an argument with a whining Jewish mother."[15] Uris's work was aspirational, not biographical, hoping to instill a new Jewish spirit in the generation raised in postwar America, a spirit that actually embodied the soul that he projected on the Jews of Israel. And in many ways it did, as American Jewish fantasies and fiction began to embrace the tough Jew that Uris helped to popularize.[16]

However, Jewish children raised in postwar America also struggled with their Jewish identity, and by the 1960s, America was so tumultuous that American youth from all backgrounds struggled with several aspects of their identity. Unlike Roth and Uris, these young Jews did not live through and remember the Second World War and the Holocaust, and their struggles were unique to their own time and place. The 1960s were years of tremendous and fast-paced change, ramping up over the decade to what several American historians identify as a year of rupture in 1968.[17] It was the peak of the Vietnam War and the antiwar movement (particularly considering the Tet Offensive and the My Lai massacre). The country was in near chaos, with riots breaking out in Washington, Chicago, and Baltimore; the assassinations of Reverend Martin Luther King Jr. and Robert F. Kennedy; an unprecedented variation and degree of protest (civil rights, university campus upsets, antiwar demonstrations, feminist rallies, gay rights protests, and Black Power demonstrations); and the rise of drug culture. Jewish students grappled with their Jewish identity in light of Israel and the Holocaust, their American identity in light of atrocities of the Vietnam War, and their place in Jewish American society in light of the civil rights movement.

In this environment, all elements of American life came into question, and gender played a particularly important role in that questioning. While women fought for equal rights, and men contemplated their future and the possibility of the draft, gender rose to the surface both as an issue in and of itself (as in the feminist and gay rights movements) and as an issue attached to other problems of the day. The war in Vietnam affected people differently based on their ethnicity, sexual orientation, level of education, and especially gender. That the American military draft during the Vietnam conflict affected men more than women is unambiguous, as the draft did not include women. In addition, the American draft also disproportionately discriminated against African Americans, ensuring that it had a disproportionate effect on different American communities.[18]

Though the Vietnam War defined and promoted ideas of hegemonic masculinity, Jewish American men did not jump at the opportunity to prove themselves by that standard any longer. Unlike both world wars, American involvement in the Vietnam War was a highly contentious issue, and those on the far left determinedly fought against it. Jews have historically tended to reside on the far left, and so in this war, Jewish men did not show up in disproportionate numbers to prove their manhood. Though there are no dependable records for Jewish enlistment, voluntary or draft, for the war in Vietnam, there are other records that show the decline in Jewish enthusiasm for service. For example, the records of Jewish Peace Fellowship, a group founded in 1941 by Jewish antiwar activists to support conscientious objectors, show their peak membership (between 1941 and the present) during the years of the conflict in Vietnam. Their newsletter, *Shalom*, also shows the leaders of the Jewish Peace Fellowship struggling to keep up with and assist the record numbers of young Jewish men attempting to obtain conscientious objector status during the conflict in Vietnam. By 1971, their fundraising materials pleaded that "in greater numbers than ever before, young men and women are turning to the Jewish Peace Fellowship" as their only Jewish pacifist option.[19] Rejecting the war and the draft (and even claiming the draft was a form of gender discrimination against men) by no means meant that Jewish men in America had lost their motivation or determination to prove their masculinity alongside their American countrymen.[20] Instead of eagerly joining the fray to demonstrate their valor and bravery in the American military, Jewish men attempted to prove it elsewhere, by entirely different means, and introduced new masculinities to the Jewish American character in the process. Rejection of the war meant rejection of what it promoted, which was multifaceted but included traditional militaristic manhood.

The Vietnam War and American Manhood

With the entrance of the United States into the Vietnam War, criticism of American militarism grew in step with fervent escalation of masculine wartime rhetoric, and this rift shook the beliefs that many Americans held about masculinity and aggressive strength. The war certainly maintained the traditional, militaristic focus on masculinity through vigor, national service, victory, and brotherhood. The Johnson administration, facing criticism at home, was particularly set on maintaining a masculine image throughout the war. The president famously stated, in a moment of bravado, that "We not only screwed Ho Chi Minh, we cut his pecker off," emasculating and metaphorically castrating the enemy.[21] The masculine theme cut both ways in this war, as leaders used it as motivation to push forward on all sides. Though Johnson claims to have emasculated Ho Chi Minh in North Vietnam, the prime minister of Singapore, Lee Kuan Yew, explained, "What is happening in Vietnam cannot be repeated. We cannot allow the same forces that have emasculated South Vietnam to emasculate the whole region."[22] This hypermasculine Cold War "measuring contest" that Johnson maintained throughout his presidency was just part of his much larger fear that he was insufficiently manly for the job.[23] His wartime attitude toward Ho Chi Minh and the Soviet bloc was well-known enough for there to have been a joke in Washington, highlighting the nervous defense of American manhood. The joke tells that the Soviet Union placed an order through the American government for hundreds of cases of twelve-inch condoms. In response, the administration, unwilling to admit to any implications of not possessing any of that size, produces the prophylactics and sends them to the Soviets in cases marked "Short."[24]

Despite the strength and longevity of wartime machismo, two other significant additions to American definitions of masculinity emerged during the war in Vietnam. The first is a change in the persistent model of masculinity provided by military service, which largely depended on the support of the nation and citizens at home. Prior to the Vietnam War, service in the military was one of the most reliable bastions of masculinity available to American men. Soldiers fighting in Vietnam, whether drafted or voluntarily enlisted, found this formerly dependable means of shoring up masculinity now criticized back home as having indulged in hypermasculine excess or a sort of false masculinity. Upon returning home, they found that Americans did not see them as paragons of manly virtue but as less manly due to their lack of discipline, chivalry, and dignity. This was particularly the case after the traumatic and public relations nightmare that was the revelations of the My Lai massacre. Not only had the event shaken public belief in the honor and chivalry of the American military, but the testimony of Hugh Thompson (the man who intervened at My Lai) attributed his own act to save civilian lives not to his military education but to the sense of values instilled by his parents.[25]

The war also created an unprecedented legion of disabled veterans, with unique emotional trauma, especially those disabled through use of Agent Orange who the government denied recognition, and therefore support for their injuries and suffering.[26] The returning wounded soldiers (whether mentally or physically) paired with the tremendous blow of American defeat, forced men searching for a masculine identity to reassert their manhood through a different sort of strength. A portion of those men returning from war found such an alternate strength based on friendship, camaraderie, and shared trauma (some as prisoners of war). In what some scholars of masculinity call the *remasculinization process* of the 1970s and '80s, American producers of film, television, and literature created a new articulation of male identity, reflecting on the Vietnam War, that focused on camaraderie and strength through brotherhood.[27]

The other new addition to the growing landscape of American masculine identities is the one American Jews fought for so long at the start of the century: the draft resister. This includes illegal dodgers, legitimately failed medical assessments, registered conscientious objectors, and those who escaped the draft through active enrollment at a university. Detractors of draft resisters criticized antiwar protestors as unmanly and draft-dodgers as cowardly. Even the terms that became commonplace when referring to supporters and detractors of the war, *hawks* (supporters of the war) and *doves* (those against the war) were feminizing. Hawks disparaged doves through feminizing language, belittling those at all levels of antiwar sentiment. Johnson attacked a member of his own cabinet as a dove; ridiculing his masculinity, he exclaimed, "Hell, he has to squat to piss."[28] And this language and antidove sentiment all had an effect, whatever an individual's feeling about the war, on their sense of compromised masculinity.[29]

At the same time, the countercultural movement in the 1960s (examined in the Jewish masculine context in the following chapter) was redefining masculinity for themselves and future generations. According to James Penner, the writers and activists of the 1950s and '60s (particularly Allen Ginsberg and Timothy Leary) were popularizing what he calls a *Dionysian masculinity*, forming a "new relationship to the mythic cultural feminine." He explains that up until this shift, previously rigid masculine ideals regarded the feminine as antithetical to the masculine, and therefore a paranoid fear of femininity or feminine contamination plagued those striving for hegemonic masculinity. He explains that the men leading the Beat and countercultural movements challenged this gender dynamic by embracing the feminine in their own personalities and biological selves.[30] Within the antiwar movement (closely connected to the countercultural movement), men were embracing a Dionysian masculinity that legitimized men adopting female attitudes, dress, and manner. This was largely due to the influence of psychedelic culture, which promoted abandoning rigid behaviors and roles and criticized aggressive masculinity.[31] The draft-dodging, long-haired hippies, therefore, did not consider themselves less masculine than previous generations (even the Old Left), whose notions of manhood pushed men to fight.

The Vietnam War severed the connection of masculinity to military heroism, instead of strengthening it, as wars had done for previous generations. The sense that a clear authority was running the show, and that the military was acting for the good of mankind, was lost to the sons of the generation who lived through the Second World War. According to Lynda E. Boose, the Vietnam War, instead of strengthening patriotism and admiration of the military hero, shattered the consensus on American masculinity in a series of events that retained its patriarchal frame but left it "with an unoccupied and no longer occupiable center. Chronologically bracketed by the assassination of the national father at one end, marked by the forced retirement of his successor at the middle, and culminating in the disgraced resignation, a few steps ahead of impeachment, of the final father of the era."[32] The loss of authority was keenly felt, as the country divided and lacked consensus about leadership, both in the present and in their national aspirations.

In the midst of the conflict in Vietnam, another war erupted abroad that did not affect Americans by and large, but had tremendous impact on the identities and politics of American Jews. While American Jews struggled with the various masculinities of tradition, suburban life, the Holocaust, and the 1960s, the tough Israeli came to the fore in 1967 with the sudden outbreak and fast-paced resolution of the Six-Day War. Jewish attitudes toward the war were complex, as they reacted not only to the war itself but to the American environment of social change, the very recent history of Nazi genocide, and the generational divide driven by the conflict in Vietnam.

American Jews Respond to Israel and the Six-Day War

American Jews, much like those in Israel, had not immediately incorporated the Holocaust as a dominant feature in their everyday lives in the decades following the horrific events. After the world learned the extent of the atrocities committed against Jews in Nazi-occupied Europe, American Jews avoided the notion of the Jewish people as mere victims, and also avoided any associations of themselves with the weakness of the slaughtered. The most popular representations in the years following the Second World War depicted the heroics of Jews during and after the war, popularized by writers like Uris. Though references to destruction of the six million were certainly present in American Jewish life, they were not nearly as popular as those focusing more on the suffering of the survivors, even in cases where the narrative also hinged on the connection between those few remaining survivors and the sabras working to save them and bring them to Palestine.[33] That piteous image, the "ignoble survivor," is recognizable today as a common trope in Jewish culture, particularly in America. Some of the most iconic and beloved Hollywood Holocaust films (at least those before the turn of the twenty-first century) have undeniably pitiful Jewish antiheroes.[34] However, for decades after the war, the international Jewish image focused largely on Israel, and when Israel was discussed or presented in the American community (though it was not yet a core of American Jewish life), Israelis were pioneers—strong and virile. American television aired representations of the Holocaust, in documentary form and in related drama, as early as the late 1940s and '50s. However, such depictions primarily focused on documentary footage and survivor testimony and were not brought to a place of prominence until the late 1960s, when the Holocaust began to serve as a moral paradigm for the global issues of the day.[35] The Six-Day War, the war in Vietnam, and even the American civil rights movement enabled Americans to bring the Holocaust to a place of primacy in their lives and culture (particularly American Jews), as they saw a correlation between the past and present as part of a related continuum.

The Six-Day War is generally accepted as a sharp turning point in the Holocaust narrative in American Jewish culture. The fear of a reprise of the Holocaust arose when the second president of Egypt, Gamal Abdel Nasser (along with several other Arab leaders) threatened to drive Israel into the sea in 1967, prompting greater Jewish attention to the Holocaust, according to many scholars.[36] Though Hasia Diner has debunked the notion of American Jewish silence about the Holocaust as a myth, that this threat propelled the State of Israel and the Holocaust into the everyday lives of American Jews to a degree it had not previously reached cannot be denied. American concern for Israel was real, in spite of the fact that Israel launched a number of preemptive strikes against Egyptian forces, causing controversy over who should bear responsibility for actually beginning the war. However, the degree to which the war terrified Jews in the United States, and worried them for the survival of Israel, has often been overstated by historians of the conflict, though there was certainly much journalistic excitement about the quick turnaround and victory for Israel.[37]

It was not only the Jews of America who watched the war unfold with eager, if anxious, anticipation. Much of America saw the Six-Day victory as a victory for the United States and its allies against the Soviet bloc. Israel was, after all, fighting Soviet-backed forces out of Egypt, and managed to defeat them, a feat the United States was desperately failing to do in Vietnam. In addition, the clearly deep-rooted but latent attachment to, and concern for, the State of Israel rose to prominence in Jewish America. From the moment the war began, American Jews were so preoccupied with the events in the Middle East that an unprecedented uniformity of focus and panic affected American Jews from all walks of life and denominations.[38]

In addition to their fear for the safety of Jews in Israel, American Jews also felt a continuing guilt for their failure to rescue the Jews of Europe. This (in conjunction with the revival of antisemitic rhetoric aired in the Arab radio reports in May of 1967) garnered greater support for Israel, American involvement in the Middle East, and a certainty that the loss of Israel meant a loss to Jewish identity everywhere. In addition, it motivated (at least in part) an antagonistic Jewish American response. According to Lucy Dawidowicz, "For the second time in a quarter of a century the Jewish people were facing annihilation. But this time, somehow, things would be different. There would be no passivity, no timidity. That was the mood of American Jews."[39] Jews in the United States had so incorporated the new image of the more masculine, tough Israeli that this now seemed a possibility—a great change from their perception during the Second World War. Their fear was quickly replaced with unprecedented pride in the Israeli state and Jewish strength, as Israel vanquished its enemies with enough speed to shock the international community. Their military victory against Soviet-backed forces inspired further support for the new state from the American public (both Jewish and otherwise), which had already been high before the war began. This clear victory for democracy, as it was seen in the Cold War context, also put Israeli men in a position closer to attaining the American masculine hegemon than Jewish men in America generally had been.

Of course, the speed at which the war approached and passed was such that volunteerism to fight was hardly as possible as it had been in the Israeli War for Independence (fighting with the Machal) or in the First World War (fighting for the Jewish Legion). So American Jewish backing of the war manifested, as it had in the past, in monetary donation and political support. Monetary contributions arrived, in part, as a result of the periodic reminders of Jewish American failure to act during the Holocaust by notable survivors, like Elie Wiesel, who used it to stir up feelings of guilt over American Jewish complacency. Wiesel published *The Jews of Silence* in 1966, which focused on the Jews of the Soviet Union but also implicated the Jews of the United States, who were enjoying the comfort of the developed and democratic world. American Jewish financial contributions escalated dramatically, especially considering the short duration of the war. In the short period from the outbreak of war to its conclusion, American Jews alone raised one hundred million dollars in support of the state.[40]

In addition to showing military strength, the war had religious meaning for global Jewry. Israel not only fought off its enemies, but it also conquered territories like the Sinai Peninsula, Gaza Strip, West Bank, and Golan Heights, and including land that was irreplaceably sacred to the Jewish religion, such as the holy sites of the Old City of

Figure 23. As Israel changed, so did Srulik, "Dosh's" cartoon embodiment of the nation. He grew taller, donned a uniform, and during the Six-Day War (not pictured) he appeared helmeted and in military boots. Kriel Gardosh, "Srulik is Growing Up," illustration, srulik.co.il, June, 29, 2023. http://srulik.co.il/%d7%a9%d7%a8%d7%95%d7%9c%d7%99%d7%a7/.

Jerusalem. These successes had implications for messianic, as well as political, Zionism. At this time, Zionism in Israel turned toward the religious, overpowering the previously dominant secular Zionist forces.[41] However, the war affected Jews and Zionists in the United States quite differently. According to political scientist Daniel Elazar, American Jews actually became less religious in the aftermath of the Six-Day War. He argued that Jewish life in America began to focus so intently on Israel (at the cost of Jewish religion) that it formed a unique "Israelotry," in which Jews came to worship the Israeli state over the God of Israel.[42] Even the anti-Zionist group, the American Council for Judaism, found themselves conflicted over the matter. After the group's director assisted the Syrian ambassador in writing a speech critical of Israel, a member of the group wrote that if the director "couldn't say anything good about Israel, why couldn't he have kept his big yap shut."[43] Sociologist Chaim Waxman wrote that individuals like this, after the war, landed in the odd position of identifying as both anti-Zionist and pro-Israel, but that for the overwhelming majority of American Jews, there was an unambiguously pro-Israel consensus. It is interesting that for Jewish identity among both Zionist and non-Zionist Jews (even among both the religious and secular), Israel became an unshakable aspect of being Jewish.

Still, marked differences in the masculine image of Israel differentiated this conflict from their earlier struggle. The image of the Israeli (previously evolved from halutz to sabra) now evolved from sabra to soldier. It was, in fact, at the outbreak of the Six-Day War that the artist Dosh revamped his comic Israeli personification, Srulik, to be a soldier. He began drawing Srulik as taller, wearing long pants, military boots, rolled up sleeves, and a military helmet.[44]

Israel established itself as the preeminent military power in the area, and their soldiers became icons of heroism and militaristic manhood (though this iconic status has since changed several times over in response to political actions and situations in Israel). While the fight in Vietnam discredited the masculinity of the American soldier, the war in Israel did the opposite for the soldiers of Israel. Through Israeli soldiers, American Jews discovered what Lucy Dawidowicz described as a "new pride in being Jewish, in the aura that radiated from General Moshe Dayan, his ruggedness, vigor, determination."[45] This change in the international Jewish image prompted two changes in the attitudes of American Jews, which reflect both their attitudes toward the State of Israel as a foreign nation and their own personal identity. They came to see Israel as a state capable of survival, one that even thrived in the initial decades of its existence. Young Jews saw Jewish heroes in Israel and the older community saw new strength and success, and a diminished sense of urgency about Jewish survival.

The sexuality of Jews in Israel was highlighted in American journalistic reports on the war, stressing the miniskirts worn by young female Jewish soldiers and the sexual relationships formed within an army that maintained compulsory service for both men and women.[46] The appeal of the Israeli soldier as personified by tough Jewish men appealed to Americans on both sides of the discussion of the conflict in Vietnam. He was a military hero, rugged and rough, but with his history of the Jewish tradition for peace, he was resignedly fighting the good fight for democracy in a Middle East fighting for its soul in the Cold War conflict.

American Jewish support had changed since the Second World War, reverted to its prewar Zionism of primarily philanthropic and political support, without military or illegal aid. The Six-Day War provided a defining moment, however, for the American Jewish relationship to the Israeli state, affecting even those who previously felt little connection. There was a tremendous drive for American youth to support the State of Israel, regardless of their earlier intentions to make aliyah themselves. It is an interesting measure of difference between the determined creation of the state and the settled reality of Israel that unlike the War of Independence, no Machal volunteers traveled to fight and bolster Israeli forces. There was not time to do so in the Six-Day War, but even after, they did not do so in any of the conflicts that followed. Though many American Jews have chosen to go to Israel to serve regardless of their intention of making aliyah (either as immigrants in the Israel Defense Forces, or taking the civilian jobs left vacant by soldiers during conflicts), the rush to do so for a specific conflict has never since arisen, and the numbers remain quite small. American Jews did, however, begin to migrate to Israel in much larger numbers. The numbers of American *olim* (new immigrants in Israel) increased tremendously in the years immediately following the Six-Day War. From 1968 to 1969, Jewish migration from America to Israel increased by over 40 percent, and then by an additional 17 percent by 1971. This increase was not permanent, however, as it all but disappeared by 1973 and declined even further in the aftermath of the Yom Kippur War.[47]

For most of America, the Six-Day War strengthened the perception of Israel as a small, scrappy new nation, acting as the biblical character David, facing down Goliath and prevailing in spite of disadvantage in size, age, and support. The Six-Day War also changed the way that American Jewish youth saw themselves as members of a religious and ethnic minority, perhaps even more than for their parents' generation. As one young woman wrote at the close of the war, "Two weeks ago, Israel was they; now Israel is we."[48] Even those who had no interest in making aliyah felt drawn to the small state's struggle for survival. Though there was little time to plan volunteerism in Israel during the conflict, about 7,500 young Americans (primarily students) volunteered for civil service (though most did not make it there before the crisis was over). However, the enthusiasm for civil service declined when the threat was over, and there was no physical danger in the journey.

This volunteerism shows a somewhat conflicted young Jewish America, as many young Jews on the political Left formed a decidedly negative view of war based on the American example in Vietnam. The war in Israel felt more personal for many Jews, and for some, far easier to see as a just war to protect a vulnerable people. This was not merely a Jewish view, but a largely American one. According to survey data from the Pew Research Center, for forty years immediately following the war, Americans were primarily sympathetic to Israel (rather than to Arab states or Palestinians), and more so than any other nation outside of the conflict.[49] However, support for Israel during and after this conflict brought much of the young Jewish Left into conflict with their non-Jewish counterparts, who considered the Israeli government and military guilty of committing atrocities of imperialism against a colonized Arab people. For some young Jews, the two situations were impossible to reconcile—loathing war and supporting the Jewish people in a unique situation. As one student at City College in New York wrote:

> The Israeli-Arab war has had a schizoid effect on my emotions.
> On the one hand, I find war and its inherent loss of life revolting
> and I could not and would not participate. On the other hand,
> I realize that Israel has been struggling for its existence while

surrounded by hostile neighbors bent on her destruction, and I
sympathize with Israel. The net result is that I sit home and curse
war and the Arabs.[50]

In the aftermath of the war, Jewish American identity came to focus
as never before on the significance of the State of Israel and the necessity
of including the Holocaust in Jewish culture and religion. Without the
fear of another Holocaust, after all, American Jews may not have rallied
as they did to aid the Jewish state. Though there doubtless would have
been support, much rationale for volunteering, supporting, and donating
was the fear of another genocide. After the fear and anxiety of the Six-
Day War, American Jews began weaving the Holocaust as never before
into their everyday public lives and religious education. Chaim Waxman
argued that in the wake of the Six-Day War, the Holocaust as a symbol
of Jewish survival became a core unifying element of Jewish civil life in
America.[51] Much as Hasia Diner debunked the popular narrative that
claimed American Jewish focus on the Holocaust emerged in reaction to
the Six-Day War, Emily Alice Katz similarly debunked the narrative that
American Jews also did not incorporate Israel into their lives until the war.
Katz demonstrated that starting in 1948, the State of Israel was already
significant (though to a lesser degree) in the everyday lives of American
Jews. So much so that they had already begun incorporating Israeli folk
dance, consumer culture, and household incorporation of Israeli imagery well before the war.[52]

The uptick in Israeli focus for American Jews after the war is still notable, however, as American Jews in larger numbers began practicing Jewish
life differently, adopting Israeli customs and even changing the way they
pronounced Hebrew words to adopt the Israeli sound (such as from *yar-
mulke* to *kippa*, or *Shabbos to Shabbat*). This "Israelotry" or "Israelization"
appeared in several areas of American Jewish life. Jewish youth groups, synagogues, and summer camps incorporated Israeli folk music and dancing.
Having Israeli art and artifacts in the home became an important element
of larger Jewish culture in the United States. In addition, this incorporation of Israeli life and culture into the lives of American Jews became more
attainable and organic with the increasing waves of immigrants moving to
the United States from Israel, which began immediately after statehood
was declared, but rose dramatically in the early 1970s.[53]

In spite of the pride American Jews felt in the aftermath of the war, and the degree to which they began integrating Israel and its brand of militant masculinity into their daily lives, American youth continued to struggle with the morality of war, particularly the role America was playing in the war in Vietnam. Jewish men and women became many of the most identifiable faces and names of the protest movements of the 1960s and '70s, and throughout their protests, Jewish men still struggled to balance their identities with their masculine image. That balance turned out to be even more complex as the 1960s drew to a close, particularly for Jewish men involved in the American antiwar movement and participating in the associated counterculture. It became difficult, for example, to enjoy the masculine pride linked to Israeli victory while still dodging the military draft in America. Those involved in civil rights protests struggled to balance identities, fighting for the rights of underserved minorities while commuting from the wealthy suburban homes of their parents. And those Jewish observers of ethnic pride movements in the United States looked to Israel, to tough Jews proving themselves abroad, as inspiration and justification for a new Jewish masculinity in America.

The Six-Day War may not have made hawks out of the doves counted among Jewish American youth, but it left some conflicted and struggling to balance their identities as American antiwar agitators (more on this in the following chapter) and as members of a global Jewish community in the aftermath of the Holocaust, fighting for continued survival.

10

Substituting the Bomb
for the Book

Jewish Men, Protest, Revolution, and Upheaval

> We were demonstrating at the Pentagon to disassociate ourselves
> from a certain kind of manhood. We were opposed, not merely to a
> foreign policy, but to a masculine identity that breeds such policies.
> We were confronting the five-sided symbol of the soldiering sex.
> Even as we opposed it, however, we embodied it. The contradic-
> tion was evident. Among us were groups who mouthed the slogan,
> "fight for peace."
>
> —Mark Gerzon[1]

The social, political, and cultural cataclysms of the 1960s had dramatic
effects on Jewish America. There was a rupture in American perceptions of gender and sex, and the Jewish community felt this acutely. In
addition to being an American minority already considered outside of
hegemonic American gender (with stereotypes specifically about both
Jewish men and women still prevalent), Jews were particularly active in
the movements that defined American counterculture and highlighted
masculinities coalescing at the margins of American society. This chapter examines the continued negotiation of Jewish masculine gender
identity in a historical moment when contradicting forces were rapidly
and aggressively redefining manhood. In examining two distinct rec-
lamations of Jewish masculinity enacted by Jewish men on the far left
(protest movement) and the far right (Jewish militancy), there are surprising similarities. Both groups expressed their masculinity within their
respective movements by dominating over women, relegating them to
the sidelines in spite of their purported support of the simultaneous

feminist movement, and in spite of the gender inclusivity of their non-Jewish comrades of parallel movements. Both identified as antiestablishment, and factions of both resorted to violent terrorism.

Counterculture, Protest, and the Jewish American Man

The antiwar movement of the 1960s contained a distinctly Jewish dimension that manifested as a highly gendered phenomenon. Among the primary actors in antiwar demonstration, Jewish men actively and disproportionally took on leadership positions, compared with their percentage of the American population. Some of the most recognizable figures of the time were Jewish, such as Jerry Rubin, Robert Alan Haber, Abbie Hoffman, Mark Rudd, Allen Ginsberg, David Gilbert, and A. J. Weberman. In spite of major disruptions to gender norms caused by multifaceted massive social change in the 1960s (second-wave feminism, antiwar protest, protesting the draft, Black nationalism, and such), Jewish men still struggled to find their own unique place in the ever-broadening landscape of American masculinities.

As nonviolent protest increased all over the country, Jews became particularly prominent among the protesters and supporters of social movements. Even in non-Jewish specific groups, Jews were quite visible in leadership and among the ranks. Two-thirds of the white Freedom Riders traveling to Mississippi were Jewish; the majority of the steering committee of the Berkeley free speech movement in 1964 was Jewish; the chapters of Students for a Democratic Society (SDS) at Columbia and the University of Michigan were both more than half Jewish; at Kent State in Ohio, where only 5 percent of the student population was Jewish, Jews constituted 19 percent of SDS membership (also worth noting that three of the four students shot by the National Guard at Kent State were Jewish).[2] This disproportional representation on college campuses is largely due to the affluence that the American Jewish community attained in the years following the war. Of the students participating in these groups, most came from middle-class Jewish families, as restrictions on Jewish attendance in American universities had become a thing of the past. With unprecedented access to higher education, Jews were overrepresented at universities overall, not only in protest. While Jews comprised 3.2 percent of the national population, the percentage of

Jewish faculty was 8.7 percent, and Jews comprised 10 percent of graduates as well as 5.3 percent of undergraduates. These numbers are even more disproportionately Jewish in the highest-ranking institutions.[3] The number of Jewish women enrolled was also unprecedented, as more than 50 percent of Jewish women of age were in college by 1970, a product, historian Paula Hyman explained, of their middle-class incomes, small family size, and instilled cultural value of education.[4]

Agitators in the antiwar movement sustained several intersecting interests and causes, not always exclusive to the goal of peace. Feminist protesters, for example, frequently participated in the antiwar movement, splitting their efforts and time between multiple movements. Nearly every feminist protestor profiled in Joyce Antler's book on Jewish radical feminism relays the experience of Jewish women involved with radical protest on multiple fronts, including union activism, garment workers, racial equality advocates, antiwar protestors, Jewish activists, Zionists, and more. Their differing interests intersected through inclusive and overarching ideologies like anticolonialism, peace activism, and the fight for American civil rights (struggles that simultaneously involved political, gendered, economic, and racial issues).

Despite the egalitarian rhetoric espoused by so many intersectional protestors, the antiwar movement suppressed female expression in a typically patriarchal fashion reflective of larger American (and Jewish) society. Dominant Jewish male leaders struggled to prove their place among the influential masculine heroes of the revolution, particularly Black nationalists. This made for a machismo-ridden climate, with men trying to prove themselves at the expense of one another, and of women. This particularly held true in more militant groups, but peaceful protests also relegated women to the sidelines, embracing a male-dominated and hypermasculine climate in the movement. Even some of the men in the movement recognized continuity between this treatment of women at meetings and the treatment of women in the Jewish community. Jerry Rubin reflected, of his years with the Youth International Party (the Yippies), "I remember during yippie meetings the 'men' talked their business and humored the women when they began to talk, not expecting to hear anything 'worthwhile.' During all that time I was seeing, not Joan, Barbara, or Laurie, but my grandma on the second floor of the synagogue watching my grandfather with the men downstairs."[5]

Because the draft comprised one of the key issues of antiwar protest, men involved in antiwar activism (both Jewish and otherwise) asserted their authority over the issue, which they felt affected them most, as it was their lives at risk if the draft continued. This male dominance relegated women to more menial tasks that would maintain their subordinate role in the movement, such as typing reports or preparing food for events. Even in the act of refusing the draft (a practice some men decried as un-American and unmanly), hypermacho rhetoric can be seen in materials produced by activists, as in the directly sexual slogan, "Girls say yes to boys who say no." Though a lot of feminists in the antiwar movement disliked the campaign, many went along with it to further the cause. Joan Baez even posed for a photo that would become a poster bearing this slogan.[6] This division of gender among antiwar activists, Sara Evans argued, gave rise to women's liberation, as female activists unwilling to be marginalized took their negative experiences in the antiwar movement and made them central issues of women's rights and inequality.[7]

At Columbia University, where multiple student movements erupted simultaneously, faculty theorized that the Jewish students in non-Jewish-specific white protest were, in part, Jewish students revolting against their middle-class parents and attempting to prove their masculinity alongside Black nationalists. These students, according to one faculty member, "regard their fathers as emasculated by suburban life and their Judaism as a 'shallow, pale thing.' . . . They hate their fathers for this—for accepting Ridgewood (the suburb) and part of their hostility to Judaism comes from this."[8] Whether Jewish students involved in the movement actually drew their motivation from tension with their parents' generation is murky guesswork, aside from the statements made by the students themselves (some of which I examine below). However, comments by the older generation of Jews, such as the faculty member above, or sociologist Lewis Feuer, provide insight to how the older generation interpreted intergenerational tension. Feuer, for example, also believed that these Jewish students were, at least in part, motivated by the emasculation of their own fathers. He highlighted the shift to suburban life far less than the post-Holocaust image of Jewish weakness, which also served to emasculate Jewish men. He explained:

> In previous generations Jewish students felt ashamed that their often cultureless parents were a persecuted people, always passive, always suffering, telling horrid stories of the indignities of pogroms. Their fathers seemed lacking in manliness. Their misfortune lacked the heroic cast, and were therefore devoid of the nobility of tragedy. Then a new generation after the Second World War heard of Jews, it was as victims, again almost always passive, of the Nazi holocaust [sic], of those who had torn from them the last shreds of human dignity as they were led in queues to abattoirs. The Jewish students of successive generations felt that their parents—orthodox, liberal, religious, agnostic—somehow shared in the psychology of passive acquiescence, that as the persecuted, they had been virtually deprived of their manhood, emasculated.[9]

This perception of shameful Jewish weakness as unmasculine is precisely the aspect of the Holocaust that affected the masculine image of Jews worldwide. The Jewish male protestor then, according to Feuer, felt it necessary to protest the injustices done to Jews and everyone else, without calling attention to his own Jewish background. Feuer argued that the basic reason for Jewish students being so involved in protest was a revolt against their fathers not for being emasculated by modern life but for being emasculated by historical antisemitism. Either way, it is both fascinating and telling that Feuer and other Jewish men from the survivor/parental generation observed the antiwar movement and highlighted their own emasculation as the cause for the student rebellion.

Sociologist Nathan Glazer gave a quite different explanation for the prominence of Jewish students in the counterculture and protest movements. He hypothesized that tensions had actually diminished between generations in families with liberal or radical parents. Nearly all Jewish parents, he believed, considered themselves at least liberal if not radical. From their own experiences, he explained, they tended to support the activism of their children. With the support of their parents, Jewish students participated more actively, knowing they still had a home and family to fall back on.[10] Regardless of the accuracy of any of these claims about the Jewish-generational motivation of student protestors, it is nonetheless clear that young Jewish men engaging in student protests attempted to take back a manlier identity, and that the older generation perceived it as such. These young men attempting to do so exerted their efforts within a larger American countercultural and political context, as opposed to forming and working through specifically Jewish groups.

When protests erupted in April and May of 1968 at Columbia University, contemporary Jewish observers understood the movement to have a distinctly Jewish component. This is evident in the papers of the American Jewish Committee Office of Information Service, which detected an identifiably Jewish presence among both student protestors and faculty supporters. Worried that the presence of Jews in the protests might spark antisemitism, the American Jewish Committee interviewed five high-ranking Jewish academics at Columbia to comment on the anxieties of the committee regarding the Jewish element in disruptions on campus. Though they gave their feedback on Jewish students as uncategorical truth, it contains much speculation and psychologizing. The theme that dominates the commentary is that Jewish activists wanted to emulate groups they saw as more masculine, like Black nationalists and African Americans fighting for civil rights. By observing Black activists and Black Power groups, young Jewish men saw a precedent of masculine civil protest that they could mimic. The faculty interviewed by the American Jewish Committee believed that for Jewish student activists the "desire to identify with revolutionary Negro experience is crucial."[11] However, this identification was ideological, not practical. "The frustration here," one faculty member explained, "probably is that they (the Jewish kids) are soft, they're not tough, they're not really experienced in life. They have to assert their masculinity, that's a fundamental challenge. They're sort of play-acting; they know when the score is over they can go back home; the others, the black kids, can't."

It is interesting that this faculty member and Nathan Glazer agreed on the sympathetic nature of the Jewish generational dialogue, that Jewish (presumably liberal) parents at home supported the activism of their sons and daughters on college campuses. However, Glazer used this point to explain why there had come to be so many Jewish students in the movement, whereas the Columbia faculty member used it as a point of frustration for the students already involved. The two ideas are not mutually exclusive, as it is entirely possible that the supportive nature of the parents allowed students to become activists, but also plagued their sense of independent masculinity. At any rate, there was no getting around the large (and visible) participation of young Jewish men in the protest movement, or the desire to manifest the masculinity that the faculty generation ascribed to them.

Indeed, Jewish students were present even in civil rights groups, which were primarily African American. This reflects a long history of Jews involved in the struggle for civil rights in the United States. Complicating this narrative with the desire of Jewish men involved to create more masculine identities for themselves not only broadens historical understanding of Jewish masculinity during this time, it also adds a necessary gendered component to the history of Jews in the movement on the whole. There were young Jews active in the early days of the Student Non-violent Coordinating Committee (SNCC) and the Congress of Racial Equality (CORE) who participated in all levels of protest. Two Jewish men from New York were famously killed while working with Black civil rights protestors in the Freedom Summer murders in Mississippi in 1964. Students for a Democratic Society, the Weathermen, and other primarily white student groups attempted to join forces with more militant protestors, like the Black Panthers and other Black nationalists. In large part, they were rejected, rather than embraced as brothers in arms in a shared struggle.

A Columbia professor used the case of Mark Rudd (the SDS member who would break off to form the more radical Weathermen in 1969), as an example of this rejection by Black nationalists, and the subsequent desire by Jewish students to assert their masculinity. He explained of the SDS takeover of an administration building on campus, "the black students in Hamilton Hall challenged Rudd . . . they challenged his masculinity in a way . . . you know. . . . They said, 'show us your way, take your own building,' and he did."[12] He is speaking here of the student takeover of a mostly administrative building on campus. The building, Hamilton Hall, was seized and occupied by a joint effort of the Student Afro-American Society (SAS) and SDS. After a disagreement in which SDS members wanted to take hostages to draw attention to their antiwar cause, the Black students of SAS asked white students to leave. The above faculty member identified Rudd's issue of one of both Jewishness and masculinity. At the time, however, the events were described in non-Jewish circles as a purely racial split, "SDS pleaded not to be evicted, the blacks ordered the whites out of the building. . . . Some went home, but about a hundred decided to take a building of their own."[13] In more recent scholarship, the Jewish identity of many leading SDS members has been recognized, but not analyzed. In his 2003 history of Columbia University, Robert McCaughey profiled key student radicals as "so-called red diaper babies," who "mostly came from New York (or from the city's surrounding suburbs, where their parents had recently moved) and were likely to be Jewish. There were few intercollegiate athletes among them, and still fewer fraternity members."[14] This profile recognizes not only the Jewishness of the members but also (at least for the male members) an absence of masculine participation outside of the movement (no athletics, no fraternities).

The ironic duality that Jewish professors described (characteristic of the Old Left generation they represented), of Jewish students struggling for acceptance with Black Nationalists only to be rejected and emasculated, is emblematic of the state of Black-Jewish relations during this period. Traditionally involved with the civil rights movement, some American Jews were positively predisposed to the Black Power movement and wanted to support it.[15] However, Black activists in this new movement did not see Jews as sharing in their struggle.[16]

In his 1963 essay, "My Negro Problem—And Ours," Norman Podhoretz showed that this desire to emulate the masculinity of African American boys was not new to Rudd's generation. He brought up Jewish masculinity explicitly when recalling the relations between Black and Jewish boys in his Brooklyn neighborhood, explaining that it was the African American boys' "superior masculinity" that Jewish boys envied.[17] He did not believe, as Rudd did, that the two groups were or should be united in their struggles as minorities but explained the tensions between them by the differences in their experiences growing up in segregated American society. He explained that growing up Jewish in Brooklyn, his impression of the Black boys in his neighborhood was that they were "free, independent, reckless, brave, masculine, erotic. . . . But most important of all," he went on, "they were tough; beautifully, enviably tough, not giving a damn for anyone or anything. To hell with the teacher, the truant officer, the cop; to hell with the whole of the adult world that held us in its grip and that we never had the courage to rebel against except sporadically and in petty ways."[18]

Rudd has made several statements that support similar assumptions about his own motivation and actions (and those of his fellow

Jewish protestors). In fact, Rudd is an excellent case study of the generational divide within his Jewish family. Both his parents' families were mass-migration-period immigrants. His mother was the first American-born in her family from Lithuania and his father emigrated from Poland and served in the American Army in World War II. Continuing to serve as a reservist, he Americanized his name from Rudnitsky to Rudd, as, according to his son, "someone had told him that a Rudnitsky could never rise above the rank of Captain, so in 1954 he shortened his name—and mine—which seemed to do the trick."[19] He eventually rose to the rank of lieutenant colonel.

The Rudd family was not particularly religious but maintained their sense of Jewish culture and apartness from the "goyim" in their relatively integrated suburban neighborhood. The teenage Rudd was desperate to escape the middle-class Jewish suburban life he resented as overly bourgeois and old-fashioned, so he joined a non-Jewish but still Jewish-dominated movement at Columbia. He remembers it as such, explaining "All of us were Jewish. It's hard to remember the names of non-Jewish Columbia SDS'ers; it was as much a Jewish fraternity as Sammie" (Sammie here refers to the fraternity Sigma Alpha Mu, a Jewish fraternity commonly known as "Sammy," or "Sammie" for its SAM abbreviation). Even so, Jewishness was not a factor that student protestors actively recognized as a unifying element of their organizations. Rudd recalls, "I don't remember one single conversation in which we discussed the fact that so many of us were Jewish. This glaring lack alone might serve as a clue to what we were up to: by being radicals we thought we could escape our Jewishness." If these Jewish men hoped to escape their Jewishness, a main feature of their dissatisfaction was with the Jewish manhood they wanted to leave behind.

Rudd acknowledges the male atmosphere, as well as the Jewishness of the group, when he compares SDS (a non-gender-specific group) to a Jewish fraternity. After he broke with SDS to found and lead the Weathermen (which would become a terrorist group pursued by the FBI), tensions between the men and women involved grew. Conflicts arose between Rudd and the Jewish women in the Weather Underground (particularly Bernadine Dohrn, Jane Alpert, and Robin Morgan) over chauvinism in the group. According to McCaughey, some women thought Rudd's chauvinism "excessive even by prevailing standards on the left."[20] Between Jewish men and women involved in the movement, Rudd argued that tension within the group was a male/female struggle that happened to be between Jews, rather than an ethnic struggle.[21] However, he made clear distinctions in his feelings toward and relationships with non-Jewish women in the movement as well. When discussing his own sexual conquests while living as a fugitive activist, he explained that to a Jewish boy like himself, sleeping with lots of women, particularly *shiksas* (non-Jewish women who are traditionally forbidden by Jewish law), was his way of living out a male fantasy.[22] Though objectifying and juvenile, his distinction shows an awareness of his own varying treatment of Jewish and non-Jewish women in the movement.

For Jewish students at Columbia, motivations for joining political protest movements were diverse and at times contradictory. They recognized and wanted to escape their suburban privilege (and Jewishness) and yearned to join the more oppressed Black student protestors, to whom they felt a kinship due to their oppressed minority status as Jews. So simultaneously they joined *because* of their Jewish past, while hoping their participation could *rid* them of their Jewish present. They felt that although there was a large Jewish population (25 percent of the Columbia student body was Jewish in the early 1960s), the school was still "dripping with goyishness."[23] Rudd explained, "Identifying with the oppressed seemed to me at Columbia and since a natural Jewish value, though one we never spoke of as being Jewish."[24] Though Rudd was not discussing his masculinity as such, he does reinforce the conclusion reached by the Columbia professor quoted earlier, who explained that Rudd's "desire to identify with revolutionary Negro experience" showed his frustration as a soft Jewish kid; not tough, not experienced, and not as oppressed as Jewish history might entitle him to feel. The fact that the Jewish membership of SDS was more heavily male and the non-Jewish membership more heavily female also indicates that men joining the movement in greater numbers as a masculine endeavor may have been largely limited to Jewish membership. This is not to say, however, that Jewish women in the movement did not also avoid openly identifying as Jewish, and for some overlapping reasons concerning privilege, historical connection to oppression, and so on. But Jewish feminists, particularly, as Joyce Antler has shown, had other reasons for not identifying religiously within the countercultural movement as well (such as the determination to align themselves with an overtly patriarchal value system).[25]

There was still a good deal of Jewish camaraderie within the protest movement at Columbia, though it emerged in separate groups, or dealing with separate issues, from the larger groups like SDS. One of the most unifying protests of Jewish students *as Jews* was to fight against the dismissal of Rabbi Goldman (sometimes called Rabbi Bruce), who served as a Jewish chaplain at Columbia University during the 1968 protests and was known as the "radical rabbi." While at Columbia, Goldman was sympathetic toward several radical movements. He supported student protests (including the destruction of property), accepted interfaith relationships among students, approved of mixed gender cohabitation (against the school's policy), and provided abortion counseling to Barnard students (the private women's liberal arts college affiliate). The fight over Rabbi Goldman, and the unity of Jewish students protesting *as Jews* directly contradicted the efforts to "pass" in American society, which the previous generations had worked toward. Those who participated in these specifically Jewish actions made their Jewishness more visible within the New Left, as did Rabbi Goldman. The Jewish Advisory Board at Columbia (drawn from the older generation) felt this jeopardized the prestige of the Jewish establishment. Jewish students defended their protest as not only right, but as being one that actually took pride in their Jewishness, unlike the Jewish Advisory Board, who they saw as cowardly, and condemned them as "a bunch of self-hating Jews faithfully ass-licking their WASP masters."[26] They did not, however, make the same comments about other Jewish students who were active only in non-Jewish protest.

Outside of the university environment (though often closely linked) young protestors staged similar demonstrations, also led by a notable number of Jewish participants, and also largely male. One of the most unusual courtroom spectacles in American history took place from 1969 to 1970 and included a public demonstration of the new Jewish manhood of the time. Although not generally presented as part of a particularly Jewish American story, the trial of the Chicago Seven (originally the Chicago Eight) is a standout event in the history of Jewish men and counterculture. The defendants were charged with conspiracy to incite the 1968 riots at the National Democratic Convention in Chicago. Of the seven defendants, three were Jews (Abbie Hoffman, Jerry Rubin, and Lee Weiner) and all were men. In addition, both defense attorneys (William

Kunstler and Leonard Weinglass) were Jewish, as was one of the two prosecuting attorneys (Richard Schultz) and the presiding judge (Julius Hoffman). Of the twelve key players in this drama, therefore, seven were Jews. And in the entire ordeal, only a few women participated as actors, all in subservient positions (stenographers and assistants), aside from the twelve jurors, ten of whom were women.[27]

It is not only because of the Jewishness or maleness of the players that I claim this trial was a Jewish masculine event. Throughout the trial, the defense played out a form of guerrilla theater that consistently commented on their own and Judge Hoffman's Jewishness. They may not have thought of the proceedings as a demonstration of male Jewishness at the time, but maleness was a recognized element of the trial. Appreciating that perceptions of gender played an important role in the case, the defense attorneys tried to eliminate jurors who might impugn the masculinity of the defendants. During the juror selection process, Judge Hoffman dismissed several questions from Kunstler and Weinglass meant to eliminate potential jurors, one of which was, "Do you believe that young men who refuse to participate in the armed forces because of their opposition to the war are cowards, slackers, or unpatriotic?" Jewish men had routinely been accused of all three of these slants over the previous century, so much so that it is unlikely the connection was unintentional. Kunstler and Weinglass intended to eliminate jurors predisposed to judge the defendants as unmanly and cowardly, demonstrating the significance of gender in the courtroom drama.[28]

Initially, the federal government charged eight defendants with conspiracy and intent to incite a riot, including one of the cofounders of the Black Panthers, Bobby Seale. The government also charged Seale (along with Dellinger, Hayden, Davis, Hoffman, and Rubin) with inciting violence.[29] Seale's attorney fell ill and entered the hospital for emergency surgery days before the trial. Judge Hoffman refused to postpone the trial or to grant Seale a new attorney (he insisted that Seale accept representation by the counsel of the other defendants). Seale protested that he needed to have his choice of attorney or exercise his right to represent himself. Unwilling to compromise, the judge had Seale bound, gagged, and eventually removed from the courtroom. The uproar over the confrontation between Seale and Judge Hoffman made the trial an instant spectacle of racial inequality.

Just as Jewish university students felt kinship with Black national-ists, so too did the Chicago Seven. They deferred to Seale's wisdom and experience when they acquiesced to have his lawyer be chief counsel for the group. Shortly after having him bound and gagged, the judge declared a mistrial for Bobby Seale, ejecting him from court and separating him from the other defendants. At this point, the racial element of the trial, which had previously dominated the courtroom, was replaced by a Jew-ish presence. The Jewish atmosphere of the courtroom was defined by two elements: the growing centrality of the Holocaust since the Six-Day War two years earlier, and the conflict between the Jewish generations: establishment and counterculture.

The defendants used the Holocaust as a tool to insult the judge, court, and system prosecuting them. They vented their frustration at the establishment, comparing them to Nazis routinely throughout the trial. Even David Dellinger, a non-Jewish defendant, vented his anger at Judge Hoffman through this language, "You want us to be like good Germans supporting the evils of our decade and then when we refused to be good Germans and came to Chicago . . . now you want us to be like good Jews, going quietly and politely to the concentration camps while you and this court suppress freedom and truth."[30] Abbie Hoffman and Jerry Rubin, in one of the most memorable theatrical stunts of the trial, entered the courtroom one day wearing black judge's robes with yellow Jewish stars affixed to their chests (commenting on their own Jewishness as well as the judge's while alluding to their own persecution).

By identifying themselves as Jews, and continually interjecting Holocaust comparisons into the proceedings, Hoffman and his fel-low defendants presented themselves to the public as the persecuted minority. They did not present themselves as passive or meek victims, however, but changed the implications of their persecution as Jewish men. Decades later, Abbie Hoffman, reflecting on his own identity and feelings toward the older generation, explained, "Deep down I am sure we felt our parents' generation was a bunch of cop outs. Six million dead and except for the Warsaw Ghetto hardly a bullet fired in resistance."[31] According to Pnina Lahav, Hoffman, his codefendants, and their entire generation of young Jews were fuming about the passivity of Jews in previous generations and were determined to right that wrong by plac-ing themselves in the line of fire, which they did (in cases like Mark

Rudd, quite literally in the form of terrorist bombings).[32] Though not fought with fists, engaging Judge Hoffman in a Jewish generational battle allowed them to "fight to the good fight," so to speak, and to distinguish themselves from those who went like lambs to slaughter, or (as in the case of Julius Hoffman) assisted in oppression, instead of fighting for the oppressed.

The Yippies (the Youth International Party founded by Hoffman and Rubin) steeped their actions in absurdity and reveled in spectacle, but not entirely without purpose. The conflict between the Jewish establishment and countercultural youth played out in this theatrical war the defendants fought against Judge Hoffman. Sharing the same Jewish last name and heritage, Abbie Hoffman led the charge of a very Jewish, and masculine, brand of ridicule against his oppressor. His brand of masculinity was not the Dionysian masculinity embraced by the New Left, but the more aggressive, vitriolic language of the Old Left and harder masculinity. James Penner explained, in his analysis of masculinity and the rhetoric of the 1960s, that Hoffman's masculinity:

> Expresses the legacy of both hard masculinity and Dionysian masculinity from the 1960s, and the various contradictions that the two trends imply. Hoffman is a key figure because he, in many respects, is the embodiment of both traditions. On one hand, Hoffman is a product of the Old Left. He is the son of radical left-wing Jewish parents, and his toughness evokes his devout commitment to progressive politics and social change. . . . Hoffman has intellectually accepted a progressive idea (feminism), but at the same time, on a psychosocial level, he is disavowing that he is in any way soft or effeminate for doing so.

The way his particular masculinity played out in the courtroom was an aggressive, yet humorous, attack on Judge Hoffman. He was a clown, but he was a tough clown, using loud, angry tactics to humiliate the judge. Initially, he threatened to change his own first name to "fuck" so that when called to testify he would legally have to be addressed as "Fuck Hoffman."[33] At times, he referred to Judge Hoffman not by their shared surname (refusing any idea of kinship) but colloquially called him "Julie," "the judge," or "Magoo" (the judge bore a striking resemblance to the cartoon character Mr. Magoo, and Hoffman led his supporters in chanting "Screw Magoo"). At one point, he also gave his own name, not as Hoffman, but as "Shaboysnakoff." Hoffman, he insisted, was his slave name.[34] This claim not only implied that he had been robbed of his Jewish identity but also implicated Judge Hoffman, who bore his own "slave name" without question. Abbie's antics in the courtroom were more spiteful than comical, clearly lashing out against sell-out, middle-class establishment Jews. "Your idea of justice is the only obscenity in this court, Julie," he shouted at the judge, "this ain't the Standard Club" (the Standard Club was an exclusive German-Jewish club to which the judge belonged).[35] Abbie spoke to him scathingly in Yiddish, "You *schtunk. Shchande vor de goyim,* huh?" Translated, this means "you skunk [or stinker], fronting for the gentiles [or, you shame us in front of the gentiles]."[36] However, when translating it himself, Abbie translated it as "front man for the WASP power elite."

The Chicago Seven trial was a demonstration of Jewish protestors embracing and using their Jewish heritage and history of oppression to their advantage in a public spectacle. They, particularly in the case of Abbie Hoffman, embraced the ideals of the New Left, while behaving in an undeniably masculine way. Whether they would have done so as vociferously, or as Jewishly, had Judge Hoffman not cast Bobby Seale from the courtroom is unknown. They had deferred to his authority as an experienced dissenter, and to his role as leader in Black American politics. Just as Mark Rudd was appealing to Black protestors at Columbia, so too did the Yippies benefit from the association and respect that came with being codefendants with Bobby Seale. It was only in Seale's absence that the Jewishness of the trial became so dominant.

The deference to Black protestors and leaders was not universal among Jews in the New Left. Nor were all Jews outside of the movement comfortable with the growing association of Jews to civil rights and organized protest. However, once the connection was forged in some instances, it was assumed in others. Some Jewish youth worried that the visibility of Jews might be used as justification for increased antisemitism in the United States, particularly on college campuses.[37] Their fears proved to be well-founded, as very public episodes of Jewish restriction ensued in response to the Jew-activist connection. At the University of Wisconsin in 1967, the Board of Regents put a system into place to restrict out-of-state students from particular "hold states," the states from which 90 percent of their Jewish students originated. One legislator clearly admitted of the restriction that: "It was to get rid of the kikes from New York and the dirty niggers."[38]

Jewish advocates became visible among wartime dissenters of all ages, but not only on college campuses. Jews participated in intellectual and political groups like Nader's Raiders (legal, political, and social advocacy group following Ralph Nader), which also brought attention to the Jewish presence in the movement. Nathan Glazer expressed his own fear that if the United States lost the war in Vietnam, Jews would be held responsible in some way, because of their prominence among the students and intellectuals speaking out against the war.

Older generations of Jewish Americans also expressed their concern that such a visible Jewish presence in varied movements pushed Jews away from Judaism and from more exclusively Jewish endeavors. When contemplating the crisis of diminishing Jewish identity on leaving their parents' home (a theme in Jewish commentary present through all of modernity, not exclusive to this decade), one American rabbi noted that though Jewish students previously found themselves barred from many (though not all) gentile student groups, the student revolts of the 1960s "destroyed these barriers," and therefore Jewish participation in exclusively Jewish student groups suffered a sharp decline.[39] The only benefit to this shift toward outside groups, in his estimation, was that when radical Jews were rejected from some groups, particularly the Black protest movement, they were forced to find a radicalism of their own, guiding those who did continue to embrace their Jewish connection to form more radical, socialist, Zionist organizations.

There is some truth to that assumption, though not necessarily that Jewish leftists reformed into Zionist organizations after rejection by Black nationalists. Certainly, when the Black nationalist movement declared Zionism a form of racist colonialism and accused Israel of oppressing a Third World people, they alienated Jewish protestors who also considered themselves Zionists.[40] One notable instance of this occurred in Chicago at the 1967 National Conference for New Politics convention, when the Black caucus condemned the Six-Day War as a war of Zionist aggression and imperialism. Within weeks of the conflict, SNCC published an article in their newsletter on "The Palestine Problem," which inarguably antagonized Israel. The article listed arguments for classifying Israeli behavior as white imperialism and even depicted a cartoon in which a hand marked with a Star of David held a double-ended noose tied around the necks of a Black man and a Palestinian man. An arm swinging a machete to cut the rope was labeled "Third World Liberation Movement."[41] A photograph in the article showed a wall with cowering men lined up against it at gunpoint with the caption, "Zionists lined up Arab victims and shot them in the back in cold blood. This is the Gaza Strip, Palestine, not Dachau." SNCC stood by this article and issued a defense in their following issue of *Movement*. They explained that SNCC is partisan, and though anti-Zionist, they make a clear effort to distinguish between the Jew and the Zionist. They explain of the article, "It is not anti-Jewish. It does not characterize Jews as a group. It carefully distinguishes between Jews and Zionists."[42]

Black nationalists were not all anti-Zionist, so the relationship between the two groups did not follow a clear trajectory. Some leaders in the movement, whether sympathetic to the Zionist cause or not, even used Zionism as an example and precedent for reparations and the creation of a Black state. Malcom X, though drawn to the Palestinian cause, suggested that the Black community use the "strategy used by the American Jews" and explained that "Pan Africanism will do for people of African decent [sic] all over the world the same that Zionism has done for Jews all over the world."[43] His view on Zionism, however, revealed little solidarity with what "Zionism has done for Jews all over the world," and much antagonism toward what he believed was the white oppression of another people of color, Palestinian Arabs. He explained, "the Jews . . . with the help of Christians in America and Europe, drove our Muslim brothers out of their homeland, there they had settled for centuries, and took over the land for themselves. . . . In America the Jews sap the very life-blood of the so-called Negros to maintain the state of Israel."[44]

The rift between African Americans (particularly those in the Black Power movement) and American Jews, already present in the mid-1960s, only widened as a result of the Israel-Palestine debate. In truth, the heart of their conflict was far closer to home and was based on the journey that Jews had worked so hard to complete in America: attaining whiteness. Whiteness in American culture is not only an aspirational goal, but is inexorably linked to masculinity. The study of whiteness acknowledges it as a racial construct encompassing an indefinite number of ethnicities and intersecting with issues not only of race, but also nationalism, class, and masculinity. As such, the perception of an American immigrant group as white acknowledges their access to elements of American acceptance that are otherwise difficult to obtain.

Many scholars of whiteness and acculturation have argued that in the journey to become Americans, Jews also became white (or in some cases, they argue, had to become white in order to become American).[45] Eric Goldstein, in his 1997 article on Jewishness and race in the nineteenth-century United States, explains that American Jews in the late 1800s claimed a racial identity of Jewishness to better align with other variations of white European ancestry. However, as Eastern European Jews came in greater numbers in the twentieth century, such emphasized racial difference became an impediment to their claims of whiteness, and so they engaged in less public talk of racial Jewishness, in favor of Jewish whiteness.[46] Historian Matthew Frye Jacobson argued that Jewishness in the public eye (in film and television) was visibly marked by Jewish phenotypes, which Jews eventually effaced through use of blackface, which brought them more firmly into the category of "white" by metaphorically standing on the shoulders of African Americans. Other scholars of whiteness have used similar arguments for American ethnic groups achieving whiteness through positive comparison to African Americans, as Noel Ignatiev did in his 1995 book, *How the Irish Became White*. That this transformation took place, and that it came at the expense of African Americans, was a common trope in African American commentary from the late 1960s and early '70s, though they did not yet have the language of whiteness theory that scholars use today.

In an essay titled "Negroes Are Anti-Semitic Because They're Anti-White," African American novelist James Baldwin explained that the tension between Jewish and Black communities in Harlem and Watts in 1967 was a result not of the Jewishness of Jews, but of the whiteness they had achieved. He explained:

> In the American context, the most ironical thing about Negro anti-Semitism is that the Negro is really condemning the Jew for having become an American white man—for having become, in effect, a

Christian. The Jew profits from his status in America, and he must expect Negroes to distrust him for it. The Jew does not realize that the credential he offers, the fact that he has been despised and slaughtered, does not increase the Negro's understanding. It increases the Negro's rage. For it is not here, and not now, that the Jew is being slaughtered, and he is never despised, here, as the Negro is, because he is an American. The Jewish travail occurred across the sea and America rescued him from the house of bondage. But America is the house of bondage for the Negro, and no country can rescue him. What happens to the Negro here happens to him because he is an American.[47]

As for the Jewish state, Baldwin explained that unlike the struggle for Black rights in America, which is largely a nonviolent movement, "no one has ever seriously suggested that the Jew be nonviolent. There was no need for him to be nonviolent. On the contrary, the Jewish battle for Israel was saluted as the most tremendous heroism." This is true, in large part *because* the Jew was previously believed to be violence-averse by nature. The opposite is true of Black men in America, who (at least in early civil rights protests) demonstrated the quiet dignity in nonviolent protest of which racist depictions claimed they were incapable. In other words, where the Jew had to disprove his presumed cowardice and unwillingness to fight, the Black man had to disprove his presumed propensity for violence. By refusing to engage in reactive violence, even in response to violence against them, Black civil rights protestors recall feeling as though they had gained a respectable manhood and a dignified calm in their measured response. Franklin McCain, a member of the Greensboro Four, explained that by protesting in this way, he had gained his manhood, but not only that, he felt as though "the manhood of a number of other black persons had been restored."[48]

Baldwin's statement on Jewish whiteness is in response, in part, to the insistence of liberal students that they were engaging in a shared struggle of Jews and African Americans. Some, like State University of New York at Albany student M. Jay Rosenberg, recognized that Jews had attained the status of whiteness in America, but explained that though it had been "won," it must be cast aside to share in the struggle of Black Nationalists:

> The blacks in America are the first to abjure the idea of assimilation, to realize the inherent lie in the concept of the melting-pot. . . . Today's young American Jew is a good bit slower. He desperately wants assimilation; Jewishness embarrasses him. . . . He cannot accept the fact that he is seen as a Jew, that his destiny is that of the Jews, and that his only effectiveness is as a Jew. But he wants to be an "American," . . . he is a ludicrous figure. He joins black nationalist groups, not as a Jew but as a white man. His whiteness, his precious whiteness, is too valuable to him for it to be relegated to a secondary position. He does not understand that his relevance to the black struggle is as a Jew and a fellow victim of endless white exploitation. . . . He must realize that his own struggle for liberation is a continuing one, that he too has much to fear and also much of which to be proud. The miracle of Israel, a national liberation deferred for 2000 years, should be his inspiration. The Jew did it alone, as the black knows he must, and he did it with guns.[49]

Though he recognizes Jewish whiteness, Rosenberg differs from Baldwin in his conclusion that the Jewish relevance to the Black struggle is as "a fellow victim of endless white exploitation." This particular association of Jews with whiteness, to Baldwin's mind, was merely more white oppression. Their particular Jewish background of oppression did not make Jews kindred, as Rosenberg believed, but emphasized their difference from the situation of African Americans. Precisely the liberation Rosenberg spoke of, that the Jew achieved alone and with guns, was an unrelatable position to the Black struggle in the United States, which did not garner the international monetary and political support of the Zionist war for statehood.

Whiteness became particularly important when contemporary commentators began to identify Israelis as white Jews, as James Baldwin and the SNCC did in their earlier statements. In doing so, American Jews (and African Americans) identify Israel as a white Jewish state, despite the fact that the majority of its inhabitants were not the image of the white-presenting, primarily Ashkenazi Jews that Zionist groups promoted. Ashkenazi Jews were only a minority of Jews in Israel by the late 1960s, the majority being Mizrahi Jews from northern Africa and central Asia. By identifying Israelis with the European minority, observers pointed to the brand of Israeli Jew that American Jews were so proud to emulate: Western European, Ashkenazi Jews. It was these Israeli Jews, specifically, that were the focus of most American discussions about Israeli toughness, and with which they could continue to associate themselves without negating their white masculinity in the United States.

This distinction that Jewish Americans (and those African American's ascribing whiteness to American Jews) made, whether consciously or unconsciously, shaped the American/Israeli connection in the American imagination. By emulating Ashkenazi Israelis as heroes, American Jews emphasized the focus on white masculinity and the compatibility of this particular Israeli manhood with the American traditional hegemon.[50] In doing so, they also solidified the impression among African Americans that oppression in Palestine, because of its white/Black dichotomy, presented a shared struggle with global pan-African and Black nationalist movements.[51] It is also worth noting that there is a worthwhile comparison to be made not only between African Americans and Palestinian Arabs, but between these groups and Mizrahi Jews, who (despite the fact that they were the majority of Jews in Israel) struggled against racism from their Ashkenazi Jewish fellow countrymen. The Ashkenazi, European Zionists in Israel attempted to "de-Orient" Oriental Jewry, in their own unironic version of Rudyard Kipling's *White Man's Burden*.[52]

By the end of the 1960s, many American Jews, including a glut of Jewish campus organizations, struggled with the dichotomy of contemporary oppression of minorities and impoverished peoples (particularly Palestinians and the PLO) and the historical oppression of Jews. In the year following his previous quote above, Rosenberg explained the difficulty of being a radical leftist who supported Israel. He felt that he had "to choose between the Fatah-supporting SDS and the ultra-middle class lox and bagel breakfast club, Hillel Society." He explained, "I felt that there had to be a third route. That third route was Zionist radicalism . . . borrowing from the black nationalists, I announced the formation of a militant, radical campus Zionist organization called the 'Hebrew Students Alliance.'"[53] This group rallied over three hundred attendees at their first meeting, providing a venue for Jewish students who felt similarly isolated yet remained determined to "not surrender their identity just so they can be accepted by their 'revolutionary' peers," or "give up their radicalism to accommodate the Jewish establishment."

These groups, many self-identified Zionists, and Jewish socialist groups courting a tense relationship with the State of Israel, examined the good and the bad emerging from the new state. Even though the most radical of the groups reveled in the reflection of Israeli society and in the *new Jew*, their pride also took an underexamined gendered form. Male students spoke of satisfaction with the state and rebuilding the Jewish people, though they did not acknowledge either the whiteness they highlighted in focusing on Ashkenazi Jews or the masculinity they were ascribing to the *new Jew*. For example, when asked why he cared so much about Israel, more so than Jewish religious life or culture, one student explained, "For me, Israel presents an alternative to American Judaism. It offers me an alternative to that ghetto mentality that I think many people have, and that I try to fight against. And it's a symbol to me of new strength and the rebirth of the Jewish people."[54]

American Jewish women, on the other hand, did recognize that this rebirth of the Jewish people in Israel was male-dominated and even oppressive of Israeli women. In the newsletter of the Jewish Socialist Committee at Oberlin College, female contributors criticized gender inequality in Israeli life. They argued that the integration of *halacha* (Orthodox Jewish Law) into national law institutionalized the oppression of women and lack of feminism in Israel. Indeed, they criticized gender inequality across all of Israeli society, but particularly in kibbutz life, where the egalitarian promises of gender equality failed to deliver. It was the fault, they explained, of the state-promoted religious law, societal structure, and the structure of the military, because all maintained such rigid gender roles.[55] The same group, interestingly, also spoke highly of anti-Nazi rallies in the United States by Meir Kahane and the Jewish Defense League, an unapologetically masculine movement, and the clearest example of the influence of Black Power on the Jewish Left.

Jewish female students acknowledged the growing popularity of the masculine sabra in Israel. Indeed, many praised the positive change to the Jewish image. However, they also occupied themselves with another gender-based struggle for change, which played out in the emerging feminist movement. As previously mentioned, the dissatisfaction with women's roles and their treatment in antiwar protest presented female activists with a dual struggle, their dedication to the movement and their growing awareness of the necessity of the fight for women's rights. It was in no small part the growing aggressive masculinity of the protest movement, and the Jewish element of that masculinity, that pushed so many Jewish women to dedicate their efforts more determinedly to gender equality. Say Burgin argued, in her 2012 article on the gendering effects of the antiwar movement on activists, that those who evaded the draft felt their masculinity was threatened by their evasion of manly duty and instilled in them a desire to assert their manliness within the antiwar movement. Within the movement, and in response to accusations of cowardice by hawks, protestors and draft resisters redefined their brand of masculinity as one that was not based on the militaristic warring archetype. They saw their resistance to needless war as a more sincere manhood, based on responsibility to society and justice. In doing so, however, they strengthened their sense of masculinity through dominance over women in the movement.

For many men, this period necessitated a complex negotiation of masculine identities, embracing the women's movement and maintaining a sense of masculine self. Even men who were sympathetic to the cause of gender equality often found that in supporting feminism, they felt emasculated by the renegotiation of male expectations.[56] Some male activists, like Abbie Hoffman, justified their continued dominant or hypermasculine behavior in a movement shared with feminists by claiming a "macho feminism," which embraced notions of equality while maintaining the attitudes and dominant behaviors of the previous generation. He used macho discourse, for example, to criticize men who did not embrace new gender roles, saying that those who "cling to old roles, I see as 'sissies' afraid to meet the challenge and adventure of a new attitude. When it comes time to clear away the dishes only cowards stay seated at the table."[57] This attitude, as Hoffman expressed it, helps to explain why men who were sympathetic to the goals of the feminist movement, who worked alongside women in protest and student organizations, acted particularly macho and abusive to one another, and at times to women as well. His calling other men "sissies" to shame them into embracing gender equality is the oxymoronic expression of a man with a masculine axe to grind.

Female activists were often on the receiving end of this determined masculinity. In Students for a Democratic Society, for example, many women felt their roles inside the organization were as gendered and devalued as were their roles outside of the movement.[58] Men in the movement often lost sight of the goals of the women's movement, with which they claimed sympathy, in their attempts to access American hegemonic masculinity through tough, aggressive leadership. Anthropologist Karen Brodkin argued that the attempt to whiten Jewish men came largely at the expense of Jewish women, by creating the stereotypes of the Jewish mother and the Jewish American princess and presenting them as smothering and emasculating Jewish men.[59] If this is the case, then abuses of Jewish women in the antiwar movement were, at least in part, a byproduct of Jewish men's attempts to attain white manhood. Amy Kesselman (a founding member of the Chicago West Side Group) explained that she started resenting Jewish men in the political movement on her college campus, both for their dominance of the scene and for the sexism she identified in Jewish American culture. She particularly identified a masculinist emphasis within her chapter of Students for a Democratic Society in Chicago and cited this as one of the motivating factors for beginning a separate women's movement on campus.[60] When women in the movement did speak out against the sexist and male-dominated atmosphere of the protest movement, they would be harassed and abused by their male comrades. One iconic example of this was when a cofounder of the radical feminist group the Redstockings, Shulamith Firestone, along with fellow activist Marilyn Webb, were harassed off a stage at an antiwar protest, with men in the crowd famously yelling for someone to "Fuck her! Take her off the stage! Rape her in the back alley!"

Many Jewish women broke from their other protest pursuits to focus on the cause of women's rights, and did so without openly acknowledging the Jewishness of so much of the feminist movement. According to members of the Boston Women's Health Collective (the group that published the widely sold and disseminated book *Our Bodies, Ourselves*, originally published in 1971), recognizing the predominance of Jewish women in the collective would have been problematic to the cause of the universal women's movement, because classifying themselves, even unofficially, as a Jewish group was far too narrow an identifier.[61] This was a common theme among feminist activists, who retrospectively discussed the heavy participation of Jewish women, but believed at the time that it would do more harm than good to the feminist movement by threatening their universalist stance.[62]

Jewish feminists did, however, use Holocaust imagery (like the defendants in the trial of the Chicago Seven did), while avoiding discussion of their Jewishness in publications. Betty Friedan, in one of the most controversial sections of her feminist classic, *The Feminine Mystique*, compares life as a housewife to life in a concentration camp—dehumanizing, infantilizing, and systematically designed to take away a person's sense of agency and self-determination. She called this the "Comfortable Concentration Camp." Even if they did not routinely discuss or promote the heavy participation of Jewish women in the movement, many of them went on to apply second-wave feminism to Jewish life, with an impact not only on Jewish women but on Jewish men as well, as Jewish life began to change to reflect modern notions of gender equality.

It was those Jewish women who were both part of the feminist movement of the late 1960s and had become more focused on Jewish life in the aftermath of the Six-Day War who began a more dedicatedly Jewish feminist movement, one that focused on change in traditional Jewish practice.[63] Jews within the American feminist movement who attempted to identify and celebrate their Jewishness felt that their Jewish particularity, which was important to them, was delegitimized by the women's movement (much as African American women had felt delegitimized by lack of recognition in the movement for their dual struggle for civil rights).[64]

In the early 1970s, Jewish feminists dedicated direct efforts toward the Jewish religious communities, creating several Jewish feminist organizations and publications, but never a comprehensive overarching Jewish feminist organization. They established groups like Lilith, Ezrat Nashim, and organizations that focused energy on Jewish feminist discussions and publications (like the North American Jewish Students Network). The Jewish Feminist Organization, which attempted to be such an overarching representative body, was short-lived. Early goals for feminist reform to Jewish life focused on making the status of women in Jewish life more equal to that of Jewish men, including positions of religious authority, and on eliminating the injustices to Jewish women based on male-focused assumptions of rabbinic law.[65] Because of these goals, Jewish feminism is not merely American feminism in the Jewish sphere but its own unique movement that adopted influences from second-wave feminism. In 1972, Hebrew Union College (of the Reform

Jewish movement) ordained the first American female rabbi, and the Reconstructionist movement soon followed (the first female rabbi in the Conservative movement would not be ordained until 1985).

This progress shows the growing recognition and significance of gender difference in the Jewish community throughout the 1960s and '70s, and the journey that so many Jewish feminists took (from anti-war and college activism to Jewish feminism) shows how significant male dominance and macho culture in Jewish America had become. This male dominance and the popularity of tough Jewish culture had a watershed moment in 1967, with the events of the Six-Day War. The war brought Israeli toughness, statehood, Jewish survival, and racial identity to the fore of Jewish American politics and changed the way Jewish Americans defined themselves on the global stage. The result of this shift is a major change in the process of Jewish American acculturation, as Jewish unification, solidarity, and defense became part of Jewish life. This also marked a shift, then, in divergent Jewish American masculinities, as achieving the hegemonic American masculine ideal became less important in the upheaval of the Jewish American self-image. Israel exemplified a new pride in masculine Jewishness, and because it was identified as white, it provided a precedent for a new, hypermasculine, American Jewish manhood that no longer required the approval of the American white mainstream. What emerged at this time, simultaneous with the movements discussed in this section, was precisely that: a militant American Jewish organization that relied on the image of tough Jews from Israel to legitimize their reclamation of a highly masculine and purely American movement.

Militant Judaism: The Jewish Defense League

Though not an explicitly male movement, Jewish militant groups—particularly in the Jewish Defense League (JDL)—were dominated by men, and much of their image was based on contemporary conceptions of mainstream American masculinity. The goal of JDL, Jewish defense, and their motto, "Never Again," implied a universal goal of protection for all Jewish people. Their rhetoric, however, was pointedly male, and the organization intended that its actions be carried out by Jewish men and boys. The JDL and the movement of which it was a part have been largely dismissed as representing fringe-fanaticism that left little mark on Jewish American history. Their lasting influence, however, was in the revitalization of a hypermasculine Jewish American ideal, which has had lasting effects on the Jewish American male image, aspiration toward American hegemony, and group identity despite having never gained widespread acceptance.[66]

Scholars have largely downplayed the lasting significance of Meir Kahane's influence on American Jewish masculinity, as Paul Breines explained, so as not to "divert attention from the more ordinary, mainstream, and widespread instances of American Jewish toughness."[67] The places in which JDL advertisements, recruiting materials, and reporting about their activities appeared, however, were more mainstream and available to the American public than were the changes to Jewish masculinity conducted in the American Jewish "mainstream" religion and culture. Indeed, the mainstream history of the Americanization of Jewish masculinity earlier in the century provides a standard against which the more extreme Jewish masculinity of the JDL stands out clearly. Far from remaining in the background, Kahane blatantly attempted to alter both the perception and the reality of Jewish men, who he saw as enfeebled by their history of persecution.

The JDL acknowledged and attempted to move away from what they believed the diaspora Jew had become: physically weak, easily cowed, and therefore disconnected from tougher, biblical images of a distant Jewish masculine past. They also saw an example of aspirational Jewish manhood in the newly formed and militarily proven State of Israel, and hoped to re-create Jews—and the perception of Jewish men—in that image, creating "tough Jews" through physical training. They encouraged Jewish men to behave in a more intimidating manner by openly carrying firearms and brawling in the streets. This was a more brazen attempt than, for example, those of the Revisionist Zionist movement during the Second World War, whose American operatives attempted to create an all-Jewish army to protect Jews and Jewish interests worldwide.[68] JDL rhetoric called back to Max Nordau's "muscle Jew" and Herzl's desire to bring the Jew up to fighting par with his countrymen. The JDL's attempt to assert Jewish strength reflected the addition of dominant American notions of aggressive manhood, typified by both the American military and emerging ethnic pride movements among other American minorities, like the Calumet Community Congress, the Puerto Rican Young Lords, the Italian American League, and the Black Power movement.[69]

The JDL emerged as one organization within this militant Jewish milieu and was unique in its significant reaction—both positive and negative—to the African American militant movement. It formed on the heels of a splintering and reconfiguring of Jewish-Black alliances that had gone from near-consensus among American Jews, who cooperated with Dr. Martin Luther King Jr., and embraced his message of interracial cooperation, to the distrust and distancing examined between American Jews and the emerging Black Power movement. The change from cooperation to parallel, and at times conflicting, struggles forced liberal American Jews to take on a more inward-focused perspective. Subsequently, the belief that Jews and African Americans shared a common struggle started to degrade, allowing Jewish activists to embrace more Jewish-centered agendas and causes. The tension also attuned American Jews more directly to their own privilege as a white ethnic minority.[70] Together, the changing relationship between Black Power activists and American Jews, the inward shift of American Jewish activism, and the tactics and aesthetic of Black Power directly influenced Meir Kahane and his followers.

Kahane was concerned with growing tensions between the Jewish and African American populations and devoted himself to the training of "husky Jewish boys in the not-so-gentle art of karate" to defend New York Jewish communities against Black antisemites. He moved his family from Queens to Brooklyn, after he claimed a group of Black militants invaded their home.[71] Though he saw Black militants as a threat to Jewish safety, he also saw the tactics of Black militarism as the answer to that threat. He therefore created a movement to change the image of young Jewish men in America through the combined influence of the masculinities embodied by Black Power and the Revisionist Zionists. Kahane simultaneously promoted his political agenda in America, the Soviet Union, and Israel, hoping to create an immediate and dramatic change to the way Jewish men interacted with the world around them.

Kahane cofounded the JDL in 1968 to protect a community under threat and ignored by police, motivations that bear a striking resemblance to those of the Black Panthers. That there could be a Jewish militant group like the JDL was possible, in part, because the group was able to harness some of the pride manifest among American Jews after the Israeli victory in the 1967 Six-Day War. The fear and anxiety for the survival of the Jewish people that defined the war for many American Jews inspired some to go to Israel, men and women eager to join the fight even after the quick conclusion to that conflict. American volunteers during the short war included both men and women, but those who became militant presented not only as aggressively pro-Israel, but aggressively male. He believed that as a result of the Six-Day War, Jews around the world were finally ready to take the responsibility for their security into their own hands, having been relieved of the burden of non-violence.[72] He further claimed that the Israeli victory allowed the rest of the world to let go of their support of the Jewish people, to "get the guilt off their back[s]" after failing to intervene in the Holocaust, and to paint Israel as an aggressor instead of a nation of survivor-victims.[73] Indeed, after the war, young American activists—particularly those involved with the Black Power movement—became increasingly critical of Israel and supportive of the Palestinian struggle.[74] He saw this criticism of Israel as a continued form of antisemitism, believing that Jews had, through their emasculated image, spent a century making themselves easy targets for blame in American society, noting: "if a minority group has an image of weakness and is at the same time affluent, it becomes an ideal scapegoat when times get hard."[75]

Kahane intended to foster Jewish pride, teach self-defense to Jewish youth, and gain political power and influence.[76] He openly criticized diaspora Jewry as emasculated and weak, and his rhetoric toward American and European Jews was openly disdainful, using the gendered language that had long been hurled at them by both antisemites and Israeli sabras to describe American Jews. In spite of his disdain toward the American diaspora, Kahane clearly believed that American Jews were not irredeemable, since he continued to address the American diaspora, long after he himself migrated to Israel.[77] Adopting what would become the slogan for Holocaust remembrance worldwide, "Never Again," as their rallying cry, the JDL mourned the loss of Jewish life and simultaneously used Holocaust victims as an example of Jewish weakness and willingness to be abused and enfeebled by others. Speaking to a crowd in Philadelphia, Kahane reinforced an old stereotype of Jews as willingly powerless, explaining that the Jewish people historically refused to help themselves, instead remaining meekly complacent. They "see a black cloud that says it's going to rain but the Jew doesn't go for an umbrella. He must first catch pneumonia."[78] Another JDL member explained, "All of us had someone among those 6,000,000 during World War II who walked quietly into German gas chambers. We won't just walk in again. Never again."[79] The JDL therefore walked a thin line between protecting the Jews they saw as meek or complacent, thus reinforcing the stereotype, and presenting their members as the embodiment of tough Jewish success, thereby attempting to disprove that stereotype.

Kahane was well suited to the project, having spent much of his youth involved in Revisionist Zionism, which already carried highly masculine imagery and intentions. Having joined Betar when he was fourteen years old, he was exposed to this movement and its goals early. Betar laid the groundwork, in many ways, for what the JDL would later build. Their practical goals included preparing American Jewish youth to fulfill their Zionist duty through psychological, moral, and physical training. They aimed to create a new Jew "out of decay and disintegration, through sweat and blood, a new people—proud, kind and refined, and tough."[80] Kahane left Betar in the wake of the creation of the State of Israel (which nullified the primary goal of Betar, support for the Irgun), and joined Bnei Akiva, which focused on the religious character of the new Jewish state.[81] However, he resurrected Betar's ideals and tactics within the JDL, though by the end of his career, Revisionist Zionism had rejected Kahane in turn.[82]

By 1969, JDL had garnered 6,500 members in seventeen American cities, growing to over 15,000 members by 1971.[83] Their recruiting tactics appealed directly to the feeling of emasculation and weakness from which so many American Jewish men wanted to break. Indeed, some of the founding members looked like ideal Jewish "tough guys." The JDL's fourth founding member, Chaim Bieber, was a renowned boxer reputed to lift cars with his bare hands.[84] The JDL even briefly attracted some figures closely associated with the peace movement, like Bob Dylan, who began supporting Kahane after the Six-Day War.[85] At the same time, the larger Jewish community did not support the JDL. The Anti-Defamation League condemned the JDL as "a self-appointed group of vigilantes whose protection the Jewish community does not need or want."[86] Jewish press around the country criticized the JDL for engaging in the very behaviors and tactics they sought to oppose. The Jewish War Veterans, arguably one of the manliest organizations of the Jewish establishment, denounced the organization as a disgraceful spectacle using "abhorrent tactics."[87]

Abhorrent or disgraceful, wanted or not, elements of the JDL speak directly to the issue of the American Jewish male self-image. While sentencing Meir Kahane for plotting violence and possession of explosives, Judge Jack B. Weinstein made this connection, declaring that, "In this country, at this time, it is not permissible to substitute the bomb for the book as the symbol of Jewish manhood."[88] Two essential elements of the JDL exemplify this goal of a new Jewish manhood in America, and particularly merit examination through the lens of Jewish gender: its determination to present itself as a distinctly American organization and its appeal as a group capable of curing Jewish men of their emasculated "bookish" condition. These aspects appealed specifically to inner-city Jews, less wealthy and established than their uptown Jewish neighbors. Libby Kahane, Meir's wife, reflected that the JDL impressed grassroots Jewry, but not the Jewish establishment:

> The ordinary Jew was heartened by Meir's efforts to change the image of the Jew from a weakling to a fighter, but the heads of the established Jewish organizations, who never had to walk alone at night in a rough neighborhood, has other concerns. Their priority was to maintain social and business connections with wealthy upper-class non-Jews. Meir was spoiling the respectable image they worked so hard to promote.[89]

The connection to the neighborhood experiences of inner-city Jews as separate from the Jewish elite was a constant thread of Kahane's rhetoric. He clearly thought that this difference, the tenacity gained from living as a Jew in a rough neighborhood, was one that highlighted the American nature of the JDL's struggle. While always supporting Israel, JDL recruiting materials were proudly American and meant to announce the "arrival" of Jewish men in the American masculine milieu. Phrases like, "We are speaking of the American Dream!" and "Are you willing to stand up for *democracy* and Jewish survival?" topped fliers and pamphlets.[90]

Followers and admirers of the JDL argued that the group represented "strength—not weakness, courage—not cowardice, and most important of all, its members are Americans first and Jews second."[91] This stress on the American-ness of the organization is key, as it put the JDL on the same playing field as the tough men of the ethnic groups it mirrored. Members of the JDL clearly saw in the Black Power movement, and even in the actions of the American Nazi Party, an aspirational goal of strength and intimidation.[92] It identified this idealized image of machismo as an inarguably American phenomenon in a political landscape dominated by ethnic pride and the minority rights revolution. The brand of masculinity unique to the JDL is a combination of both this particularly American masculine influence and the ideals of the Revisionist Zionist militants to which Kahane and many of his followers adhered. Combining these influences added components that, in the end, created a movement quite apart from the Revisionists; it was determinedly American, and proudly religious.[93]

Highlighting their connection to these other ethnic American movements, supporters of the JDL criticized mainstream Jewish organizations for being "un-American" and even "Jewish 'Uncle Toms'" because of their lack of self-defense and pride. Kahane called them "Uncle Irvings," who had never had to live in fear of street violence from ethnic minorities.[94] These rich Jews were, in the eyes of the JDL, less American because of their distance from the most American of experiences, ethnic tension and ethnic pride. In spite of Kahane's fear of Black aggression, several of the JDL's slogans were directly taken from the Black Panthers, like the call to "put some Jewish-is-beautiful spirit back in the Jew," and even the image of a raised fist in its logo.[95] This is an especially interesting appropriation given the JDL's determination to protect New York's Jewish community specifically from radical Black leftists.[96]

The JDL famously lashed out against Black militants, most notably when Student Non-Violent Coordinating Committee leader James Forman announced that he would interrupt services at Temple Emanu-El in New York City to read a manifesto calling for reparations for past exploitation from local churches and synagogues.[97] A group of JDL members stood guard at Temple Emanu-El with chains, sticks, and bats, though Forman never appeared. A JDL coordinator explained, "Reparations imply guilt, and the Jew has always felt his moral obligation to the black man. Heads would have been broken if Forman had showed . . . if they can enter our synagogues, it is just as well that they bring on the machine guns now."[98] The paradoxical relationship that the JDL maintained with Black militancy meant that although the militants of the JDL acknowledged their debt to Black Power, they still felt a constant need to defend themselves against accusations of white privilege and exercising white power over people of color. The Black Panther Party was a constant point of reference for Kahane's image for the JDL, but the Panthers were never as purely male an organization as the JDL. Black women held leadership positions and participated in greater numbers among their ranks, just as they had done throughout the civil rights movement.[99]

The calls to arms that the JDL used to rally support directly appealed to the desire of Jewish men to regain (or gain) some measure of performatively tough masculinity. In fact, the JDL's recruiting materials, advertisements, and publications used the words *boys* and *men* to the point of redundancy, never mentioning female members, of which there were very few. There was a JDL Women's Group in Brooklyn, composed primarily of married, middle-aged women whose activities were explicitly limited to "female projects."[100] Janet Dolgin explained that the JDL aimed to embody two types at once, the scholar and the *chaya* (fighter), and though one may have included women, the other did not. "The scholar was an educator; the chaya, a fighter. The scholar's role recalled a religious tradition; the chaya's, a fully profane world. The scholar might be a bureaucrat; the chaya, an activist. Scholars were men or women; chayas were men."[101]

In 1969, the JDL ran a three-column advertisement in the *New York Times* targeting their prime audience: Jewish men of high school and college age. The image atop the ad shows six presumably Jewish men wearing sunglasses, some carrying clubs, and all looking intentionally menacing. They stand in front of a New York City synagogue. The advertisement reads:

Question: Is This Any Way for Nice Jewish Boys to Behave?

Answer: Maybe. Maybe there are times when there is no other way to get across to the extremist that the Jew is not quite the patsy some think he is. Maybe there is only one way to get across a clear

A young JDL member stands
guard with a baseball bat.
"Is this any way for
nice Jewish boys to behave?"

● DAILY NEWS, MONDAY, JULY 27, 1970

Figure 24. Jewish Defense League promotional materials. I-374, Records of the Jewish Defense League, box 1, folder 6. Photo courtesy of the American Jewish Historical Society.

response to people who threaten the seizure of synagogues and extortion of money. Maybe nice Jewish boys do not always get through to people who threaten to carry teachers out in pine boxes and to burn down merchants' stores. Maybe some people and organizations are too nice. Maybe in times of crisis, Jewish boys should not be that nice. Maybe—just maybe—nice people build their own road to Auschwitz.

It goes on to add, "Nice Jewish, Christian, white and black boys should create a society of justice and equality in which people can get back to being nice."[102] This is a direct appeal to young Jewish men and their desire as "nice Jewish boys" to be on equal footing with more tough "Christian, white and black boys." Though the ad embraced the nice Jewish boy archetype as desirable, it clearly dismisses it as ineffective in securing peace and safety for the Jewish people, "Maybe—just maybe—nice people build their own road to Auschwitz."[103]

The image of these Jewish tough guys, however, does little to counteract the assumption that Jewish boys remain nice or unthreatening. Aside from the dark sunglasses they wear, they do not resemble any sort of gang or military operation. They do not wear berets like the Black Panthers, badges, matching boots, or anything resembling a uniform, though this would change later in the life of the JDL. They stand, hands in their pockets, at their sides, or gripping clubs, looking exactly how one might imagine nice Jewish boys would look with clubs in hand, wearing regular street clothes: jeans or slacks, button-down shirts, and neckties. In some of their demonstrations, they do look a bit more organized, and possibly intimidating, than in the *New York Times* advertisement, but for the most part, photographs of the JDL show otherwise average Jewish men who happen to have weapons (sticks, chains, bats, and such) in hand.[104]

The tone of the JDL is far removed from previous American Jewish attempts to "become men" by succeeding in masculine pursuits in American institutions; in fact, it rejected most existing institutions: right and left, Jewish and gentile, criminal and government. And as a result, membership consisted mainly of youth on the fringes of Jewish society: teens from broken homes, residents of poor and neglected neighborhoods, children of Holocaust survivors, *ba'alei teshuvah* (a Jew who returns to Orthodoxy, or who becomes Orthodox for the first time), the unemployed, and the unbalanced.[105] The ad, in spite of the group's support of the Israeli state, makes no mention of Israel or Israeli strength, again emphasizing the American nature of this particular Jewish masculinity, intent on protecting democracy and the American way of life.

Arguably, the JDL had few real successes, they carried out some of their plans; however, the group remained on the sidelines of Jewish America. They held classes for tactical self-defense in major cities, several specifically restricted registration to men, even if they did not restrict the courses to JDL members, or even to Jewish men.[106] They also sent members to intervene in issues of the larger Jewish community as part of their commitment to defend Jewish rights. In many of these cases, the JDL's actions were not violent but were still very intentionally performing and cultivating masculinity. For example, during a New York gravediggers union strike in 1970, the JDL sent out young volunteers to dig Jewish graves to ensure their chance for timely burial. When some of the volunteering boys got tired of the chore and decided to abandon their task, a JDL office manager pointedly asked girls to replace them to shame the boys into resuming their stations digging.[107]

The JDL set up an eight-week summer camp for Jewish boys in Woodbourne, New York, called Camp Jedel (Jedel was the shorthand for Jewish Defense League in its early days, before the acronym JDL caught on), that trained them in karate, firearms, discipline, and included study of the history of Jewish underground fighters. The camp reflected Kahane's own youthful experiences in the Revisionist Zionist summer camp, Camp Betar, where he received military training as well as classes on Jewish history. In his camp days, the goals of Betar and its parent organization, Brith Trumpeldor of America, were to train and send Jewish boys to Palestine to fight for statehood.[108] The JDL also promoted aliyah among its members, but it was not the primary goal. The rhetoric maintained that Israel would be the only safe place where Jews looked out for Jewish interests, but its stated goal was to create a tough Jewish body to do the work of Jewish defense in America. The JDL thus added the influence of the Black Power movement and structure (defense of their own community where America had failed) to the masculine indoctrination of Betar.

The slogan of the camp was not subtle in its goals, "They used to send us to camps . . . but NEVER AGAIN. Now we have our own camps to make sure . . . NEVER AGAIN."[109] Like some Jewish camps of previous generations, this camp promised to turn boys into men, but in a much more aggressive fashion than those seen in prewar America that emphasized a return to nature. The aggressive weapons training program was in line with Kahane's motto, "Every Jew, a Twenty-Two."[110] In its first summer of operation, the camp supported one female student, who made clear in an interview that she decided to attend the camp to support the ideology. She explained that in the city it's good to have karate skills and that "the camp's a bit primitive, but it gets the JDL message across."[111] Perhaps in using the word "primitive" she was referring to the determinedly nonintellectual, hypermasculine, brutal training tactics. A reporter for the *National Observer* explained of a training session:

> Two lines of sweaty, grimy young men stood rigidly at attention in the 90 degree weather. . . . A young instructor walked down the lines, kicking about every fourth lad hard in the solar plexus. Each doubled over momentarily and looked as though he might vomit; then he straightened up proudly. Three weeks of five-hour daily karate lessons had toughened the young men.[112]

Whether the "toughening" process successfully made them into "husky Jewish boys" or not, the trainees saw the desired change. One camper, after attending the first two years of Camp Jedel, explained, "I am not a karate expert nor am I a sharpshooter. There is, however, one change which Camp Jedel has burned into me: I am damn proud to be a Jew."[113]

The JDL was never a large movement (at its own highest estimate about one quarter of a percent of the American Jewish population in 1971), but it demonstrated the combined influence on Jewish America of Israeli masculinity, the Holocaust, and the countercultural and political movements of the 1960s.[114] It showed the most extreme manifestation of the very real feelings among young Jewish men that their manhood was called into question and needed to be redeemed through radical reconstruction. Using the strength of Israeli men as examples of how Jewish manhood could and ought to be, the JDL connected strong masculine Jews throughout history in one tough narrative. One supporter wrote that this stalwart Jewish group behaved "in the tradition of the Maccabees, the Warsaw Ghetto, and the Haganah," bringing together the few popularly glorified examples of tough Jewish manhood: the ancient heroes of Jewish history, the few violent resisters of the Holocaust, and the fighting forces in modern-day Israel.[115]

The connection was one that Kahane pushed hard. An administrator at the Stephen Wise Free Synagogue of New York described Kahane after he gave a guest lecture to the congregation as "tieless, shirt open at the neck, and collar draped over his suit jacket, he affectuates [sic] the appearance of the young Israeli, and his broad frame and muscular demeanor gives one a feeling of strength and power."[116] Kahane promoted himself as a masculine hero, explaining to *Women's Wear Daily* that he was an active baseball and football player and that his people trusted him because he wouldn't ask anything of them that he wouldn't do himself, including "beating up Nazis, throwing bottles at the cops, invading offices and painting slogans."[117]

Kahane and his followers argued that this toughness was desperately needed to combat rising antisemitism, which they largely blamed, not really on the Black Panthers and similar movements for ethnic pride, but on the antiwar liberal left, particularly for their lack of support for the State of Israel during the Six-Day War. According to the Camp Jedel director, "we have never aligned ourselves with the bigots of the reactionary right. Now the radical-liberal left—white and black—is turning on us, picking the Jew to be their scapegoat."[118] JDL members were particularly worried at the number of young Jews drawn to radical social and antiwar movements, which largely remained anti-Israel (or at least highly critical of Israel's military activity). A brochure for Camp Jedel warned:

> The growth of extremism, and more important, its ability to capture the allegiance of so many Jewish youngsters is a danger of the first magnitude. This is due to the fact that there is no group or framework which presents the other side, the true facts, concerning these groups and individuals plotting revolution and anarchy in America. At the same time, the sheer physical threat on the part of extremists has become alarming. Threats of force and its use on campus, beatings and robbery of youngsters in their own neighborhoods are all a part of an increasing phenomenon today. We are, therefore, operating a camp which will train Jewish youth for proud leadership—strong both in mind and body. The program, a rugged and difficult one, will turn out the type of Jewish youngster who is loyal and responsible to his own and his people's needs.[119]

Even while criticizing far left and militant Black nationalist movements, Kahane openly discussed the fact that he happily adopted their tactics and welcomed the comparison.

In an interview with *Playboy* magazine in 1972 (one would be hard-pressed to find a more masculine venue for such a discussion), Kahane was asked to comment on the appropriation of Black militant images and tactics and responded, "The Talmud says, 'Who is wise? He who learns from all people.' We're happy when people call us Panthers, because we know a Panther doesn't mess with a Panther."[120] It's also worth noting that of all the famous and impressive figures interviewed and published in *Playboy* during its heyday, Kahane, as a Jewish leader, was an outlier. In his recent book on Kahane, Shaul Magid suggested that he was, in fact, the most Jewish interview in the history of the magazine.[121] Kahane likely saw a good audience for the topic of remasculinizing previously assumed effeminate Jewish men in the readers of *Playboy*.

For their part, the radical Jews on the left criticized the tough Jewish image emerging from both the JDL and Israel as detrimental to peace and Jewish identity. These Jews tended to equate Israeli culture with fostering a harmful sort of hypermasculinity, which blamed the cultivated machismo of Israeli men for the destruction of Jewish unity and for warmongering on the global stage. The JDL was an example of that negative effect on American Jewry. However, Kahane's reception in Israel shows that the JDL's particular manifestation of hypermasculinity, though it took cues from Israeli manhood, was a purely American blending of a masculine Israeli image with American aggression and problems. Upon arriving in Israel, Kahane found few Israelis initially interested in his racially based, hypermasculine, aggressive political agenda. As Shaul Magid deftly demonstrates in *Meir Kahane: The Public Life and Political Thought of an American Jewish Radical*, Kahane's political career in Israel was precisely the opposite of what the American Jewish Left had asserted, it was an imposition of his own very American practices and problems onto Israeli society. While the Six-Day War made some American Jewish men prouder to be Jews, members of the JDL attempted to emulate Israeli toughness in the United States and to look back into their own histories, as Americans, to find other examples of Jewish toughness. What they created was a Jewish American masculinity that found masculine inspiration in the people of Israel.

The upheaval that occurred in American society during this period, the Vietnam War, the antiwar movement, and the rise of an antiestablishment counterculture all served to complicate the identities of young American men, Jews included. The addition of the Six-Day War and the acuteness with which it affected American Jewish culture made the late 1960s and early 1970s a period in which American Jews reevaluated their position as world citizens and as men. This reevaluation did not follow any clear trajectory but a fracturing and reconfiguring of Jewish male identities in the United States. Each of the groups that show the tumult (antiwar protestors, militants, radical Zionists) represent the fringes of American Jewry, not the majority. It is, however, in examining these outliers that we learn about what we might call a mainstream American Jewish manhood. Those who strayed from the norm to claim a new masculine identity help to define the masculinity with which they remained dissatisfied.

Meir Kahane envisioned an America in which Jewish boys brawled in the streets alongside other tough minorities, defending Jewish interests. He wanted to change the way that the rest of American society perceived Jews; he explained, "We're out to change the traditional image of the Jew as a patsy. We want our young people to stand straight and tall."[122] His true goal, recognized or not, was not merely about changing the image of Jews as "people," his goal was to fully reinvent Jewish manhood in America. The past century has had continuous examples of Jewish men struggling against a feminized image, but none more overtly than the JDL in its claims of Jewish power and pride.

But did it make a dent in the nice Jewish boy image? The JDL is still active, and the few remaining leaders are trying to revive it even now in 2022, but it was a fleeting heyday. I would argue that the overt call to American Jewish men to stand up for themselves, and to be brutal, did indeed take root in the American Jewish imagination. Starting while the JDL was most active and continuing to this day, tough (even brutal) Jewish characters have made their way into popular culture and entertainment. And they have continued to become more American, more hard-boiled, as the new Jewish male archetype has matured. Growing from the early "tough Jews" of midcentury literature scrutinized by Paul Breines and Warren Rosenberg to brutal Jews like Donny Donowitz (the "Bear Jew" of Quentin Tarantino's *Inglourious Basterds*), this image of Jewish men has proven determinedly resistant to criticism, and consistently popular among Jewish audiences. The JDL did not succeed in its mission to create a feared and respected street army of Jewish toughs that made antisemites shake in their boots, but it did give early permission for American Jewish boys to idolize the image of the sabra and Israeli soldier as tough Jewish heroes and assured them they were not alone in their belief that there was truth behind the emasculated Jewish stereotype or in their desire to change themselves and the face of Jewish manhood.

Conclusion

The Bear versus the Giant Lobster

Throughout all the struggles of Jewish men to rid their masculine image of its unique qualities, it has diversified, and competing images have emerged, but the primary Jewish male archetype remains largely unchanged. This is evident in the thread of like-minded actors intent on changing the position and perception of Jewish men: Theodore Roosevelt hoped that Jews would emulate the "Maccabee or fighting Jewish type"; the City Athletic Club and agricultural associations trained Jewish New Yorkers of the upper and lower classes to become manly Americans; Jewish Americans enlisted and fought in both American and Jewish armed forces, and then, as Jewish war veterans, fought for the recognition of Jewish American heroes; Bugsy Siegel poured money into the fight for Israeli statehood to train Jews to kill their enemies; Jewish men in the countercultural movement of the 1960s and '70s struggled to redefine their own masculinity through protest and rebellion; Meir Kahane trained Jewish boys to brawl in the street to defend Jewish interests. The past century has a continuum of examples of the Jewish male struggle against a feminized image that remains, though more complex than ever, to this day.

The story of Jewish life in the United States is not one of unswerving upward mobility, nor is it one of consistent antisemitic impediments. As a history of an immigrant group, this book followed the progress of American Jews up the slippery slope of acculturation. For the most part the Jewish trajectory has trended upward, but with periodic backslides of varying severity. Setbacks in the Jewish experience of Americanization demonstrate the tension between the religious and the secular, the old and the young, and the native-born and recent immigrants. Motivated by the concept that each of these points of conflict contained a gendered element (which focused on the male as the model of a successful immigrant), this study recognized and followed the trajectory of Jewish acculturation that held American hegemonic masculinity as the highest goal of American acculturation and highlighted instances of antisemitism in American history as similarly gendered, using the successes or failures of Jewish men to be American as motivation for discrimination.

Excellent preexisting studies concerning the Jewish experience in the military, university life, agriculture, finance, civil rights and women's rights movements, counterculture and protest, crime, sports, and many other aspects supported this research. What I have attempted to reveal is that one of the connecting threads between these elements of Jewish life in America is the component of masculinity, perceptions about it, and access to it. Examining Jewish participation in the civil rights movement, for example, is a fruitful field of study that has produced fascinating theses about Jewish altruism, motivation, and politics. It is worth adding to this field the awareness that Jewish men participated aggressively in protest, mimicked tactics from many Black movements, and fought to be recognized as men in a related struggle. The Jewish experience in the American military, particularly antisemitic encounters involving servicemen, is better illuminated if the particularly emasculating form of antisemitism they faced is examined. In nearly every element of Jewish history in America, especially relationships between Jewish men and women, adding a consideration of the role played by Jewish men engaging with issues of masculinity adds much-needed depth to our historical understanding of Jewish life and identity. In the debate over sustaining Jewish culture, which Sylvia Barack Fishman revitalized in her 2008 work, *Matrilineal Ascent/Patrilineal Descent: The Gender Imbalance in American Jewish Life*, Jewish men are often blamed for the loss of Jewish culture. For answers about the motivation of secularizing Jewish men, engaging issues of masculinity in the United States can only serve to productively complicate the discussion.

As a sweeping history from the turn of the century through 1973, this book only scratched the surface of several areas of the history of Jewish American masculinity worthy of examination. I make no claims that Jews have or have not been successful in their goal of achieving American masculinity, largely because there has never been a consensus among Jews in America about how they should practice, assimilate, retain culture, perform masculinity, or anything else. I have instead attempted to demonstrate that this goal, whether attainable or not, was ever-present among some elements of American Jewry, and help to explain some of the actions taken, and the ways in which Jewish men orchestrated such action over the century. What is clear through this work is that the view of Jewish men as weak or effeminate has been a constant strain among popular sentiments about Jewish manhood in America, and there has always been a corresponding strain of Jewish men attempting to remedy this sentiment through proving or improving their manhood. It is also clear that antisemitism itself is a gendered bigotry, manifesting in different ways across different nations, and America has not proven itself an exception. Recognizing the gendered nature of this particular bigotry, and refocusing our study of Jewish history through the lens of a uniquely Jewish masculine struggle, provides insight into and a deeper understanding of the American Jewish experience.

In the fifty years which have elapsed since the close of the periodization of this book in 1973, much has changed for international Jewry, primarily concerning the role of Israel on a global stage. Israel engaged in several international conflicts as well as movements to relocate hundreds of thousands of Jews from the Soviet Union and Ethiopia. The victories of the small nation in these endeavors have had tremendous effects on the self-image of American Jews and their perceptions of Jewish strength, and still continue to influence the political shifts among large portions of American Jewry. Changes in the presentation of Jewish strength connected to the violent conflicts alone are enough to be worthy of an entirely separate examination of Jewish masculinity. However, the American focus of the present study cannot extend into our current era of digital communications and globalization. Certainly, more factors than the State of Israel have arisen to complicate the Jewish masculine narrative. The prominent Jewish leadership and participation in the American neoconservative movement, which rejected the New Left and many of the ideals and movements covered in Chapters 9 and 10, also worked to alter perceptions of Jewish American manhood. Additional Jewish types have become part of mainstream popular culture, including the Israeli Mossad as super-soldier and the vengeful super Jew, both evolved from the earlier types of sabra and resistance fighter. But alongside popular images of these types, are the same representations that there were in the century before. For every Zohan flexing his muscles is a Hebrew Hammer bickering with his mother. Alongside visibly Jewish actors in hypermasculine violent roles (like Jon Bernthal playing the Punisher, or Eli Roth as the Bear Jew) are the ever-present Jewish nebbish and shlemiel characters, so ubiquitous they need not even be human to be recognizable, as is the case with Dr. Zoidberg (the giant lobster alien discussed in the introduction).

What does it mean, then, for the image of the Jewish nebbish to have lived on, so dominantly, well into the twenty-first century in spite of emerging new Jewish male types? In the years that have elapsed since beginning this project in 2013, so much has come to the fore in popular discussion that makes this timeless subject more timely and significant than I could have imagined. The #MeToo movement and subsequent considerations of toxic masculinity have made this previously niche subject both relevant and applicable to current debates. Considerations abound over alternative masculinities and the rearing of feminist men. In addition, the combination of contemporary political and academic shifts has brought issues of white privilege, previously absent from mainstream discussions, to nearly all areas of historical and contemporary discussion. The connection between masculinity and whiteness and the inherent privilege of both have opened conversations concerning access and equity that expand our understanding of the past as well as our interpretation of events in our present. The issue of masculinity has been gaining importance and recognition by both mainstream and academic observers. The release and positive reception of Sarah Imhoff's book on Jewish masculinity in 2017 confirmed the necessity for such a discussion and opened the field that this book appreciatively joins. The history recounted across the preceding chapters gives us insight into what these current discussions of masculinity have to do with Jewish men, and in what ways the perception of Jews has changed in the last hundred years.

During the 2016 presidential campaign, many comparisons were drawn between Jewish—though secular—Democratic candidate Bernie Sanders and nominally Christian Republican, Donald Trump. However, observers at times seemed less concerned with this religious distinction than with the two men's alternate forms of masculinity. In a comparison of the candidates, a journalist notes that Trump's German background and family emphasized pride in being attackers and fighters, while Sanders, whose father escaped Nazi Europe, "does not so much fight, as he fights back."[1] She continues, "It is not a coincidence that the first time a woman is a serious contender for the presidency, and the first time a Jew wins delegates in a presidential primary or caucus, we also have the first presidential candidate to tout his own penis size" (though Lyndon Johnson famously nicknamed his own genitals "Jumbo"). This marked a real difference from the two previous presidential elections, which focused on religion and race, particularly on Mitt Romney's Mormonism and the accusations that Barak Obama had Muslim affiliations.

The 2016 comparisons make some unexpected connections and works on assumptions about both "white" and Jewish masculinity, part of an emerging scholarly field with limited but increasing research. How could Sanders, a liberal socialist, be read as so aggressively against the grain of the establishment, and yet still be the gentle Jewish victim fighting only in defense? If Bernie Sanders presented as a gentler sort of man, a Jew in the most stereotypical sense, how did he attract such an aggressive male following that Robinson Meyer (writing for *The Atlantic*) dubbed them the "Bernie Bros?"[2] How can a man conduct himself as a loud, hard-hitting communicator from Brooklyn, yet also be named an "honorary woman" by Gloria Steinem?[3] While European images of Jewish men have been historically emasculated or gentle, American images of Jewish men are disparate and contradictory and can only be understood through the history of Jewish male representation and masculine achievement.

With the recent Russian invasion of Ukraine in 2022, the American Jewish community responded to the emerging celebrity of Ukrainian president Volodymyr Zelenskyy with unprecedented excitement and masculine hyperbole. Overnight the Jewish leader became the most discussed man on the internet, and, for a leader actively under siege and threat of death, he was sexualized to a degree that many commentators found shocking and inexplicable.[4] Comments, memes, blogs, articles, and entire Twitter accounts abounded, praising Zelenskyy's masculinity, sex appeal, physique, and even the size of his genitals. Given that Zelenskyy is not American, the overwhelming online American Jewish response of exaltation was a curious development, but the answer lies in the history of Jewish manhood. Zelenskyy was, in many ways, the hero American Jewish men have been waiting for, which for all of the reasons laid out in this book, they have yet to achieve.[5]

Zelenskyy is not American, but he presents a long-awaited manifestation of Jewish masculinity, and his own journey leading to politics mirrors many American Jewish stories. He's a comedian turned politician, like American Jew Al Franken. He won the Ukrainian version of *Dancing with the Stars*, a victory recently shared by an American Jew (Alan Bersten), celebrated in the American Jewish press for his victory and his athleticism. He is the descendant of Holocaust survivors, and more importantly, of Jews who fought Nazis during the Holocaust. Unlike many Israeli macho men, Zelenskyy still looks the part of an Eastern European Jew, the Ashkenazi DNA that dominates American Jewish archetypes. Unlike many masculine Jewish heroes, Zelenskyy's Jewishness has been highlighted, not downplayed. Unlike Bernie Sanders, Zelenskyy's sudden political celebrity is as a wartime leader, not a dissenting political voice in the United States Senate. Zelenskyy, unlike all hopeful American Jewish politicians who ran, successfully won the presidency with an astounding majority. As a result of these manifestations of long-awaited Jewish manhood, American commentators seized the opportunity to present Zelenskyy as the antidote to emasculated Jews, and one that is not reliant on the often-contentious State of Israel. It is a reaction to a long history of Jewish masculinity in America of which contemporary American Jews are only vaguely historically aware, but the results of which have affected them greatly.

We need not rely only on popular representations of Jews to define realities of Jewish manhood. Certainly not when the historical realities provide us with tangible examples of Jewish manhood that account for those fictional or fictionalized representations. Studies of the changing images of Jewish men in film and literature are fascinating in what they teach about male Jewish desires, but the historical questions that begged for answers were about the realities of Jewish life in America, the masculine ideals they influenced and worked toward, and how these ideals, in turn, guided the course of modern Jewish history.

Glossary

Aliyah: Hebrew, literally translated as "going up." Aliyah refers to the immigration of Jews from diaspora communities to the land of Israel/Palestine.

Aliyah Bet: The code name given to the illegal immigration of Jews to Palestine under the British Mandate, mostly composed of Holocaust survivors and refugees fleeing Nazi Europe.

Ba'alei Teshuvah: Translates literally from the Hebrew as "a master of return." In practical usage, it is used to refer to Jews from secular or non-orthodox backgrounds who become observant.

Chutzpah: Yiddish term for audacity, used both pejoratively and positively, as in the cases of the English "cheekiness" or "irreverence."

Edelkayt: Yiddish. According to Daniel Boyarin, this is a rabbinic model of masculinity established thousands of years ago, recognizable for its gentle, timid, non-phallocentric nature. As it resisted gentile assumptions about masculinity, Edelkayt helped to confirm Western stereotypes of the feminized Jewish man. See also: mensch.

Eretz Israel: The traditional Jewish name for the pre-statehood Land of Israel. Because it is the identification for the ancestral homeland, it had no definable geographical boundaries.

First Aliyah: The first wave of Jewish immigration to Palestine between 1882 and 1903. Also called the agricultural aliyah.

Galut: Hebrew name given for life in the Jewish diaspora or exile. It at times refers to the spaces that diaspora Jews occupy but can also be used to indicate the condition of Jews in the diaspora, uprooted and persecuted.

Goldene Medine: Yiddish phrase meaning "golden land" or "land of gold."

Goy/Goyim: Yiddish, often pejorative term for a non-Jew.

Halacha: The laws and ordinances of Judaism that regulate religious observances and the daily life and conduct of the Jewish people. Translates from Hebrew as "the way."

Halutz(im): A Jewish immigrant to pre-state Palestine, usually represented as a farmer or pioneer, creating and building Jewish settlements in Palestine.

Kavod: Hebrew word meaning honor and respect.

Kehillah: Hebrew word meaning "congregation." In the early twentieth century, however, the word also refers to a local Jewish communal structure.

Kibbutz(im): A collective community in Israel (or in pre-state Palestine), typically an agriculturally based commune. Kibbutznik is a name for a member of the kibbutz.

Landsmanschaftn: Mutual benefit societies formed by Jewish immigrants from the same villages, towns, and cities in Central and Eastern Europe.

Mauschel: A derogatory term with antisemitic overtones, meaning to talk like a Jewish peddler. The term was also used by Theodor Herzl to describe a type of Jew he categorized as "crooked, 'low and repugnant,' frightened, unresponsive to beauty, passive, queer, effeminate."

Mensch: Yiddish word for a person of honor or one with integrity.

Momzer/Momzerim: A pejorative term coming from the Greek, mamzer, meaning "son of a prostitute." In Yiddish, the term has come to mean "bastard" and has a connotation of contemptibility or deception.

Moshav(im): A cooperative community of farmers in Israel. Unlike a kibbutz, a moshav is not a commune but a cooperative agricultural community composed of several farms.

Naches (and *Goyim Naches*): Yiddish expression meaning pleasure, satisfaction, delight; proud enjoyment. *Goyim naches* is a term used by Daniel Boyarin in his 1999 book *Unheroic Conduct*, which he defines as "games goyim play."

Nebbish: From the Yiddish *nebekh*, meaning "poor thing." A person, most often a man, regarded as submissive, timid, unfortunate, or ineffectual.

Olim: New immigrants to Israel.

Sabra: A Jew born in Israel or in pre-state Palestine. They were named for a thorny prickly pear found in Palestine, one with a harsh exterior, but containing sustenance and sweetness inside.

Sheygetz: A Yiddish term for a gentile boy or man, often derogatory.

Shiksa: A Yiddish term for a gentile woman or girl, often derogatory.

Shande: Yiddish for an embarrassment, shame, disgrace, or scandal. The term is usually used to describe the actions of a Jew in front of an audience of non-Jews, bringing shame on the Jewish people.

Sheref: Arabic word meaning honor and respect.

Shomer/Shomrim: Hebrew word for "guard," used in this work to describe those members of pre-state Palestine who acted as guards over the Jewish settlements to protect them from potential attack.

Yishuv: Hebrew for "settlement," refers to the Jewish entity in Palestine from the Ottoman period through the British Mandate. The Yishuv had reached about 650,000 members before the end of the British Mandate.

Notes

Introduction

1 Philip Roth, *Patrimony* (New York: Vintage Books, 1996), 159.
2 His voice is a tacit implication of his Jewishness as well, based on the marble-mouthed Jewish accented voices of vaudevillian George Jessel and character actor Lou Jacobi, and *Futurama* writers created his dialogue to clearly invoke Jewishness, with phrases like "And then, a wonderous thing happened, why not?" in *Futurama*, season 4, episode 4, "Love and Rocket," directed by Brian Sheesley, written by Matt Groening, David X. Cohen, Dan Vebber, Kristin Gore, and David Mirsky, aired February 10, 2002, on Fox.
3 *Futurama*, season 4, episode 9, "Future Stock," directed by Brian Sheesley, written by Matt Groening, David X. Cohen, Aaron Ehasz, Kristin Gore, and Jeff Westbrook, aired March 31, 2002, on Fox.
4 *Futurama*, season 2, episode 9, "Why Must I Be a Crustacean in Love?" directed by Brian Sheesley and Bret Haaland, written by Matt Groening, David X. Cohen, Eric Kaplan, and Jeff Westbrook, aired February 6, 2000, on Fox.
5 Jacob Rader Marcus, *The American Jew, 1585–1990: A History* (Brooklyn: Carlson Publishing, 1995), 336.
6 I do so in the full acknowledgment that true assimilation is nonexistent, but that Jews experienced a form of *blocked assimilation*. Jews experienced what Susan Brown and Frank Bean called a blocked assimilation model, in which they are blocked from full entry into American society based on a discriminating factor, in this case, their religious and ethnic identity as Jews. This also fits Ruby Jo Reeves Kennedy's theory of three melting pots: Catholic, Protestant, and

Jewish (though she was looking primarily at intermarriage). Within the Jewish melting pot, we see partially assimilated/blocked American Jews working to assimilate new Jewish immigrants into their own American melting pot, in which they were highly acculturated Jews. For explanations of these definitions see Susan K. Brown and Frank D. Bean, "Assimilation Models, Old and New: Explaining a Long-Term Process," Migration Policy Institute, accessed September 22, 2018, www.migrationpolicy.org/article/assimilation-models-old-and-new -explaining-long-term-process; Matt O'Brien, "The Important Difference between Assimilation and Integration," ImmigrationReform .com, accessed September 22, 2018, https://immigrationreform.com/ 2016/09/29/the-important-difference-between-assimilation-and -integration/; Ruby Jo Reeves Kennedy, "Single or Triple Melting-Pot? Intermarriage Trends in New Haven, 1870–1940," *American Journal of Sociology* 49, no. 4 (January 1944): 331–39.

7 For a particularly interesting critique of the use of the term in the work of R. W. Connell, see Demetrakis Z. Demetriou, "Connell's Concept of Hegemonic Masculinity: A Critique," *Theory and Society* 30, no. 3 (June 2001): 337–61.

8 R. W. Connell, *Masculinities*, 2nd ed. (Berkeley: University of California Press, 2005), 37.

9 Meaning to demonstrate the conventions through which the identity of man is established and upheld. Michael Schwalbe, 2005; Schrock and Schwalbe, "Men, Masculinity, and Manhood Acts."

10 This definition of *manhood acts* is in line with that laid out by Douglas Schrock and Michael Schwalbe in their 2009 article "Men, Masculinity, and Manhood Acts," *Annual Review of Sociology* 35 (2009): 277–95.

11 Judith Butler, "Performative Acts and Gender Constitution: An Essay in Phenomenology and Feminist Theory," in *Performing Feminisms: Feminist Critical Theory and Theatre*, ed. Sue-Ellen Case (Baltimore: Johns Hopkins University Press, 1990).

12 For an overview of the history and development of queer theory, see Annamarie Jagose, *Queer Theory: An Introduction* (New York: New York University Press, 1997).

13 Stephen D. Moore, *God's Beauty Parlor: And Other Queer Spaces in and around the Bible* (Stanford, CA: Stanford University Press, 2001), 14.

14 It is equally important to recognize that by using the language of queer theory to scrutinize and write about a group of primarily heterosexual men, the goal is not appropriation but the proliferation of its finding and insights. Calvin Thomas, "Introduction: Identification, Appropriation, Proliferation," in *Straight with a Twist: Queer Theory and the Subject of Heterosexuality*, ed. Calvin Thomas (Urbana: University of Illinois Press, 2000), 1–7.

15 Michael Kimmel, "Masculinity as Homophobia: Fear, Shame, and Silence in the Construction of Gender Identity," in *Race, Class, and Gender in the United States: An Integrated Study*, ed. Paula S. Rothenberg (New York: Worth Publishers, 2004), 82.

16 Schrock and Schwalbe, "Men, Masculinity, and Manhood Acts," 285.

17 Daniel Boyarin, *Unheroic Conduct: The Rise of Heterosexuality and the Invention of the Jewish Man* (Berkeley: University of California Press, 1997), 25–29. For more on the history of LGBTQ Jews, see Daniel Boyarin, Daniel Itzkovitz, and Ann Pellegrini, eds., *Queer Theory and the Jewish Question* (New York: Columbia University Press, 2003), and Steven Greenberg, *Wrestling with God and Men: Homosexuality in the Jewish Tradition* (Madison: University of Wisconsin Press, 2004). For a brief history of Jews in the early movement for gay rights, see "Homophobia and Tolerance in Judaism," in Jonathan Friedman's *Rainbow Jews: Jewish and Gay Identity in the Performing Arts* (New York: Lexington Books, 2007).

18 For readings on Jewish masculinity in Europe, see Baader, Gillerman, and Lerner's edited volume *Jewish Masculinities: German Jews, Gender, and History*, and many of Sander Gilman's publications, including *Freud, Race, and Gender*, *The Jew's Body*, *Smart Jews: The Construction of the Image of Jewish Superior Intelligence*, *Making the Body Beautiful: A Cultural History of Aesthetic Surgery*, and *Jewish Frontiers: Essays on Bodies, Histories, and Identities*. For studies dealing tangentially with Israeli masculinity, see Mayer's *Women and the Israeli Occupation*, Almog's *The Sabra: The Creation of the New Jew*, and Presner's *Muscular Judaism: The Jewish Body and the Politics of Regeneration*.

19 See Paul Breines's *Tough Jews: Political Fantasies and the Moral Dilemma of American Jewry*, Boyarin's *Unheroic Conduct*, Rosenberg's *Legacy of Rage: Jewish Masculinity, Violence, and Culture*, Brod and Zevit's *Brother Keepers: New Perspectives on Jewish Masculinity*, Moscowitz's *A Culture*

of Tough Jews: Rhetorical Regeneration and the Politics of Identity, and Hollander's *From Schlemiel to Sabra: Zionist Masculinity and Palestinian Hebrew Literature*.

Chapter 1

1 Theodor Herzl, *The Complete Diaries of Theodor Herzl, Volume 1*, ed. Raphael Patai (New York: Herzl Press, 1960), 9.

2 John Higham, *Send These to Me* (Baltimore: Johns Hopkins University Press, 1984), 117–52.

3 In "Neither 'Sissy' Boy nor Patrician Man: New York Intellectuals and the Construction of American Jewish Masculinity," for example, Ronnie A. Grinberg explains, "Whereas elite Protestant constructions of masculinity stressed traits like strength and athleticism, Jewish masculinity emphasized intellect and combative debate." Literature scholars begin from this assumption and build on it to make arguments about changing masculinity. For example, Yaron Peleg explains that to masculinize a Jewish character, the author Moshe Smilansky endowed the characters with "non-Jewish" traits, and "construct[ed] him in the image of a goy. The desired change from a weak and diminutive Torah scholar to a strong and courageous farmer and soldier is achieved here by internalizing traditionally non-Jewish values" [emphasis added]. Ronnie A. Grinberg, "Neither 'Sissy' Boy nor Patrician Man: New York Intellectuals and the Construction of American Jewish Masculinity," *American Jewish History* 98, no. 3 (July 2014): 128. Yaron Peleg, "Heroic Conduct: Homoeroticism and the Creation of Modern, Jewish Masculinities," *Jewish Social Studies* 13, no. 1 (Autumn 2006): 31–58, at 39–40.

4 For a thorough and interesting account of the use of manhood and the First World War in *Ost und West*, see the fifth chapter ("Antisemitism and the German-Jewish Male") of David A. Brenner's *Marketing Identities: The Invention of Jewish Ethnicity in Ost und West* (Detroit: Wayne State University Press, 1998), 159–82.

5 Sander Gilman dates this particular belief to Tomás de Cantimpré's *Miraculorum et exemplorum memorabilium sui temporis libri duo* (Douai: Baltazris Belleri, 1605), and it emerges again in Thomas Calvert's 1648 book, *The Blessed Jew of Marocco; Or, a Blackmoor Made White*. Quoted in David S. Katz, "Shylock's Gender: Jewish Male

Menstruation in Early Modern England," *Review of English Studies* 50, no. 200 (November 1999): 440–62.

6 Sander L. Gilman, "Whose Body Is It Anyway? Hermaphrodites, Gays, and Jews in N. O. Body's Germany," in *German Jews, Gender, and History*, ed. Benjamin Maria Baader (Bloomington: Indiana University Press, 2012), 148.

7 Katz, "Shylock's Gender," 456.

8 Katz, "Shylock's Gender," 457.

9 For more on Otto Weininger and Jewish gender, aside from his own 1903 book, *Sex and Character: An Investigation of Fundamental Principles*, trans. Ladislaus Löb (Bloomington: Indiana University Press, 2005), see Chandak Sengoopta, *Otto Weininger: Sex, Science, and Self in Imperial Vienna* (Chicago: University of Chicago Press, 2000); Nancy A. Harrowitz and Barbara Hyams, eds., *Jews and Gender: Responses to Otto Weininger* (Philadelphia: Temple University Press, 1995); Susan C. Anderson, "Otto Weininger's Masculine Utopia," *German Studies Review* 19, no. 3 (October 1996): 433–53; and Christina Von Braun's "Sexual Images in Racist Anti-Semitism" ("Sexualisierung: Der Körper des Juden als, Konversionssymptom"), accessed August 8, 2018, www.christinavonbraun.de/_pdf/Sexual%20Images%20in%20Anti -semitism.pdf.

For more specifically on Jewish self-hatred, see Sander Gilman's work, particularly *Jewish Self-Hatred: Anti-Semitism and the Hidden Language of the Jews* (Baltimore: Johns Hopkins University Press, 1986); Allan Janick, "Viennese Culture and the Jewish Self-Hatred Hypothesis: A Critique," in *Jews, Assimilation, and Culture in Vienna*, ed. Ivar Oxaal et al. (New York: Routledge, 1987): 75–88; Paul Reitter, "The Jewish Self-Hatred Octopus," *German Quarterly* 82, no. 3, German-Jewish and Jewish-German Studies (Summer 2009): 356–72.

10 Weininger, *Sex and Character*, 274.

11 Weininger, *Sex and Character*, 272.

12 Weininger, *Sex and Character*, 278.

13 Weininger, *Sex and Character*, 279.

14 Weininger, *Sex and Character*, 286.

15 Weininger, *Sex and Character*, 280.

16 Weininger, *Sex and Character*, 275.

17 Patricia Szobar, "Telling Sexual Stories in the Nazi Courts of Law: Race Defilement in Germany, 1933–1945," in *Sexuality and German Fascism*, ed. Dagmar Herzog (New York: Berghahn Books, 2005), 147.

18 Andrea Dworkin wrote that traditional antisemitism habitually portrayed Jews as rapists of Christian women. The sexual nature of this act, she argued, did not make Jewish men more masculine, but dehumanized them—implying that they must be castrated or imprisoned. The idea that a Jewish man could become dehumanized and dangerous and need to be fixed by physical removal of male organs contributes an interesting perspective to the discussion of masculinity in antisemitic rhetoric. It implies that excluding Jews from Christian society resulted not only in their emasculation and comparison to women by antisemitic rhetoric, but in their exclusion from manhood altogether. Andrea Dworkin, "The Sexual Mythology of Anti-Semitism," in *A Mensch among Men: Explorations in Jewish Masculinity*, ed. Harry Brod (Freedom, CA: Crossing Press, 1988), 119.

19 For historical examples, see Weininger or Havelock Ellis, and for historiographical references, see Gilman, Von Braun, Bederman, and Anderson.

20 This distinction is especially significant when examining the motivations of some Jewish to Christian converts, as Sarah Imhoff does in *Masculinity and the Making of American Judaism*. This issue as well as the work that Imhoff conducted is covered in the final section of the following chapter, "Accepting Jewish Weakness."

21 Weininger, *Sex and Character*, 81.

22 Weininger, *Sex and Character*, 281.

23 Daniel Boyarin, "What Does a Jew Want?; or, The Political Meaning of the Phallus," *Discourse* 19, no. 2 (Winter 1997): 26.

24 Sander Gilman, *Freud, Race, and Gender* (Princeton, NJ: Princeton University Press, 1993), 38–39.

25 Raine Dozier, "Beards, Breasts, and Bodies: Doing Sex in a Gendered World," *Gender and Society* 19, no. 3 (June 2005): 297–316.

26 Hauser quoted in Von Braun, "Sexual Images," 12–13.

27 For more on the connection of masculinity to maleness as it pertains to women, see Jack Halberstam, *Female Masculinity* (Durham, NC: Duke University Press, 1998).

28 Barbara Breitman, "Lifting Up the Shadow of Antisemitism: Jewish Masculinity in a New Light," in *A Mensch among Men: Explorations in Jewish Masculinity*, ed. Harry Brod (Freedom, CA: Crossing Press, 1988), 106–7.

29 As quoted in the epigraph at the start of this chapter, Herzl wrote, "All these sufferings rendered us ugly and transformed our character which had in earlier times been proud and magnificent." Theodor Herzl, *The Complete Diaries of Theodor Herzl, Volume 1*, ed. Raphael Patai (New York: Herzl Press, 1960), 9.

30 This is true of Jewish women attempting to acculturate in both European and American culture, where the middle-class domestic role for women dominated. Paula Hyman, *Gender and Assimilation in Modern Jewish History: The Roles and Representation of Women* (Seattle: University of Washington Press, 1995), 25–32.

31 Marion Kaplan, "Tradition and Transition: Jewish Women in Imperial Germany," in *Jewish Women in Historical Perspective*, ed. Judith R. Baskin (Detroit: Wayne State University Press, 1998), 231–32.

32 Benjamin Maria Baader, "Jewish Difference and the Feminine Spirit of Judaism in Mid-Nineteenth-Century Germany," in *Jewish Masculinities: German Jews, Gender, and History*, ed. Benjamin Maria Baader, Sharon Gillerman, and Paul Lerner (Bloomington: Indiana University Press, 2012), 50–71.

33 Boyarin shows images taken from a Passover Haggadah, in which the "Evil Son" is represented as a "Muscle Jew" in contemporary European dress. Boyarin, *Unheroic Conduct*, 77–78.

34 George L. Mosse, *The Image of Man* (New York: Oxford University Press, 1996), 29.

35 Yaron Ben-Naeh, "Urban Encounters: The Muslim-Jewish Case in the Ottoman Empire," in *The Ottoman Middle East: Studies in Honor of Amnon Cohen*, ed. Eyal Ginio and Elie Podeh (Leiden: Brill, 2014), 178.

36 Yaron Ben-Naeh, "Honor and Its Meaning among Ottoman Jews," *Jewish Social Studies* 11, no. 2 (Winter 2005): 22.

37 See Sarah Abrevaya Stein on images of Jewish men and women in advertisements in Yiddish and Ladino presses. Sarah Abrevaya Stein, *Making Jews Modern: The Yiddish and Ladino Press in the Russian and Ottoman Empires* (Bloomington: Indiana University Press, 2003), 183–85.

38 Simon Wendt and Pablo Dominguez Andersen used this position of Jews as the perfect example of a male group marginalized from the hegemonic masculine ideal in Europe, in their introduction to a more global analysis of other masculinities and their roles in nation building. "Introduction," in Wendt and Andersen, *Masculinities and the Nation in the Modern World: Between Hegemony and Marginalization* (New York: Palgrave, 2015), 7.

39 Zionism was not the only Jewish answer to developing European nationalism and modern political movements. There were additional Jewish territorial movements as well as nonterritorial Jewish nationalist movements across Europe. For more on Jewish territorialism, see Laura Almagor's *Beyond Zion: The Jewish Territorialist Movement* (New York: Oxford University Press, 2022), which follows Israel Zangwill's Jewish Territorial Organisation (the ITO) and the Freeland League for Jewish Colonization under the leadership of Isaac Steinberg.

40 Robert A. Nye referred to this process as the "embourgeoisement" of the duel in *Masculinity and Male Codes of Honor in Modern France* (New York: Oxford University Press, 1993), 132–33. Also see Steven A. Riess, "Antisemitism and Sport in Central Europe and the United States," in *Jews in the Gym: Judaism, Sports, and Athletics*, ed. Leonard Greenspoon (West Lafayette, IN: Purdue University Press, 2012), 99–100.

41 Kevin McAleer, *Dueling: The Cult of Honor in Fin-de-Siècle Germany* (Princeton, NJ: Princeton University Press, 1994), 143. Mosse, *Image of Man*, 22.

42 Sander L. Gilman, *Making the Body Beautiful: A Cultural History of Aesthetic Surgery* (Princeton, NJ: Princeton University Press, 1999), 124.

43 Gilman, *Making the Body Beautiful*, 69.

44 Jacques Kornberg, "Theodor Herzl: Zionism as Personal Liberation," in *Theodor Herzl: From Europe to Zion*, ed. Mark H. Gelber and Vivian Liska (Tübingen, Germany: Max Niemeyer, 2007), 50–51. For more on Albia and Herzl's entry into the fraternity, see Kornberg, *Theodor Herzl: From Assimilation to Zionism* (Bloomington: Indiana University Press, 1993), 42.

45 Kornberg, *Theodor Herzl: From Assimilation to Zionism*, 70.

46 Quote cited in Julius H. Schoeps, "Modern Heirs of the Maccabees: The Beginning of the Vienna Kadimah, 1882–1897," *LBIYB* 27 (1982): 167.

47 Marion A. Kaplan, "As Germans and as Jews in Imperial Germany," in *Jewish Daily Life in Germany, 1618–1945*, ed. Marion A. Kaplan (New York: Oxford University Press, 2005), 213–14.

48 Roc Morin, "Fighting for Facial Scars in Germany's Secret Fencing Frats: The Secret Duels, Conducted by a Small Number of University Fraternities in Germany, Austria, and Switzerland, Are All That Remain of a Once Widespread Practice Called *Mensur*," Vice.com, March 19, 2015, www.vice.com/en_uk/article/av4bp4/frauleins-dig-them-0000573-v22n2.

49 Schoeps, "Modern Heirs of the Maccabees," 164.

50 Max Nordau, *Degeneration* (New York: D. Appleton, 1968), 40–41.

51 Nordau, *Degeneration*, 541.

52 "Nervous Diseases," Jewish Encyclopedia, accessed July 9, 2018, www.jewishencyclopedia.com/articles/11446-nervous-diseases.

53 Charles Seligman Bernheimer, *The Russian Jew in the United States: Studies of Social Conditions in New York, Philadelphia, and Chicago, with a Description of Rural Settlements* (Philadelphia: John C. Winston, 1905), 294–95.

54 Mosse, "Max Nordau, Liberalism, and the New Jew," 568.

55 The only English translation of the article ("Muskeljudentum") is excerpted in Todd Presner's "'Clear Heads, Solid Stomachs, and Hard Muscles': Max Nordau and the Aesthetics of Jewish Regeneration," *Modernism/modernity* 10, no. 2 (April 2003): 269–96.

56 For an analysis of distributed material among Zionists presenting Jewish rejuvenation in Palestine, see Michael Berkowitz's chapter "Art and Zionist Popular Culture," in *Zionist Culture and West European Jewry before the First World War* (New York: Cambridge University Press, 1993), 119–42.

57 Judith Solis Cohen quoted in "Womankind: A Woman's Impression of the Zionist Congress, Edited by Sarah Kassy," *Jewish Exponent* (1887–1990), January 9, 1914; ProQuest Historical Newspapers, *Jewish Exponent*, 5.

58 *Die Jüdische Turnzeitung* 2, no. 11 (1900). English translation from Presner, "Clear Heads," 283.

59 Thomas Hughes, *Tom Brown at Oxford: A Sequel to School Days at Rugby, Volume 2* (Boston: Ticknor and Fields, 1868), 170.

60 Jacques Kornberg made this argument and supported it clearly in his chapter "The Dreyfus Legend," in *Theodor Herzl: From Assimilation to Zionism*.

61 An idea that, oddly, fits very well in Otto Weininger's assertion that, "The Jews would have to overcome Judaism before they could be ripe for Zionism." Boyarin, *Unheroic Conduct*, 311. Weininger, *Sex and Character*, 282.

62 Gilman, *Freud, Race, and Gender*, 34, 89; Gilman, *Jewish Self-Hatred*; Boyarin, *Unheroic Conduct*, 308.

63 Theodor Herzl, "Mauschel," *Selected Writings of Theodor Herzl* (Tel Aviv: M. Neuman, 1897), 176–80.

Chapter 2

1 Theodore Roosevelt, *Works: The Strenuous Life* (New York: Century, 1901), 3–4.

2 Steven J. Gold. "'The Jazz Singer' to 'What a Country!' A Comparison of Jewish Migration to the United States, 1880–1930 and 1965–1998," *Journal of American Ethnic History* 18, no. 3, The Classical and Contemporary Mass Migration Periods: Similarities and Differences (Spring 1999): 117.

3 On racial science and Jews in the United States, see Robert Singerman, "The Jew as Racial Alien: The Genetic Component of American Anti-Semitism," in *Anti-Semitism in American History*, ed. David Gerber (Urbana: University of Illinois Press, 1987).

4 William F. Pinar, *The Gender of Racial Politics and Violence in America: Lynching, Prison Rape, and the Crisis of Masculinity* (New York: P. Lang, 2001), 321–416.

5 Matthew Frye Jacobson, *Whiteness of a Different Color: European Immigrants and the Alchemy of Race* (Cambridge, MA: Harvard University Press, 1998), 173–75.

6 Gail Bederman, *Manliness and Civilization: A Cultural History of Gender and Race in the United States, 1880–1917* (Chicago,: University of Chicago Press, 2008), 171.

7 Bederman, *Manliness and Civilization*, 170–71. David McCullough, *Mornings on Horseback: The Story of an Extraordinary Family, a Vanished Way of Life, and the Unique Child Who Became Theodore Roosevelt*

(New York: Simon and Schuster, 2007), 256. Michael Kimmel, *Manhood in America: A Cultural History* (New York: Oxford University Press, 2012), 132. Theodore Roosevelt, *An Autobiography* (New York: Charles Scribner's Sons, 1913), 148.

8 Roosevelt, *Autobiography*, 119.

9 For a history of antisemitic caricatures and images of Jews, see Abraham Foxman's *Jews and Money: The Story of a Stereotype* (New York: Palgrave, 2010), and Henry Kellerman's *Greedy, Cowardly, and Weak: Hollywood's Jewish Stereotypes* (Fort Lee, NJ: Barricade Books, 2009). And for histories of Jews and money, see Eliyahu Stern's *Jewish Materialism: The Intellectual Revolution of the 1870s* (New Haven, CT: Yale University Press, 2018); Julie L. Mell's *The Myth of the Medieval Jewish Moneylender, Volumes I and II* (New York: Palgrave Macmillan, 2017); and for American specific history of Jews in business, see Hasia Diner's (editor) *Doing Business in America: A Jewish History* (West Lafayette, IN: Purdue University Press, 2018).

10 Theodore Roosevelt in a letter to Lyman Abbott, May 29, 1908, *Letters of Theodore Roosevelt*, 1043.

11 Letter from Theodore Roosevelt to Anna Roosevelt Cowles. Theodore Roosevelt Collection. MS Am 1834 (532). Harvard College Library. www.theodorerooseveltcenter.org/Research/Digital-Library/Record?libID=0283837. Theodore Roosevelt Digital Library. Dickinson State University.

12 Letter to George Briggs Alton, May 15, 1901, *Letters of Theodore Roosevelt*, 78.

13 Theodore Roosevelt, letter to George Briggs Alton, May 15, 1901, *Letters of Theodore Roosevelt*, 78.

14 Nell Irvin Painter, *The History of White People* (New York: W. W. Norton, 2010), 304–5.

15 Thomas G. Dyer, *Theodore Roosevelt and the Idea of Race* (Baton Rouge: Louisiana State University Press, 1980), 124–25.

16 Letter to Arthur Train, August 13, 1918, SC-10293, American Jewish Historical Society, New York and Boston.

17 Arthur Train, "The Flag of His Country," *McClure's Magazine* 50, no. 10 (August 1918): 9–11, 45–46.

18 "'Teaching Our Sons to Do What We Have Been Teaching the Savages to Avoid': G. Stanley Hall, Racial Recapitulation, and the Neurasthenic Paradox," in Bederman, *Manliness and Civilization*.

19   Theodore Roosevelt, *American Problems* (New York: Charles Scribner's Sons, 1926), 155.

20   Roosevelt, *American Problems*, 131.

21   Roosevelt in a letter to George Briggs Alton, May 15, 1901, *Letters of Theodore Roosevelt*, 79.

22   Letter from Theodore Roosevelt to Robert M. O'Reilly. Theodore Roosevelt Papers, Library of Congress Manuscript Division. www.theodorerooseveltcenter.org/Research/Digital-Library/Record?libID=0183334. Theodore Roosevelt Digital Library. Dickinson State University.

23   Theodore Roosevelt in a letter to Madison Grant, December 30, 1918, *Letters of Theodore Roosevelt*, 1419.

24   Letter from James Andrew Drain to Theodore Roosevelt, Theodore Roosevelt Papers, Library of Congress Manuscript Division. www.theodorerooseveltcenter.org/Research/Digital-Library/Record?libID=068930. Theodore Roosevelt Digital Library. Dickinson State University.

25   Letter from Theodore Roosevelt to James Andrew Drain, www.theodorerooseveltcenter.org/Research/Digital-Library/Record?libID=0292410. Theodore Roosevelt Digital Library. Dickinson State University.

26   Roosevelt, *Autobiography*, 186.

27   Theodore Roosevelt in a letter to Lyman Abbott, May 29, 1908, *Letters of Theodore Roosevelt*, 1042.

28   The numbers vary a bit across Roosevelt's recollections. In his autobiography he cites "a score or two" (p. 187), but this quote and number come from his letter to George Briggs Alton, May 15, 1901, *Letters of Theodore Roosevelt*, 78.

29   In his 2006 book, *Jews in Blue*, Jack Kitaeff features only thirteen notable NYPD Jews as notable in his profile of high-ranking NYPD officers.

30   For a more thorough examination of US military concerns on "International Jewry," see Joseph W. Bendersky, *The "Jewish Threat": Anti-Semitic Politics of the U.S. Army* (New York: Basic Books, 2000).

31   Estimate of soldiers in the Continental Army from John Whiteclay Chambers, ed., *The Oxford Companion to American Military History* (New York: Oxford University Press, 1999), 187. Total population from

Evarts Boutell Greene and Virginia Draper Harrington, *American Population before the Federal Census of 1790* (New York: Columbia University Press, 1932), 7.

32 Simon Wolf, *The American Jew as Patriot, Soldier, and Citizen* (Philadelphia: Levytype, 1895), 424. Also see Adam D. Mendelsohn, *Jewish Soldiers in the Civil War: The Union Army* (New York: New York University Press, 2022).

33 Solomon Grayzel, *A History of the Jews: From the Babylonian Exile to the Present, 5728–1968* (New York: Meridian, 1984), 483.

34 Jonathan D. Sarna and Adam Mendelsohn, eds., *Jews and the Civil War: A Reader* (New York: New York University Press, 2010), 29.

35 This number came from Wolf (*American Jew as Patriot, Soldier, and Citizen*, 425–26), though numbers ranging by up to 800 can be found in varying sources, including the number 7884, listed by the *New York Post* on the two hundred and fiftieth anniversary of Jews in the United States proceedings publication appendixes in 1905, pages 213–14.

36 United States War Department, *Revised United States Army Regulations of 1861* (Washington, DC: Government Printing Office, 1863), 36.

37 Historical Note, Board of Delegates of American Israelites Records, February–April 2003; 1-2, finding guide, American Jewish Historical Society, New York and Boston.

38 Jonathan D. Sarna, *When General Grant Expelled the Jews* (New York: Schocken, 2012), 6–20.

39 Board of Delegates of the American Israelites Resolutions, January 9, 1863; Board of Delegates of American Israelites Records; 1-2; box 4; folder 8; American Jewish Historical Society, New York and Boston.

40 Bendersky, *Jewish Threat*, 33.

41 Amy Kaplan, "Romancing the Empire: The Embodiment of American Masculinity in the Popular Historical Novel of the 1890s," *American Literary History* 2, no. 4 (Winter 1990): 662.

42 Ellen M. Umansky, "Spiritual Expressions: Jewish Women's Religious Lives in the United States in the Nineteenth and Twentieth Centuries," in *Jewish Women in Historical Perspective*, ed. Judith R. Baskin (Detroit: Wayne State University Press, 1998), 343.

43 Rev. Dr. Henry Berkowitz, "Woman's Part in the Drama of Life," *American Jewess* 1, no. 2 (May 1895): 66.

44   Meyer Cohn, "The Young Man and the Synagogue," *American Hebrew and Jewish Messenger*, November 13, 1914, 1.

45   "Improvements Needed," *Jewish Messenger*, March 23, 1866.

46   "Improvements Needed," *Jewish Messenger*, March 23, 1866.

47   David Kaufman, "Temples in the American Athens: A History of the Synagogues of Boston," in *The Jews of Boston*, ed. Jonathan D. Sarna et al. (New Haven, CT: Yale University Press, 1995), 181.

48   Max Heller, "Moral Courage: The Test of American Manhood: Sermon," preached at the Jewish Union Service, Hill Auditorium, University of Michigan, Ann Arbor, Michigan, February 21, 1915, 7.

49   Von Braun, "Sexual Images in Racist Anti-Semitism," 1–15.

50   Hasia Diner, *Roads Taken: The Great Jewish Migrations to the New World and the Peddlers Who Forged the Way* (New Haven, CT: Yale University Press, 2015).

51   For more on the existence of female Jewish peddlers, see Carolyn Eastwood and Beatrice Michaels Shapiro, *Chicago's Jewish Street Peddlers* (Chicago: Chicago Jewish Historical Society, 1991), 21.

52   This does not mean that there were no instances of Jewish peddlers engaging in extramarital relations with their married clients, of course, but if they did, it is certainly less well documented and commented on in relevant literature.

53   Todd Presner, "'Clear Heads, Solid Stomachs, and Hard Muscles," 270. For more on Jewish "self-hatred," see Sander Gilman's *Jewish Self-Hatred: Anti-Semitism and the Hidden Language of the Jews* (Baltimore: Johns Hopkins University Press, 1986).

54   Paul Breines, *Tough Jews: Political Fantasies and the Moral Dilemma of American Jewry* (New York: Basic Books, 1990), 167.

55   Heller, "Moral Courage," 4.

56   Marcus Eli Ravage, *An American in the Making* (New Brunswick, NJ: Rutgers University Press, 2009), 142. For more analysis of Marcus Eli Ravage's *An American in the Making*, see Dana Mihailescu's "Jewish Men and the Early Twentieth-Century American Code of Masculinity through Ethnic Lenses," *Atenea* 28 (June 2008): 87–102.

57   Mihailescu, "Jewish Men," 216.

58   Imhoff, *Masculinity*, 58.

59   Eli Lederhendler, *Jewish Responses to Modernity: New Voices in America and Eastern Europe* (New York: New York University Press, 1994), 113–15.

60 Jesse Isidor Straus, "David Blaustein," *Publications of the American Jewish Historical Society*, no. 22 (1914): 206–11. David Blaustein, "The Making of Americans," *Jewish Charity III*, no. 3 (December 1903): 70.

61 Yaakov Ariel, *Evangelizing the Chosen People: Missions to the Jews in America, 1880–2000* (Chapel Hill: University of North Carolina Press, 2000), see chapter "The Converts."

62 Perhaps the most oft-questioned of these converts is Otto Weininger, who, though he insisted that a Jew could overcome his Jewish masculinity to become a "real man," still decided to end his life shortly after his own conversion. For an in-depth discussion of Weininger's view of masculinity and the Jewish body, see Anderson, "Weininger's Masculine Utopia," 433–53.

63 For a succinct explanation, see the introduction to *Fighting to Become Americans: Assimilation and the Trouble between Jewish Women and Jewish Men* (Boston: Beacon Press, 1999).

64 Ted Merwin, *In Their Own Image: New York Jews in Jazz Age Popular Culture* (New Brunswick, NJ: Rutgers University Press, 2006), 50–51.

65 Louis Grossmann, "The Opinion of an Individual," *American Israelite*, January 17, 1895, 4.

Chapter 3

1 Diary entry, Rabbi David Philipson, September 25, 1905, MS-35, American Jewish Archives, Cincinnati, Ohio.

2 Gold, "'The Jazz Singer' to 'What a Country!'" 117.

3 Beth Wenger, "Federation Men: The Masculine World of New York Jewish Philanthropy, 1880–1945," *American Jewish History* 101, no. 3 (July 2017): 377–99.

4 Boris D. Bogen, "The Children of the Jewish Poor," *American Hebrew* (1879–1902); September 12, 1902; ProQuest Historical Newspapers, *American Hebrew and Jewish Messenger*, 461.

5 For more on these relationships and Jewish women's role in early twentieth-century criminal activity, see Albert Fried's *The Rise and Fall of the Jewish Gangster in America*; Jenna Weissman Joselit's *Our Gang: Jewish Crime and the New York Jewish Community, 1900–1940*, which both also draw heavily from Abraham Shoenfeld's investigation for Judah Magnes in 1912, found in the Judah L. Magnes Collection in

the Central Archives for the History of the Jewish People (CAHJP) in Jerusalem.

6 Mary Linehan showed this in her examination of the sex industry in Chicago at the turn of the century in her essay "Prostitution in the US: Chicago," in *Selling Sex in the City: A Global History of Prostitution, 1600s–2000s*, ed. Magaly Rodriguez Garcia, Lex Heerma van Voss, and Elise van Nederveen Meerkerk (Boston: Brill, 2017), 386–413.

7 The Committee of Fourteen, *The Social Evil in New York City: A Study of Law Enforcement by the Research Committee of the Committee of Fourteen* (New York: A. H. Kellogg, 1910), 39.

8 Imhoff, *Masculinity*, 217.

9 See Moscowitz, Breines, Cohen, Rockaway, and especially Bergoffen on this phenomenon of revival of the image to transform Jewish past.

10 "Club Revelation: An Experiment with Delinquent Boys" report, American Jewish Congress, records, I-77, box 391, folder 10, American Jewish Historical Society, New York and Boston. Oral History Transcript, 1965, 1974 (1 of 2); Abraham Shoenfeld Papers, P-884, box 5a, folder 10, American Jewish Historical Society, New York and Boston.

11 Morris S. Lazaron, "The American Jew: His Problems and His Psychology," *Journal of Religion* 1, no. 4 (July 1921): 388.

12 The latter pejoratives from Imhoff, *Masculinity*, 209.

13 George Jackson Kneeland, *Commercialized Prostitution in New York City* (New York: Twentieth Century, 1913), 215. Edward J. Bristow, *Prostitution and Prejudice: The Jewish Fight against White Slavery, 1870–1939* (New York: Schocken Books, 1982), 162.

14 Albert Fried, *The Rise and Fall of the Jewish Gangster in America*, rev. ed. (New York: Columbia University Press, 1993), 10.

15 Bristow, *Prostitution and Prejudice*, 151.

16 Sarah Imhoff thoroughly scrutinizes the highly masculine language used by Bingham to disparage the Jewish community, in *Masculinity*, 205–22.

17 Judah Leon Magnes, *Dissenter in Zion: From the Writings of Judah L. Magnes*, ed. Arthur A. Goren (Cambridge, MA: Harvard University Press, 1982), 94–95.

18 "Wrong about Jews, Bingham Admits: Statement That They Supplied Half New York Criminals Was an Error. His Statistics were bad. Didn't Collect Them Himself for His North American Review

Article—Jewish Citizens Satisfied," *New York Times* (1857–1922), September 17, 1908, 16.

19 "The American Jew," Box #4, Folder #1. MS-35, David Philipson Papers, American Jewish Archives, Cincinnati, Ohio.

20 Letter from Jacob Schiff explaining the necessity of the New York "Jewish Community" (Kehillah), forwarded to Dr. Philipson, June 10, 1909, Box #1, Folder #20. MS-35. David Philipson Papers, American Jewish Archives, Cincinnati, Ohio.

21 New York Crime Buster, unpublished, undated, unnumbered pages, Abraham Shoenfeld Papers; P-884, box 5b, folder 6, American Jewish Historical Society, New York and Boston.

22 Both of which have been dealt with at length by excellent scholars in the field and need not be further examined in this study. For an examination of these two cases specifically in terms of Jewish masculinity, see Imhoff, *Masculinity*, chapters 8, 9.

23 New York Crime Buster, unpublished, undated, unnumbered pages, Abraham Shoenfeld Papers, P-884, box 5b, folder 6, American Jewish Historical Society, New York and Boston.

24 Mir Yarfitz, *Impure Migration: Jews and Sex Work in Golden Age Argentina* (New Brunswick, NJ: Rutgers University Press, 2019), 130.

25 Goren, *New York Jews and the Quest for Community*, 160.

26 New York Crime Buster, unpublished, undated, unnumbered pages, Abraham Shoenfeld Papers, P-884, box 5b, folder 6, American Jewish Historical Society, New York and Boston.

27 See "Dissenter: Pacifist and Radial, 1917–1922," in *Dissenter in Zion*, 157–200.

28 See Robert A. Rockaway, *But He Was Good to His Mother: The Lives and Crimes of Jewish Gangsters* (New York: Gefen Publishing, 2000).

29 This is much the same argument that Sarah Imhoff demonstrated: Jews used in the case of Leopold and Loeb, to downplay their Jewishness therefore separating them from the Jewish community at large, without denying their culpability. "The Problem of the Gangster," *American Hebrew and Jewish Messenger* (1903–1922), January 15, 1915, ProQuest Historical Newspapers, *American Hebrew and Jewish Messenger*, 300. Imhoff, *Masculinity*, 244–69.

30 Oral History Transcript, page 54, 1965, 1974 (1 of 2), Abraham Shoenfeld Papers, P-884, box 5a, folder 10, American Jewish Historical Society, New York and Boston.

31   John J. Daly, "'Gangster Eat Gangster,' Might Prove Best Policy," *Washington Post* (1923–1954), July 23, 1931, ProQuest Historical Newspapers, *Washington Post*, 2.

32   Warren Grover, *Nazis in Newark* (Piscataway Township, NJ: Transaction Publishers, 2003), 54.

33   "Nazi Armed with Lead Pipe Arrested as Newark Police Break Up Anti-Nazi Riot," *Jewish Telegraphic Agency*, October 18, 1933.

34   Tim Newark, *The Mafia at War: The Shocking True Story of America's Wartime Pact with Organized Crime* (New York: Skyhorse Publishing, 2012), 72–73.

35   Newark, *Mafia at War*, 75.

36   Kenneth Daniel Williams, "The Saga of Murder, Inc.: A German Propaganda Victory," accessed May 1, 2018, www.merkki.com/murderinc.htm. "Nazis Name U.S. Flier A 'Typical' Gangster: Downed Man's Fortress Bore Title: 'Murder Inc.'" *New York Times* (1923–Current file); New York, December 22, 1943, 4.

37   John J. Daly, "'Gangster Eat Gangster,' Might Prove Best Policy," *Washington Post* (1923–1954), July 23, 1931, ProQuest Historical Newspapers, *Washington Post*, 2.

38   Numerical data extracted from Paul Ritterband, "Counting the Jews of New York, 1900–1991: An Essay in Substance and Method," in *Papers in Jewish Demography 1997; Selected Proceedings of the Demographic: Sessions Held at the 12th World Congress of Jewish Studies, Jerusalem, 1997*, ed. Sergio Della Pergola and Judith Even (Jerusalem: Hebrew University, 2001), 199–228. Estimates of Jewish delinquency from Hon. Julius M. Mayer, "The Problem of the Delinquent Child," *Jewish Charity III*, no. 4 (January 1904): 89. Boris D. Bogen, "The Jewish Boy Criminal," *Jewish Charity IV*, no. 4 (January 1905): 126. New York City census demographics from the official website of the city of New York, "Total and Foreign-Born Population: New York Metropolitan Region by Subregion and County, 1900–2000," nyc.gov, accessed March 4, 2016, https://www.nyc.gov/assets/planning/download/pdf/data-maps/nyc-population/nny2000/nny_table_5_3.pdf.

39   As scholars and critics of the current American justice system have noted, high numbers of specific minority groups in crime statistics may reflect systemic and police bias as much as the reality of over-representation of a particular demographic in crime. However, even

if the police in New York at the turn of the century were more apt to arrest and prosecute Jewish delinquents than others, the numbers are still high compared to their overall numbers in the city.

40 "The Jewish Press: Jewish Boy Criminals," *American Hebrew and Jewish Messenger* (1903–1922), February 10, 1905, ProQuest Historical Newspapers, *American Hebrew and Jewish Messenger*, 348. Bogen, "Jewish Boy Criminal," 126–29.

41 He did, however, include women in his discussion of the modernization of Jewish charity, explaining that though women provided the kindness necessary in charitable work, they lacked the organizational skills for large-scale reform. Quoted in Wenger, "Federation Men," 381, original source Boris D. Bogen, *Jewish Philanthropy: An Exposition of Principles and Methods of Jewish Social Service in the United States* (1917; reprint, Montclair, NJ: Patterson Smith, 1969), 319–20.

42 "Science Studies the Origin of the Gangster: Professor Thrasher's Praiseworthy Effort to Find Out Why the Gangs Which It Is So Natural for Boys to Form Often Become Nurseries of Crime," *Washington Post* (1923–1954), Washington, DC, March 13, 1927, SM6.

43 Marion Weinstein, "Woman and Her Interests: Consider the Immigrant Mother Our Neglect of Her the Root of Social Evils," *American Hebrew and Jewish Messenger* (1903–1922), June 16, 1916, ProQuest Historical Newspapers, *American Hebrew and Jewish Messenger*, 184.

44 Gil Ribak, "'The Jew Usually Left Those Crimes to Esau': The Jewish Responses to Accusations about Jewish Criminality in New York, 1908–1913," *AJS Review* 38, no. 1 (April 2014): 1–28.

45 Jewish Protectory and Aid Society, "Annual Report of the Jewish Protectory and Aid Society," accessed May 2, 2018, catalog.hathitrust.org/Record/011474686.

46 For more on Noah and his misadventures in Jewish leadership, see Jonathan D. Sarna's biography, *Jacksonian Jew: The Two Worlds of Mordecai Noah* (New York: Holmes and Meier, 1981).

47 Uri D. Herscher, *Jewish Agricultural Utopias in America, 1880–1910* (Detroit: Wayne State University Press, 1981), 29.

48 "Establishing a New Jerusalem in Sholam," *Olde Ulster* 9, no. 8 (August 1913): 226, 228.

49 Gabriel Davidson, "The Tragedy of Sholam," *Jewish Tribune* (June 16 and 23, 1922): 3, 5.

50 Davidson, "Tragedy of Sholam," 6.

51 Accounts of each of these settlements, their benefactors, and their failures can be found in several publications and records held by the American Jewish Committee, the Baron de Hirsch Foundation, and the Jewish Agricultural Society. For more thorough accounts, one can also consult Uri D. Herscher's *Jewish Agricultural Utopias*; Leonard G. Robinson's, *Agricultural Activities*; and Gabriel Davidson's, *Our Jewish Farmers: The Story of the Jewish Agricultural Society*.

52 United States, Commission on Industrial Relations, *Industrial Relations: Final Report and Testimony, Volume 8* (Washington, DC: Government Printing Office, 1916), 7526.

53 Imhoff, *Masculinity*, 97–127.

54 Robinson, *Agricultural Activities*, 69–71. Also see Sarah Imhoff's analysis of the Woodbine experiment and perceived Jewish masculinity, in *Masculinity*.

55 Robinson, *Agricultural Activities*, 4.

56 Robinson, *Agricultural Activities*, 95.

57 This is not to say there are not Jewish farmers, indeed there have been more in recent decades as part of environmental sustainability movements. Even accounting for recent years, however, it is not at the forefront of Jewish occupations. For more on recent developments in Jewish agriculture, see the work of Dr. Adrienne Krone, "Growing Food: Ecological Ethics in the Jewish Community Farming Movement," in *Feasting and Fasting: The History and Ethics of Jewish Food*, ed. Aaron Gross, Jody Myers, and Jordan Rosenblum (New York: New York University Press, 2019), 273–86.

58 "The Jewish Boy Criminal," *American Hebrew and Jewish Messenger* (1903–1922), January 20, 1905, ProQuest Historical Newspapers, *American Hebrew and Jewish Messenger*, 263.

59 Sabsovich, "Farming and Farm Schools," 183–86.

60 M. V. Ball, "The Dispersion of the Immigrant," *Jewish Charity III*, no. 7 (April 1904): 168–69.

61 Numbers from Jonathan D. Sarna, "The Crucial Decade in Jewish Camping," in *A Place of Our Own: The Rise of Reform Jewish Camping*, ed. Michael M. Lorge and Gary P. Zola (Tuscaloosa: University of Alabama Press, 2006), 29.

62 Sarna, "Crucial Decade," 30.

63 Marcie Cohen Ferris, "'God First, You Second, Me Third': An Explora-
    tion of 'Quiet Jewishness' at Camp Wah-Kon-Dah," *Southern Cultures*
    8, no. 1 (Spring 2012): 58–70.

64 Camp Kawaga flier, undated, Bernard C. Ehrenreich Papers; P-26, box 1,
    folder 4, American Jewish Historical Society, New York and Boston.

65 "Kawaga Heritage," Camp Kawaga, accessed June 3, 2018, https://
    kawaga.com/heritage.

66 Advertisement, *The Jewish Exponent* (1887–1990), May 30, 1924, Pro-
    Quest Historical Newspapers, *Jewish Exponent*, 13.

67 Camp Port Indian brochure, Box 2, Young Men's and Young Women's
    Hebrew Association of Philadelphia, Nearprint Collection, American
    Jewish Archives, Cincinnati, Ohio.

68 An argument furthered by David S. Koffman in his 2019 book, *The Jews'
    Indian: Colonialism, Pluralism, and Belonging in America* (New Bruns-
    wick, NJ: Rutgers University Press, 2019).

69 For an examination of white men appropriating Indian appearances as a
    masculine act, see Michael Taylor, *Contesting Constructed Indian-ness: The
    Intersection of the Frontier, Masculinity, and Whiteness in Native American
    Mascot Representations* (Lanham, MD: Lexington Books, 2013), 18–19.

70 David I. Macleod, *Building Character in the American Boy: The Boy
    Scouts, YMCA, and Their Forerunners, 1870–1920* (Madison: University
    of Wisconsin Press, 1983).

71 As Sharon Bird found in their 1996 study on masculinity and homo-
    social constructions, the mere separation between men and women
    (or boys and girls) enforces that being masculine means being "not-
    female," and places all men involved into a masculine group by defini-
    tion, strengthening masculine identity. Sharon R. Bird, "Welcome to
    the Men's Club: Homosociality and the Maintenance of Hegemonic
    Masculinity," *Gender and Society* 10, no. 2 (April 1996): 120–32.

72 Emphasis original, "The Jew and the Club," *The Atlantic*, October, 1924,
    www.theatlantic.com/magazine/archive/1924/10/the-jew-and-the
    -club/306258/.

73 Lisa Fetheringill Zwicker, "Performing Masculinity: Jewish Students
    and the Honor Code at German Universities," in *Jewish Masculinities:
    German Jews, Gender, and History*, ed. Benjamin Maria Baader, Sharon
    Gillerman, and Paul Lerner (Bloomington: Indiana University Press,
    2012), 117–19.

74   Don C. Seitz, *Famous American Duels: With Some Account of the Causes That Led to Them* (New York: Thomas Y. Crowell, 1929), eBook.

75   Gil Ribak, "'Beaten to Death by Irish Murderers': The Death of Sadie Dellon (1918) and Jewish Images of the Irish," *Journal of American Ethnic History* 34, no. 4 (Summer 2013): 63.

76   Steven, A. Riess, "Tough Jews: The Jewish American Boxing Experience, 1890–1950," in *Sports and the American Jew*, ed. Steven Riess (Syracuse, NY: Syracuse University Press, 1998), 64–66.

77   Herbert Sussman, *Masculine Identities: The History and Meanings of Manliness* (Santa Barbara: CA: Praeger, 2012), 127.

78   For more on Jewish boxers and their nicknames, see Mike Silver's *Stars in the Ring: Jewish Champions in the Golden Age of Boxing* (Lanham, MD: Rowman and Littlefield, 2016).

79   Mike Silver, *Stars in the Ring: Jewish Champions in the Golden Age of Boxing* (Guilford, CT: Lyons Press, 2016), 10–11, 60.

80   Stephen H. Norwood, "'American Jewish Muscle': Forging a New Masculinity in the Streets and in the Ring, 1890–1940," *Modern Judaism* 29, no. 2 (May 2009): 179–80.

81   Riess, "Tough Jews," 103.

82   "The City Athletic Club," *American Hebrew and Jewish Messenger* (1903–1922), November 20, 1908, ProQuest Historical Newspapers, *American Hebrew and Jewish Messenger*, 74.

83   "City Athletic Club," 74.

84   References to members' activities and successes in these sports are scattered throughout the City Athletic Club records, particularly their monthly journal, *The Arrow*. City Athletic Club Records, I-533, Box 173–75, American Jewish Historical Society, Boston and New York.

85   There was a long-standing policy of objectivity regarding the Jewish community put in place by Adolph Ochs and maintained by his son-in-law Arthur Hayes Sulzberger. See Laurel Leff, *Buried by the Times: The Holocaust and America's Most Important Newspaper* (New York: Cambridge University Press, 2005). One instance of controversy in which the *Times* might have been expected to mention the Jewish nature of the club was in 1968, when their alleged discriminatory practices led to a "boycott by Negro athletics" at one of their track meets at Madison Square Garden. It was at this point that City

Athletic Club opened membership to "all persons regardless of race, creed, color or national origin." From "City Athletic Club Agrees to Open Membership to All," *New York Times* (1923–Current file), March 26, 1968, ProQuest Historical Newspapers, *New York Times*, 25.

86 "Full Membership Reached," *New York Times* (1857–1922), January 24, 1909, ProQuest Historical Newspapers, *New York Times*, S3.

87 Board of Governors Minutes, multiple books, 1908–29, City Athletic Club Records, I-533, American Jewish Historical Society, New York and Boston.

88 Multiple mentions in the Temple Bulletin Collection, MS-882d, American Jewish Archives, Cincinnati, Ohio.

89 "Objects," Constitution and Bylaws of the City Athletic Club, circa 1909. From the Board of Governors minutes, August 1908–October 1910. City Athletic Club Records, I-533, Box 177, Box 1, American Jewish Historical Society, Boston and New York.

90 "City Athletic Club to Build: President Guggenheim Reports a Membership of More Than 1,000," *American Hebrew and Jewish Messenger* (1903–1922), April 2, 1920, ProQuest Historical Newspapers, *American Hebrew and Jewish Messenger*, 622.

91 Oral History Transcript, page 80, 1965, 1974 (1 of 2), Abraham Shoenfeld Papers, P-884, box 5a, folder 10, American Jewish Historical Society, New York and Boston.

92 Later on, The Boy's Club also refused to participate in the funding or selection of American athletes for the Maccabia Games in Israel because they included only Jewish Americans, going against the complete nondiscrimination policy the club had adopted. Multiple letters, 1939–55, Grand Street Boys' Association Records, I-312, box 1, folder 2, American Jewish Historical Society, New York and Boston.

93 Bogen, "The Children of the Jewish Poor," 461.

94 "Activity of the Jews in Athletics," by Morris J. Frank, in *The American Hebrew and Jewish Messenger* (1903–1922); September 18, 1908, ProQuest Historical Newspapers, *American Hebrew and Jewish Messenger*, 477.

95 Sidney Cohen, "The Jew as Athlete," *American Hebrew and Jewish Messenger* (1903–1922), September 10, 1920, ProQuest Historical Newspapers, *American Hebrew and Jewish Messenger*, 438.

96 "The City Athletic Club," 74.

97 Rabbi quoted in "Because You're a Jew," by Sydney Reid, *The Independent*, November 26, 1908, ProQuest Historical Newspapers, American Periodicals, 1212.

98 Capitalization from original. Reid, "Because You're a Jew," 1212.

99 Theodor Herzl, as previously discussed, had been a member of a dueling fraternity at the University of Vienna, but resigned when the group began endorsing increasingly popular antisemitic views. Marianne R. Sanua, *Going Greek: Jewish College Fraternities in the United States, 1895–1945* (Detroit: Wayne State University Press, 2003), 32.

100 Marianne R. Sanua, "Jewish College Fraternities in the United States, 1895–1968: An Overview," *Journal of American Ethnic History* 19, no. 2 (2000): 5.

101 In her notes on the fraternity referring to entries in the *Universal Jewish Encyclopedia*, her own research at the American Jewish Archives, and in Yale University Records, Marianne Sanua conclusively identifies two of the three founders' Jewish identities and presents very convincing evidence to reach the conclusion that the third founder was Jewish as well. Sanua, *Going Greek*, 47–48.

102 "Pi Lambda Phi History," Pi Lambda Phi website, accessed March 8, 2018, www.pilambdaphi.org/site/c.plKXL7MPIqG/b.3609919/k.A021/Pi_Lam_History.htm (now unavailable), and October 11, 2023, https://www.pilambdaphi.org/about/history/.

103 Clarence K. Weil's *Z B T 1898, 1923: The First 25 Years*, a history of the organization compiled for their Silver Jubilee Convention. Published by Zeta Beta Tau Fraternity (New York City, 1923), 14.

104 Bulletin, August 1914, box 2, folder 1, MS-497, Pi Tau Pi Fraternity Records, American Jewish Archives, Cincinnati, Ohio. Quote from Sanau, *Going Greek*, 55.

105 Quote is from the foreword of Clarence K. Weil's *Z B T 1898, 1923: The First 25 Years*, a history of the organization compiled for their Silver Jubilee Convention. Published by Zeta Beta Tau Fraternity (New York City, 1923). Inconsistent capitalization original.

106 "Fundamentals," editorial in *ZBTQ* 4, no. 4 (May 1920): 28–30, quoted in Sanau, *Going Greek*, 61.

107 "Fundamentals."

108 Bernard M. L. Ernst, "The Greek Letter Societies and the Jew," *American Israelite* (1874–2000), November 3, 1904, ProQuest Historical Newspapers, *American Israelite*, 1.

109 "Say Fraternities Are Unamerican," *New York Times* (1857–1922), May 22, 1910, ProQuest Historical Newspapers, *New York Times*, 10.

110 Jacob Turchinksy, "The Case against Jewish Fraternities," *Octagonian* 2, no. 5 (May 1913), 1. Quoted in Sanua, *Going Greek*, 91.

111 *Bulletin* (page 7), July 1917, box 1, folder 2, MS-497, Pi Tau Pi Fraternity Records, American Jewish Archives, Cincinnati, Ohio.

112 *Bulletin* (page 8), July 1917, box 1, folder 2, MS-497, Pi Tau Pi Fraternity Records, American Jewish Archives, Cincinnati, Ohio.

113 *Hai Resh Bulletin* 6, no. 6, July 1917, box 1, folder 2, MS-497, Pi Tau Pi Fraternity Records, American Jewish Archives, Cincinnati, Ohio.

114 Continued discussions appear in the pages of the *Pitaupian* and the Bulletin of Pi Tau Pi, box 2, various folders, MS-497, Pi Tau Pi Fraternity Records, American Jewish Archives, Cincinnati, Ohio.

115 *The Pitaupian* (honorary member edition), August 1919, box 2, folder 2, MS-497, Pi Tau Pi Fraternity Records, American Jewish Archives, Cincinnati, Ohio.

116 Alvin Austin Silverman, Bulletin, August 1914, box 2, folder 1, MS-497, Pi Tau Pi Fraternity Records, American Jewish Archives, Cincinnati, Ohio.

Chapter 4

1 Bartley C. Crum, *Behind the Silken Curtain: A Personal Account of Anglo-American Diplomacy in Palestine and the Middle East* (New York: Simon and Schuster, 1947), 192.

2 There were, in fact, many arguments against Zionism by a variety of critics, Jews and non-Jews, antisemites, Jewish territorialists, religious arguments from the Orthodox, and American assimilationists. For more on the criticisms of the movement, see Walter Laqueur, *A History of Zionism: From the French Revolution to the Establishment of the State of Israel* (New York: Schocken Books, 2009), chapter 8: "Zionism and Its Critics."

3 Laqueur, *A History of Zionism*, 589.

4 William Schack, "The Jews Thrive on Persecution," *Forum and Century* 90, no. 1 (July 1933): 56.

5 See Michael Berkowitz chapter, "Zionist Heroes and New Men," in *Zionist Culture and West European Jewry before the First World War* (New York: Cambridge University Press, 1993), 99–118.

6 Quoted in Mark A. Raider, *The Emergence of American Zionism* (New York: New York University Press, 1998), 79–80.

7 More information about David Tidhar is available online, provided by the Tidhar family and Touro College, including the monumental nineteen-volume *Encyclopedia of the Founders and Builders of Israel*, which David Tidhar compiled and published over the twenty-three years from 1947 until his death. www.tidhar.tourolib.org/.

8 Quoted in Arthur A. Goren, *The Politics and Public Culture of American Jews* (Bloomington: Indiana University Press, 1999), 169. Original source cited as Eva Leon, "With the Chalutzim," *New Palestine* 6, no. 16 (April 18, 1924): 324.

9 This expression was a common Zionist trope, particularly in the early years of Jewish settlement in Palestine. However, there were inhabitants in Palestine who farmed and worked the land long before Zionist settlers made their way to settle and work the land.

10 Jonathan Krasner, "'New Jews' in an Old-New Land: Images in American Jewish Textbooks Prior to 1948," *Journal of Jewish Education* 69, no. 2, (2003): 12.

11 Goren, *Politics and Public Culture of American Jews*, 170–71.

12 "Jewish Minute Men," *Young Judean*, October 1912, 20, 1-61, Jewish Student Organizations, American Jewish Historical Society.

13 Raider, *Emergence of American Zionism*, 78–79.

14 Bartley Crum quoted in Amy Kaplan, *Our American Israel: The Story of an Entangled Alliance* (Cambridge, MA: Harvard University Press, 2018), from 29 to 32.

15 "About Men and Things: Physical Culture among Jews," *Jewish Exponent* (1887–1990), May 6, 1904, ProQuest Historical Newspapers, *Jewish Exponent*, 4.

16 "Dr. Eliot's Remarkable Address: Verbatim Report of Noted Educator's Talk before the Harvard Zionist Society," *Jewish Exponent* (1887–1990), January 2, 1925, ProQuest Historical Newspapers, *Jewish Exponent*, 8.

17 "President Eliot on Football," *School Journal* 70 (February 18, 1905): 188–89.

18 Inconsistent spelling, grammar, and punctuation original. Rabbi Max J. Merritt, "Palestine's Agricultural Colleges: What Jewish Farmers Are Doing to Regenerate the Holy Land," *American Israelite* (1874–2000), November 6, 1913, ProQuest Historical Newspapers, *American Israelite*, 1.

19 "The Jewish Theological Seminary and Zionism: Letter from Louis Marshall," *American Hebrew and Jewish Messenger* (1903–1922), September 20, 1907, ProQuest Historical Newspapers, *American Hebrew and Jewish Messenger*, 488.

20 Diary entry, Rabbi David Philipson, September 25, 1905, MS-35, American Jewish Archives, Cincinnati, Ohio.

21 "The Jewish Theological Seminary and Zionism: Letter from Louis Marshall," *American Hebrew and Jewish Messenger* (1903–1922), September 20, 1907, ProQuest Historical Newspapers, *American Hebrew and Jewish Messenger*, 488. Orm Øverland, *Immigrant Minds, American Identities: Making the United States Home, 1870–1930* (Urbana: University of Illinois Press, 2000).

22 Evyatar Friesel, "American Zionism and American Jewry: An Ideological and Communal Encounter," *American Jewish Archives* 40, no. 1 (1988): 5–7.

23 Ben Halpern, "The Americanization of Zionism, 1880–1930," *American Jewish History* 69, no. 1 (September 1979): 17.

24 Leslie Stein, *The Hope Fulfilled: The Rise of Modern Israel* (Westport, CT: Praeger, 2003), 200.

25 Rafael Medoff, *Militant Zionism in America: The Rise and Impact of the Jabotinsky Movement in the United States, 1926–1948* (Tuscaloosa: University of Alabama Press, 2002), 16–19.

26 Louis Lipsky quote from Deborah Esther Lipstadt, "The Zionist Career of Louis Lipsky, 1900–1921" (PhD diss., Brandeis University, 1976). Mary McCune, "Social Workers in the Muskeljudentum: 'Hadassah Ladies,' 'Manly Men,' and the Significance of Gender in the American Zionist Movement, 1912–1928," *American Jewish History* 86, no. 2 (June 1998): 143.

27 Quoted in Melvin I. Urofsky, *American Zionism from Herzl to the Holocaust* (Lincoln: University of Nebraska Press, 1975), 151.

28 Imhoff, *Masculinity*, 182.

29 Meyer W. Weisgal, "The Land of Israel," *American Israelite* (1874–2000), July 29, 1926, ProQuest Historical Newspapers, *American Israelite*, 1.

30 Hadassah *Bulletin*, no. 33 (June 1917): 11–12 (quoted in McCune, "Social Workers in the Muskeljudentum," 135).

31 For more on the shift of American Jewish philanthropy into a masculine enterprise, see Wenger, "Federation Men," 377–99.

32   The issue of *feminism* and Zionism is a different discussion, and one that
     is more highly complicated than the history of women in Zionism (see
     "No, You Can't Be a Feminist and a Zionist" in *The Forward* or "Yes, I
     Can Be a Zionist and a Feminist" in the *Huffington Post*). The argument
     over the compatibility of Zionism and feminism hit a new crescendo
     in January of 2017, when the Women's March movement in the United
     States banned Zionist women's groups from participating, citing their
     presence as possibly too triggering of other participants' traumas.
33   Berkowitz, *Zionist Culture and West European Jewry*, 19.
34   "Proceedings of the Tenth Annual Convention July 2–July 3, 1924," 219;
     Annual and Mid-Winter National Conventions Records in the Hadas-
     sah Archives on Long-Term Deposit at the American Jewish Historical
     Society, I-578/RG 3, box 1, folder 15, American Jewish Historical Soci-
     ety, Boston and New York. McCune, "Social Workers in the Muskelju-
     dentum," 140–41, 146–47.
35   Louis Dembitz Brandeis, *Brandeis on Zionism: A Collection of Addresses
     and Statements* (Union, NJ: Law Book Exchange, 1999), 77. Commas
     original.
36   McCune, "Social Workers in the Muskeljudentum," 138.
37   "Proceedings of the Tenth Annual Convention July 2–July 3, 1924,"
     220–21; Annual and Mid-Winter National Conventions Records in
     the Hadassah Archives on Long-Term Deposit at the American Jewish
     Historical Society, I-578/RG 3, box 1, folder 15, American Jewish His-
     torical Society, Boston and New York.
38   "Womankind: A Woman's Impression of the Zionist Congress, Edited
     by Sarah Kassy," *Jewish Exponent* (1887–1990); January 9, 1914, Pro-
     Quest Historical Newspapers, *Jewish Exponent*, 5.
39   Berkowitz, *Zionist Culture and West European Jewry*, 19.
40   Naomi Wiener Cohen, "The Reaction of Reform Judaism in America
     to Political Zionism (1897–1922)," *Publications of the American Jewish
     Historical Society* 40, no. 4 (June 1951): 361–94.
41   Isaac Wise, box 4, folder 9, MS-35, David Philipson Papers, American
     Jewish Archives, Cincinnati, Ohio.
42   Correspondence with Jacob Schiff, box 1, folder 1, MS-35, David Philip-
     son Papers, American Jewish Archives, Cincinnati, Ohio.
43   Address in Nashville, Tennessee, October 9, 1934, box 4, folder 1, MS-35,
     David Philipson Papers, American Jewish Archives, Cincinnati, Ohio.

44 Letter to Jacob Schiff, August 26, 1907, box 1, folder 1, MS-35, David Philipson Papers, American Jewish Archives, Cincinnati, Ohio.

45 Friesel, "American Zionism and American Jewry," 12.

46 Quotes from two letters, August 10 (1909) and September 3 (1918), box 1, folder 20, MS-35, David Philipson Papers, American Jewish Archives, Cincinnati, Ohio.

47 Letter to Dr. Philipson, September 5, 1918, box 1, folder 20, MS-35, David Philipson Papers, American Jewish Archives, Cincinnati, Ohio.

48 Caitlin Carenen, "Complicating the Zionist Narrative in America: Jacob Schiff and the Struggle over Relief Aid in World War I," *American Jewish History* 101, no. 4 (October 2017): 441–63.

49 For more on the territorialist movement, see Almagor, *Beyond Zion*. Quoted in Urofsky, *American Zionism*, 213.

50 Several letters from 1918, box 1, folder 1, MS-35, David Philipson Papers, American Jewish Archives, Cincinnati, Ohio.

51 "Zionists throughout Country Welcome Weizmann-Marshall Accord," February 15, 1927, Jewish Telegraphic Agency. Accessed June 21, 2018, www.jta.org/1927/02/15/archive/zionists-throughout-country-welcome-weizmann-marshall-accord.

52 "Reform Judaism and Zionism: A Centenary Platform," Central Conference of American Rabbis, accessed May 21, 2019, www.ccarnet.org/rabbinic-voice/platforms/article-reform-judaism-zionism-centenary-platform.

53 For more on this group, see Thomas Kolsky, *Jews against Zionism: The American Council for Judaism, 1942–1948* (Philadelphia: Temple University Press, 1990).

54 For more on all of these shifts, see Laqueur, *History of Zionism*, 171–81.

Chapter 5

1 Italics original. Jewish War Veterans of the United States pamphlet, *Jews in the World War: A Study in Jewish Patriotism and Heroism* (New York: Jewish War Veterans of the United States, 1941), 2.

2 Boyarin, *Unheroic Conduct*, 284–86.

3 Rabbi Gustav N. Hausmann, "The Great War and the Hope of the Jew," a lecture delivered before Congregation Pincus Elijah and before Young Israel December 12, 1914 (New York: S.N., 1915), 11–13.

4 Hausmann, "Great War and the Hope of the Jew," 31–34.

5 Office of the Provost Marshal General, *Manual of Instructions for Medical Advisory Boards* (Washington, DC: Government Printing Office, 1918), 92.

6 Punctuation original. Lewis P. Brown, "The Jew Is Not a Slacker," *North American Review* 207, no. 751 (June 1918): 858.

7 Quoted in Nancy Gentile Ford, *Americans All!: Foreign-Born Soldiers in World War I* (College Station: Texas A&M University Press, 2001), 37.

8 Scholarly numbers vary from about 200,000 to about 250,000. It is yet unknown how many of these Jews were immigrants and how many native-born, given the massive immigration during this period, with the American Jewish population increasing from 250,000 in 1880 to four million by 1920.

9 American Jewish Committee, *The War Record of American Jews: First Report of the Office of War Records* (New York: American Jewish Committee, 1919), 6.

10 Saul Friedlander, "Political Transformations during the War and Their Effect on the Jewish Question," in *Hostages of Modernization: Germany, Great Britain, France* (New York: Walter de Gruyter, 1992), 153–54.

11 "A Jew," by Damon Runyon, published in *The Cosmopolitan*, November, 1922.

12 Martin Zielonka, "Sam Dreben, D.S.C.: The Fighting Jew, 1878–1925," *Western States Jewish Historical Quarterly* 44, no. 1 (2011): 79–84, 83.

13 Jessica Cooperman, "'A Little Army Discipline Would Improve the Whole House of Israel': The Jewish Welfare Board, State Power and the Shaping of Jewish Identity in World War I America" (PhD diss., New York University, 2010), 248–49.

14 Hausmann, "Great War and the Hope of the Jew," 16.

15 Horace Meyer Kallen, "Nationality and the Jewish Stake in the Great War," an address delivered at the Third Annual Menorah Convention, at the University of Cincinnati, in Cincinnati, Ohio, December 22, 1914. Published in the *Menorah Journal* 1, no. 2 (April 1915): 13.

16 Hagdud Haivri League, Inc., Program of the formal establishment of Bet Hagdudim in Avi-chail, 1955. Jewish Legion collection, I-429, box 1, folder 1, American Jewish Historical Society, New York and Boston.

17 "Jewish Battalions Paved Way to Statehood," *Jerusalem Post*, n.d., Jewish Legion collection, I-429, box 1, folder 9, American Jewish Historical Society, New York and Boston.

18 William Braiterman, "The Jewish Legion of World War I," *Sun Magazine*, April 23, 1967. Jewish Legion collection, I-429, box 1, folder 10, American Jewish Historical Society, New York and Boston. William Braiterman, oral history interview, 1974. Jewish Legion collection, I-429, box 1, folder 8, American Jewish Historical Society, New York and Boston.

19 Roman Freulich, *Soldiers in Judea: Stories and Vignettes of the Jewish Legion* (New York: Herzl Press, 1964), 33.

20 Francine Klagsbrun, *Lioness: Golda Meir and the Nation of Israel* (New York: Schocken Books, 2017), 70.

21 Elias Gilner, *Jews Who Fought*, pamphlet, printing and date unknown. American Jewish Historical Society, New York and Boston.

22 Gilner, *Jews Who Fought*.

23 Hagdud Haivri League, Inc., program of the formal establishment of Bet Hagdudim in Avi-chail, 1955. Jewish Legion collection, I-429, box 1, folder 1, American Jewish Historical Society, New York and Boston.

24 Freulich, *Soldiers in Judea*, 114.

25 Freulich, *Soldiers in Judea*, 28.

26 Major H. D. Myer, "Soldiering of Sorts," unpublished transcript, page 149. Jewish Legion collection, I-429, box 1, folder 14, American Jewish Historical Society, New York and Boston.

27 Jewish War Veterans of the United States pamphlet, *Jews in the World War: A Study in Jewish Patriotism and Heroism* (New York: Jewish War Veterans of the United States, 1941), 23.

28 Leonard Dinnerstein, *Antisemitism in America* (New York: Oxford University Press, 1994), 112.

Chapter 6

1 Mac Davis, *Jews Fight Too!* (New York: Jordan Publishing, 1945), author's note.

2 Nancy Bernhard, *U.S. Television News and Cold War Propaganda, 1947–1960* (New York: Cambridge University Press, 1999), 19.

3 For a more in-depth analysis of World War II films and their re-creation of manhood, see Lary May's, *The Big Tomorrow: Hollywood*

and the Politics of the American Way (Chicago: University of Chicago Press, 2000).

4   "How to Serve Your Country in the WAVES or SPARS," Gjenvick-Gjønvik Archives, accessed September 16, 2017, https://www .ggarchives.com/Military/NavyArchives/Brochures/WAVESorSPARS -1943.html.

5   Much of the series of "Jenny of the Job" illustrations are available on the Northwestern University Libraries website in their World War II Poster Collection, https://dc.library.northwestern.edu/collections/ faf4f60e-78e0-4fbf-96ce-4ca8b4df597a.

6   Philip Wylie, *Generation of Vipers* (Normal, IL: Dalkey Archive Press, 1996).

7   Letters and newspaper clippings, American Jewish Congress, records, I-77, box 709, folder 26, American Jewish Historical Society, New York and Boston.

8   Bendersky, *Jewish Threat*, 295–96.

9   Cited in Boyarin, *Unheroic Conduct*, 77.

10 Statement of the Central Conference, 1936, Central Conference of American Rabbis, *Yearbook* 46 (Cape May, NJ: Bloch).

11 Letter, July 1, 1936, Jewish War Veterans of the United States of America collection, I-32, box 1, folder 8, American Jewish Historical Society, New York and Boston.

12 Leon Schwarz, Jewish War Veterans of the United States of America collection, I-32, box 1, folder 2, American Jewish Historical Society, New York and Boston.

13 Yearbook, page 122, #30725 (Central Conference of American Rabbis), American Jewish Historical Society, Center for Jewish History.

14 Jewish War Veterans of the United States of America collection undated, 1923–93, 2003 (box 1, folder 8), included as an added text to a letter to the CCAR from Leon Schwarz, a former Major of Mobile Alabama, included in a packet sent to the CCAR from Julius Klausner, Jr of the JWV.

15 Letter titled "Jews Want No Exemption," Jewish War Veterans of the United States of America collection, I-32, box 1, folder 8, American Jewish Historical Society, New York and Boston.

16 Letter to the CCAR from Leon Schwarz, a former Major of Mobile, Alabama, Jewish War Veterans of the United States of America collection,

1-32, box 1, folder 8, American Jewish Historical Society, New York and Boston.

17 Derek Penslar, *Jews and the Military: A History* (Princeton, NJ: Princeton University Press, 2013), 88.

18 Deborah Dash Moore, "When Jews Were GIs: How World War Two Changed a Generation and Remade American Jewry," in *American Jewish Identity Politics*, ed. Deborah Dash Moore (Ann Arbor: University of Michigan Press, 2008), 29.

19 Moore, *GI Jews*, 169.

20 Ben Ewing, interview, Oral History Collection, Holocaust Memorial Center Archives. Holocaust Memorial Center Zekelman Family Campus, Farmington Hills, Michigan.

21 AJA-Archive notes and images\MS-780_ American Jewish Committee\Box B8, Folder 16, "In the Nation's Service." Article originally published by King Feature's Syndicate, 1942, in his segment, Damon Runyon's *The Brighter Side*.

22 *Pitaupian*, October 1942, page 5, box 2, MS-497, Pi Tau Pi Fraternity Records, American Jewish Archives, Cincinnati, Ohio.

23 "Mother's Day Message" by Mrs. Victor Frank, *Pitaupian*, April 1943, page 8, box 2, MS-497, Pi Tau Pi Fraternity Records, American Jewish Archives, Cincinnati, Ohio.

24 "Business as Usual" by Dr. Phillip David Bookstabber, *Pitaupian*, October 1942, page 3, box 2, MS-497, Pi Tau Pi Fraternity Records, American Jewish Archives, Cincinnati, Ohio.

25 In "Jews in the Armed Forces," by the Army and Navy Public Relations Committee, National Jewish Welfare Board. National Jewish Welfare Board Bureau of War Records, undated, 1940–69 (bulk 1943–46), box 90, folder 9, pages 21–22.

26 "In the Nation's Service." Article originally published by the *Atlanta Constitution*, "One Word More with Ralph McGill" (July 13, 1942), box 8, folder 16, MS-780, American Jewish Committee Records, American Jewish Archives, Cincinnati, Ohio.

27 In a back-and-forth correspondence between Samuel Leff and Milton Weill, begun April 8, 1942; National Jewish Welfare Board, Bureau of War Records, 1940–69, 1-52, box 10, folder 1, American Jewish Historical Society, New York and Boston.

28 Letter to Mrs. Jane Wise, Chairman, War Records Committee of the Jewish Federation of Trenton, National Jewish Welfare Board, Bureau of War Records, 1940–69, I-52, box 10, folder 3, American Jewish Historical Society, New York and Boston.

29 Morris Eisenstein, interview [30699]. Visual History Archive, USC Shoah Foundation Institute. Accessed online at http://vhaonline.usc.edu/ on November 14, 2013.

30 Moore, GI Jews, 159.

31 Lee Kennett, G.I.: The American Soldier in World War II (New York: Charles Scribner's Sons, 1987), 89.

32 Howard Cwick, interview [33870]. Visual History Archive, USC Shoah Foundation Institute. Accessed online at http://vhaonline.usc.edu/ on November 5, 2013.

33 For a history of the abuse of French women by American liberating troops, see Mary Louise Roberts, What Soldiers Do: Sex and the American GI in World War II France (Chicago: University of Chicago Press, 2013).

34 Harry Zaslow, interview, Oral History Collection, Holocaust Memorial Center Archives, Holocaust Memorial Center Zekelman Family Campus, Farmington Hills, Michigan.

35 Zaslow, interview.

36 Harold Baldwin, interview, Oral History Collection, Holocaust Memorial Center Archives, Holocaust Memorial Center Zekelman Family Campus, Farmington Hills, Michigan.

37 Harold Baldwin, interview, Oral History Collection, Holocaust Memorial Center Archives, Holocaust Memorial Center Zekelman Family Campus, Farmington Hills, Michigan.

38 Ernest James, Interview [34954]. Visual History Archive. USC Shoah Foundation Institute. Accessed online at http://vhaonline.usc.edu/ on November 5, 2013.

39 Conference proceedings, January 1939, box 1, folder 1, MS-266, National Federation of Temple Youth Records, American Jewish Archives, Cincinnati, Ohio.

40 Conference proceedings, January 1939.

41 Bitter Herb by Herby Groelinger, 1947, box 1, folder 3, MS-266, National Federation of Temple Youth Records, American Jewish Archives, Cincinnati, Ohio.

Chapter 7

1 K. Shabbetai, *As Sheep to the Slaughter? The Myth of Jewish Cowardice* (New York: World Federation of the Bergen-Belsen Survivors Association, 1963), 31.

2 Translation of the *Daily Digest of Foreign Broadcasts*, British Broadcasting Cooperation, quoted in "The Covenant of the Gangsters," by Ernst Kris, *Journal of Criminal Psychopathology* 4, no. 3 (1943): 450.

3 Dworkin, "Sexual Mythology," 119.

4 Christiane Kohl, *The Maiden and the Jew: The Story of a Fatal Friendship in Nazi Germany* (Hanover, NH: Steerforth Press, 1997), 144.

5 For perspectives and firsthand accounts, see the recollections of Einsatzgruppen referenced by Christopher Browning's *Ordinary Men: Reserve Police Battalion 101 and the Final Solution in Poland* (New York: Harper Perennial, 1992), and for alternative interpretations of same and similar sources, see Daniel Jonah Goldhagen, *Hitler's Willing Executioners: Ordinary Germans and the Holocaust* (New York: Vintage Books, 1996).

6 Shlomo Shafir explains this negotiation of tactics in "American Jewish Leaders and the Emerging Nazi Threat (1928–January 1933)," in *America, American Jews, and the Holocaust: American Jewish History*, ed. Jeffrey Gurock (New York: Routledge, 1998), 159.

7 American League for a Free Palestine Records, I-278, box 2, folder 3, American Jewish Historical Society, New York and Boston.

8 Jeffrey Gurock, *Jews in Gotham: New York Jews in a Changing City, 1920–2010* (New York: New York University Press, 2013), 109–10.

9 Address to the American Jewish Congress delivered by Dr. Wise for the twentieth anniversary of the founding of the organization, June 12, 1938, Stephen S. Wise Collection, MS-49, box 5, folder 8, American Jewish Archives, Cincinnati, Ohio.

10 Correspondence, June 16, 1939, Stephen S. Wise Collection, MS-49, box 5, folder 8, American Jewish Archives, Cincinnati, Ohio.

11 Excerpted text from a Boston paper, November 30, 1932, Stephen S. Wise Collection, MS-49, box 5, folder 8, American Jewish Archives, Cincinnati, Ohio.

12 Speech in March and radio address in September of 1935, Stephen S. Wise Collection, MS-49, box 5, folder 8, American Jewish Archives, Cincinnati, Ohio.

13 November 1943, Stephen S. Wise Collection, MS-49, box 5, folder 8, American Jewish Archives, Cincinnati, Ohio.

14 For an explanation of how and when Rabbi Wise became aware of the details of the mass killing through the American State Department, see Urofsky, *A Voice That Spoke for Justice*, 319–22. Robert A. Michael, *The Holocaust: A Chronology and Documentary* (Lanham, MD: Jason Aronson Publishing, 1998), 177.

15 For an examination of the diversity of Jewish New York's reaction to the war, Holocaust, and attempts to create a Jewish state, see the third chapter of Gurock, *Jews in Gotham*, 104–31.

16 K. Shabbetai, *As Sheep to the Slaughter? The Myth of Jewish Cowardice* (New York: World Federation of the Bergen-Belsen Survivors Association, 1963).

17 According to Barbie Zelizer, by 1944 the US Signal Corps shot 50 percent of all of the still images published in US newspapers, books, and journals. *Remembering to Forget: Holocaust Memory through the Camera's Eye* (Chicago: University of Chicago Press, 1998), 22.

18 Barbie Zelizer, "Gender and Atrocity: Women in Holocaust Photographs," in Zelizer, *Visual Culture and the Holocaust* (New Brunswick, NJ: Rutgers University Press, 2001), 249.

19 Richard Middleton-Kaplan, "The Myth of Jewish Passivity," in *Jewish Resistance against the Nazis*, ed. Patrick Henry (Washington, DC: Catholic University of America Press, 2014), 8.

20 Passivity and femininity have been firmly connected in Western notions of gender analysis since Freud. Jessica Benjamin, "Deconstructing Femininity: Understanding 'Passivity' and the Daughter Position," in *The Annual of Psychoanalysis Vol. 32*, ed. Jerome A. Winer and James W. Anderson (New York: Routledge, 2004), 45–57.

21 Quoted in Bonnie Gurewitsch, "American Soldiers Confront the Holocaust," in *Ours to Fight For: American Jewish Voices from the Second World War*, ed. Jay M. Eidelman (New York: Museum of Jewish Heritage, 2003), 64.

22 On the various relief organizations and their early interactions with survivors through Jewish members of the American military, see Abraham S. Hyman, *The Undefeated* (Jerusalem: Gefen House, 1993); Rabbi Herschel Schacter, "Sholom Aleichem Yidn, Ihr Zeit Frei!" in *Ours to Fight For: American Jewish Voices from the Second World War*,

ed. Jay M. Eidelman (New York: Museum of Jewish Heritage, 2003); and Oscar A Mintzer, *In Defense of the Survivors: The Letters and Documents of Oscar A. Mintzer, AJDC Legal Advisor, Germany, 1945–46* (Berkeley, CA: Judah Magnes Museum, 1999).

23 Leon Bass, interview 44720 (Visual History Archive, USC Shoah Foundation, 1998), accessed October 2017, segment 43.

24 From the report of Earl G. Harrison (US representative on the Intergovernmental Commission on Refugees) to Harry S. Truman, September 30, 1945, *Department of State Bulletin* 13, no. 326 (September 30, 1945), 456–63.

25 "Displaced Persons in Germany Letter from President Truman to General Eisenhower Transmitting Report of Earl G. Harrison," *Department of State Bulletin* 13, no. 326 (September 30, 1945), 455–63. Melvin Price's appeal from the Congressional Record: Proceedings and Debates of the 79th Congress First Session, *Appendix* Volume 91-Part 12, A3924.

26 This was still in accordance with the paper's continuing policy to remain impartial to Jewish matters, as referenced in chapter 4. See Leff, *Buried by the Times*.

27 James Carroll, "Shoah in the News: Patterns and Meanings of News Coverage of the Holocaust," Discussion Paper D-27, Joan Shorenstein Center—Press, Politics, and Public Policy, Harvard University, Cambridge, Massachusetts, October 1997, pages 4–6.

28 Data from Karl Frucht, "Clem Has Been Here: Second Thoughts on the American Soldiers in Europe," *Commentary* 1, no. 5 (March 1946): 42.

29 Diana T. Meyers, *Victims' Stories and the Advancement of Human Rights* (New York: Oxford University Press, 2016), eBook.

30 Meyers, *Victims' Stories*, chapter 1.

31 For more on the gendered captioning of liberation images in the press, see Zelizer, "Gender and Atrocity," 258–61.

32 "Conditions in the Displaced Persons Camps," September 9, 1945, Abraham Klausner Papers, P-879, box 1, folder 27, American Jewish Historical Society, New York.

33 Hyman, *The Undefeated*, 157, 331–32.

34 Boyarin, *Unheroic Conduct*, 13–15.

35 Samuel Lubell, "The Second Exodus of the Jews," *Saturday Evening Post* 219 (October 5, 1946): 16–17, 86. Quotation found in Novick, *The Holocaust in American Life*, chapter 4.

36 Letter from Survivors to Joint Distribution Committee, box 2, folder 16, P-879 (Rabbi Abraham Klausner Papers), American Jewish Historical Society, Center for Jewish History.

37 *Lest We Forget; The Massacre of the Warsaw Ghetto: A Compilation of Reports Received by the World Jewish Congress and by the Representation of Polish Jewry* (New York: Spett Printing, 1943), 35. Accessed through the Leo Baeck Institute in New York. Deborah E. Lipstadt, *Holocaust: An American Understanding* (New Brunswick, NJ: Rutgers University Press, 2016), 32.

Chapter 8

1 See extract in Arthur Hertzberg, *The Zionist Idea: A Historical Analysis and Reader* (New York: Meridian Books, 1959), 431.

2 And indeed, Roosevelt had advocated the foundation of a Jewish state in Palestine after the Balfour Declaration, even suggesting that one of the Allies' conditions for peace should have been the creation of a Jewish state in Palestine. Given his other statements about Jews, that a return to the rugged life would suit them and rebuild the Jewish man, the pioneering opportunities in Palestine clearly seemed ideal. By that time, he had owned his ranch in the Dakota territories for two decades and spent much time on the frontier, where he believed the emasculated moralities of upper-class city life (the particular problem plaguing the Jewish people) could be remedied. Isaiah Friedman, *The Question of Palestine: British-Jewish-Arab Relations, 1914–1918* (New Brunswick, NJ: Transaction Publishers, 1992), 312.

3 Additional data and analysis on pre-state and post-Holocaust migration to Israel, see Sergio Della Pergola, "Demography in Israeli Palestine: Trends, Prospects, Policy Implications," paper presented at IUSSP General Conference. Salvador, Brazil, August 2001, 9–10 (figure 1). Also see "עלייה והגירה—שנתון סטטיסטי לישראל," Publications, Central Bureau of Statistics (Israel), accessed March 21, 2019, www.cbs.gov.il/he/subjects/Pages/עלייה-והגירה-בין-לאומית.aspx. To review a helpful map with charts of migration flows and numbers, see Elie Barnavi, ed., *A Historical Atlas of the Jewish People: From the Time of the Patriarchs to the Present* (New York: Schocken Books, 1992), 194–95. Lastly, for a more cohesive study of the displaced persons across Europe at the close of the war, see David

Nasaw's *The Last Million: Europe's Displaced Persons from World War to Cold War* (New York: Penguin Press, 2020).

4 Martin Van Creveld, *The Sword and the Olive: A Critical History of the Israeli Defense Force* (New York: Perseus Books Group, 1998), 14.

5 Etan Bloom, "Toward a Theory of the Development of the Modern Hebrew Handshake," in *Jewish Masculinities: German Jews, Gender, and History*, ed. Benjamin Maria Baader, Sharon Gillerman, and Paul Lerner (Bloomington: Indiana University Press, 2012), 157.

6 Van Creveld is referring to the *Circassians*, a Palestinian minority that used to work as guards for Jewish settlements in Palestine, along with some Druze and Arab groups. Van Creveld, *The Sword and the Olive*, 12.

7 Michael Berkowitz, *Western Jewry and the Zionist Project, 1914–1933* (New York: Cambridge University Press, 1997), 9.

8 Major-General Derek Tulloch, *Wingate: In Peace and War* (London: Macdonald, 1972), 45.

9 Christopher Sykes, *Orde Wingate: A Biography* (Cleveland: World Publishing, 1951), 111.

10 Sykes, *Orde Wingate*, 151.

11 About 3,500 volunteers, according to Derek Penslar, a much smaller volunteer core, proportionately, to Canada, South Africa, and several other nations. Penslar, *Jews and the Military*, 237.

12 Oz Almog, *The Sabra: The Creation of the New Jew* (Berkeley: University of California Press, 2000), 132–35.

13 Almog, *The Sabra*, 4.

14 Nahum Sokolow, *History of Zionism, 1600–1918: Volume 1* (New York: Longmans, Green, 1919), xvii.

15 Tom Segev, *1949: The First Israelis* (New York: Free Press, 1986), 290.

16 For more on the mentality of the sabra, and the negative, at times patronizing, attitude toward diaspora Jews, see Almog, *The Sabra*, chapter 2: "The Elect Son of the Chosen People."

17 An overheard conversation between two young sabras recounted in K. Shabbetai, *As Sheep to the Slaughter? The Myth of Jewish Cowardice* (New York: World Association of the Bergen-Belsen Survivors Association, 1963), 9–10.

18 Avner Holtzman, "'They Are Different People': Holocaust Survivors as Reflected in the Fiction of the Generation of 1948," *Yad Vashem Studies* 30 (2002): 344, 337–68.

19 Gilner, *Jews Who Fought.*

20 "Leader Says Jews Will Fight As Unit," *New York Times*, March 14, 1940, 6.

21 Monty Noam Penkower, "In Dramatic Dissent: The Bergson Boys," *American Jewish History* 70, no. 3 (March 1981): 284.

22 Advertisement, *New York Times*, January 5, 1942, 13.

23 Advertisement, *New York Times*, December 7, 1942, 14.

24 Eran Kaplan, "A Rebel with a Cause: Hillel Kook, Begin, and Jabotinsky's Ideological Legacy," *Israel Studies* 10 (2005): 92–93.

25 Medoff, *Militant Zionism in America*, 61.

26 Norman Mailer's *The Naked and the Dead*, Irwin Shaw's *The Young Lions*, Ira Wolfert's *An Act of Love*, Merle Miller's *That Winter*, and Stefan Heym's *The Crusaders*. Discussed in Deborah E. Lipstadt, *Holocaust: An American Understanding* (New Brunswick, NJ: Rutgers University Press, 2016), 31.

27 Translated from Hebrew, "שרוליק: נולד," http://srulik.co.il, accessed September 27, 2018, http://srulik.co.il/שרוליק. For an English publication of the Dosh cartoons in these early years, see Dosh, *To Israel, With Love* (New York: Thomas Yoseloff, 1960).

28 For illustration of the character's evolution, see figure 25 in the following chapter.

29 David Malet, *Foreign Fighters: Transnational Identity in Civic Conflicts* (New York: Oxford University Press, 2013), 132.

30 Penslar, *Jews and the Military*, 238.

31 Ricky-Dale Calhoun, "Arming David: The Haganah's Illegal Arms Procurement Network in the United States, 1945–49," *Journal of Palestine Studies* 36, no. 4 (Summer 2007): 23–24.

32 For a more thorough history of the Sonneborn Institute, see the seventh chapter of Derek Penslar's *Jews and the Military*, as well as Murray S. Greenfield and Joseph M. Hochstein's, *The Jews' Secret Fleet*.

33 Quote provided by Derek Penslar, *Jews and the Military*, 241–44.

34 Imhoff, *Masculinity*, 195.

35 Rockaway, *But He Was Good to His Mother*, 247–48.

36 Gurock, *Jews in Gotham*, 128–29.

37 Jewish Telegraph Agency, October 2, 1946. Accessed online at http://pdfs.jta.org/1946/1946-10-02_226.pdf on January 2, 2018.

38 Hillel Kook, "Kol Koreh me-et ha-Umah ha-Ivrit" (A Manifesto of the Hebrew Nation), accessed through Kaplan's "Rebel with a Cause," 93.

39 *For Survival and Freedom*, American League for a Free Palestine Records, I-278, box 2, folder 5, American Jewish Historical Society, New York and Boston.

40 The organizations are the American Friends of a Jewish Palestine, the Committee for a Jewish Army of Stateless and Palestinian Jews, the Emergency Committee to Save the Jewish People of Europe, and the American League for a Free Palestine. *For Survival and Freedom*, American League for a Free Palestine Records, I-278, box 2, folder 5, American Jewish Historical Society, New York and Boston.

41 "A Proclamation," *New York Times*, December 7, 1942, 14.

42 Adina Hoffman, *Ben Hecht: Fighting Words, Moving Pictures* (New Haven, CT: Yale University Press, 2019), 154–55.

43 For more on the *Eternal Road* and its cultural and historical significance, see Jonathan C. Friedman, *The Literary, Cultural, and Historical Significance of the 1937 Biblical Stage Play* The Eternal Road (Lewiston, NY: E. Mellen Press, 2004).

44 *A Flag Is Born* (Script), 1946, page 23. American League for a Free Palestine Records, I-278, box CB 2, folder 4, American Jewish Historical Society, New York and Boston.

45 Ben Hecht, *A Child of the Century* (New York: Simon and Schuster, 1954), 518.

46 David S. Wyman, "The Bergson Group, America, and the Holocaust: A Previously Unpublished Interview with Hillel Kook/Peter Bergson," *American Jewish History* 89, no. 1 (March 2001): 11–13.

47 Various disclaimers by American Zionist organizations, American League for a Free Palestine Records, I-278, box 2, folder 3, American Jewish Historical Society, New York and Boston.

48 Zionists vs. League: Dispute Flares up in Boston Area, *Jewish Weekly Times*, February 2, 1947, 1, 5.

49 Quoted in Judith Tydor Baumel's *The "Bergson Boys" and the Origins of Contemporary Zionist Militancy* (Syracuse, NY: Syracuse University Press, 2005), 122–23.

50 *This Is Betar*, pamphlet, Brit Trumpeldor of America (New York, 1940), 48. Accessed through the YIVO Library Collection at the Center for Jewish History.

51 *This Is Betar*, 22.

52 "Youths Drill Here to Free Palestine," *New York Times*, January 14, 1946.

53 *The Avukah Problem: A Special Report by the American Zionist Youth Commission, 1942*, 18; Campus Zionism collection, I-428, box 1, folder "Avukah convention Reports," American Jewish Historical Society, New York, and Boston.

54 Statements from both students (whose praesidium included future neoconservative Nathan Glazer) and faculty advisors are used here from "Militant Student Zionism," Summary Report of the Seventeenth Annual Convention of Avukah, June 15, 1942, Campus Zionism collection, I-428, box 1, folder "Avukah convention Reports," American Jewish Historical Society, New York and Boston.

55 *The Avukah Problem: A Special Report by the American Zionist Youth Commission, 1942*, Campus Zionism collection, I-428, box 1, folder "Avukah convention Reports," American Jewish Historical Society, New York and Boston.

56 Sumner Alpert, "Zionism on the Campus," *Jewish Education* 18, no. 2 (February/March 1947): 41.

57 Carole Joffe, "Changes in Campus Zionism," *The Maccabean: Forum for American Jewish Youth* 2, no. 2 (Fall 1965): 15–24. Accessed through the American Jewish Historical Society, New York and Boston.

Chapter 9

1 Martin Jezer, "The Futility of This Most Recent War," June 30, 1967 (clipping); Jewish Counter Culture Collection, I-504, box 5, folder 4, American Jewish Historical Society, Boston and New York.

2 *This Is Betar*, 4.

3 Lila Corwin Berman, "American Jews and the Ambivalence of Middle-Classness," *American Jewish History* 93, no. 4 (December 2007): 412.

4 See Paul Breines's *Tough Jews: Political Fantasies and the Moral Dilemma of American Jewry*, Warren Rosenberg's *Legacy of Rage: Jewish Masculinity, Violence, and Culture*, Daniel Boyarin's *Unheroic Conduct*, Harry Brod and Shawn Israel Zevit's, *Brother Keepers: New Perspectives on Jewish Masculinity*, and David Moscowitz's *A Culture of Tough Jews: Rhetorical Regeneration and the Politics of Identity*.

5 Breines, *Tough Jews*, 59.

6 See Kaplan, *Our American Israel*, 72–73.

7 For more on American shifting views of Israel in the 1980s, see Kaplan, *Our American Israel*, 136–77.

8 Weininger, *Sex and Character*, 281.

9 For a more thorough reading of *Portnoy's Complaint*, sexual deviance, and sexual failure, read Josh Lambert's analysis in *Unclean Lips: Obscenity, Jews, and American Culture* (New York: New York University Press, 2014), 123–28.

10 "Blueprint for Hebrew Freedom: A Letter from Peter H. Bergson to Dr. Chaim Weizmann," American League for a Free Palestine Records, I-278, box 2, folder 3, American Jewish Historical Society, New York and Boston.

11 Quoted in Joseph Wershba, "Daily Closeup: Leon Uris, Author of 'Exodus,'" *New York Post*, July 2, 1959, 34.

12 Quote from Philip Roth, "The New Jewish Stereotypes," *American Judaism* 11, no. 2 (Winter 1961): 11.

13 Wershba, "Daily Closeup," 34.

14 Roth, "New Jewish Stereotypes," 49.

15 M. M. Silver, *Our Exodus: Leon Uris and the Americanization of Israel's Founding Story* (Detroit: Wayne State University Press, 2010), 114–15.

16 In his 1990 book, *Tough Jews: Political Fantasies and the Moral Dilemma of American Jewry*, Paul Breines identifies a conflict inspired by the two great shifts of the Jewish twentieth century: the Holocaust and the establishment of Israel. The two created a conflict of Jewish self-identity, as the former resulted in the disillusionment with universal values and the latter provided the military means to disregard such values entirely. Hence the emergence of "tough Jews" in literature.

17 For further reading on the significance of 1968, see Todd Gitlin, *The Sixties: Years of Hope, Days of Rage* (New York: Bantam Books, 1987); Mark Kurlansky, *1968: The Year That Rocked the World* (New York: Random House, 2004); Elaine Carey and Alfred J. Andrea, eds., *Protests in the Streets: 1968 Across the Globe* (Indianapolis: Hackett Publishing, 2016); and Grzegorz Kość, Clara Juncker, Sharon Monteith, and Britta Waldschmidt-Nelson, eds., *The Transatlantic Sixties: Europe and the United States in the Counterculture Decade* (Bielefeld, Germany: Transcript, 2013).

18 For an examination of the specific effect of the draft on African Americans, see James E. Westheider, *Fighting on Two Fronts: African Americans and the Vietnam War* (New York: New York University Press,

1999), chapter 2 ("'I'm Not a Draft Evader . . . I'm a Runaway Slave': African Americans and the Draft").

19 *Shalom: The Jewish Peace Fellowship Newsletter*, Jewish Peace Fellowship Records, I-189, box number 18, folder number 4, American Jewish Historical Society, New York.

20 Jewish Peace Fellowship Records, I-189, box number 5, folder number 5, American Jewish Historical Society, New York.

21 David Halberstam, *The Best and the Brightest* (New York: Random House, 1972), chapter 18, eBook.

22 Kuan Yew quote from Kahane, *The Jewish Stake in Vietnam* (New York: Crossroads Publishing, 1967), 183.

23 For more on Johnson and desperate masculinity, see the eighth chapter of Kimmel, *Manhood in America*, titled "The Masculine Mystique."

24 Joke related in Andrew Bard Schmookler, *Out of Weakness: Healing the Wounds That Drive Us to War* (New York: Bantam Books, 1988), 126.

25 Michael A. Newton, *The United States Department of Defense Law of War Manual: Commentary and Critique* (New York: Cambridge University Press, 2019), 138–39.

26 The substance was not acknowledged as harmful to humans, or the effected veterans granted disability benefits, until 2015.

27 This was a dominant trend in media, but of course not the only representation of the war and masculinity. For more on this remasculinization process in film and television, see Susan Jeffords, *The Remasculinization of America: Gender and the Vietnam War* (Bloomington: Indiana University Press, 1989).

28 Myrian Miedzian, *Boys Will Be Boys: Breaking the Link between Masculinity and Violence* (New York: Lantern Books, 2002), chapter 2, eBook.

29 Say Burgin, "Understanding Antiwar Activism as a Gendering Activity: A Look at the U.S.'s Anti-Vietnam War Movement," *Journal of International Women's Studies* 13, no. 6 (2012): 26.

30 James Penner, *Pinks, Pansies, and Punks: The Rhetoric of Masculinity in American Literary Culture* (Bloomington: Indiana University Press, 2010), 157–60.

31 Penner, *Pinks, Pansies, and Punks*, 168–69.

32 Lynda E. Boose, "Techno-Muscularity and the 'Boy Eternal': From the Quagmire to the Gulf," in *Gendering War Talk*, ed. Miriam Cooke and Angela Wollacott (Princeton, NJ: Princeton University Press, 1993), 88.

33 Hasia Diner demonstrates this well in discussion of Israel, survivors, and American advocacy, particularly concerning the dominance of Uris's *Exodus* over Ruth Gruber's *Israel without Tears*. Diner, *We Remember with Reverence and Love*, 186–87.

34 For an analysis of postmillennium changes to this popular image in Holocaust cinema, see Miriam Eve Borenstein, "Heroes, Victims and Villains: Character Inversion in Holocaust Cinema" (master's thesis, West Chester University of Pennsylvania, 2009).

35 Jeffrey Shandler, *While America Watches: Televising the Holocaust* (New York: Oxford University Press, 1999), 82.

36 For a good summary of the accepted narrative, see Diner's conclusion in *We Remember with Reverence and Love*, 370–75.

37 Kaplan, *Our American Israel*, 97.

38 Michael L. Morgan, *Beyond Auschwitz: Post-Holocaust Jewish Thought in America* (New York: Oxford University Press, 2001), 79–80. The significance of that fear within the Jewish community, the sudden need to support the state, is how Alan Dershowitz explained the lack of connection that American Jews of Generation X felt toward Israel compared with the previous generations who lived through the brief but terrifying conflict. Alan M. Dershowitz, *The Vanishing American Jew: In Search of Jewish Identity for the Next Century* (Boston: Little, Brown, 1997), 90.

39 Lucy Dawidowicz, "American Public Opinion," *American Jewish Yearbook* 69 (1968): 204.

40 Dawidowicz, "American Public Opinion," 206–9.

41 "How the Six-Day War Transformed Religion: Six Perspectives on How the 1967 Arab-Israeli Conflict Changed Islam, Judaism, Christianity, and Mormonism," *The Atlantic*, accessed August 1, 2018, www .theatlantic.com/international/archive/2017/06/how-the-six-day-war -changed-religion/528981/.

42 Howard M. Sachar, *A History of the Jews in America* (New York: Vintage Books, 1992), 890.

43 Quoted in Chaim I. Waxman, *America's Jews in Transition* (Philadelphia: Temple University Press, 1983), 113.

44 Translated from Hebrew, "שרוליק מתבגר," http://srulik.co.il, accessed September 27, 2018, http://srulik.co.il/שרוליק.

45 Dawidowicz, "American Public Opinion," 205.

46   For more on American reporting of Israeli military style and sexuality, see Kaplan, *Our American Israel*, 100–110.

47   David M. Szonyi, "American Aliyah: Will It Go Up?" *Ruach Chaim*, Spring 1976. Jewish Student Organizations Collection, I-61, box 53, folder 19, American Jewish Historical Society, New York and Boston.

48   Nancy Weber, "The Truth of Tears," *Village Voice*, June 15, 1967. Quoted in Dawidowicz, "American Public Opinion," 211.

49   Robert Ruby, "A Six-Day War: Its Aftermath in American Public Opinion," May 30, 2007, www.pewforum.org/2007/05/30/a-six-day-war-its-aftermath-in-american-public-opinion.

50   Dawidowicz, "American Public Opinion," 212–13.

51   Waxman, "The Pendulum Shift, 1965–1975," in *America's Jews*, 104–34.

52   Emily Alice Katz, *Bringing Zion Home: Israel in American Jewish Culture, 1948–1967* (Albany: State University of New York Press, 2015).

53   Amnon Kapeliuk, "Israel Emigrants," *Journal of Palestine Studies* 6, no. 4 (Summer 1977): 165–69.

Chapter 10

1   Mark Gerzon, *A Choice of Heroes* (Boston: Houghton Mifflin, 1982), 85.

2   Statistics for Berkely from Bettina Aptheker, *Intimate Politics* (Emeryville, CA: Seal Press, 2006), and Phillip Mendes, "'We Are All German Jews': Exploring the Prominence of Jews in the New Left," *Melilah: Manchester Journal of Jewish Studies* 6 (2009). Numerical data on Students for a Democratic Society chapters from *A Tale of Two Utopias*. For more on the Jewish students killed at Kent State, see the article from Jonah Lowenfeld's "Remembering Kent State as an American Tragedy with a Jewish Face," *Forward* April 28, 2010, https://forward.com/news/127615/remembering-kent-state-as-an-american-tragedy-with/ (accessed December 10, 2017). Paul Berman, *A Tale of Two Utopias: The Political Journey of the Generation of 1968* (New York: W. W. Norton, 1996), 44–45.

3   Stephen Steinberg, *The Academic Melting Pot: Catholics and Jews in American Higher Education* (New York: McGraw-Hill, 1974), 167–69, see table on 101.

4   Paula E. Hyman, "Jewish Feminism Faces the American Women's Movement," in *American Jewish Identity Politics*, ed. Deborah Dash Moore (Ann Arbor: University of Michigan Press, 2008), 223.

5 Jerry Rubin, *Growing (Up) at 37* (Lanham, MD: Rowman and Little-field, 2014), 159.

6 Burgin, "Understanding Antiwar Activism," 20–21.

7 Sara Evans, *Personal Politics: The Roots of Women's Liberation in the Civil Rights Movement and the New Left* (New York: Vintage Books, 1980), 170–71.

8 Report by the American Jewish Committee's Information Service on the *Faculty Thoughts on the Jewish Role in the Student Disorders at Columbia University*, November 1968, box 95, folder 2, MS-603. Rabbi Marc H. Tanenbaum Collection, American Jewish Archives, Cincinnati, Ohio.

9 Lewis S. Feuer, *The Conflict of Generations: The Character and Significance of Student Movements* (New York: Basic Books, 1969), 429–30.

10 Nathan Glazer, "The Jewish Role in Student Activism," *Fortune Magazine*, January 1969, 126.

11 Report by the American Jewish Committee's Information Service on the *Faculty Thoughts on the Jewish Role in the Student Disorders at Columbia University*, November 1968, box 95, folder 2, General correspondence, memos and working papers, 1968. American Jewish Archives, Cincinnati, Ohio.

12 Report by the American Jewish Committee's Information Service on the *Faculty Thoughts on the Jewish Role in the Student Disorders at Columbia University*, November 1968, box 95, folder 2, General correspondence, memos and working papers, 1968. American Jewish Archives, Cincinnati, Ohio.

13 Louis Lusky and Mary H. Lusky, "Columbia 1968: The Wound Unhealed," *Political Science Quarterly* 84, no. 2 (June 1969): 169–288.

14 Robert A. McCaughey, *Stand, Columbia: A History of Columbia University* (New York: Columbia University Press, 2003), 429.

15 For nuanced analyses that also recount the complex historiographies of this topic, see both Marc Dollinger's *Black Power, Jewish Politics: Reinventing the Alliance in the 1960s* (Lebanon, NH: Brandeis University Press, 2018) and Cheryl Lynn Greenberg's *Troubling the Waters: Black-Jewish Relations in the American Century* (Princeton, NJ: Princeton University Press, 2006).

16 In his recent book *Black Power, Jewish Politics: Reinventing the Alliance in the 1960s*, Marc Dollinger complicates the narrative of Jewish Black

relations, demonstrating how the shifting priorities and motivations in the civil rights movement and Black power struggle altered the trajectories of both groups, and in many ways, drove a wedge between them.

17 Norman Podhoretz, "My Negro Problem—And Ours," *Commentary*, accessed April 17, 2019, www.commentarymagazine.com/articles/my-negro-problem-and-ours

18 For more analysis of Podhoretz's article and Jewish-Black relations, see Michael R. Fischbach, *Black Power and Palestine: Transnational Countries of Color* (Stanford, CA: Stanford University Press, 2018), "The Fire This Time: SNCC, Jews, and the Demise of the Beloved Community"; Karen Brodkin, *How Jews Became White Folks and What That Says about Race in America* (New Brunswick, NJ: Rutgers University Press, 2002), 149; quote is from Podhoretz, "My Negro Problem—And Ours."

19 Mark Rudd, "Why Were There So Many Jews in SDS? (Or, the Ordeal of Civility)," accessed December 10, 2017, Markrudd.com, www.markrudd.com/indexcd39.html?about-mark-rudd/why-were-there-so-many-jews-in-sds-or-the-ordeal-of-civility.html.

20 McCaughey, *Stand, Columbia*, 437.

21 Mark Rudd, "After Words with Mark Rudd," filmed March 24, 2009, for BookTV on C-SPAN2, Video, 41:25.

22 Rudd, "After Words with Mark Rudd," 11:00

23 See table on page 6 of Alfred Jospe's study, "Jewish Students and Student Services at American Universities: A Statistical and Historical Study," Hillel International, accessed October 24, 2018, https://www.bjpa.org/search-results/publication/4538.

24 Rudd, "Why Were There So Many Jews in SDS?"

25 Antler, *Jewish Radical Feminism*, 296.

26 Michael E. Staub, *Torn at the Roots: The Crisis of Jewish Liberalism in Postwar America* (New York: Columbia University Press, 2002), 1–4.

27 Pnina Lahav, "Theater in the Courtroom: The Chicago Conspiracy Trial," *Law and Literature* 16, no. 3 (2004): 408, 407.

28 Rita James Simon, "The American Jury: Instrument of Justice or of Prejudice and Conformity?" *Sociological Inquiry* 47, no. 3–4 (July 1977): 275.

29 Jon Weiner, ed., *Conspiracy in the Streets: The Extraordinary Trial of the Chicago Eight* (New York: New Press, 2006), 14.

30 United States, District Court (Illinois: Northern District), *Contempt, Transcript of the Contempt Citations, Sentences, and Responses of the Chicago Conspiracy 10* (Chicago: Swallow Press, 1970), 72.

31 David Farber, *Chicago '68* (Chicago: University of Chicago Press, 1988), 5–6.

32 Lahav, "Theater in the Courtroom," 435.

33 Pnina Lahav, "The Chicago Conspiracy Trial as a Jewish Morality Tale," in *Lives in the Law*, ed. Austin Sarat, Lawrence Douglas, and Martha Merrill Umphrey (Ann Arbor: University of Michigan Press, 2006), 33.

34 Harry Brod, "Toward a Male Jewish Feminism," in *A Mensch among Men*, ed. Harry Brod (Freedom, CA: Crossing Press, 1988), 185.

35 "Judge Hoffman Is Taunted at the Trial of the Chicago Seven after Silencing Defense Counsel," *New York Times*, February 6, 1970, 41.

36 Spelling of the transliteration from Wiener, *Conspiracy in the Streets*, 205.

37 Hillel Schenker, "A New Antisemitism? Reflections on the Extreme Right," *The Maccabean: Forum for American Jewish Youth* 2, no. 2 (Fall 1965): 5–14.

38 Dorothy Rabinowitz, "Are Jewish Students Different?" *Change* 3, no. 4 (Summer 1971): 49.

39 Ezra Spicehandler, "National and Social Characteristics of Jewish Youth in the U.S.A.," in *Youth Today: A Collection of Articles and Essays*, edited by Yehuda Gotthelf (Tel-Aviv: World Labour Zionist Movement, 1970), 129. Accessed through YIVO at the Center for Jewish History.

40 Marc Dollinger's *Black Power, Jewish Politics* contains a chapter on the interactions between (and intersecting interests/issues of) Black Power and American Zionism, which fleshes out some of the involved issues in more detail, beyond interests in masculinities.

41 *SNCC Newsletter* 1, no. 4 (June/July 1967): 5 (accessed through the online repository at Duke University).

42 *The Movement* 3, no. 2 (September 1967): 2 (accessed through the online library at UCSD).

43 "Malcolm X Makes It Home from Mecca," *Amsterdam News*, May 23, 1964.

44 Fischbach, *Black Power and Palestine*, "Malcolm X, Global Black Solidarity, and Palestine," eBook.

45 For more scholarly works dealing with Jews and whiteness, see Brodkin, *How Jews Became White Folks and What That Says about Race in America*; Matthew Frye Jacobson, *Whiteness of a Different Color*

(Cambridge, MA: Harvard University Press, 1998); Eric L. Goldstein, *The Price of Whiteness: Jews, Race, and American Identity* (Princeton, NJ: Princeton University Press, 2006); David R. Roediger, *Working toward Whiteness: How America's Immigrants Became White: The Strange Journey from Ellis Island to the Suburbs* (New York: Basic Books, 2005).

46   Eric L. Goldstein, "'Different Blood Flows in Our Veins': Race and Jewish Self-Definition in Late Nineteenth Century America," *American Jewish History* 85, no. 1 (March 1997): 29–55.

47   James Baldwin, "Negroes Are Anti-Semitic Because They're Anti-White," New York Times Digital Archive, accessed April 16, 2019, https://archive.nytimes.com/www.nytimes.com/books/98/03/29/specials/baldwin-antisem.html.

48   D'Weston Haywood, *Let Us Make Men: The Twentieth-Century Black Press and a Manly Vision for Racial Advancement* (Chapel Hill: University of North Carolina Press, 2018), 170.

49   M. Jay Rosenberg, "To Uncle Tom and Other Such Jews," 1969; Jewish Counter Culture Collection, I-504, box 5, folder 3, American Jewish Historical Society, New York.

50   For more on the Euro-centricity (and lack of diversity) of Jewish American life and scholarship, see Melanie Kaye/Kantrowitz, *The Colors of Jews: Racial Politics and Radical Diasporism* (Bloomington: Indiana University Press, 2007).

51   Fischbach, *Black Power and Palestine*, "The Fire This Time: SNCC, Jews, and the Demise of the Beloved Community," eBook.

52   For more on the relationship between European Zionists and Mizrahi Jews in the early years of Israeli statehood, see Bryan K. Roby, *The Mizrahi Era of Rebellion: Israel's Forgotten Civil Rights Struggle, 1948–1966* (Syracuse, NY: Syracuse University Press, 2015).

53   "My Evolution as a Jew," by M Jay Rosenberg, 1970; Jewish Student Organizations Collection, I-61, box 15, folder 10, American Jewish Historical Society, New York and Boston.

54   *Nimrod*, issue 4, Spring 1981, Jewish Student Organizations Collection, I-61, box 15, folder 10, American Jewish Historical Society, New York and Boston.

55   *Nimrod*, issue 1, Fall 1979, and *Nimrod*, issue 2, Spring 1980 Jewish Student Organizations Collection, I-61, box 15, folder 10, American Jewish Historical Society, New York and Boston.

56 See the chapter "Unmanly Guilt" in Ray Raphael's *The Men from the Boys: Rites of Passage in Male America* (Lincoln: University of Nebraska Press, 1988), 144–80.

57 Quoted and analyzed in Penner. Also see Penner for a gendered analysis of Abbie Hoffman's public vasectomy project, which speaks to his particular brand of "Macho Feminism." Penner, *Pinks, Pansies, and Punks*, 214.

58 Joyce Antler, *Jewish Radical Feminism: Voices from the Women's Liberation Movement* (New York: New York University Press, 2018), 36–37.

59 eHer assertion about this relationship is largely based on the various writings of Riv-Ellen Prell, Paula Hyman, and the critique of literature by Philip Roth and his contemporaries. Brodkin, *How Jews Became White Folks*, 160–62.

60 Antler, *Jewish Radical Feminism*, 34.

61 Antler, *Jewish Radical Feminism*, 200–201.

62 For an analysis of Friedan's use of Holocaust imagery and its implications for historical assumptions about Jewish American reactions to the Holocaust before the Six-Day War, see Kirsten Fermaglich, "'The Comfortable Concentration Camp': The Significance of Nazi Imagery in Betty Friedan's 'The Feminine Mystique' (1963)," *American Jewish History* 91, no. 2 (June 2003): 205–32.

63 Judith Hauptman, "Conservative Judaism: The Ethical Challenge of Feminist Change," in *The Americanization of the Jews*, ed. Robert M. Seltzer and Norman J. Cohen (New York: New York University Press, 1995), 296–97.

64 Hyman, "Jewish Feminism Faces the American Women's Movement," 226.

65 Paula E. Hyman, "Ezrat Nashim and the Emergence of a New Jewish Feminism," in *The Americanization of the Jews*, ed. Robert M. Seltzer and Norman J. Cohen (New York: New York University Press, 1995), 285.

66 In his recent book on Meir Kahane, Shaul Magid acknowledged this connection between the JDL, masculinity, and American assimilation and commented on the lack of gender critique in current scholarship on Kahane as an area in need of examination. Shaul Magid, *Meir Kahane: The Public Life and Political Thought of an American Jewish Radical* (Princeton, NJ: Princeton University Press, 2021), eBook.

67 Breines, *Tough Jews*, 14.

68 For more on Hillel Kook and the American leaders of the Revisionist Zionists, see Baumel, "*Bergson Boys.*"

69 Many of these groups even formed alliances with one another. For example, branches of the JDL had alliances at various times with the Italian American League, various Black Power groups (including the Black Panthers), and anti-Islamic groups across the United States and Canada. For an analysis of the phenomenon of white (and white ethnic) men appropriating Black masculinities from the civil rights era to benefit from the image of powerful Black masculinities, see Katharine Bausch's *He Thinks He's Down: White Appropriations of Black Masculinities in the Civil Rights Era* (Vancouver: University of British Columbia Press, 2020).

70 Dollinger, *Black Power, Jewish Politics*, 63.

71 "Never Again Cries Head of Jewish Defense Body," *Jewish Post and Opinion*, October 3, 1969.

72 An editorial in the *Jewish Post and Opinion* showed the similarity of motivations between the spirit of the Six-Day War response in the United States and the JDL. Speaking about Kahane, the writer explained, "His message strikes a responsive chord in young Jews unlike anything in recent years except the Six-Day War, and both have an underlying thread of similarity." "ADL Policy Needs Revising," *Jewish Post and Opinion*, August 27, 1971.

73 Walter Goodman, "Rabbi Kahane says: 'I'd Love to See The J.D.L. Fold Up. But—,'" *New York Times*, November 21, 1971, 32.

74 See Dollinger's chapter on Black Power and American Zionism in *Black Power, Jewish Politics*.

75 "*Playboy* Interview: Meir Kahane," *Playboy Magazine*, October 1972, 71.

76 The most famous example of its attempted influence being the JDL's attempt to threaten Soviet-American détente relations enough to force the USSR to free Soviet Jews for migration to Israel.

77 For more on Kahane's perception of the American diaspora, as well as his commentary on Kahane's continued work in the United States, see Magid, *Meir Kahane*.

78 "Three Hundred Hear Rabbi Kahana [sic] in Philadelphia," clipped from the *Jewish Post and Opinion*, exact date unknown. Records of the Jewish Defense League, I-374, box 1, folder 3, American Jewish Historical Society, New York and Boston.

79 John Peterson, "Jewish Defense League: Camp Builds Cadre of Street Fighters," *National Observer*, July 28, 1969.

80 *This Is Betar*, 22.

81 Libby Kahane, *Rabbi Meir Kahane: His Life and Thought—Volume One: 1932–1975* (New York: Institute for the Publication of the Writings of Rabbi Meir Kahane, 2008), 25.

82 Kahane had a dramatic, conflict-riddled public relationship with Menachem Begin, one of the most famous followers of Jabotinsky, and was completely rejected by both Begin and the political party he founded, Likud. When Kahane entered Israeli politics, he was a supporter of Begin, content that even if Begin was not a religious Jew, he at least didn't desecrate the Sabbath in public and kept the religious in mind when crafting legislation. Libby Kahane, *Rabbi Meir Kahane: His Life and Thought—Volume Two: 1976–1983* (New York: Institute for the Publication of the Writings of Rabbi Meir Kahane, 2016), 74.

83 Numbers compiled from various news sources in the AJHS Jewish Defense League collection. It is worth noting that many established Jewish institutions denied these high numbers of membership that the JDL claimed, if not the number of supporters who did not register as members. Various sources include clippings from Jewish and non-Jewish newspapers, *Newsweek*, *Time*, and *New York Magazine*. As small as this organization may seem, even if we assume that these numbers are exaggerated, compared with the American Jewish population, it cannot be dismissed as insubstantial. Even at the height of their recruiting, the Black Panthers only ever reached five thousand members. Jeffrey O. G. Ogbar, *Black Power: Radical Politics and African American Identity* (Baltimore: Johns Hopkins University Press, 2019), 189.

84 Shlomo Mordechai Russ, "The 'Zionist Hooligans': The Jewish Defense League" (PhD diss., City University of New York, 1981), 74.

85 Anthony Scaduto, "Won't You Listen to the Lambs, Bob Dylan?," *Rolling Stone*, November 28, 1971, 34. "Dylan's Jewishness," unknown source clipping, June 17, 1971, Records of the Jewish Defense League, I-374, box 1, folder 3, American Jewish Historical Society, New York and Boston. Dafna Arad, "The Jewish Couple That Taught Bob Dylan Hebrew and Introduced Him to Zionism," *Haaretz*, July 4, 2016, www.haaretz.com/israel-news/culture/.premium.MAGAZINE-the-lost-bob-dylan-nyc-tapes-1.5404956.

86 Anti-Defamation League General Counsel Arnold Foster in "Jewish Militants Step Up Activity," *New York Times*, June 25, 1969, 25.

87 Anti-Defamation League General Counsel Arnold Foster.

88 Russ, "The 'Zionist Hooligans,'" 524.

89 L. Kahane, *Rabbi Meir Kahane: His Life and Thought—Volume One: 1932–1975* (Jerusalem: Urim Publications, 2008), 121.

90 From assorted clippings in the Records of the Jewish Defense League, I-374, box 1, American Jewish Historical Society, New York and Boston; italics added.

91 Clipping from 1969 in the Records of the Jewish Defense League, I-374, box 1, folder 3-, American Jewish Historical Society, New York and Boston.

92 When asked if the only difference between the JDL and the American Nazi Party was that the JDL was right and the Nazis were wrong, Kahane replied, "I can't put it better than that." "*Playboy* Interview," *Playboy*, 70.

93 The JDL did not require its members to practice Orthodox Judaism, and most did not. However, as an Orthodox rabbi, Kahane maintained the Jewish Defense League as a political-religious organization.

94 Phillip P. Brown and Seymour C. Lechter, letters to the editor from (clippings), original newspapers unknown, Records of the Jewish Defense League, I-374, box 1, folder 3, American Jewish Historical Society, New York and Boston. Meir Kahane, *Never Again! A Program for Survival* (New York: Pyramid Books, 1972), 52–72.

95 The same author of that statement was quick to point out that those who hurled "abuses" at the JDL ("white-collar donkeys who claim to represent Boston Jewry") "have never had the guts to assail to the same degree Black Militants." P. Baram Brookline, letter to the editor "Jellyfish Jews," *Jewish Advocate*, December 4, 1969, 2.

96 It was, in fact, rising racial tension in the New York City schools that precipitated the founding of the JDL, as Blacks demanded more Black teachers in primarily Black schools in the Ocean Hill–Brownsville neighborhoods of Brooklyn, inspired by Black Power and the desire to be taught by educators who spoke the cultural language of Black children. Of the white teachers they sought to displace, many were Jewish, and Jewish communities felt there was rising Black antisemitism. This culminated in the New York City teacher's strike of 1968,

and attacks on teachers in Jewish neighborhoods. The Jewish Defense League was founded largely on the notion that these attacks were being ignored by the police and going unreported by non-Jewish presses. Kahane argued that this was cause for Jews to step in and take care of it themselves, like the Panthers in Oakland or the Puerto Rican Young Lords in Chicago.

97 He had already disrupted several church services in the city, first at New York's Riverside Church, then several others, to read what he called the "Black Manifesto."

98 Murray Schneider, date unknown, Records of the Jewish Defense League, I-374, box 1, folder 3, American Jewish Historical Society, New York and Boston.

99 For more on women in the Black Panther Party and the Black civil rights movement, see Davis W. Houck and David E. Dixon, eds., *Women and the Civil Rights Movement, 1954–1965* (Jackson: University of Mississippi Press, 2009). In addition, see Suzanne Cope's recent book on women and food in the movement, *Power Hungry: Women of the Black Panther Party and Freedom Summer and Their Fight to Feed a Movement* (Chicago: Chicago Review Press, 2021).

100 The highest numbers of participating women at an actual JDL event that I have found was an incident in which twenty men and seven women affiliated with a JDL protest of Jewish arrests in the Soviet Union were themselves arrested in New York City in June 1970. According to Janet Dolgin, women in the league occasionally grumbled about being on the periphery of the group but generally accepted their roles on the sidelines. Janet L. Dolgin, *Jewish Identity and the JDL* (Princeton, NJ: Princeton University Press, 1977), 80, 94. Clipping, Records of the Jewish Defense League, I-374, box 1, folder 4, American Jewish Historical Society, New York and Boston.

101 Dolgin, *Jewish Identity and the JDL*, 80.

102 Inconsistent capitalization in the original. Advertisement, *New York Times*, June 24, 1969, 31.

103 Advertisement, *New York Times*, June 24, 1969, 31.

104 A slightly more intimidating image can be found in "The Jewish Defense League," Anti-Defamation League Bulletin, November 1969. Records of the Jewish Defense League, I-374, box 1, folder 3, American Jewish Historical Society, New York and Boston.

105 Yair Kotler, *Heil Kahane* (New York: Adama Books, 1986), 37. Also see Magid, *Meir Kahane.*

106 The *Jewish Advocate* published an announcement of a tactical self-defense course in Boston open to "males, both members of JDL and non-members." "Self-Defense Course for JDL," *Jewish Advocate*, January 15, 1970.

107 L. Kahane, *Volume One*, 150.

108 Medoff, *Militant Zionism in America*, 26. "Youths Drill Here to Free Palestine," *New York Times*, January 14, 1946.

109 Camp Jedel Flier, Records of the Jewish Defense League, I-374, box 1, folder 13, American Jewish Historical Society, New York and Boston.

110 "*Playboy* Interview," *Playboy*, 76.

111 Though pictured in an article, Fran Grossman (the only female camper) wears a different uniform from the all-male students with whom she is training, who all wear white karate robes. Fran wears dark pants and a dark tunic. John Peterson, "Jewish Defense League."

112 Peterson, "Jewish Defense League."

113 L. Kahane, *Volume One*, 115.

114 "Population data taken from the National Jewish Population Survey (NJPS) 1971," Berman Jewish DataBank, accessed December 08, 2017, www.jewishdatabank.org/studies/details.cfm?StudyID=304.

115 "Defends JDL," unknown source clipping, December 5, 1969, Records of the Jewish Defense League, I-374, box 1, folder 3, American Jewish Historical Society, New York and Boston.

116 Stephen Wise Free Synagogue of New York Newsletter, Records of the Jewish Defense League, I-374, box 1, folder 4, American Jewish Historical Society, New York and Boston.

117 Trucia D. Kushner, "Meir Kahane-The Unorthodox Rabbi of the JDL," *Women's Wear Daily*, December 1970. Records of the Jewish Defense League, I-374, box 1, folder 4, American Jewish Historical Society, New York and Boston.

118 Peterson, "Jewish Defense League."

119 Quote from Camp Jedel Flier. Though the heyday of the camp was in the early 1970s before Kahane migrated to Israel, it was reopened under the name Camp Meir shortly after Meir's assassination in 1990. It had a revival in the early 1990s after the Crown Heights Riots, and there is some video footage available on the internet, though finding

reputable sources is difficult. For one recruiting video, see "Camp Meir," accessed September 14, 2018, www.youtube.com/watch?v= vwBONwXTEu0. A Flier for Camp Meir from 1990 shows similar goals and language as the original Camp Jedel materials.

120   Kahane backed up this statement in another interview with a story about the JDL's confrontation of activist Sonny Carson (who was propagating antisemitic rhetoric). He and fourteen JDL members confronted Carson as panther peers. He explained, "You don't sit down with Sonny Carson. Sonny Carson does not listen. With Sonny Carson, you walk in and you say, 'Sonny, baby, you gonna get out? Or do we have to cut you up?' And he says, 'Now man, now sit down, let's talk.' He says, 'Now we understand. Now we're speaking Panther to Panther.'" Goodman, "Rabbi Kahane says," 32. "*Playboy* Interview," *Playboy*, 74.

121   For an interesting analysis of the *Playboy* interview and what it reveals about Kahane's mission and interpretation of his own movement, see Magid, *Meir Kahane*, "Liberalism. Meir Kahane's American Pedigree: Radicalism and Liberalism in 1960s American Jewry."

122   Unknown source clipping, January 12, 1970, Records of the Jewish Defense League, I-374, box 1, folder 4, American Jewish Historical Society, New York and Boston.

Conclusion

1   Jen Graves, "What Kind of Men Are These? The Straight Drag of Donald Trump, and the Jewish Masculinity of Bernie Sanders," *The Stranger*, accessed September 18, 2018, www.thestranger.com/slog/2016/03/17/23739302/what-kind-of-men-are-donald-trump-and-bernie-sanders.

2   He defined the Bernie Bro as "male . . . white; well-educated; middle-class (or, delicately, 'upper middle-class'); and aware of NPR podcasts and jangly bearded bands." Meyer Robinson, "Here Comes the Bernie-bro," *The Atlantic*, accessed September 18, 2017, www.theatlantic.com/politics/archive/2015/10/here-comes-the-berniebro-bernie-sanders/411070/.

3   Tim Murphy, "The Time Gloria Steinem Made Bernie Sanders an 'Honorary Woman,'" *Mother Jones*, September 20, 2017, www

.motherjones.com/politics/2016/01/time-bernie-sanders-became
-honorary-woman/.

4   Tita Smith, "Hotter Than Trudeau! Ukrainian president's defiant
heroics and combat gear photos defending Kyiv turn him into an
unlikely sex symbol," last modified February 27, 2022, www.dailymail
.co.uk/news/article-10556123/Fans-swoon-Ukraine-President
-Volodymyr-Zelenskyy-fights-Russian-invasion.html.

5   For a more thorough examination of the response to Zelenskyy's
Jewish masculinity, see Miriam Eve Mora, "'Standing Up to Russian
Aggression Really Brings Out His Eyes': Zelenskyy Thirst-Trapping,"
Journal of Feminist Studies in Religion: Blog (April 2022), www.fsrinc
.org/standing-up-to-russian-aggression-really-brings-out-his-eyes
-zelenskyy-thirst-trapping/.

Bibliography

Almagor, Laura. *Beyond Zion: The Jewish Territorialist Movement*. New York: Oxford University Press, 2022.

Almog, Oz. *The Sabra: The Creation of the New Jew*. Berkeley: University of California Press, 2000.

Anderson, Susan C. "Otto Weininger's Masculine Utopia." *German Studies Review* 19, no. 3 (October 1996): 433–53.

Antler, Joyce, ed. *Jewish Radical Feminism: Voices from the Women's Liberation Movement*. New York: New York University Press, 2018.

———. *Talking Back: Representations of Jewish Women in American Culture*. Hanover, NH: University of New England Press, 1997.

Aptheker, Bettina. *Intimate Politics*. Emeryville, CA: Seal Press, 2006.

Ariel, Yaakov. *Evangelizing the Chosen People: Missions to the Jews in America, 1880–2000*. Chapel Hill: University of North Carolina Press, 2000.

Arkush, Allan. "Review: *Tough Jews: Political Fantasies and the Moral Dilemma of American Jewry* by Paul Breines." *Modern Judaism* 12 (1992): 219–22.

Aschheim, Steven E. *Brothers and Strangers: The East European Jew in German and German Jewish Consciousness, 1800–1923*. Madison: University of Wisconsin Press, 1982.

Avineri, Shlomo. *The Making of Modern Zionism: The Intellectual Origins of the Jewish State*. New York: Basic Books, 1981.

Baader, Benjamin Maria, Sharon Gillerman, and Paul Lerner, eds. *Jewish Masculinities: German Jews, Gender, and History*. Bloomington: Indiana University Press, 2012.

Baker, Cynthia. *Jew*. New Brunswick, NJ: Rutgers University Press, 2017. eBook.

Barnavi, Elie, ed. *A Historical Atlas of the Jewish People: From the Time of the Patriarchs to the Present*. New York: Schocken Books, 1992.

Barnouw, Dagmar. *Germany 1945: Views of War and Violence*. Bloomington: Indiana University Press, 1996.

Baskin, Judith R., ed. *Jewish Women in Historical Perspective*. Detroit: Wayne State University Press, 1998.

———. "Review: *Unheroic Conduct: The Rise of Heterosexuality and the Invention of the Jewish Man* by Daniel Boyarin." *Criticism* 41, no. 1 (1999): 124–28.

Baum, Charlotte, Paula Hyman, and Sonya Michel. *The Jewish Woman in America*. New York: Dial Press, 1976.

Baumel, Judith Tydor. *The "Bergson Boys" and the Origins of Contemporary Zionist Militancy*. Syracuse, NY: Syracuse University Press, 2005.

Beck, Evelyn Torton. "The Politics of Jewish Invisibility." *NWSA Journal* 1 (1988): 93–102.

Bederman, Gail. *Manliness and Civilization: A Cultural History of Gender and Race in the United States, 1880–1917*. Chicago: University of Chicago Press, 2008.

Bell, Daniel. *The End of Ideology: On the Exhaustion of Political Ideas in the Fifties*. Cambridge, MA: Harvard University Press: 2001.

Bendersky, Joseph W. *The "Jewish Threat": Anti-Semitic Politics of the U.S. Army*. New York: Basic Books, 2000.

Ben-Naeh, Yaron. "Honor and Its Meaning among Ottoman Jews." *Jewish Social Studies* 11, no. 2 (Winter 2005): 19–50.

Bergoffen, Wendy H. "Guardians, Millionaires, and Fearless Fighters: Transforming Jewish Gangsters into a Usable Past." *Shofar: An Interdisciplinary Journal of Jewish Studies* 25, no. 3 (Spring 2007): 91–110.

Berkowitz, Michael. *Western Jewry and the Zionist Project, 1914–1933*. New York: Cambridge University Press, 1997.

———. *Zionist Culture and West European Jewry before the First World War*. New York: Cambridge University Press, 1993.

Berman, Paul. *A Tale of Two Utopias: The Political Journey of the Generation of 1968*. New York: W. W. Norton, 1996.

Bernheimer, Charles Seligman. *The Russian Jew in the United States: Studies of Social Conditions in New York, Philadelphia, and Chicago, with a Description of Rural Settlements*. Philadelphia: John C. Winston, 1905.

Bernstein, Deborah, and Hannah Ashley. "The Soul of a New Yishuv: Pioneers and Homemakers; Jewish Women in Pre-State Israel." *Bridges* 5 (1995): 94–100.

Biale, David. *Eros and the Jews: From Biblical Israel to Contemporary America*. Berkeley: University of California Press, 1997.

———. *Not in the Heavens: The Tradition of Jewish Secular Thought*. Princeton, NJ: Princeton University Press, 2015.

Birnbaum, Ervin. *In the Shadow of the Struggle*. Jerusalem: Gefen Publishing House, 1990.

Borenstein, Miriam Eve. "Heroes, Victims, and Villains: Character Inversion in Holocaust Cinema." Master's thesis, West Chester University of Pennsylvania, 2009.

Boyarin, Daniel. *Unheroic Conduct: The Rise of Heterosexuality and the Invention of the Jewish Man*. Berkeley: University of California Press, 1997.

———. "What Does a Jew Want?; or, The Political Meaning of the Phallus." *Discourse* 19, no. 2 (Winter 1997): 21–52.

Boyarin, Daniel, coedited with Jonathan Boyarin. *Jews and Other Differences: The New Jewish Cultural Studies*. Minneapolis: University of Minnesota Press, 1997.

Boyarin, Daniel, coedited with Daniel Itzkovitz and Ann Pellegrini. *Queer Theory and the Jewish Question*. New York: Columbia University Press, 2003.

Boyd, Stephen B., W. Merle Longwood, and Mark W. Muesse, eds. *Redeeming Men: Religion and Masculinities*. Louisville, KY: Westminster John Knox Press, 1996.

Brandeis, Louis Dembitz. *Brandeis on Zionism: A Collection of Addresses and Statements*. Union, NJ: Law Book Exchange, 1999.

Breines, Paul. "An Assimilated Jew Speaks: Notes on 'Jews without Memory.'" *American Literary History* 13 (2001): 530–39.

———. "Germans, Journals and Jews/Madison, Men, Marxism and Mosse: A Tale of Jewish-Leftist Identity Confusion in America." *New German Critique* 20 (1980): 81–103.

———. *Tough Jews: Political Fantasies and the Moral Dilemma of American Jewry*. New York: Basic Books, 1990.

Brenner, David A. *Marketing Identities: The Invention of Jewish Ethnicity in Ost und West*. Detroit: Wayne State University Press, 1998.

Brenner, Michael, and Gideon Reuveni. *Emancipation through Muscles: Jews and Sports in Europe*. Lincoln: University of Nebraska Press, 2006.

Brewer, Susan A. *Why America Fights: Patriotism and War Propaganda from the Philippines to Iraq*. New York: Oxford University Press, 2009.

Bristow, Edward J. *Prostitution and Prejudice: The Jewish Fight against White Slavery, 1870–1939*. New York: Schocken Books, 1982.

Brod, Harry. *The Making of Masculinities: The New Men's Studies*. Boston: Allen and Unwin, 1987.

Brod, Harry, ed. *A Mensch among Men: Explorations in Jewish Masculinity*. Freedom, CA: Crossing Press, 1988.

Brod, Harry, coedited with Shawn Israel Zevit. *Brother Keepers: New Perspectives on Jewish Masculinity*. Harriman, TN: Men's Studies Press, 2010.

Brodkin, Karen. *How Jews Became White Folks and What That Says about Race in America*. New Brunswick, NJ: Rutgers University Press, 2002.

Brown, Susan K., and Frank D. Bean. "Assimilation Models, Old and New: Explaining a Long-Term Process." Migration Policy Institute. Accessed September 22, 2018. www.migrationpolicy.org/article/assimilation-models -old-and-new-explaining-long-term-process.

Browning, Christopher. *Ordinary Men: Reserve Police Battalion 101 and the Final Solution in Poland*. New York: Harper Perennial, 1992.

——. *Origins of the Final Solution: The Evolution of Nazi Jewish Policy, September 1939–1942*. Lincoln: University of Nebraska Press, 2004.

Bruscino, Thomas. *A Nation Forged in War: How World War II Taught Americans to Get Along*. Knoxville: University of Tennessee Press, 2010.

Burgin, Say. "Understanding Antiwar Activism as a Gendering Activity: A Look at the U.S.'s Anti-Vietnam War Movement." *Journal of International Women's Studies* 13, no. 6 (2012): 18–31.

Burleigh, Michael, and Wolfgang Wippermann. *The Racial State: Germany, 1933–45*. New York: Cambridge University Press, 1991.

Butler, Judith. "Performative Acts and Gender Constitution: An Essay in Phenomenology and Feminist Theory." In *Performing Feminisms: Feminist Critical Theory and Theatre*, edited by Sue-Ellen Case. Baltimore: Johns Hopkins University Press, 1990.

Calhoun, Ricky-Dale. "Arming David: The Haganah's Illegal Arms Procurement Network in the United States, 1945–49." *Journal of Palestine Studies* 36, no. 4 (Summer 2007): 22–32.

Carenen, Caitlin. "Complicating the Zionist Narrative in America: Jacob Schiff and the Struggle over Relief Aid in World War I." *American Jewish History* 101, no. 4 (October 2017): 441–63.

Carey, Elaine, and Alfred J. Andrea, eds. *Protests in the Streets: 1968 Across the Globe*. Indianapolis: Hackett Publishing, 2016.

Carey, Maddy. *Jewish Masculinity in the Holocaust: Between Destruction and Construction*. London: Bloomsbury Publishing, 2017.

Carroll, Bret, ed. *American Masculinities: A Historical Encyclopedia*. Thousand Oaks, CA: SAGE Publications, 2003.

Carver, Terrell. "Men and Masculinities in International Relations Research." *Brown Journal of World Affairs* 21, no. 1 (Fall 2014): 113–26.

Chambers, John Whiteclay, ed. *The Oxford Companion to American Military History*. New York: Oxford University Press, 1999.

Cohen, Naomi Wiener. *The Americanization of Zionism, 1897–1948*. Lebanon, NH: Brandies University Press, 2003.

———. "The Reaction of Reform Judaism in America to Political Zionism (1897–1922)." *Publications of the American Jewish Historical Society* 40, no. 4 (June 1951): 361–94.

Cohen, Rich. *Tough Jews: Fathers, Sons, and Gangster Dreams*. New York: Simon and Schuster, 1998.

Connell, R. W. *Masculinities*. 2nd ed. Berkeley: University of California Press, 2005.

Cooperman, Jessica. "'A Little Army Discipline Would Improve the Whole House of Israel': The Jewish Welfare Board, State Power, and the Shaping of Jewish Identity in World War I America." PhD diss. New York University, 2010.

Crim, Brian E. *Antisemitism in the German Military Community and the Jewish Response, 1914–1938*. Lanham, MD: Lexington Books, 2014.

Davidson, Gabriel. *Our Jewish Farmers: The Story of the Jewish Agricultural Society*. New York: L. B. Fischer Publishing, 1943.

Dawidowicz, Lucy. "American Public Opinion." *American Jewish Yearbook* 69 (1968): 198–229.

Dekel, Mikhal. *The Universal Jew: Masculinity, Modernity, and the Zionist Moment*. Evanston, IL: Northwestern University Press, 2010.

DellaPergola, Sergio. "Demography in Israeli Palestine: Trends, Prospects, Policy Implications." Paper Presented at IUSSP General Conference. Salvador, Brazil, August 2001.

Demetriou, Demetrakis Z. "Connell's Concept of Hegemonic Masculinity: A Critique." *Theory and Society* 30, no. 3 (June 2001): 337–61.

Dershowitz, Alan M. *The Vanishing American Jew: In Search of Jewish Identity for the Next Century*. Boston: Little, Brown, 1997.

Diner, Hasia. *Her Works Praise Her: A History of Jewish Women in America from Colonial Times to the Present*. New York: Basic Books, 2002.

———. *Roads Taken: The Great Jewish Migrations to the New World and the Peddlers Who Forged the Way*. New Haven, CT: Yale University Press, 2015.

———. *We Remember with Reverence and Love: American Jews and the Myth of Silence after the Holocaust*. New York: New York University Press, 2009.

Diner, Hasia, ed. *Doing Business in America: A Jewish History*. West Lafayette, IN: Purdue University Press, 2018.

Dinnerstein, Leonard. *Antisemitism in America*. New York: Oxford University Press, 1994.

Dosh. *To Israel, With Love*. New York: Thomas Yoseloff, 1960.

Dworkin, Andrea. "The Sexual Mythology of Anti-Semitism." In *A Mensch among Men: Explorations in Jewish Masculinity*, edited by Harry Brod. Freedom, CA: Crossing Press, 1988.

Dyer, Thomas G. *Theodore Roosevelt and the Idea of Race*. Baton Rouge: Louisiana State University Press, 1980.

Eastwood, Carolyn, and Beatrice Michaels Shapiro. *Chicago's Jewish Street Peddlers*. Chicago: Chicago Jewish Historical Society, 1991.

Eidelman, Jay M., ed. *Ours to Fight For: American Jewish Voices from the Second World War*. New York: Museum of Jewish Heritage, 2003.

Eilberg-Schwartz, Howard, ed. *The People of the Body: Jews and Judaism from an Embodied Perspective*. New York: State University of New York Press, 1992.

Endelman, Todd M. *Leaving the Jewish Fold: Conversion and Radical Assimilation in Modern Jewish History*. Princeton, NJ: Princeton University Press, 2015.

Erens, Patricia. "Gangsters, Vampires, and J.A.P.'s: The Jew Surfaces in American Movies." *Journal of Popular Film* 4, no. 3 (1975): 208–22.

Evans, Sara. *Personal Politics: The Roots of Women's Liberation in the Civil Rights Movement and the New Left*. New York: Vintage Books, 1908.

Farber, David. *Chicago '68*. Chicago: University of Chicago Press, 1988.

Fast, Howard. *My Glorious Brothers*. Naperville, IL: Sourcebooks, 2011.

Fehrenbach, Heide, and Davide Rodogno, eds. *Humanitarian Photography: A History*. New York: Cambridge University Press, 2015.

Ferris, Marcie Cohen. "'God First, You Second, Me Third': An Exploration of 'Quiet Jewishness' at Camp Wah-Kon-Dah." *Southern Cultures* 8, no. 1 (Spring 2012): 58–70.

Feuer, Lewis S. *The Conflict of Generations: The Character and Significance of Student Movements*. New York: Basic Books, 1969.

Fischbach, Michael R. *Black Power and Palestine: Transnational Countries of Color*. Stanford, CA: Stanford University Press, 2018.

Fishman, Sylvia Barack. *A Breath of Life: Feminism in the American Jewish Community*. Brandeis Series in American Jewish History, Culture, and Life. Waltham, MA: Brandeis University Press, 1995.

Ford, Nancy Gentile. *Americans All!: Foreign-Born Soldiers in World War I*. College Station: Texas A&M University Press, 2001.

Foxman, Abraham. *Jews and Money: The Story of a Stereotype*. New York: Palgrave, 2010.

Frankel, Jonathan, ed. *Jews and Gender: The Challenge to Hierarchy*. New York: Oxford University Press, 2000.

Freulich, Roman. *Soldiers in Judea: Stories and Vignettes of the Jewish Legion*. New York: Herzl Press, 1964.

Fried, Albert. *The Rise and Fall of the Jewish Gangster in America*. New York: Columbia University, 1993.

Friedan, Betty. *The Feminine Mystique*. New York: W. W. Norton, 2010.

Friedlander, Saul. "Political Transformations during the War and Their Effect on the Jewish Question." In *Hostages of Modernization: Germany, Great Britain, France*, edited by Herbert Arthur Strauss, 150–64. New York: Walter de Gruyter, 1992.

Friedman, Isaiah. *The Question of Palestine: British-Jewish-Arab Relations, 1914–1918*. New Brunswick, NJ: Transaction Publishers, 1992.

Friedman, Jonathan C. *The Literary, Cultural, and Historical Significance of the 1937 Biblical Stage Play* The Eternal Road. Lewiston, NY: E. Mellen Press, 2004.

———. *Rainbow Jews: Jewish and Gay Identity in the Performing Arts*. Lanham, MD: Lexington Books, 2007.

———. *Speaking the Unspeakable: Essays on Sexuality, Gender, and Holocaust Survivor Memory*. Boston: University Press of America, 2003.

Friesel, Evyatar. "American Zionism and American Jewry: An Ideological and Communal Encounter." *American Jewish Archives* 40, no. 1 (1988): 5–23.

Fuchs, Esther, ed. *Israeli Women's Studies: A Reader*. New Brunswick, NJ: Rutgers University Press, 2005.

Fussell, Paul. *Wartime: Understanding and Behavior in the Second World War*. New York: Oxford University Press, 1989.

Gage, Nicholas. *The Mafia Is Not an Equal Opportunity Employer*. New York: McGraw-Hill, 1971.

Gilman, Sander. *FAT BOYS: A Slim Book*. Lincoln: University of Nebraska, 2004.

———. *Freud, Race, and Gender*. Princeton, NJ: Princeton University Press, 1993.

———. *Jewish Frontiers: Essays on Bodies, Histories, and Identities*. New York: Palgrave Macmillan, 2003.

———. *Jewish Self-Hatred: Anti-Semitism and the Hidden Language of the Jews*. Baltimore: Johns Hopkins University Press, 1986.

———. *The Jew's Body*. New York: Routledge, 1991.

———. *Making the Body Beautiful: A Cultural History of Aesthetic Surgery*. Princeton, NJ: Princeton University Press, 1999.

———. *Smart Jews: The Construction of the Image of Jewish Superior Intelligence*. Lincoln: University of Nebraska Press, 1996.

Ginio, Eyal, and Elie Podeh, eds. *The Ottoman Middle East: Studies in Honor of Amnon Cohen*. Leiden, The Netherlands: Brill, 2014.

Ginsburg, Faye, and Anna Lowenhaupt Tsing, eds. *Uncertain Terms: Negotiating Gender in American Culture*. Boston: Beacon, 1990.

Gitlin, Todd. *The Sixties: Years of Hope, Days of Rage*. New York: Bantam Books, 1987.

Glenn, Susan A. *Daughters of the Shtetl: Life and Labor in the Immigrant Generation*. Ithaca, NY: Cornell University Press, 1990.

———. "The Vogue of Jewish Self-Hatred in Post–World War II America." *Jewish Social Studies* 12 (2006): 95–136.

Gold, Steven J. "'The Jazz Singer' to 'What a Country!' a Comparison of Jewish Migration to the United States, 1880–1930 and 1965–1998." *Journal of American Ethnic History* 18, no. 3, The Classical and Contemporary Mass Migration Periods: Similarities and Differences (Spring 1999): 114–41.

Goldenberg, Myrna, and Amy H. Shapiro, eds. *Different Horrors, Same Hell: Gender and the Holocaust*. Seattle: University of Washington Press, 2013.

Goldhagen, Daniel Jonah. *Hitler's Willing Executioners: Ordinary Germans and the Holocaust*. New York: Vintage Books, 1996.

Goldstein, Eric L. *The Price of Whiteness: Jews, Race, and American Identity*. Princeton, NJ: Princeton University Press, 2006.

Goren, Arthur A. *New York Jews and the Quest for Community: The Kehillah Experiment, 1908–1922*. New York: Columbia University Press, 1970.

———. *The Politics and Public Culture of American Jews*. Bloomington: Indiana University Press, 1999.

Gordan, Rachel. "Post-WWII American Judaism: How Judaism Became an American Religion." PhD diss., Harvard University, 2011.

Gotthelf, Yehuda, ed. *Youth Today: A Collection of Articles and Essays*. Tel-Aviv: World Labour Zionist Movement, 1970.

Grayzel, Solomon. *A History of the Jews: From the Babylonian Exile to the Present, 5728–1968*. New York: Meridian, 1984.

Greenberg, Steven. *Wrestling with God and Men: Homosexuality in the Jewish Tradition*. Madison: University of Wisconsin Press, 2004.

Greene, Evarts Boutell, and Virginia Draper Harrington. *American Population before the Federal Census of 1790*. New York: Columbia University Press, 1932.

Greenfield, Murray S., and Joseph M. Hochstein. *The Jews' Secret Fleet: The Untold Story of North American Volunteers Who Smashed the British Blockade*. Jerusalem: Gefen Publishing House, 1987.

Greenspoon, Leonard, ed. *Jews in the Gym: Judaism, Sports, and Athletics*. East Lafayette, IN: Purdue University Press, 2012.

Grinberg, Ronnie A. "Neither 'Sissy' Boy nor Patrician Man: New York Intellectuals and the Construction of American Jewish Masculinity." *American Jewish History* 98, no. 3 (July 2014): 127–51.

Grossmann, Atina. "Victims, Villains, and Survivors: Gendered Perceptions and Self-Perceptions of Jewish Displaced Persons in Occupied Postwar Germany." *Journal of the History of Sexuality* 11 (2002): 291–318.

Grover, Warren. *Nazis in Newark*. Piscataway Township, NJ: Transaction Publishers, 2003.

Gurock, Jeffrey, ed. *America, American Jews, and the Holocaust: American Jewish History*. New York: Routledge, 1998.

——. *Jews in Gotham: New York Jews in a Changing City, 1920–2010*. New York: New York University Press, 2013.

Haiman, Miecislaus. "The Polish American Contribution to World War II." *Polish American Studies* 3, no. 1/2 (January–June 1946): 35–37.

Halberstam, David. *The Best and the Brightest*. New York: Random House, 1972.

Halberstam, Jack. *Female Masculinity*. Durham, NC: Duke University Press, 1998.

Halpern, Ben. "The Americanization of Zionism, 1880–1930." *American Jewish History* 69, no. 1 (September 1979): 15–33.

Halkin, Hillel. *Jabotinsky: A Life*. New Haven, CT: Yale University Press, 2014.

Harrowitz, Nancy A., and Barbara Hyams, eds. *Jews and Gender: Responses to Otto Weininger*. Philadelphia: Temple University Press, 1995.

Haywood, Chris, Thomas Johansson, Nils Hammarén, Marcus Herz, and Andreas Ottemo. *The Conundrum of Masculinity: Hegemony, Homosociality, Homophobia, and Heteronormativity*. New York: Routledge, 2018.

Hecht, Ben. *A Child of the Century*. New York: Simon and Schuster, 1954.

Heller, Max. "Moral Courage: The Test of American Manhood: Sermon." Preached at the Jewish Union Service, Hill Auditorium, University of Michigan, Ann Arbor, February 21, 1915.

Henry, Patrick, ed. *Jewish Resistance against the Nazis*. Washington, DC: Catholic University of America Press, 2014.

Herscher, Uri D. *Jewish Agricultural Utopias in America, 1880–1910*. Detroit: Wayne State University Press, 1981.

Hertzberg, Arthur. *The Zionist Idea: A Historical Analysis and Reader*. New York: Meridian Books, 1959.

Herzl, Theodor. *The Complete Diaries of Theodor Herzl, Volume 1*, edited by Raphael Patai. New York: Herzl Press, 1960.

Herzog, Dagmar, ed. *Sexuality and German Fascism*. New York: Berghahn Books, 2005.

Higham, John. *Strangers in the Land: Patterns of American Nativism, 1860–1925*. New Brunswick, NJ: Rutgers University Press, 1955.

Hoffman, Adina. *Ben Hecht: Fighting Words, Moving Pictures*. New Haven, CT: Yale University Press, 2019.

Hollander, Philip. "Contested Zionist Masculinity and the Redemption of the Schlemiel in Levi Aryeh Arieli's 'Allah Karim!'" *Israel Studies* 17 (2012): 92–118.

———. *From Schlemiel to Sabra: Zionist Masculinity and Palestinian Hebrew Literature*. Bloomington: Indiana University Press, 2019.

Holtzman, Avner. "'They Are Different People': Holocaust Survivors as Reflected in the Fiction of the Generation of 1948." *Yad Vashem Studies* 30 (2002): 337–68.

Horlacher, Stefan. *Configuring Masculinity in Theory and Literary Practice*. Boston: Brill Rodopi, 2015.

Hughes, Thomas. *Tom Brown at Oxford: A Sequel to School Days at Rugby, Volume 2*. Boston: Ticknor and Fields, 1868.

Hyman, Abraham S. *The Undefeated*. Jerusalem: Gefen House, 1993.

Hyman, Paula. *Gender and Assimilation in Modern Jewish History: The Roles and Representation of Women*. Seattle: University of Washington Press, 1995.

———. "Gender and the Shaping of Modern Jewish Identities." *Jewish Social Studies* 8 (2002): 153–61.

Ignatiev, Noel. *How the Irish Became White*. New York: Routledge Press, 1995.

Imhoff, Sarah. "Making Jewish Gender: Religion, Race, Sexuality, and American Jews, 1910–1924." PhD diss., University of Chicago, 2010.

———. *Masculinity and the Making of American Judaism*. Bloomington: Indiana University Press, 2017.

Jackson, Ronald L., and Murali Balaji, eds. *Global Masculinities and Manhood*. Urbana: University of Illinois, 2011.

Jacobson, Matthew Frye. *Roots Too: White Ethnic Revival in Post–Civil Rights America*. Cambridge, MA: Harvard University Press, 2006.

———. *Whiteness of a Different Color*. Cambridge, MA: Harvard University Press, 1998.

Jagose, Annamarie. *Queer Theory: An Introduction*. New York: New York University Press, 1997.

Janick, Allan. "Viennese Culture and the Jewish Self-Hatred Hypothesis: A Critique." In *Jews, Assimilation, and Culture in Vienna*, edited by Ivar Oxaal et al., 75–88. New York: Routledge, 1987.

Jansz, Jeroen. "Masculine Identity and Restrictive Emotionality." In *Gender and Emotion: Social Psychological Perspectives*, ed. Agneta H. Fischer, 166–89. New York: Cambridge University Press, 2000.

Jeffords, Susan. *The Remasculinization of America: Gender and the Vietnam War*. Bloomington: Indiana University Press, 1989.

Joselit, Jenna Weissman. *Our Gang: Jewish Crime and the New York Jewish Community, 1900–1940*. Bloomington: Indiana University Press, 1983.

Joskowicz, Ari, and Ethan B. Katz, eds. *Secularism in Question: Jews and Judaism in Modern Times*. Philadelphia: University of Pennsylvania Press, 2015.

Kahane, Meir. *The Jewish Stake in Vietnam*. New York: Crossroads Publishing, 1967.

———. *Never Again! A Program for Survival*. New York: Pyramid Books, 1972.

Kalmar, Ivan. The *Trotskys, Freuds, and Woody Allens: Portrait of a Culture*. Toronto: Penguin Books, 1994.

Kaplan, Amy. *Our American Israel: The Story of an Entangled Alliance*. Cambridge, MA: Harvard University Press, 2018.

———. "Romancing the Empire: The Embodiment of American Masculinity in the Popular Historical Novel of the 1890s." *American Literary History* 2, no. 4 (Winter 1990): 659–90.

Kaplan, Eran. "A Rebel with a Cause: Hillel Kook, Begin, and Jabotinsky's Ideological Legacy." *Israel Studies* 10, no. 3 (Fall 2005): 87–103.

Kaplan, Marion A. *Between Dignity and Despair: Jewish Life in Nazi Germany*. New York: Oxford University Press, 1998.

———. *The Making of the Jewish Middle Class: Women, Family, and Identity in Imperial Germany*. New York: Oxford University Press, 1991.

Kaplan, Marion A., ed. *Jewish Daily Life in Germany, 1618–1945*. New York: Oxford University Press, 2005.

Kaplan, Marion A., coedited with Deborah Dash Moore. *Gender and Jewish History*. Bloomington: Indiana University Press, 2011.

Katz, David S. "Shylock's Gender: Jewish Male Menstruation in Early Modern England." *Review of English Studies* 50, no. 200 (November 1999): 440–62.

Katz, Emily Alice. *Bringing Zion Home: Israel in American Jewish Culture, 1948–1967*. New York: State University of New York Press, 2015.

Kavieff, Paul R. *The Purple Gang: Organized Crime in Detroit, 1910–1945*. New York: Barricade Books, 2000.

Kaye/Kantrowitz, Melanie. *The Colors of Jews: Racial Politics and Radical Diasporism*. Bloomington: Indiana University Press, 2007.

Keene, Jennifer D. *World War I*. Westport, CT: Greenwood Press, 1962.

Kellerman, Henry. *Greedy, Cowardly, and Weak: Hollywood's Jewish Stereotypes*. Fort Lee, NJ: Barricade Books, 2009.

Kennedy, Ruby Jo Reeves. "Single or Triple Melting-Pot? Intermarriage Trends in New Haven, 1870–1940." *American Journal of Sociology* 49, no. 4 (January 1944): 331–39.

Kennett, Lee. *G.I.: The American Soldier in World War II*. New York: Charles Scribner's Sons, 1987.

Kimmel, Michael S. *Angry White Men: American Masculinity at the End of an Era*. New York: Nation Books, 2015.

———. *Manhood in America: A Cultural History*. New York: Oxford University Press, 2012.

———. "Masculinity as Homophobia: Fear, Shame, and Silence in the Construction of Gender Identity." In *Race, Class, and Gender in the United States: An Integrated Study*, edited by Paula S. Rothenberg, 81–92. New York: Worth Publishers, 2004.

Kimmel, Michael S., ed. *The Politics of Manhood: Profeminist Men Respond to the Mythopoetic Men's Movement (and the Mythopoetic Leaders Answer)*. Philadelphia: Temple University Press, 1995.

Kitaeff, Jack. *Jews in Blue: The Jewish American Experience in Law Enforcement*. Youngstown, NY: Cambria Press, 2006.

Klagsbrun, Francine. *Lioness: Golda Meir and the Nation of Israel*. New York: Schocken Books, 2017.

Klapper, Melissa R. *Jewish Girls Coming of Age in America, 1860–1920*. New York: New York University Press, 2005.

Kneeland, George Jackson. *Commercialized Prostitution in New York City*. New York: Twentieth Century, 1913.

Kohl, Christiane. *The Maiden and the Jew: The Story of a Fatal Friendship in Nazi Germany*. Hanover, NH: Steerforth Press, 1997.

Kolsky, Thomas. *Jews against Zionism: The American Council for Judaism, 1942–1948*. Philadelphia: Temple University Press, 1990.

Koppes, Clayton R., and Gregory D. Black. "What to Show the World: The Office of War Information and Hollywood, 1942–1945." *Journal of American History* 64, no. 1 (June 1977): 87–105.

Kornberg, Jacques. *Theodor Herzl: From Assimilation to Zionism*. Bloomington: Indiana University Press, 1993.

———. "Theodor Herzl: Zionism as Personal Liberation." In *Theodor Herzl: From Europe to Zion*, edited by Mark H. Gelber and Vivian Liska, 43–56. Tübingen, Germany: Max Niemeyer, 2007.

Kość, Grzegorz, Clara Juncker, Sharon Monteith, and Britta Waldschmidt-Nelson, eds. *The Transatlantic Sixties: Europe and the United States in the Counterculture Decade*. Bielefeld, Germany: Transcript, 2013.

Kotler, Yair. *Heil Kahane*. New York: Adama Books, 1986.

Kranson, Rachel. *Ambivalent Embrace: Jewish Upward Mobility in Postwar America*. Chapel Hill: University of North Carolina Press, 2017. www.jstor.org .proxy.lib.wayne.edu/stable/10.5149/9781469635446_kranson.

Krasner, Jonathan B. *The Benderly Boys and American Jewish Education*. Waltham, MA: Brandeis University Press, 2011.

———. "'New Jews' in an Old-New Land: Images in American Jewish Textbooks Prior to 1948." *Journal of Jewish Education* 69, no. 2, (2003): 7–22.

Kris, Ernst. "The Covenant of the Gangsters." *Journal of Criminal Psychopathology* 4, no. 3 (1943): 445–58.

Kurlansky, Mark. *1968: The Year That Rocked the World*. New York: Random House, 2004.

Lahav, Pnina. "The Chicago Conspiracy Trial as a Jewish Morality Tale." In *Lives in the Law*, edited by Austin Sarat, Lawrence Douglas, and Martha Merrill Umphrey, 21–54. Ann Arbor: University of Michigan Press, 2006.

———. "Theater in the Courtroom: The Chicago Conspiracy Trial." *Law and Literature* 16, no. 3 (2004): 381–474.

Lederhendler, Eli. *Jewish Responses to Modernity: New Voices in America and Eastern Europe*. New York: New York University Press, 1994.

Leff, Laurel. *Buried by the Times: The Holocaust and America's Most Important Newspaper*. New York: Cambridge University Press, 2005.

Lipstadt, Deborah E. *Holocaust: An American Understanding*. New Brunswick, NJ: Rutgers University Press, 2016.

Lorge, Michael M., and Gary P. Zola, eds. *A Place of Our Own: The Rise of Reform Jewish Camping*. Tuscaloosa: University of Alabama Press, 2006.

Macleod, David I. *Building Character in the American Boy: The Boy Scouts, YMCA, and Their Forerunners, 1870–1920*. Madison: University of Wisconsin Press, 1983.

Magnes, Judah Leon. *Dissenter in Zion: From the Writings of Judah L. Magnes*, edited by Arthur A. Goren. Cambridge, MA: Harvard University Press, 1982.

Malet, David. *Foreign Fighters: Transnational Identity in Civic Conflicts*. New York: Oxford University Press, 2013.

Marcus, Jacob Rader. *The American Jew, 1585–1990: A History*. Brooklyn: Carlson Publishing, 1995.

Markowitz, Sidney L. *What You Should Know about Jewish Religion, History, Ethics, and Culture*. New York: First Carol Publishing, 1992.

Mart, Michelle. *Eye on Israel: How America Came to View the Jewish State as an Ally*. Albany: State University of New York Press, 2006.

Martel, Elise. "From Mensch to Macho? The Social Construction of a Jewish Masculinity." *Men and Masculinities* 3, no. 4 (2001): 347–69.

May, Lary. *The Big Tomorrow: Hollywood and the Politics of the American Way*. Chicago: University of Chicago Press, 2000.

McAleer, Kevin. *Dueling: The Cult of Honor in Fin-de-Siècle Germany*. Princeton, NJ: Princeton University Press, 1994.

McCullough, David. *Mornings on Horseback: The Story of an Extraordinary Family, a Vanished Way of Life, and the Unique Child Who Became Theodore Roosevelt*. New York: Simon and Schuster, 2007.

McCune, Mary. "Social Workers in the Muskeljudentum: 'Hadassah Ladies,' 'Manly Men,' and the Significance of Gender in the American Zionist Movement, 1912–1928." *American Jewish History* 86, no. 2 (June 1998): 135–65.

Mearsheimer John J., and Stephen M. Walt. *The Israel Lobby and U.S. Foreign Policy*. New York: Farrar, Straus and Giroux, 2007.

Medoff, Rafael. *Militant Zionism in America: The Rise and Impact of the Jabotinsky Movement in the United States, 1926–1948*. Tuscaloosa: University of Alabama Press, 2002.

———. "Recent Trends in the Historiography of American Zionism." *American Jewish History* 86, no. 1 (March 1998): 117–34.

Medoff, Rafael, with Chaim I. Waxman. *The A to Z of Zionism*. Lanham, MD: Scarecrow Press, 2009.

Mell, Julie L. *The Myth of the Medieval Jewish Moneylender, Volumes I and II*. Durham, NC: Palgrave Macmillan, 2017.

Mendes, Phillip. "'We Are All German Jews': Exploring the Prominence of Jews in the New Left." *Melilah: Manchester Journal of Jewish Studies* 6 (2009): 22–38.

Mendes-Flohr, Paul, and Jehuda Reinharz. *The Jew in the Modern World: A Documentary History*. New York: Oxford University Press, 1980.

Merwin, Ted. *In Their Own Image: New York Jews in Jazz Age Popular Culture*. New Brunswick, NJ: Rutgers University Press, 2006.

Meyers, Diana T. *Victims' Stories and the Advancement of Human Rights*. New York: Oxford University Press, 2016.

Michael, Robert A. *The Holocaust: A Chronology and Documentary*. Lanham, MD: Jason Aronson Publishing, 1998.

Miedzian, Myriam. *Boys Will Be Boys: Breaking the Link between Masculinity and Violence*. New York: Lantern Books, 2002.

Mihailescu, Dana. "Jewish Men and the Early Twentieth-Century American Code of Masculinity through Ethnic Lenses." *Atenea* 28 (June 2008): 87–102.

Mintzer, Oscar A. *In Defense of the Survivors: The Letters and Documents of Oscar A. Mintzer, AJDC Legal Advisor, Germany, 1945–46*. Berkeley, CA: Judah Magnes Museum, 1999.

Moore, Deborah Dash. *At Home in America: Second Generation New York Jews*. New York: Columbia University Press, 1981.

———. *GI Jews: How World War II Changed a Generation*. Cambridge, MA: Harvard University Press, 2006.

Moore, Deborah Dash, ed. *American Jewish Identity Politics*. Ann Arbor: University of Michigan Press, 2008.

Moore, Deborah Dash, coauthored with Jeffrey S. Gurock, Annie Polland, Howard B. Rock, and Daniel Soyer. *Jewish New York: The Remarkable Story of a City and a People*. New York: New York University Press, 2017.

Morgan, Michael L. *Beyond Auschwitz: Post-Holocaust Jewish Thought in America*. New York: Oxford University Press, 2001.

Morin, Roc. "Fighting for Facial Scars in Germany's Secret Fencing Frats." Last modified March 19, 2015, www.vice.com/en_uk/article/av4bp4/frauleins-dig -them-0000573-v22n2.

Moscowitz, David. *A Culture of Tough Jews: Rhetorical Regeneration and the Politics of Identity*. New York: Peter Lang, 2015.

——. "Nice Jewish Boys: Trope, Identity, and Politics in the Rhetorical Representation of Contemporary Tough Jews." PhD diss., Indiana University, 2004.

Moss, Richard. *Creating the New Right Ethnic in 1970s America: The Intersection of Anger and Nostalgia*. Lanham, MD: Rowman and Littlefield, 2017.

Mosse, George L. *The Crisis of German Ideology: Intellectual Origins of the Third Reich*. New York: Universal Library, 1964.

——. *The Image of Man: The Creation of Modern Masculinity*. New York: Oxford University Press, 1996.

——. "Max Nordau, Liberalism, and the New Jew." *Journal of Contemporary History* 27 (1992): 565–81.

——. *Nationalism and Sexuality: Respectability and Abnormal Sexuality in Modern Europe*. New York: Howard Fertig, 1985.

Murray, Susan. "Ethnic Masculinity and Early Television's Vaudeo Star." *Cinema Journal* 42 (2002): 97–119.

Newark, Tim. *The Mafia at War: The Shocking True Story of America's Wartime Pact with Organized Crime*. New York: Skyhorse Publishing, 2012.

Nordau, Max. *Degeneration*. Translated by George Mosse. Lincoln: University of Nebraska Press, 1968.

Norwood, Stephen H. "'American Jewish Muscle': Forging a New Masculinity in the Streets and in the Ring, 1890–1940." *Modern Judaism* 29, no. 2 (May 2009): 167–93.

Novick, Peter. *The Holocaust in American Life*. Boston: Houghton Mifflin, 1999.

Nye, Robert A. *Masculinity and Male Codes of Honor in Modern France*. New York: Oxford University Press, 1993.

O'Brien, Matt. "The Important Difference between Assimilation and Integration." ImmigrationReform.com, accessed September 22, 2018. https://immigrationreform.com/2016/09/29/the-important-difference-between-assimilation-and-integration/.

Ogbar, Jeffrey O. G. *Black Power: Radical Politics and African American Identity*. Baltimore: Johns Hopkins University Press, 2019.

Øverland, Orm. *Immigrant Minds, American Identities: Making the United States Home, 1870–1930*. Urbana: University of Illinois Press, 2000.

Pain, Gill. *Literature of the 1940s: War, Postwar, and "Peace."* Edinburgh: Edinburgh University Press, 2013.

Paldiel, Mordecai. *Saving One's Own: Jewish Rescuers during the Holocaust*. Lincoln: University of Nebraska Press, 2017.

Parco, James E., and David A. Levy, eds. *Attitudes Aren't Free: Thinking Deeply about Diversity in the U.S. Armed Forces*. Maxwell Airforce Base, AL: Air University Press, 2010.

Peleg, Yaron. "Heroic Conduct: Homoeroticism and the Creation of Modern, Jewish Masculinities." *Jewish Social Studies* 13, no. 1 (Autumn 2006): 31–58.

Penkower, Monty Noam. "In Dramatic Dissent: The Bergson Boys." *American Jewish History* 70, no. 3 (March 1981): 281–309.

Penslar, Derek J. *Jews and the Military: A History*. Princeton, NJ: Princeton University Press, 2015.

Peskowitz, Miriam, and Laura Levitt, eds. *Judaism since Gender*. New York: Routledge, 1997.

Pinzer, Maimie. *The Maimie Papers*. Old Westbury, NY: Feminist Press, 1977.

Postal, Bernard. *Encyclopedia of Jews in Sports*. New York: Bloch Publishing, 1965.

Prell, Riv-Ellen. "The Begetting of American's Jews: Seeds of American Jewish Identity in the Representations of American Jewish Women." *Journal of Jewish Communal Service* 669 (1993): 4–23.

———. *Fighting to Become Americans: Assimilation and the Trouble between Jewish Women and Jewish Men*. Boston: Beacon Press, 1999.

———. *Women Remaking American Judaism*. Detroit: Wayne State University Press, 2007.

Presner, Todd Samuel. "'Clear Heads, Solid Stomachs, and Hard Muscles': Max Nordau and the Aesthetics of Jewish Regeneration." *Modernism/modernity* 10, no. 2 (April 2003): 269–96.

———. *Muscular Judaism: The Jewish Body and the Politics of Regeneration*. New York: Routledge Press, 2007.

Rabinowitz, Dorothy. "Are Jewish Students Different?" *Change* 3, no. 4 (Summer 1971): 47–50.

Raider, Mark A. *The Emergence of American Zionism*. New York: New York University Press, 1998.

Raider, Mark A., Jonathan D. Sarna, and Ronald W. Zweig, eds. *Abba Hillel Silver and American Zionism*. New York: Frank Cass Publishers, 1997.

Rausch, David A. *Friends, Colleagues, and Neighbors: Jewish Contributions to American History*. Grand Rapids, MI: Baker Books, 1996.

Rebhun, Uzi. "Jewish Identity in America: Structural Analyses of Attitudes and Behaviors." *Review of Religious Research* 46 (2004): 43–63.

Reeser, Todd W. *Masculinities in Theory: An Introduction*. Malden, MA: Wiley-Blackwell, 2010.

Reitter, Paul. "The Jewish Self-Hatred Octopus." *The German Quarterly* 82, no. 3, German-Jewish and Jewish-German Studies (Summer 2009): 356–72.

Ribak, Gil. "'Beaten to Death by Irish Murderers': The Death of Sadie Dellon (1918) and Jewish Images of the Irish." *Journal of American Ethnic History* 34, no. 4 (Summer 2013): 41–74.

———. "'The Jew Usually Left Those Crimes to Esau': The Jewish Responses to Accusations about Jewish Criminality in New York, 1908–1913." *AJS Review* 38, no. 1 (April 2014): 1–28.

Riess, Steven A., ed. *Sports and the American Jew*. Syracuse: Syracuse University Press, 1998.

Riis, Jacob August. *How the Other Half Lives: Studies among the Tenements of New York*. New York: Scribner's Sons, 1914.

Ritterband, Paul. "Counting the Jews of New York, 1900–1991: An Essay in Substance and Method." In *Papers in Jewish Demography 1997; Selected Proceedings of the Demographic: Sessions Held at the 12th World Congress of Jewish Studies, Jerusalem, 1997*, edited by Sergio Della Pergola and Judith Even, 199–228. Jerusalem: Hebrew University, 2001.

Roberts, Mary Louise. *What Soldiers Do: Sex and the American GI in World War II France*. Chicago: University of Chicago Press, 2013.

Robinson, Leonard G. *The Agricultural Activities of the Jews in America*. New York: American Jewish Committee, 1912.

Roby, Bryan K. *The Mizrahi Era of Rebellion: Israel's Forgotten Civil Rights Struggle, 1948–1966*. Syracuse, NY: Syracuse University Press, 2015.

Rockaway, Robert A. "American Jews and Crime: An Annotated Bibliography." *American Studies International* 31, no. 1 (February 2000): 26–41.

———. *But He Was Good to His Mother: The Lives and Crimes of Jewish Gangsters*. New York: Gefen Publishing House, 2000.

———. "Hoodlum Hero: The Jewish Gangster as Defender of His People, 1919–1949." *American Jewish History* 82, no. 1/4 (1994): 215–35.

———. "The Rise of the Jewish Gangster in America." *Journal of Ethnic Studies* 8, no. 2 (1980): 31–44.

Roediger, David R. *Working toward Whiteness: How America's Immigrants Became White: The Strange Journey from Ellis Island to the Suburbs*. New York: Basic Books, 2005.

Roosevelt, Theodore. *American Problems*. New York: Charles Scribner's Sons, 1926.

——. *An Autobiography*. New York: Charles Scribner's Sons, 1913.

——. *The Letters of Theodore Roosevelt*. Edited by Elting E. Morison, 8 vols. Cambridge, MA: Harvard University Press, 1951–54.

——. *Theodore Roosevelt: Letters and Speeches*. Edited by Louis Auchincloss. Cambridge, MA: Harvard University Press, 2004.

——. *Works: The Strenuous Life*. New York: Century Company, 1901.

Rosenberg, Warren. *Legacy of Rage: Jewish Masculinity, Violence, and Culture*. Amherst: University of Massachusetts Press, 2001.

Rosenfeld, Gavriel D. *Hi Hitler! How the Nazi Past Is Being Normalized in Contemporary Culture*. Cambridge: Cambridge University Press, 2015.

Rosenthal, Monroe. *Wars of the Jews: A Military History from Biblical to Modern Times*. New York: Hippocrene Books, 1990.

Roth, Philip. "The New Jewish Stereotypes." *American Judaism* 11, no. 2 (Winter 1961): 10–11, 49–51.

Rotundo, E. Anthony. *American Manhood: Transformations in Masculinity from the Revolution to the Modern Era*. New York: Basic Books, 1993.

——. *Growing (Up) at 37*. Lanham, MD: Rowman and Littlefield, 2014.

——. *We Are Everywhere*. New York: Harper and Row, 1976.

Ruspini, Elisabetta, ed. *Men and Masculinities around the World: Transforming Men's Practices*. New York: Palgrave Macmillan, 2011.

Sachar, Howard M. *A History of the Jews in America*. New York: Vintage Books, 1992.

Sanua, Marianne R. *Going Greek: Jewish College Fraternities in the United States, 1895–1945*. Detroit: Wayne State University Press, 2003.

——. "Jewish College Fraternities in the United States, 1895–1968: An Overview." *Journal of American Ethnic History* 19, no. 2 (2000): 3–42.

Sarna, Jonathan D., and Adam Mendelsohn, eds. *Jews and the Civil War: A Reader*. New York: New York University Press, 2010.

Sarna, Jonathan D., Ellen Smith, and Scott-Martin Kosofsky, eds., *The Jews of Boston*. New Haven, CT: Yale University Press, 1995.

Sasson-Levy, Orna. "Individual Bodies, Collective State Interests: The Case of Israeli Combat Soldiers." *Men and Masculinities* 10 (2007): 296–321.

Schapkow, Carsten. *Role Model and Countermodel: The Golden Age of Iberian Jewry and German Jewish Culture during the Era of Emancipation*. London: Lexington Books, 2016.

Schmookler, Andrew Bard. *Out of Weakness: Healing the Wounds That Drive Us to War*. New York: Bantam Books 1988.

Schoeps, Julius H. "Modern Heirs of the Maccabees: The Beginning of the Vienna Kadimah, 1882–1897." *LBIYB* 27 (1982): 155–70.

Searles, George J., ed. *Conversations with Philip Roth.* Jackson: University Press of Mississippi, 1992.

Segal, Lynne. "Gender, War, and Militarism: Making and Questioning the Links." *Feminist Review* 88 (2008): 21–35.

Segev, Tom. *1949: The First Israelis.* New York: Free Press, 1986.

Seitz, Don C. *Famous American Duels: With Some Account of the Causes That Led to Them.* New York: Thomas Y. Crowell, 1929.

Seltzer, Robert M., and Norman J. Cohen, eds. *The Americanization of the Jews.* New York: New York University Press, 1995.

Sengoopta, Chandak. *Otto Weininger: Sex, Science, and Self in Imperial Vienna.* Chicago: University of Chicago Press, 2000.

Shabbetai, K. *As Sheep to the Slaughter? The Myth of Jewish Cowardice.* New York: World Association of the Bergen-Belsen Survivors Association, 1963.

Shandler, Jeffrey. *While America Watches: Televising the Holocaust.* New York: Oxford University Press, 1999.

Silver, M. M. *Our Exodus: Leon Uris and the Americanization of Israel's Founding Story.* Detroit: Wayne State University Press, 2010.

Silver, Mike. *Stars in the Ring: Jewish Champions in the Golden Age of Boxing.* Guilford, CT: Lyons Press, 2016.

Simon, Rita James. "The American Jury: Instrument of Justice or of Prejudice and Conformity?" *Sociological Inquiry* 47, no. 3–4 (July 1977): 254–93.

Sion, Liora, and Eyal Ben-Ari. "Imagined Masculinity: Body, Sexuality, and Family among Israeli Military Reserves." *Symbolic Interaction* 32 (2009): 21–43.

Skrentny, John David. *The Minority Rights Revolution.* Cambridge, MA: Belknap Press of Harvard University Press, 2002.

Smith, Mitchell. *Baseballs, Basketballs, and Matzah Balls: What Sports Can Teach Us about the Jewish Holidays.* Bloomington, IN: Author House, 2009.

Staub, Michael E. *Torn at the Roots: The Crisis of Jewish Liberalism in Postwar America.* New York: Columbia University Press, 2002.

Stein, Leslie. *The Hope Fulfilled: The Rise of Modern Israel.* Westport, CT: Praeger Publishers, 2003.

Stein, Sarah Abrevaya. *Making Jews Modern: The Yiddish and Ladino Press in the Russian and Ottoman Empires.* Bloomington: Indiana University Press, 2003.

———. "Sander Smarts: Gilman's 'Smart Jews.'" *Jewish Social Studies* 4, no. 2 (Winter 1998): 180–87.

Steinberg, Stephen. *The Academic Melting Pot: Catholics and Jews in American Higher Education*. New York: McGraw-Hill, 1974.

Sterba, Christopher. *Good Americans: Italian and Jewish Immigrants during the First World War*. New York: Oxford University Press, 2003.

Stern, Eliyahu. *Jewish Materialism: The Intellectual Revolution of the 1870s*. New Haven, CT: Yale University Press, 2018.

Sussman, Herbert. *Masculine Identities: The History and Meanings of Manliness*. Santa Barbara, CA: Praeger, 2012.

Sykes, Christopher. *Orde Wingate: A Biography*. Cleveland: World Publishing, 1951.

Tasker, Yvonne. *Spectacular Bodies: Gender, Genre, and the Action Cinema*. New York: Routledge, 1993.

Taylor, Michael. *Contesting Constructed Indian-ness: The Intersection of the Frontier, Masculinity, and Whiteness in Native American Mascot Representations*. Lanham, MD: Lexington Books, 2013.

Thomas, Calvin, ed. *Straight with a Twist: Queer Theory and the Subject of Heterosexuality*. Urbana: University of Illinois Press, 2000.

Thomas, Pat. *Did It! From Yippie to Yuppie: Jerry Rubin, an American Revolutionary*. Seattle: Fantagraphics Books, 2017.

Tobin, Gary A., and Sharon L. Sassler. *Jewish Perceptions of Antisemitism*. Berlin: Springer Science Business Media, 1988.

Tucker, Spencer C., ed. *The Encyclopedia of the Arab-Israeli Conflict: A Political, Social, and Military History*. Santa Barbara, CA: ABC-CLIO, 2008.

Tulloch, Derek. *Wingate: In Peace and War*. London: Macdonald, 1972.

United States War Department. *Revised United States Army Regulations of 1861*. Washington, DC: Government Printing Office, 1863.

Uris, Leon. *Exodus*. New York: Bantam Books, 1983.

Urofsky, Melvin I. *American Zionism from Herzl to the Holocaust*. Lincoln: University of Nebraska Press, 1975.

———. *A Voice That Spoke for Justice: The Life and Times of Stephen S. Wise*. Albany: State University of New York Press, 1982.

Van Creveld, Martin. *The Sword and the Olive: A Critical History of the Israeli Defense Force*. New York: Perseus Books Group, 1998.

Von Braun, Christina. "Sexual Images in Racist Anti-Semitism" ("Sexualisierung: Der Körper des Juden als, Konversionssymptom"). Accessed August 8, 2018. www.christinavonbraun.de/_pdf/Sexual%20Images%20in%20Anti-semitism.pdf (now unavailable).

Warren, Mary Anne. *Gendercide: The Implications of Sex Selection*. Totowa, NJ: Rowman and Allenheld, 1985.

Warshow, Robert. "The Gangster as Tragic Hero." In *The Oxford Book of Essays*, edited by John Gross, 581–86. Oxford: Oxford University Press, 1998.

Watt, Martin. *The Jewish Legion and the First World War*. New York: Palgrave Macmillan, 2004.

Waxman, Chaim I. *America's Jews in Transition*. Philadelphia: Temple University Press, 1983.

Weininger, Otto. *Sex and Character: An Investigation of Fundamental Principles*. Translated by Ladislaus Löb. Bloomington: Indiana University Press, 2005.

Wendt, Simon, and Pablo Dominguez Andersen, eds. *Masculinities and the Nation in the Modern World: Between Hegemony and Marginalization*. New York: Palgrave, 2015.

Wenger, Beth S. *The Jewish Americans: Three Centuries of Jewish Voices in America*. Garden City, NY: Doubleday, 2007.

———. *History Lessons: The Creation of American Jewish Heritage*. Princeton, NJ: Princeton University Press, 2012.

Wenger, Beth S., coeditor. *Gender in Judaism and Islam: Common Lives, Uncommon Heritage*. New York: New York University Press, 2014.

Wertheimer, Jack, ed. *Imagining the American Jewish Community*. Waltham, MA: Brandeis University Press, 2007.

Westheider, James E. *Fighting on Two Fronts: African Americans and the Vietnam War*. New York: New York University Press, 1999.

Wiener, Jon. *Conspiracy in the Streets: The Extraordinary Trial of the Chicago Eight*. New York: New Press, 2006.

Wiesel, Elie. *The Jews of Silence: A Personal Report on Soviet Jewry*. New York: Schocken Books, 1966.

Williams, John Alexander. *Turning to Nature in Germany: Hiking, Nudism, and Conservation, 1900–1940*. Stanford, CA: Stanford University Press, 2007.

Wilson, Thomas C. "Compliments Will Get You Nowhere: Benign Stereotypes, Prejudice, and Anti-Semitism." *Sociological Quarterly* 37 (1996): 465–79.

Wolf, Simon. *The American Jew as Patriot, Soldier, and Citizen*. Philadelphia: Levytype, 1895.

Wylie, Philip. *Generation of Vipers*. 1942. Reprint, Normal, IL: Dalkey Archive Press, 1996.

Wyman, David S. *The Abandonment of the Jews: America and the Holocaust, 1941–1945*. New York: New Press, 2007.

———. "The Bergson Group, America, and the Holocaust: A Previously Unpublished Interview with Hillel Kook/Peter Bergson." *American Jewish History* 89, no. 1 (March 2001): 3–34.

Yezierska, Anzia. *Bread Givers*. New York: Persea Books, 2003.

Yosef, Raz. *Beyond Flesh: Queer Masculinities and Nationalism in Israeli Cinema.* New Brunswick, NJ: Rutgers University Press, 2004.

Zangwill, Israel. *From the Ghetto to the Melting Pot: Israel Zangwill's Jewish Plays.* Edited by Edna Nahshon. Detroit: Wayne State University Press, 2006.

Zaretsy, Natasha. "Feminists of the 1960s and 1970s." In *Women's Rights: People and Perspectives*, edited by Crista DeLuzio, 191–206. Santa Barbara, CA: ABC-CLIO, 2010.

Zelizer, Barbie. *Remembering to Forget: Holocaust Memory through the Camera's Eye*. Chicago: University of Chicago Press, 1998.

———. *Visual Culture and the Holocaust*. New Brunswick, NJ: Rutgers University Press, 2001.

Zielonka, Martin. "Sam Dreben, D.S.C.: The Fighting Jew, 1878–1925." *Western States Jewish Historical Quarterly* 44, no. 1 (2011): 211–17.

Index